"This is no ordinary war book. It is the private exchanges of a devoted couple who were able to see beyond the horizon of conflict and envision a joint mission that would serve all humanity."

— *G. William Whitehurst, World War II veteran, historian, and member of Armed Services Committee, United States House of Representatives (1969-1987) Second Congressional District of Virginia.*

"A deeply touching love story during the horrors of the Second World War and the triumph of marriage and medicine."

— *Robert Edwards, PhD, DSc, CBE, Cambridge University, UK, the scientist responsible for the world's first test tube baby and the winner of the U.S. Lasker Award.*

"*War and Love* describes the Joneses' personal and professional goals during a time when the rest of the country could not look past tomorrow."

— *Elizabeth Carr, America's first test tube baby and now online reporter for the Poynter Institute for Medical Studies.*

War and Love

War and Love

A Surgeon's Memoir of Battlefield Medicine
During World War II With Letters
to and from Home

By

Howard W. Jones Jr., M.D.

Georgeanna Seegar Jones, M.D.

To order additional copies of this book, contact:
Xlibris Corporation
1-888-795-4274
www.Xlibris.com
Orders@Xlibris.com
24700

Contents

Acknowledgments

GEORGEANNA, MY WIFE, IS COAUTHOR OF *WAR AND Love*. Except for minor insertions, the letters from home are hers, verbatim. For more than sixty years, she and I lovingly and happily collaborated on many projects. But the wear and tear of time has prevented her active participation in assembling the material for this volume. Nevertheless, as her letters attest, she is the coauthor of this work.

The daily letters she sent to me while I was overseas are essential components of our long love story—and this book. Without them, this volume would not be titled *War and Love*. The letters from home for the most part have been isolated into separate chapters. While this gives a sort of ping-pong effect that, in truth, is the way it was during the war. For the individual soldier, there was a flood of outdated letters and then nothing but uncertainty for an indeterminate interval. Individual instantaneous worldwide communication even in the time of war was a much-later development.

We also need to note that this volume could not have been put together without the competent and enthusiastic efforts of our longtime administrative assistant, Nancy Garcia. She has painstakingly and accurately deciphered my more-than-fifty-year-old handwritten letters, as well as Georgeanna's. In addition, she has typed and retyped and organized the entire work with skill and devotion. Simply stated, this volume would not exist without her superlative efforts.

We are also very grateful to Glenn Allen Scott, a retired associate editor of the *Virginian-Pilot* opinion pages, who has edited the entire work. He converted medical jargon into English that everyone can understand. However, he was more than a copy editor, as he contributed several passages elucidating events of a half century ago and immensely helped to make *War and Love* readable.

Finally, the manuscript has been critically read by Dr. Theodore Baramki, a longtime friend and colleague, whose early training in the Queen's English sensitized him to word usage and grammatical correctness. The manuscript has benefited from his reading, and we are grateful to him.

Despite all this high-level screening, there may be errors that have escaped the eye of the author, who was the final reader, and therefore rightly accepts responsibility for any mistakes that appear in print.

HWJ Jr.
Norfolk, Virginia
30 August 2004

About the Authors

GEORGEANNA EMORY SEEGAR AND HOWARD W. Jones Jr. were married 22 June 1940.

Georgeanna had graduated from Johns Hopkins Medical School in 1936 and Howard in 1935. During that era, it was not acceptable for members of the residency staff to be married.

My surgical residency was completed on 20 June. Georgeanna and I expected to marry immediately after completion of my residency, which would have been 21 June. But that happened to be a Friday. Georgeanna's mother said she had never heard of anybody marrying on a Friday; so we were married Saturday night 22 June 1940 in the Episcopal church in Towson, Maryland, in which Georgeanna's mother and father had been married.

Georgeanna and I had dated for eight years, the first real date being Thanksgiving Day 1932, after meeting for a second time. That second meeting took place in medical school over the dissecting table in the anatomy laboratory; she and Donnie Boyle were teamed with Al and Hal Swartz.

I was tracking down Al Swartz, who was a graduate of Amherst College, where I had gone, so that I could welcome him to Baltimore and Hopkins. When I found him, I rediscovered my future wife.

HWJ Jr.

Howard and Georgeanna Jones

Prologue

*T*HIS BOOK FLOWS FROM SEVERAL UNRELATED BUT serendipitous events.

At Christmas 1998 I received two copies of Tom Brokow's *The Greatest Generation*. Having participated in World War II, I took up that book with great interest.

I could not avoid an inward smile at the presumptuous title. After all, there were other great generations: the Age of Pericles, the Renaissance, the Enlightenment, and, of course, the generations that gave us steam power in the Industrial Revolution, usable electricity, and the internal-combustion engine; all of which led to the automobile, the airplane, radio, TV, and other gadgets of the E-age, and more.

Nevertheless, World War II, aside from the achievement of its political objectives, served as a school for millions of Americans in uniform. Until reading *The Greatest Generation*, I had never considered that my World War II experience had influenced in any way my subsequent career. After reading Brokaw's book, I realized that it had. *War and Love*—a mix of memoirs, commentary, surgical records, battlefield diary, and letters—is the fruit of that realization.

Another serendipitous event occurred at Christmas 1999: I received a third copy of *The Greatest Generation*, which I passed on to my son Larry. Despite its being the Christmas season, an urgent project demanded that I root among sealed packing boxes in the family storeroom for documents about the early days of in vitro fertilization (IVF).

During this archival search, I came upon a long-forgotten notebook in which I had kept a World War II diary. Together with this notebook diary were two companion notebooks containing a case-by-case record of each wounded soldier upon whom I had operated during the war in Europe, from two months after the invasion of Normandy to meeting the Russians on the Baltic Sea. I had long thought and hoped that the surgical notebooks were stored somewhere, but I had no recollection whatsoever of a diary.

From September 1944, when I arrived at my first field hospital, which was situated in a French cow pasture, until the collapse of the Third Reich, I performed three hundred operations.

Nearly all were performed on "nontransportable" battlefield wounded. The patients were primarily U.S. enlisted men and officers. Some were prisoners of war. A few others were civilians.

In my surgical notebooks, I recorded the name, rank, and serial number of each casualty. I described the wound and the medical procedures used to deal with them. I reported the medical outcome of each operation.

Yet another serendipitous event occurred in the spring of 2000 upon opening one more sealed box in the storeroom: There, carefully preserved, was apparently every letter I had written from Europe and Asia to Georgeanna, my wife, as well as several military documents. The box also contained many letters from Georgeanna to me, carried by me across the world to end up in the family storeroom.

The diary, letters, other documents, memory, and general reading are the sources of my recollection of World War II—from the beginning, well behind the battle lines, to later, from two miles to ten miles behind the front, where I surgically treated severely wounded men. I operated within earshot of the battleground to the sounds of the murderous weapons created by men attempting to violently impose their will on other men.

The values derived from the wartime army experience doubtlessly did influence my subsequent life, as it did the lives of millions of others. The most spectacular and important of these influences were recorded in *The Greatest Generation*.

How the war had influenced the lives of millions of U.S. veterans was spotlighted by the Public Broadcasting System's *Jim Lehrer News Hour* on 4 July 2000. A segment of that newscast was devoted to the impact of the GI Bill of Rights, which was signed into law by President Roosevelt soon after the Normandy landings on 6 June 1944—D-Day.

Among other benefits, the GI Bill guaranteed a college education and low-interest housing loans to veterans meeting specified requirements.

The commentators on the Jim Lehrer newscast—historians Stephen Ambrose, Doris Kerns Goodwin, and Michael Beschloss and journalist Haynes Johnson—enthusiastically made the point that the GI Bill was the key force in dramatically transforming the United States after World War II.

The number of U.S. high school graduates who went to college after the war was far greater than the numbers who did so in the prewar years. The flood of veterans overflowing college classrooms compelled a beneficial expansion of the higher education system. The veterans studied hard and did well in their courses.

After graduation they performed important jobs and demanded good housing, fueling general economic expansion. For example, of the thirteen million houses built in the 1950s, eleven million were financed with GI Bill loans.

Stephen Ambrose emphasized that the Americans who fought in the war had matured and were motivated to realize the American Dream. They had seen in the military that a job done well led to promotion. They had learned how to succeed in life. The war and the GI Bill opened the gateway to the middle class and to successful lives for millions who otherwise would not have "gotten ahead in the world."

What are the army lessons that carried over to later life?

The army values duty, loyalty, reliability, integrity, accountability, and honesty. Please understand that I do not claim to exhibit these admirable qualities. But please, also understand that I admire them. I find it pleasant and possible to come to workable solutions to challenges when dealing with people who exhibit them. I find it unpleasant and frustrating and often counterproductive to deal with people exhibiting the opposite qualities.

Such admirable qualities should be acquired within the family and in schools and community contacts. I was fortunate to have had great exposure to them while growing up. But the army certainly reinforced them.

There are other qualities that, with some exceptions, are almost unique to a very large organization such as the military: organization; delegation of responsibility; improvisation when necessary; cooperation (teamwork); planning (a venerable army rubric, abbreviated to PPP—Prior Planning Pays); accountability—and a work ethic regulated, not by clock or calendar, nor even necessarily influenced by the weather, but by the mission.

In the military, one can also acquire the ability to understand, to deal with, and when necessary for the common good, to circumvent rigid bureaucracy. I believe that some of these qualities did rub off on me and expressed themselves in later life.

To those who have served in the military, the foregoing paragraphs may sound more like the spin of a recruiting officer than a tale from the medical trenches. It is standard operating procedure (SOP) among many to view the military as one big SNAFU (situation normal—all fouled up). But consider: In the European Theater of Operations alone, the U.S. military equipped and supplied more than two million soldiers from a democracy to defeat aggression by ruthless dictatorships.

The United States of America was essentially united in wishing to crush Nazism and Fascism in Europe and Japanese Militarism in Asia and the Pacific Ocean. Those ends could be accomplished only with an organization, a framework, and standard operating procedures that delegated responsibility downward through the chain of command to carry out a plan, the many details of which had to be formulated and executed by commanders down the line.

What happened when a crippling SNAFU occurred? The responsible commander was replaced. This happened many times in Europe; commanding officers up to and including corps commanders were replaced when they fouled up. Hosts of people in the academic world—and many other fields—must often secretly wish for some military practices that could do away with micromanagement from the top and ongoing toleration of mediocre performance.

It seems to me that some members of the present generation may not have the virtues I esteem. On the other hand, some members of generations who never experienced military service have acquired them in spades. Few of those who gave us the E-world have ever slept in a foxhole or a pup tent. However, on balance, I must agree with the theme of *The Greatest Generation*: The military provides excellent training in skills needed to cope successfully with challenges future life presents.

Whether as an individual involved in a micromission or macromission, the lessons of organization, delegation, improvisation, accountability, and all the other excellent qualities cited previously should help get the job done. Indeed, getting a job done— accomplishing a mission—is key to the inner contentment that makes life such a happy adventure. Those without a useful mission are missing that happiness.

This book was originally intended solely for our children. But here at the start of the Third Millennium, it arrives too late to benefit our offspring, who seem to be doing quite well without military exposure (although Howard III *was* in the peacetime army).

Perhaps grandchildren—nieces and nephews or their children— will find this story interesting and even helpful. Perhaps their reading of the diary and letters written fifty years ago, along with information and commentary provided a half century later, will enable them to appreciate the origin and application of some of the qualities that make life so much fun.

Howard W. Jones Jr., M.D.
30 August 2004

Chronology of World War II Military Service of Howard W. Jones Jr., M.D.

18 Jun 1943	Entered U.S. Army and Medical Field Service School, Carlisle, Pennsylvania.
31 Jul 1943	Graduated Medical Field Service School, Carlisle, Pennsylvania
5 Jul 1943	Arrived at Fort Sam Houston, Texas (5th Auxiliary Surgical Group).
16 Jul 1944	Departed Fort Sam Houston.
19 Jul 1944	Arrived Camp Kilmer, New Jersey.
22 Jul 1944	Departed Camp Kilmer for New York City.
23 Jul 1944	Departed New York City aboard *Queen Mary*.
28 Jul 1944	Arrived Greenock, Scotland.
29 Jul 1944	Disembarked *Queen Mary*.
30 Jul 1944	Arrived at Marbury Hall, Northwich, England.
23 Aug 1944	Moved to Chilworth Manor, Eastleigh.
26 Aug 1944	Boarded *Leopoldville* at Southampton.
27 Aug 1944	Sailed from Southampton.
29 Aug 1944	Disembarked Utah Beach, France. Bivouacked Fourcarville (apple orchard).

31 Aug 1944	Moved to cow pasture, Sainte-Marie-du-Mont
10 Sep 1944	Moved to Le Vésinet.
12 Sep 1944	Visited Paris.
14 Sep 1944	Departed Le Vésinet for Brittany.
16 Sep 1944	Arrived Ploudalmézeau (53rd Field Hospital, 1st Platoon).
24 Sep 1944	Moved to Plouay (53rd Field Hospital, 2nd Platoon).
30 Sep 1944	Departed Plouay, arrived Chartres.
1 Oct 1944	Departed Chartres 6:45 AM, arrived Jonchery-Sur-Suippe 5:30 PM.
2 Oct 1944	Departed Jonchery-Sur-Suippe 6:30 AM, arrived Bastogne, Belgium, 2:30 PM.
3 Oct 1944	Departed Bastogne 7:30 AM, arrived Saint-Vith, at noon.
7 Oct 1944	Moved into town of Saint-Vith (53rd Field Hospital, 3rd Platoon).
14 Oct 1944	Moved to Tongeren, Belgium, bivouacked Hammel with Duke de Grune.
17 Oct 1944	Moved to Nuth, Netherlands.
9 Nov 1944	Moved to Eygelshoven, Netherlands.
17 Nov 1944	Moved to Niewenhagen, Netherlands (53rd Field Hospital, 3rd Platoon).
4 Dec 1944	Moved to Übach, Germany (48th Field Hospital, 3rd Platoon).
24 Dec 1944	Moved to Bocholtz, Netherlands.
29 Dec 1944	Moved from Bocholtz to Wellen, Belgium.
8 Feb 1945	Moved to Baesweiler, Germany (48th Field Hospital, 3rd Platoon).
1 Mar 1945	Moved to Hostert (63rd Field Hospital, 3rd Platoon).
5 Mar 1945	Moved to Krefeld (Lemmenhof).
14 Mar 1945	Moved to Dülken (48th Field Hospital, 3rd Platoon).
24 Mar 1945	Moved to Kempen (108th Evacuation Hospital).

26 Mar 1945	Moved to Friedrichsfeld (48th Field Hospital, 3rd Platoon).
4 Apr 1945	Moved to Dorsten (41st Evacuation Hospital).
20 Apr 1945	Visited Schöppenstedt (108th Evacuation Hospital).
20-21 Apr 1945	Moved to Gebshardshagen (67th Field Hospital, 1st Platoon) to do one case and returned to the 108th Evac.
26 Apr 1945	Moved to Gebshardshagen (67th Field Hospital, 1st Platoon).
26 Apr 1945	Moved to Rosche.
6 May 1945	Moved to Wittenberg.
19 May 1945	Moved to headquarters at Wolfenbüttel.
23 May 1945	Moved with headquarters to Weidenbrück.
7 Jun 1945	Moved with headquarters to Marburg.
10 Jun 1945	Traveled to Nancy, France.
11 Jun 1945	Traveled to Gex, France.
12 Jun 1945	Traveled to Marseilles.
16 Jul 1945	Boarded *Admiral Benson* with two fellow officers at Marseilles 11 AM.
17 Jul 1945	Departed Marseilles 7 AM.
15 Aug 1945	Truman announces capitulation of the Japanese as we enter the harbor of Ulithi (a Pacific atoll used as U.S. Navy anchorage).
22 Aug 1945	Arrived Manila, Philippines, Casual Camp No. 5.
24 Aug 1945	Disembarked from *Admiral Benson*. Entered transit camp—the 5th Replacement Depot—without orders.
4 Sep 1945	Moved without orders to 51st General Hospital. Cable received from War Department authorizing the Pacific Command to absorb the three officers.
20 Sep 1945	Returned to 5th Replacement Depot.
25 Sep 1945	Arrived Batangas, bivouacked with the 54th General Hospital.

30 Sep 1945	Embarked for Japan on APA No. 6 *Charles Heywood*, formerly *City of Baltimore* of the Baltimore Mail Line.
15 Oct 45	Arrived Tokyo, Doai Memorial Hospital (54th General Hospital).
1-9 Nov 1945	Billeted 4th Replacement Depot, Atsugi.
9 Nov 1945	Embarked for U.S. West Coast.
18 Nov 1945	Arrived Fort Lewis, Tacoma, Washington.
22 Nov 1945	Demobilized from U.S. Army.

Maps

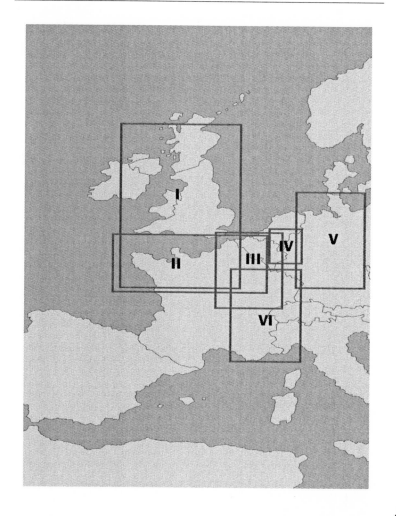

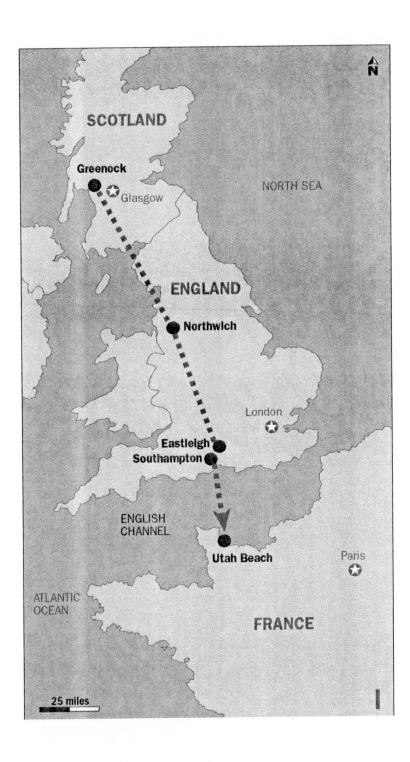

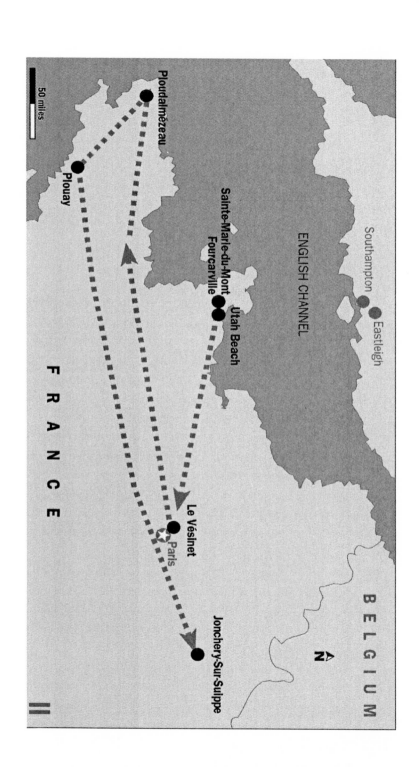

ENGLISH CHANNEL

Southampton

Eastleigh

FRANCE

BELGIUM

Ploudalmézeau

Plouay

Sainte-Marie-du-Mont

Fourcarville

Utah Beach

Le Vésinet

Paris

Jonchery-Sur-Suippe

50 miles

N

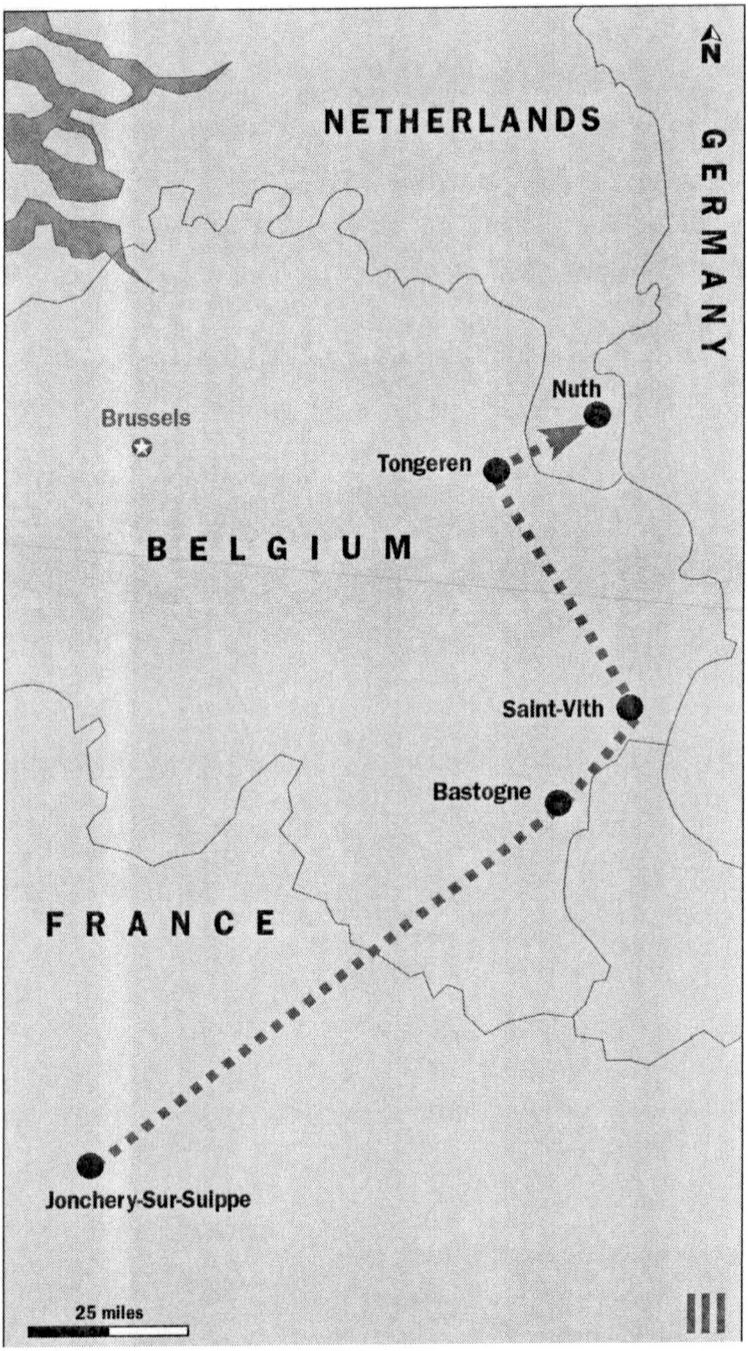

NETHERLANDS

GERMANY

N

Brussels

Nuth

Tongeren

BELGIUM

Saint-Vith

Bastogne

FRANCE

Jonchery-Sur-Suippe

25 miles

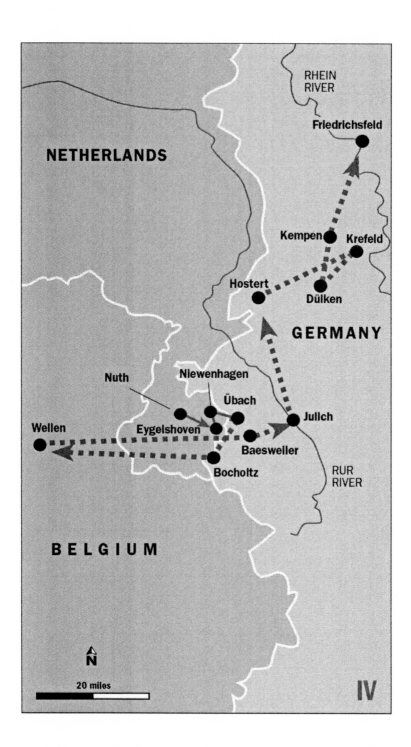

RHEIN
RIVER

Friedrichsfeld

NETHERLANDS

Kempen   Krefeld

Hostert   Dülken

GERMANY

Nuth   Niewenhagen

Übach

Wellen   Eygelshoven   Julich

Baesweller

Bocholtz   RUR
RIVER

BELGIUM

N

20 miles

IV

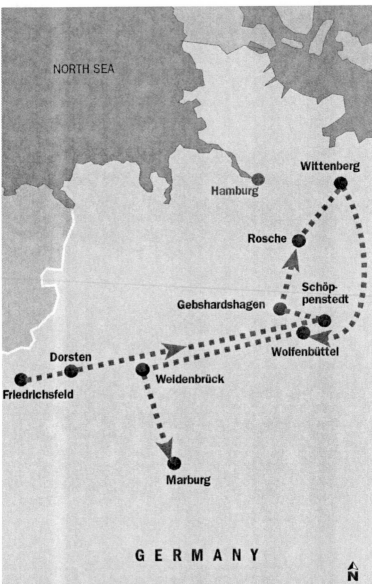

NORTH SEA

Wittenberg

Hamburg

Rosche

Schöp-
penstedt

Gebshardshagen

Wolfenbüttel

Dorsten

Friedrichsfeld

Weldenbrück

Marburg

GERMANY

N

50 miles

V

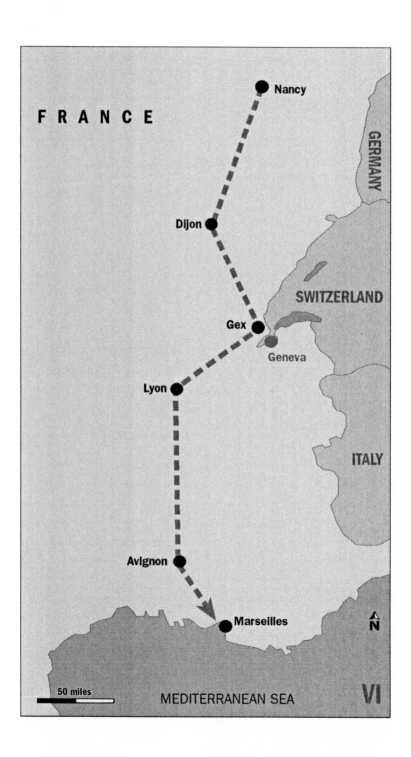

Chapter 1

France
29 August-19 September 1944

*P*ARIS HAD BEEN LIBERATED FOUR DAYS BEFORE I stepped ashore at Utah Beach on the northern coast of France on 29 August 1944. I was a battlefield surgeon, with the rank of captain, assigned to the U.S. Army's 5th Auxiliary Surgical Group.

I had entered the army 18 June 1943 and had been indoctrinated in military customs and military medicine at the Medical Field Service School in Carlisle, Pennsylvania, before being further trained at Fort Sam Houston, Texas.

On 16 September I arrived at the 53rd Field Hospital at Ploudalmézeau in Brittany. The armies of the Axis Powers—Germany, Italy, Japan—were being pushed back on every front by Allied forces.

Three months after the Normandy landings on D-Day 6 June 1944, millions of Allied soldiers were ashore in France and the Low Countries. Others had long been fighting in Italy. The Soviet Army had crossed the Danube River into Romania. The U.S. 2nd, 8th, and 29th Divisions had begun an all-out battle to wrest the fiercely defended port city of Brest, in Brittany, from the German Army.

DIARY ENTRY: 16 September 1944

We found the 1st Platoon of the 53rd Field Hospital in a farmer's field adjacent to the French town of Ploudalmézeau at the tip of Brittany. I was a stranger in a strange land, and I felt like one.

Members of the 5th Aux surgical teams weaved their way through the blackout baffle into the triage tent—also called the receiving tent—to which wounded men were brought. About a dozen recently arrived wounded lay on litters neatly arranged like beds in an open ward; but the litters, of course, were only a few inches off the ground.

Bottled glucose was being fed intravenously into each wounded man—the bottles suspended from a pole about six feet high beside each litter.

Members of the shock teams, whose job it was to treat, triage (that is, assess the seriousness of a wound and assign a priority for definitive treatment), and evaluate and render aid to the wounded, were milling around. As we arrived, an ambulance pulled up with two newly wounded.

The triage tent was quiet inside. We whispered, so that we would not disturb the work of the triage teams. We soon realized that the litter carriers moving the wounded were German prisoners of war. Actually, more POWs than American corpsmen or officers were standing around.

Imagine my surprise when I looked up and recognized an American officer—Tommy Dukehart, my back-door neighbor in the Baltimore Roland Park neighborhood! We saw each other at least once a week in Roland Park; our children were of the same age and played together daily. It was immediately apparent to me that we were supporting the Army's 29th Division—the National Guard division from Maryland and Virginia that had stormed onto Omaha Beach on D-Day.

Tommy was the 29th Division's public information officer. He was suited well for the post, because in civilian life he was a radio-industry public-relations man. The 29th Division had trained for months in the United Kingdom for the invasion of Hitler's Europe.

What were the probabilities that I would operate upon someone I knew from Baltimore?

The 5th Aux surgical teams were to take over on the morning of 16 September. Our teams had planned to work 12-hour shifts, either a day shift or a night shift. The teams not working would sleep. Because we had four teams, two teams worked days and the other teams worked nights.

I was to start the next-day shift.

That night I didn't sleep well, although I had a comfortable bed in a ward tent used as sleeping quarters for officers. I had not been surgically active for more than a year, and that troubled me. The only surgery I had performed was on dogs at Fort Sam.

While that experience was helpful, the difference between operating on a dog and operating on a human being is a big one. I wondered throughout that restless night whether I would be nervous or unable to do the required surgery after such a lengthy absence from an operating room. I had never doubted my surgical skills before.

MY FIRST PATIENT on that long-ago first day in the field was a private—P. H., Serial Number 15338833—who had an open sucking wound of the left chest. The hole had been plugged by gauze impregnated with Vaseline and covered with a field dressing.

The wounding missile had presumably entered the abdomen by the umbilicus (belly button) and exited through the chest, leaving a large opening. I made a long abdominal incision that disclosed no damage to the intestines. But the missile had dug a shallow ditch across the dome of the liver. Although it had clearly entered the chest, I could feel no penetration of the wounded man's diaphragm (the muscular partition separating the chest cavity from the abdominal cavity).

After assuring myself of the absence of major bleeding or other damage in the abdomen, I closed the wound with stitches. Our team then removed a fractured rib associated with the exit wound and found a three-inch rip in the diaphragm. I closed the rip easily with interrupted stitches.

The lung had been penetrated, but there seemed to be no bleeding. I closed the wound gently with a few fine stitches that pulled the ragged edges together.

As was the practice, we employed "water-seal draining" of the chest; as the patient breathed, a water trap prevented air from entering the thoracic cavity.

A water trap was a half-full gallon jug with the tube from the chest cavity going to the bottom of the water. When the patient exhaled, air in the chest cavity came out through the tube and bubbled through the water. On inhaling, some water would rise a few inches in the tube, but not into the chest. The traps worked very well.

PRIVATE P.H. responded well to the surgery. He was in fine condition when he was transported to the evacuation hospital. He did collect some fluid in his right chest, which I removed with needle and syringe.

I also responded well to the surgery, which consumed two hours. As I began to operate, I no longer worried that I had not operated for more than a year.

The surgical team was handicapped by the immovable government-issued light above the operating table. We had experienced difficulty seeing into the far part of the incision.

I then remembered that our equipment included a light that could be worn with a band around the head. The headlight was connected to a battery box. I tried out the headlight after completing my first operation and used it during the next operation. Because I could see better what I was doing, I used a headlight throughout the campaign in Europe.

I OPERATED ON two other freshly wounded riflemen that first day in the field. One had been hit six hours before by a machine-gun bullet. His case exemplified the extraordinary character of some of the wounds treated in battlefield surgeries.

The wounded rifleman had a very large first-aid dressing strapped across his lower chest and upper abdomen. When the dressing was removed, I was shocked by the sight of several loops of small intestine outside the body on the chest and abdomen.

These loops of bowel were thickened and dusky, as with a strangulated hernia. After anesthesia had been administered, we examined the bowel and were both amazed and delighted to discover no perforation of the intestine.

I opened the abdomen by enlarging the wound made by the bullet. The team was again pleasantly surprised upon finding no damage to the bowel or any other contents of the abdomen. The bullet had made a surgical incision, so to speak, through which the bowel herniated (protruded). The rifleman recovered swiftly. His bowels functioned normally, and his wound healed without any sign of infection.

Surgical experience in civilian life had led us to believe that such an injury would necessarily be followed by a severe wound infection, if not by peritonitis, a deadly inflammation of the bowels and the serous membrane of the abdominal cavity.

Peritonitis had been a merciless killer throughout history. But the Allied military during World War II had gained a revolutionary weapon that defeated infection: penicillin. We administered to the wounded twenty thousand units of penicillin every six hours for two days. We attributed subsequent healings to the absence of infection because we used penicillin.

But the twenty-thousand units every six hours for two days commonly dispensed in World War II was a puny dose compared with the millions of units used in later years. The lethal organism that caused infection had never before encountered anything like penicillin; it was particularly vulnerable to the new cure for infection.

Of course, we also had sulfanilamide powder and sprinkled it into the wounds. Between the powder and the penicillin, we had an effective method of combating infection.

THE THIRD WOUNDED soldier I operated on that day also had a penetrating wound of the abdomen and holes in the omentum (a fold of the serous membrane lining of the abdominal cavity) and small bowel. We closed these wounds, and they healed perfectly.

The rifleman also had a bad through-and-through wound of the right thigh. We treated that by unroofing (with an incision) the track of the missile, sprinkling the wound with sulfanilamide, and dressing it with Vaseline gauze. Numerous army medical bulletins had warned us not to close such wounds, as it had been found that infection and wound breakdown would surely follow.

The wounded we treated on that first day in the field illustrated the mission of the U.S. Army's auxiliary surgical groups: We were to take care of those who could not be transported beyond the division clearing company.

By definition, the nontransportable wounded had abdominal or chest wounds or were in bad shock and could not be transferred farther back from the front. Those who witnessed the healing of abdominal and thoracic wounds treated in field hospitals quickly understood that the handling of the seriously wounded in World War II was a lifesaving improvement over the grisly experience in World War I.

THE FOURTH PATIENT upon whom I operated that first day also had an abdominal wound. A missile had entered the soldier's body on one side and exited the other. All four patients recovered well.

Next day, 17 September, I operated on a prisoner of war who had a gunshot wound through the chest. The bullet entered just to the right of his heart, exiting almost directly opposite through his back. He also recovered well.

The following day I sat down to write one of my almost-daily letters to my wife, Georgeanna. A practicing gynecologist in Baltimore, Georgeanna was also rearing our two offspring—Willie, age two, and Georgeanna, age five months, whom we called B.

Georgeanna was already receiving my letters from France. She had much to report after getting my first missive from French soil.

Thursday, September 7, 1944
9:15 P.M.

Dearest Honey Bunny,

Today I received your first letter from—don't mention it—France. It was really quite thrilling for me. In a way, I feel I share your experiences. I would not have had it this way, but as it has happened, I would not have it otherwise. Such a world-shaking experience, as World War II should certainly be shared by some member of the family.

I am sure you will make the most of the experience, get the best out of it, and be able to leave the unhappiness and unpleasantness behind. I, too, hope that you can make your letters full enough to recall those things that you cannot say.

I find your letters most interesting and very informative—not at all incoherent, as you seem to think them. But do remember, just a little line is better than no letter at all as you grow busier.

*I am glad to know that you and Bill Falor [5th Auxiliary Surgical Group surgeon] will be able to be together, as I am sure it will be congenial. But don't forget, I don't want **you** taking any women out, even if they are friends of the family! I am a jealous woman.*

Willie [Howard III] told Ess [Howard Jr.'s mother] today that "Genze came home to see Hurk." We were amazed, as we didn't even know that he knew [Georgeanna's cousin] Jane's baby was called Hurk. He now answers questions very intelligently. Mother asked him this morning, "Is Pop [Georgeanna's father] ready?"—then he said, "No, Pop's going to shave."

He also knows the location of everything in the city. Pointed out the bakery to Father after being there once—today. They were a block away from the office, approaching Johns Hopkins (he had never been that way before), when he said, "Mary over there." B makes a bridge—standing on her hands and feet now. Do take care of yourself for me.

Regards to Bill and best love to you, Papa. Mama

I was in good spirits as I wrote to Georgeanna about my initiation into battlefield surgery.

Monday, September 18, 1944
2:00 P.M.

Dearest Ginny,

These regular hours of leisure since going to work have given me more free time than any other time since leaving Fort Sam. Most of the men here are complaining about not having time to write letters, but having 12 hours in which to do nothing but sleep and do such things as write is a luxury.

Last night, my second operation was not as busy as the first. Only one case, a through-and-through bullet wound of the chest of a POW. He did very well, and so did I, because it was an easy case. We are getting numerous POWs, as any army does as it goes forward. We are giving them good treatment—as good, I hope, as they are giving our boys, if they are getting any.

The contrasts of war are terrific. All about us the French farmers are going about their business, working in the fields, bringing over eggs, tomatoes, etc., to barter for cigarettes. People dressed up on Sunday are going to church, and yet a few miles away other people are shooting it out. In the nearby town [Ploudalmézeau] shops are open for business as usual.

This sleeping in the day is OK, but my bladder is still on the other shift—too much coffee, I think.

Love, H

ON 18 SEPTEMBER, while walking around the tent hospital for exercise and fresh air, I encountered the farmer on whose property we were encamped. All of us had encountered him before. Deprived of his land as he was, he seemed to be keeping a close eye on us.

He was a pleasant fellow, a typical peasant, and could have been a model for the painter Jean François Millet. He wore wooden clogs, ragged cap, and ragged clothes. In the mind's eye, he was the typical French peasant farmer.

On this encounter, he was all smiles. "*Brest est tombé*," he said. To this day, I remember that *tombé* means "fallen"—"Brest has fallen."

Our wounded stopped, except for the sixth wounded soldier I operated on at Ploudalmézeau. He was an American injured by an accidental discharge of his buddy's No. 12 rifle. The bullet had entered the right chest just below the clavicle and exited below the tip of the scapula posteriorly. He was brought to the 53rd Field Hospital at 4:30 PM on the eighteenth. He was in shock, his blood pressure barely obtainable.

He had received three units of plasma. We gave him two units of blood. By 8 PM his shock showed very little improvement, and we thought that he continued to have internal bleeding. At 9 PM we operated upon him and found at least two thousand cubic centimeters of blood in his chest cavity.

So there was indeed active bleeding, as we expected, but we seemed to be able to control this with sutures. During the operation, the patient received two thousand cubic centimeters of blood and two more units of plasma. By 4:30 AM on the nineteenth, the soldier seemed to be in reasonable condition. At 8 AM his blood pressure had come up to 110, and he seemed very much improved.

I did not see him after this, as I was off to sleep. When I returned to the field hospital, I was told that he had died in shock an hour after I had departed. This was the first loss we had had and, unfortunately, of an American serviceman shot by another American serviceman after the battle was over.

U.S. soldiers' shooting fellow soldiers became a pattern repeated after other battles. I was never quite sure why, but I suspect it was partly attributable to celebrating victories by drinking alcohol or cleaning guns or both. Such deaths seemed so preventable, but we encountered the phenomenon again and again.

The experience with the American GI highlighted an unsolved problem. Casualties in severe shock from blood loss sometimes recovered when the bleeding was stopped. Such was the hope with our GI. But at other times, despite control of the bleeding and ample blood replacement, irreversible shock and death followed. Never before had I seen death from irreversible shock. An autopsy revealed no further internal bleeding after the operation.

———————————

Tuesday, September 19, 1944
6:00 P.M.

Dearest Ginny,

Action has stopped on the front immediately before us. Last night I had but one case, and there have been no cases today. The one case I did was a thoracotomy for a through-and-through bullet wound. The chest was full of blood from an artery between the ribs. I'm happy to say that everyone was very complimentary on how nicely things went. It is a relief to feel that, after the 15-month layoff, I am not so rusty.

We will probably not move immediately. But this, of course, is uncertain. I have mentioned that we have comfortable living quarters. But I have only just realized that we are in a cow pasture, and we have cows sticking their heads into the tent now and again. The French people also flock around and want to trade eggs, chickens, etc., for cigarettes, which are hard for them to obtain. A gendarme from a nearby town is stationed here to keep the civilians under control.

Love and kisses to all, H

Wednesday, September 20, 1944
4:00 P.M.

Dearest Ginny,

This morning Mac and I had an opportunity to go forward and see what was left in the city before us [Brest], in which the fighting has passed through. The infantry had already left and there was none there, except the engineers with their bulldozers clearing the debris from the streets. There is not a house or building in the city that is suitable for habitation. The entire city must be rebuilt.

We had an opportunity to visit a German hospital, which was still functioning. The doctor there was a surgeon and seemed to have taken good care of his patients. He was proud of the fact that he had operated upon ten Americans who were taken wounded to his hospital.

The debris in the streets is beyond imagination. It is piled up to the second story in some places, and it is no inconsiderable job to get the place cleaned up. It is the same in every city that has been fought over.

Last night we had a movie at the hospital, The Uninitiated. *It is a ghost story that seems to prove that there is such a thing as a ghost. I would rather the movie had been something funny.*

Love as always, H

Thursday, September 21, 1944

Dearest Ginny,

The damnedest thing about this existence is the complete loss of the ability to tell what day, month, and year it is. One day is like another and, although we are constantly doing different things, there is no real routine that helps identify the days.

Today some of the others had an opportunity to go into Brest and brought back the greatest collection of souvenirs—helmets, guns, uniforms, etc. I cannot get much enthusiasm for these things, as they have to be carried along or sent home. If sent home, they accumulate, or would you like to have a nice German bayonet?

We are hoping that tomorrow or the next day Joe Redline will come in from Paris with the mail. I trust that by now things at home are quieted down and that you are able to devote all your time to the babies and to the hospital. It was never meant that you would have to devote much energy to the drudgery of existence.

Love, H

AFTER A FEW days with no casualties at Ploudalmézeau, on 24 September, our team was transferred to the 3rd Platoon of the 53rd Field Hospital at Plouay, supporting a division involved in the investment of Lorient.

Presumably with Brest under control, an assault on Lorient was to take place next. But we received no casualties at Plouay. The high command wisely concluded that the German forces in Lorient and

Saint-Nazaire, having been cut off from their supply lines, were isolated and posed no immediate threat. Considering the cost in materiel and manpower required for the reduction of Brest, the high command opted for simply containing the Germans in Lorient and St. Nazaire.

Monday, September 25, 1944

Dearest Ginny,

I cannot help but comment again on how charming is the countryside of this part of France. It is beautiful rolling green land with numerous rivers and bays. It is a characteristic of this war that the countryside, even where there is war, has actually been little damaged.

It is the towns that have been fought over that are damaged, and many of them are level to the ground. Others have half the buildings knocked down, and so on. There are no such things as battlefields as we knew in other wars. No Gettysburg or Bull Run, but, rather, Saint-Lô and Brest. All cities and towns are destroyed as the war passes through.

You might be interested in a word about our hospital, which, as you have probably gathered, is not set up all in one place.

I shall never forget the first impression of the postoperative ward. It was three ward tents laced together and containing about 50 patients, all in folding cots on which the litter is placed, so that a man need not be taken from a litter from the time he is picked up until he is ready to get up himself.

But the striking thing about this ward was that each patient was desperately sick. About three-quarters have Wangenstein suction tubes, several more draining tubes from the chest to a water-sealed bottle, and then probably two dozen at a time are receiving blood plasma or other intravenous fluids. There are also some indwelling catheters.

The general impression is one of a chemical lab with bottles and tubes running in all directions. At first, it is a tremendously depressing sight, but as one has a chance to live with it a few days, one realizes that the patients are really seriously wounded and are getting expert, if not Park Avenue nursing, and they will all get well. Penicillin and sulfanilamide undoubtedly have a lot to do with it.

Today I also got my presidential-election ballot, and I am sending it in with this letter.

Do write me about any idea you might have about our postwar world, for although it may be still far off, it helps to think about it.

Love, H

Monday,September 25, 1944
6:00 P.M.

Dearest Ginny,

We liked the setup where we were and hated to leave. But after looking this over, I think we have bettered ourselves, and so we are content.

Although we all hope this war will quickly be over, everyone is planning as if it will not, and necessarily so. We have been greatly hindered in doing intravenous work and thoracotomies, as we do not have three-way stopcocks. Oddly enough, they are not medical-department items and are unobtainable over here.

In a very sick patient the other night, we improvised a three-way system with the stethoscope and had one person pinch off the proper tube at the proper time. This enabled us to give 500 cc of blood in 10 minutes and was exactly what we needed. What I am getting at is this: Could you pick up a few stopcocks around the hospital and mail them over? I would suggest one at a time in a letter, so that one might get through fairly soon. Small packages seem to get through OK.

Incidentally, none of the packages you have mentioned sending have yet come.

All my love, H

Tuesday, September 26, 1944

Dearest Ginny,

This period of waiting and waiting while someone else figures out what we are going to do is most welcome. Ordinarily before, I have had to figure out routes, loads in vehicles, timetables, etc. Now that I am with the hospital, it is my professional training that is supposed to be used, and this is a welcomed change. We still do not know where we will go from here, but we are anticipating some change from our present situation. Where and when and if is still a question.

Every now and again we all have a session discussing some of the things we will do after the war. One of the things talked about is food. While moving, we have K rations, and after a few days of that, the boys started talking about steaks, fried chicken, lobster, etc. However, we are fairly well-off here, and today we had a turkey dinner with turkey stuffing, potatoes, corn, and fruit salad for dessert. Not bad.

Another thing that always comes up for discussion is a bathroom. Slit trenches serve the purpose, but many say that the first thing they will do after the war is spend the first week in the bathroom and sleep in the tub.

I hope I don't give the impression that this life particularly bothers me, because you know I like it and, as yet, I am glad to say, have not gotten tired of it. We are living here in pyramidal tents and have a gasoline stove to heat water.

We can have an electric light and radio. I did not bring my radio, but left it at headquarters. Baths are difficult, but now and again a quartermaster shower company will come through, and that gives us a chance to get a real cleaning. Otherwise, bathing is out of a helmet. This does very well and will until the weather takes a turn for the cold, as it will sometime.

Love to our little family, H

Diary Entry: Sunday 24 September 1944
[Plouay, 53rd Field Hospital, 3rd Platoon]

Yesterday, while still at Ploudalmézeau, I went up to the 108th Evacuation Hospital from the 1st Platoon of the 53rd Field Hospital to get a list of the linen on the surgical truck that Fritz Joachim had there and also to see the boys there. Fritz Joachim and his team of Kipen and Nelson and John Munal with Mintz and King are there, as well as a shock team.

Mac asked us to be back by 3:00 P.M., which seemed strange. The 108th is about seven miles from the 1st Platoon. They all seem well and happy and gave us a drink of some wine taken from Brest and some nonalcoholic apple juice, which tasted like a very fine cider—almost like champagne. We were back by 3:00.

The boys at the evac were pleased with their situation. I looked over the list of 12 cases that Fritz had done. All casualties (except one) had wounds to the extremities, which required debridement and a cast without too much attention to approximation of any fracture. There was one belly case, with which they were very pleased. Their cases are not nearly as sick as ours.

Contrast this with our first six cases: two chests, one thoracoabdominal, and three abdominal. Ours are sick and really nontransportable. Fritz told me of one case in which it was necessary to apply a cast. A few hours later he wanted to see if the cast was dry and found that the patient had been evacuated. This illustrates the difference between evac and field-hospital patients.

The 108th must have a stuffy CO. Bartunek (CO of the 1st Platoon of the 53rd Field Hospital) told us of a patient who had gone through their field hospital with an abdominal wound and some extremity injury. Because they were swamped at the moment, he thought it would be satisfactory to evacuate the patient straightaway to the 108th.

In an hour or so (7-mile distance), the ambulance was back with a note saying that the evac could not take the patient because he was considered nontransportable and, therefore, according to the present standard operating procedure (SOP), should have been admitted to the field hospital in the first place.

Whenever Bartunek found it necessary to send a patient on to the 108th, it was always necessary to also send along a note of explanation and persuasion to be sure that he would be admitted.

The other night we had an abdominal wound and, therefore, a field-hospital case—but complicated by a severe eye injury. The 108th had an eye team. It was considerably desirable to send the patient along. In the midst of a war it was necessary to stop and write a note of explanation to the 108th to be sure the patient was not sent back as nontransportable—besides which the evac had a good surgeon also (a 5th Aux team member: Fritz Joachim).

At any rate, at 3:00 P.M. yesterday Mac returned from VIII Corps and said that the 3rd Platoon of the 53rd was being equalized as to teams, and I would go to the 3rd Platoon to join Dave Monahan to make two teams there. Jean Bennett was also going to the 3rd Platoon from the 2nd with his shock team. Harry Talmadge was sent to the 102nd Evac. This left Mac and Bill Boukalik at the 1st Platoon, with Stephens and Jenkins as shock teams.

The platoon had a good esprit de corps, and we were sorry to leave. They had us convinced that it was the best of the three platoons. They had a tent arrangement that they considered unique and the best of any field-hospital platoon in Europe.

We were convinced, although our first impression of Bartunek had changed, and we had begun to wonder if he really had something on the ball or if he antagonized people.

At any rate, we set off in a personnel carrier at 0600 to the 2nd Platoon, which is located near Plouay, some 75 miles over dusty roads, arriving at noon. Our first impression was very favorable. It soon developed that the 1st Platoon did not have the only good platoon of a field hospital, and actually this may be better.

We have a tent in which to sit down and eat, for instance. We have an electric light in the pyramidal tent in which we are living, etc. Above all, the CO, Major Hanrahan, talks sense and seems to be very easy to get along with. Dave Monahan is well and happy and in a much better frame of mind than he is when not working. All in all, we are delighted.

Diary Entry: Monday, 25 September 1944
[Plouay, 53rd Field Hospital, 3rd Platoon]

We continue to be pleased with this platoon and think we have bettered ourselves. During the week at Platoon No. 1, some interesting things happened. There were about a dozen prisoners of war (POWs) who were working about the hospital. They lived in shelter halves (American) just behind the American enlisted area and just beside the officers' ward tent. To get from the hospital itself to our living quarters, it was necessary to work your way through the pup tents of the prisoners. In the complete blackout and without a moon, it is a wonder that someone did not fall headlong into a tent.

More than once, while walking over this way in pitch-black, we all thought of the possibility of being attacked by a prisoner who, alone with himself, may have arrived at the conclusion that he himself did not matter and if he could do away with an officer or two before being stopped, it would be more than an even exchange and pleasing to der Führer.

Furthermore, weapons became available to them. One afternoon, after the fall of Brest, all the 5th Aux, except Mac and me, went into Brest. When they came home, they looked like a reinforced infantry squad. Every man had two or more bayonets, guns, cartridges, etc., which were picked up in Brest. As our tent was close to the tents of the POWs, [the captive Germans] immediately gathered around and were happy to demonstrate how to use the weapons.

Many times our tent was left unattended during the day. Therefore, it would have been a simple matter for the POWs to take back once again a weapon that a short time previously had belonged to their comrades. I mentioned this once or twice, but nothing ever happened.

On another occasion, about nine new prisoners arrived. They had been captured that morning and were corpsmen from a German hospital. Within a few minutes the other POWs had gathered around; then some GIs and even some officers. How were things in Brest? How much longer can it last? Etc.

It was like old home week. It made you wonder what this war is and how it works. One moment this man is your enemy; the next moment the same man is your friend, and you talk over the battle as you would a football game. I am not sure I understand it.

THE DECISION OF the high command to simply contain Lorient and Saint-Nazaire meant that the need for auxiliary surgical teams in Brittany had come to an end. We hoped there would be no more nontransportable wounded.

So on 29 September we were off to the east, where the Ninth Army had been inserted into the line between the First and Third armies. We ended up in two towns, Saint-Vith and Bastogne. Both were to become household names during the Battle of the Bulge only three months away.

Ploudalmézeau, France, September 1944. The receiving (or "triage") tent.

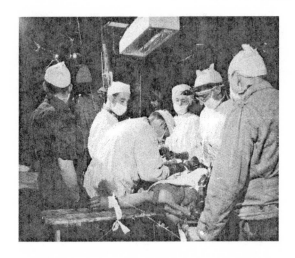

Operating at Ploudalmézeau. Left to right: Howard Yost, the assistant (who does not seem to be scrubbed); an unidentified captain; Frentzel, who is helping with the surgery; Alice Ridzon, a nurse; Howard Jones, the surgeon; Elmer Carlson, administering anesthesia. Note the headlamp worn by Jones—it proved very useful when trying to look into the depths of a wound.

Brest, France, 20 September 1945. A street scene forty-eight hours after the Germans surrendered the city.

Brest, 20 September 1945. A German-constructed blockhouse; in this case, used as a lazaret (field hospital). These blockhouses were very common and used for varied purposes.

Chapter 2

Letters from Home
7 September-30 September 1944

*T*HE 1944 PRESIDENTIAL CAMPAIGN WAS IN FULL swing when Georgeanna penned her letter of 7 September from our home in Roland Park, Baltimore.

President Franklin D. Roosevelt, despite his swiftly declining health, was seeking an unprecedented fourth term in the White House. The Republican Party's candidate was New York Governor Thomas E. Dewey, who had first gained national attention as an effective prosecutor of criminal gangs.

Georgeanna and I had been writing each other almost daily since my arrival at Camp Kilmer, New Jersey, from Fort Sam Houston, Texas, on 19 July 1944.

On that day the Soviet army had trapped five German army divisions in the Ukraine and the 2nd British Division in Normandy evicted the Germans from several towns on both banks of the Orne River.

Next day German army officers opposed to the Nazi regime attempted to assassinate Hitler with explosives brought into the Führer's "Wolf Lair" in Rastenburg. Hitler survived the blast, with deadly consequences for his would-be assassins.

Georgeanna was in her parents' house, rearing our two youngsters and working at Johns Hopkins Hospital as a physician specializing in the treatment of infertility.

Friday, September 8, 1944
11:30 P.M.

Dearest Honey Bunny,

I miss you always, but tonight, above all, I miss you for many reasons.

First, I am back in our bed with our furniture around me, and sleeping in our own room for the first time, having just got the cribs moved out and the baby settled across the hall.

Second, Father [J.K.B.E. Seegar, M.D.] is very sick again. He is sure it is a cardiac fatigue, and I'm not sure it is not some peculiar pancreatic attack; however, it is very worrisome. I really did not know how much I depended upon him for everything.

I now know that in the far corners of my mind was always the wonderful thought that, no matter what happened, I shall have Howard and he will know what to do and how to comfort me. And strange as it is, I still do have you, although you are not touchable, and still my thoughts of you sustain me.

I only hope that I have enough practical knowledge and strength to cope with the situations as they arise. It is pretty strenuous trying to run the household, take care of Father, see that Mother [Elizabeth Seegar] and Smitty [the Jones family's nanny] don't work themselves into an attack of illness, and run the laboratory at the same time. Today I even took Father's office practice and made his hospital rounds.

Your second letter from France arrived today, in which you said you had seen Bill Korb. I suppose you will be running into more people you know. Both babies are well and as sweet as usual. I only hope B is still little and cuddling when you get home. She is so nice to hold now.

My very best love and oodles of kisses, Ginny

P.S. Saturday A.M.—Father had ½ grain of morphine last night again, but feels better this A.M.

Sunday, September 10, 1944

Dearest Honey Bunny,

Yesterday I missed my tryst with you, as I was just too sleepy to stay awake another minute. It was really just as well, as Willie awoke at 5:30, waking B, and between the two we had not much sleep thereafter. Father was more comfortable and took only codeine through the night. He has needed nothing today, but has been very drowsy.

It is such a pity that you are missing the cute cuddly stage of B. She is really adorable now,—cooing, smiling, laughing, and blowing bubbles. She doesn't spit as much as Willie did and, although she is still very active, is not as "wiggly."

Willie actually counted lemons up to six yesterday, much to my amazement. At the table yesterday, he said, "One Mama, one Bessie, and two Marys."

We got our reservations for the trip to Norfolk yesterday, and I am hoping Father will be well enough for us to go. We are looking forward to the trip, and I am sure it will hold many pleasant memories of Papa.

We finally located a calendar among Smitty's affairs. I have marked over our own personal birthdays and anniversaries. If you can't figure which is which, I will not give you any more hints. Here's hoping you won't need it beyond the first anniversary, "Willie's birthday."

We are so disgusted with the political situation in respect to even the war that even Father is almost convinced to vote Republican. Mother picked up a lady downtown last week who had been treated by that "lovely young Dr. Jones at the Kelly Clinic"—she didn't get her name.

"May God Bless and keep us while we are absent one from another."

Best love, Ginny

Monday, September 11, 1944
9:30 P.M.

Dearest Honey Bunny,

As I look at my little clock, which is always kept at your time, I am impressed with the fact that you are usually sound asleep when I am thinking of you most. I hope you are asleep now, but the news is so impressive of heavy losses on the Western Front that perhaps even at this moment you are still working.

I feel sure that you must be doing some professional work now. I do hope that it won't be for long and that the fall of Germany will be followed quickly by the fall of Japan. It seems that the Philippine battle is really on.

I took Father's office practice again today from 4:00 to 6:00. He is feeling much better, but has promised to stay quiet for a few more days. I still am not sure of the diagnosis.

A man from King's [Georgeanna's brother] unit called to say he was back in the United States on rotation. So it seems that some of them are still being sent home but I'm afraid King's chances are slim.

Willie and B are both fine, and Smitty seems to have just about recovered. She has been up all day for three days now, with no ill effects. If only Father will maintain his present improvement, perhaps we could acquire an even keel again.

I hope you like the pictures—the slides are of course better, but I think these are quite cute.

If you can pick up a watch at a bargain for me, please do so. It would be a great convenience to have two. The baby knocked the crystal off mine two weeks ago, and I still haven't had the opportunity to have it recemented. Otherwise, aside from Papa, I have everything my heart desires.

Do try to anticipate your moves and warn me when I shall not get mail. You have really done so thus far, and it is a great help to know. I expect I must look for great irregularities now.

My best love and all my kisses, Ginny

> *Tuesday, September 12, 1944*
> *10:30 P.M.*

Dearest sweetheart,

I have just received your three lovely letters, which arrived today. They told me of your daily routine. I like to hear such things, as it enables me to visualize you better—of your trip to Saint-Lô, of your trip to the 2nd General Hospital, when you saw Fin Calhoun, and the arrival of bedrolls and some mail by way of Joe Redline.

I'm glad you liked the snaps of Willie. I think there are still some black-and-white photographs you have not received. I have already sent airmail stamps, but be sure to let me know about them before you run out this time.

I am depressed about the news. It looks as if Germany will fight to the last man and I won't see you by Christmas or our 1st of January anniversary.

Everyone joins me in love. Don't forget for one minute that I am thinking of you always.

All my love, Ginny

Wednesday, September 13, 1944
11:00 P.M.

Dearest sweetheart,

Today your letter about Christmas presents arrived. Of course I think you're right. I see no sense sending a gift for the sake of sending something. We'll save it for a trip when you come home. I shall send you another box of hors d'oeuvres and perhaps a book on French history, if I can locate a good one.

I am wondering if you are attached to Simpson's 9th Army. It is just getting into headlines here. The action is quite slow now, as is to be expected, I suppose. The last few months seem inexcusable to me.

I went down at 5 o'clock again today and took Father's practice. It surely is an easy way to make money. I'd hate to do it for a living, as I much prefer the laboratory.

Had a nice letter from Ann Falor [wife of Bill Falor] today. She seems to be well, but impatient. She mentioned the English Channel crossing. You have never actually said anything about it. Were you sick?

My darling, I can't tell you how much your letters mean to me. It has been wonderful to receive them so regularly. I only hope that can continue. May God be with you and guide you and keep you.

All my love, Ginny

Tuesday, September 13, 1944
11:30 P.M.

Dearest sweetheart,

Last night Louise Monahan [wife of David Monahan] and I had supper together, and by the time we had finished exchanging news, it was eleven o'clock! Dissipation for me. I also bought a tomato-red blouse for my "exclusive model."

As you have said, and I have also found, I miss you more, not less. I live for our postwar world.

All my love, Ginny

September 14, 1944
11:30 P.M.

Dearest Honey Bunny,

Here I am getting to bed, and you, I imagine, are just sighing in your sleep at the thought of getting up in a short while. Sometime write me about your routine, if you have a semblance of such. Especially what you are apt to be doing at 2:30 P.M.

You never did tell me about Don Woodruff [a Johns Hopkins colleague], and Carol Jackson is very eager for news of Art Grennan (he is a medical man in the same unit). Also, Carrington Owen blew in today and said that her sister Ruth is in the 2nd General Hospital. If you have a chance again, inquire about her, but remember—not even a friend of the family will I tolerate!

I am all packed, ready for our trip tomorrow. Would that you would be going along with me. The biggest hurricane since 1932 just swept up the coast, so I hope there will be something left of Virginia Beach.

We had quite a rain and blow here, and the top to Lib's car leaks. I went out to go home and found the driver's seat soaking. There was nothing to do but lift up my skirts and sit down—you know my usual dress and underwear, so you can imagine it was a bit chilly.

I am my usual healthy self, but living with my mind alone—my emotions are wholly with you.

All my love, Ginny

P.S. Someday I will get the girls in photography to take a picture of Mama, but it will have to be strictly glamorous!

IN SEPTEMBER, GEORGEANNA, son Willie, and sister-in-law Jane Seegar sailed from Baltimore in an Old Bay Line steamer down Chesapeake Bay to Norfolk, to vacation at Virginia Beach.

September 16, 1944
Saturday night

Dearest sweetheart,

Well, here we are in Virginia Beach, and Jane and I are very happy, but Willie has been uncertain. He really needs Papa to help him, but so do we.

He was fascinated by the boat, but considered only the deck a boat, so that when we went into the stateroom to go to bed, he kept saying, "Got to go there on the boat." He finally got to sleep at 9:00 P.M., woke at 2:00, and didn't go to sleep again until 5:30, and then it was about time to get off.

He loves the sand, but is not sure about the "big swimming cool." In fact, he cried when Jane and I went in, but finally let me take him in once. I think the noise scared him. He has been terrible in the dining room, and tonight I had to bring him out just as dinner was being served, but we are hoping for better things tomorrow.

Jane and I have just put him to bed and are in the lobby hoping to hear some news—the papers are so full of the smashing of the Siegfried Line, and we are wondering where Papa is. Tomorrow the lights go on in London. Perhaps it shouldn't be so long before our lights are on again too, but there is always a light burning in my heart—before my own personal altar—for Papa.

Best love, my dear, Ginny

Sunday, September 17, 1944
8:15 P.M.

Dearest Honey Bunny,

We are now in the stateroom waiting for Willie to tire himself out. I'm afraid it's a tough job. He enjoyed his second day at the beach better, ate and slept better. When Viola Hodge [Howard's first cousin] came, he told her, "Papa is in France." I don't know who told him that.

I am completely tired out myself (nicely so) and don't see why he isn't ready to collapse, but he certainly isn't. He loves the boat, which is what I had hoped. I trust that when you get home, he will be nicely "hotel-broke." We expect to take him to restaurants—once a week, at least—when the infantile paralysis season is over.

We have had no news, of course. No mail, so trust we will have plenty of both when we get home.

My thoughts are with you constantly. Would that I knew specifically where to direct them.

All my love, Ginny

Monday, September 18
10:00 P.M.

Dearest Honey Bunny,

Just a wee note to say I love you.

Henry Rigdon came in today with the news that the 42nd General Hospital is packed and a boat was in the harbor September 9th to move to destinations unknown. But rumor has it that he may see your cousin then in India. He says rotation will continue, and that all should be rotated by spring.

Father was out today and seems quite well. He finally developed a very tender spot on deep pressure in the left upper quadrant. I can't imagine what he has had. Elmer at long last received the soap. If you don't get yours faster than that, it'll be weeks before you get the hors d'oeuvres.

Best love, Ginny

GEORGEANNA FEARED THAT I might be killed or wounded by one of Germany's V-1 flying bombs or V-2 rockets. Each terror weapon was equipped with a one-ton warhead.

First aimed at London and later, after the Allies were rushing toward Germany, also at Antwerp and Liège, the V-1s and V-2s killed tens of thousands of mainly civilians, seriously wounded many tens of thousands more, and destroyed many thousands of dwellings and other buildings.

Tuesday, September 19, 1944
9:45 P.M.

Dearest Honey Bunny,

There is more news today about the German use of robot bombs. These terrify me, and I do hope that they will not continue.

Today we again developed home complications. Smitty—after being perfectly well one week—developed her diarrhea all over again while I was away. This morning she went into tetany [lockjaw] again.

Mother is, of course, driving Father around, so I had to take Willie to work with me. He had a wonderful time. I finished all the experimental work and dispensary, then rushed home, fed both babies, did the laundry, put the babies to bed, then back to work. Smitty is now much better, and I hope the relapse was only temporary.

M.R. [medical-school classmate] is in the Payne Whitney Psychiatric Ward with a "nervous collapse" from managing two children and a job while her husband is away in the Navy. I certainly am fortunate to have the home setup I have. Although I think it is trying at times, my situation is so much better than that of any of my friends.

The news is very slow and discouraging to me, but I will feel better when I get your letters.

With all my love, Ginny

Wednesday, September 20, 1944

Dearest Honey Bunny,

Today I received your airmail of September 13 with the enclosed money order for $100. It made me feel a little easier about my two jaunts. And now I know certainly that you must be on active duty—I do hope for not too long.

I can't help but worry about you, of course, although I do try to control myself. I'm sure I'll feel better when mail gets through saying what type of work you are doing and your battle location, if possible.

The news is still discouragingly slow—all my optimism has almost petered out. B was five months old today. She crawls, plays with toys, takes three meals a day with vegetables, fruits, pabulum and laughs and talks all the time and sits on her potty once a day. All in all, she is a very satisfactory child.

Willie continues to advance by leaps and bounds. Cuts up too easily. His favorite sentence is, "No, no, Mommy—go away." By the way, he calls me Mommy now, his own abbreviation.

Please don't continuously apologize for your letters. They are lovely, and besides, if you do write two sentences—"I'm well. I love you"—that's all I really have to know, but do know that each means so much. Will mail the sox tomorrow.

Best love, Ginny

Thursday, September 21, 1944
9:30 P.M.

Dearest Howard,

This morning's news broadcasts were most gloomy, reporting heavy casualties. I hate to think of you in the midst of this holocaust. I do hope that what experiences you have will increase your tolerance and mellow you rather than embitter you, as it did so many in the last war. Of course, my dear, I am certain they won't, but still I worry.

It is just these experiences that I wished so much to share, as I am always so afraid that being separated I will have no chance to help influence your reactions and to be myself influenced by yours. Do remember that my thoughts and love and prayers are with you always.

Tonight we left B with Mrs. Ebeling and went to the China Inn for dinner. As we had learned at Virginia Beach that olives keep Willie quieter than almost anything, we supplied ourselves with a large bottle, and he was splendid. After coming home, I took some more pictures of B. Willie is not changing so rapidly, and besides, he is very difficult to photograph these days.

Everyone is getting along fairly well here. The bank balance is satisfactory in spite of my extravagances in travel. I am waiting for a propitious moment in order to see John Young about purchasing some shares of Remington Arms, probably sometime next week, when I hope the Siegfried Line will have been cracked.

I am anxiously awaiting your next letter. I do hope you will be able to tell me about your activities, which I hope will not continue long.

Best of love and kisses, Ginny

Friday, September 22, 1944
10:30 P.M.

Dearest Honey Bunny,

Here I am in New York without Papa again! It is very nice, though, as every corner brings some happy memory of you and the lovely times we've had together. The unhappy thought is where you may be tonight. I am afraid you may be very busy with very tragic business.

Would that I were there! But seeing how really necessary I am at home does console me a bit! Your mother will take Willie tomorrow, and Geneva is coming Sunday, so I think they should be able to manage. I feel very guilty about this vacation, however.

I am anxiously awaiting news of your work.

My best love, and do take care of yourself for me, Ginny

Saturday, September 23, 1944
12:30 P.M.

Dearest,

We have had a very lovely day here. I have thought of Papa almost constantly. No matter what you may be experiencing, I know you would want us to go on, but somehow I feel unreal. My thoughts are of what we have done here and of what we may do when you return. It may not be right to think about these things, but it is inevitable.

We had breakfast at our favorite restaurant—a sticky bun for me. Then shopped for your socks, and I'm sorry that I could find only 10% wool. Write if this is not good enough, and I'll shop for others.

Bought some books for the children, but couldn't find anything I wanted for you.

Had lunch at a place on 59th St.; very good and inexpensive. Went to see Jacobowsky and the Colonel after being separated from Betty on the 5th Ave. bus. The bus pulled off with me on and Betty off. She didn't know where we were going, but we finally caught up with each other.

We saw the movie Wilson, the story of Woodrow Wilson, which of course depressed me; but was really very good, and had dinner at 11 o'clock at a barbecue place. It reminded me of when we were together at Fort Sam Houston, Texas. Everything reminded me of Papa, so I was very happy. How is it possible for me still to get goose-pimply all up and down just thinking about Papa? And after all these years!

Before I left Baltimore, the girls took a picture of me. If it turns out, I'll send it, but it's got to be glamorous or I won't.

My dear, how I hope you are safe and not too busy and are happy and that you love me best of all.

With all my love, Ginny

Sunday, September 24, 1944
10:30 P.M.

Dearest Honey Bunny,

Well, we arrived home at 8:30 after a very nice weekend indeed. I find everyone well at this end. Howard was in bed, so I have not seen him awake. B grows every day. She has her second tooth now—must have cut it since Friday. You would love her. She is so jolly and laughing—really "Ha-has" right out loud now.

This morning we went to the Dutch Reform Church of St. Nicholas on 5th Ave., as Lib [my sister] liked the preacher so much. He was really one of the best I have ever heard. His topic was "The Changing World." He said only a man of little faith would want a static world and that a government which promised security to all was leading them back down into totalitarianism.

But the really lovely part of his sermon was his concept of change. He said no lovely or worthwhile thing perished until the ideals and ideas behind them perished. Just as no lovely thing was created without first having the dream.

I would like you to hear him preach someday, as I am sure you would enjoy him

We then started for dinner, and I heard in the church of a place at 12 W. 59th St. Well, when we were already on the 5th Ave. bus, I looked again and it was 12 W. 59th St. Betty nearly died! She said, "How does Howard stand such uncertainties?" I said, "Oh, he finds life with one woman very exciting and never a dull moment."

We of course looked up another place in the proper direction, and it turned out to be very good. Walked in Central Park and so to the hotel and home.

All my love to you, my dearest, and remember to say a little prayer for us often.

With kisses, Ginny

Tuesday, September 26, 1944
11:45 A.M.

Dearest Honey Bunny,

Last night was one of those times when I really missed you more than ever, so thought it best to wait until morning to write.

It has really been just a little over two months since I have seen you, but if it were in any way possible, another month would not elapse without my taking steps to get me there. However, I feel that, under the circumstances, it is absolutely impossible at this moment.

The news is so depressing to me, mainly because I was foolishly overoptimistic. I hate to read about the rainy, cold weather, as I can visualize you in the midst of it. Do be warm and don't catch cold. Every day I hope for news, but I know I should not expect it.

I do hope you are nicely situated and not in danger, and also that you are busy and happy.

All my love, Ginny

Tuesday, September 26, 1944
10:15
(4:15 A.M. your time. Is that right?)

Dear Honey Bunny,

Today I have been better, although the war news is still discouraging. I do hope you are not out in all the mud and rain. I want you home, but I want you home well and healthy.

I just had a phone call from Louise Monahan. It seems that she has taken a job in the Edgewood Arsenal and will be in Baltimore for the "duration." She is staying at the Southern Hotel and sounded very well and cheerful. Said she had heard from Dave in a letter dated Sept. 12th. We are going to meet for dinner tomorrow to catch up on all the news.

Had lunch today with Bill Rienhoff and Monty Firor [senior surgeons at Johns Hopkins]. They both inquired about you and your whereabouts.

The election is the chief topic of conversation, and everyone concedes it to Roosevelt.

I haven't seen Dr. Stone [very senior surgeon at Johns Hopkins] since I've been back. He has been on vacation, and also does not eat in this dining room much.

Willie and B are both well. Willie is more and more fond of books, and he knows all the nursery rhymes now. Can't quote them in full, but can finish the line after our favorite fashion of testing knowledge or attention. Goldilocks is his favorite. I hope his Papa has not outgrown those tendencies!

Mother and Father take Willie with them on hospital rounds always, and they say he is no trouble at all. I trust that the children will be trained so well when you return (in a few months) that you'll appreciate the enclosed jokes.

As yet, no word from Ann Falor, but I trust the baby has arrived.

With all my love and oodles of kisses, Ginny

Wednesday, September 27, 1944
11:00 P.M.

Dearest Honey Bunny,

We are really at the end of our rope here. I am putting Smitty in the hospital in the morning. I suppose I'll just have to stay home until I get someone to help out, which looks pretty difficult at this point.

These are just the things I have dreaded—me with my troubles and you with yours; both so different instead of being the same, and so difficult for both of us to realize or appreciate the other's. But just the thought of our love and life together is my sustaining force.

I had dinner with Louise Monahan tonight. She is looking very well, although thin. It was good to talk to someone who is so vitally interested in all the little things about the 5th Auxiliary Surgical Group that I am. We are both hoping for our next letter soon, but are really not expecting it. The war news continues to be bad—the only bright spot is that we do not seem to be retreating, and you said as long as the front was not moving backwards, not to worry.

Howard is very cute these days. He plays train, boat, or chimes with everything. He straddles the baseboard at the foot of our bed and plays pony by the hour. He climbs the bedposts like a monkey, and today, when on a particularly dangerous pinnacle, he looked down and said, "Howard break his neck"—very gleefully.

If only there were some way possible for Willie and me to come to Paris! Can't you think up a scheme? I'm sure I could do something useful, even if it involved pediatrics.

My dear, I love you above all else, and this is my only mainstay. I looked at our honeymoon pictures last night and had a lovely time. But most of them do not have Papa and, when they do, they are too small. I'm going to try to enlarge some and have them printed on coarse-grain sepia paper. They might be nice for your office after the war.

All my love, Ginny

Thursday, September 28, 1944

Dearest Howard,

All day I have had the sick weight in my tummy thinking of the possibility of a whole year without you. I realize that when I am discouraged and things seem impossible, it is only because you are not here or I have not heard from you. Really, we are getting along quite well. Tomorrow I am going to interview a colored girl who "loves children and housework," probably to the tune of $25 a week.

Another thing that made me unhappy was my classmate Mary Goodwin. At the lunch table, she was asking about you and said, "By the way, I had a patient come in to talk to me today about taking her child to France. If she can do it, why can't you?" The idea that there might be a possibility of such a thing just sets me crazy. It is absolutely insane to be so in love with your husband, but that's a fact.

Had a busy morning teaching in the dispensary. I'll never get used to the temerity of medical students. But I do enjoy it. Unfortunately, there were no really good cases.

I hardly dare hope for mail in the morning. Won't go to the door anymore because it is such a disappointment, even though I know I really can't expect any. I hope that when you get back, you'll find some of your packages. I certainly feel as if they've been sent into the wind.

I spend a great deal of my idle time thinking up ways and means of being a better wife, so I hope you'll find me improved for the interim—just so I don't lose my sense of humor.

All my love, Ginny

Saturday, September 30, 1944
11:30 P.M.

Dearest Honey Bunny,

Tonight I would like to write you a four-page letter, but I can tell I won't be able to keep my eyes open that long. The news is even worse. I do hope you aren't in the snow and that, no matter where you are, you have a roof over your head. What trying times for you. And how I do wish I could be with you.

Yesterday B went to work with me, and we got along famously. I fed her before going to lunch, and she talked and cooed until 2:30, then slept all afternoon. I had to wake her up at 5:20, when I left for home. I drove home with her sitting in my lap and taking in all the sights.

Howard was a lamb all morning, so Mother said. She took him to market with her and then on hospital rounds with Father, so he didn't get to nap before 2:30. But then he slept until 5:45, so everyone had a good afternoon's rest. Mary and I washed the clothes and finished at 12 o'clock! We carefully hung them outside in a good stiff breeze under a lovely moon, but this morning rain was pouring down.

I do hope I won't have to stay home, as the work at the lab is getting interesting. Also, I have to keep an eye on my cases with Dave Cheek around. He has no discretion at all, and he is the first resident in years who has ever treated any of my cases without consulting me.

I miss you more and more, instead of less and less. The only nice thing about this will be how perfectly amazingly wonderful it will seem to have our family together again.

All my love, Ginny

Chapter 3

Belgium and Netherlands
2 October–9 November 1944

*W*HEN I SAT DOWN IN BASTOGNE, BELGIUM, ON 2 October 1944 to write in my diary, the German army had completed its suppression of the Warsaw Uprising after two months of savage fighting. All the while, the Soviet army waited outside the city. Stalin held back his forces to allow the Germans to destroy the anti-Communist Polish Home Army that had risen up against the Nazis.

Meanwhile, the U.S. Army's 30th Division was battering the Siegfried Line between Aachen and Geilenkirchen in Germany.

Diary Entry: 2 October 19, 1944
[Bastogne, Belgium, 53rd Field Hospital, 3rd Platoon]

Today we arrived at Bastogne, Belgium. We were supposed to have left Plouay at 9:00 A.M. on the 29th of September. Trucks were to be supplied by the Army (Ninth) and were due in on the 28th.

By noon on the 29th they had not arrived and Major Hanrahan

called Army headquarters. They, of course, were amazed that no trucks had arrived and dispatched 13 trucks at once from Rennes. These trucks arrived about 10:00 P.M. and we left the hospital location at 2:00 A.M. on the 30th.

It had been planned to bivouac at Rennes on the night of the 29th-30th, but in view of the hour, it was decided to go straight through to the bivouac area at Chartres, which had been the scheduled stopover for the nights of 30th-31st. This we did.

Gene Bennett, Howard Yost, Elmer Carlsen, Cpl. McNitt, T/5 Cantrell, T/5 Covert, Lt. Dryfuss, and I were in back of an ambulance (8 in all). We could not sleep sitting up, so Carlsen and I finally curled up on the floor and slept for about one hour.

This was the only sleep until Chartres. We bivouacked in an open field about two miles north of town. Saw Bill Falor and others from the 1st and 2nd Platoons, which had already arrived at Chartres ahead of us. After a good night's sleep the remaining two days of the trip were relatively easy. Cantrell and Covert finally found a place in another truck, so the six of us in the back of the ambulance made out all right.

Played bridge yesterday and today. Dryfuss and I usually taking on Carlsen and Bennett or Yost and Bennett. Tonight we are in bivouac at a so-called concentration area. It was necessary to unload the 13 quartermaster trucks and send them back, so that when we start up, it will be necessary to reload. We are setting up the surgical tent tonight and will sleep in that.

Coming through Sedan today we saw a few buildings knocked down. Weeds and general appearance could have dated them from 1940, but there was no indication of a real battle, such as at Saint-Lô, etc. The French apparently folded very quickly.

The K rations have been supplemented by French bread. We are able to barter from the moving ambulance for a package of cigarettes. Cigarettes make good barter and can be sold in Paris for 100 Fr ($2.00).

Diary Entry: 4 December 1944
[Saint-Vith, Belgium, 53rd Field Hospital, 3rd Platoon]

After setting up the surgical tent on 2 October in anticipation of the stay of a few days at Bastogne, the 3rd Platoon was ordered by Col. William E. Shambora (surgeon, 9th Army) to proceed to Saint-Vith in order to back up the 2nd Division, then going into position. We were to be ready to receive patients by 6:00 P.M. and were to be on the road by 7:30 A.M., in order to clear the road for the 2nd Division, which was taking over from the 4th Division.

Dave Monahan and all of us thought we were getting a break in being the first into action, and we figured that the 3rd Platoon had been selected, in view of the fact it had not been as busy as the other two that were in action at Brest.

Upon arriving at Saint-Vith, it was found that the 2nd Division was not yet in line and the 4th Division Clearing Company was still set up, as well as the 42nd Field Hospital, which was supporting the 4th Division. Incidentally, all three platoons of the 42nd were on the spot in support of the 4th Division Clearing Company, but only one was set up, the others being in bivouac.

We, therefore, went into bivouac beside the 2nd Platoon of the 42nd, which was also in bivouac. Because we had been ordered to be ready to receive patients by 6:00 P.M., Major Hanrahan set up the tents in operational order, but did not unpack the trucks.

During the afternoon and evening, heavy guns could be heard both north and south of us. Some thought that the noise was incoming shells. I can't tell. There is also small-arms firing—probably GIs trying out their weapons. The nearest Germans are supposed to be about three miles away, but no one knows for sure.

Last night there was trouble with the blackout. Tents newly set up were always bad, but the thing that amazed Dave and me was the apparent nonchalance of some of our own officers, who were lax in displaying lights.

Bill seemed set on having lights in the ward tent the officers were using as quarters come hell or high water. Finally, a plane identified as German by the asynchrony of its motors, went over, and our blackout problem was quickly solved by turning out the lights; but too late, I am afraid, to keep us from being observed. However, we were not shelled.

Today we spent cleaning up a bit and drying out after yesterday's rain. We got cigarette rations today.

Diary Entry: 7 October 1944
[Saint-Vith, 53rd Field Hospital, 3rd Platoon]

Since arriving at Saint-Vith we have been set up on a hill in a space that contained no pine trees, contrary to everywhere else in the Ardennes Forest. It is adjacent to the 2nd Division Clearing Company. The days have been quiet, but each night the artillery has been firing at one-to-two-hour intervals—harassing fire, they call it.

The first night or two, we were uncertain as to what was going out and what was coming in, but last night we were certain that most of it was outgoing. There is one battery of heavy guns just east of us, another south of us, and last night we had firing overhead.

Each evening there have been planes overhead identified as Germans by the asynchrony of the motors. I am not at all sure that this is a reliable method of identification. It is important, because we have had trouble blacking out this tent where the stovepipe goes through, so that when a plane is heard, we turn out the lights and sit in the dark until no sound can be heard.

Last night we heard Allied bombers continuously for 25 minutes, going in the general direction of Koblenz, Germany.

The night before last a patient arrived at 9:00 P.M. We were only partially set up, because it was known that we were moving to town today. There was no blood, no heat in the tent, and the operating room was by no means set up. However, blood was borrowed from the clearing company, a fire was started, and the OR set up in short order.

Dave took care of the patient, who fortunately was not badly hurt. B/P was 92. Blood was started and the patient promptly had a chill, so the blood had to be discontinued and plasma used. His chest wound proved to be only of the wall and not penetrating, so that only a debridement (cleansing) was necessary. He is OK today, and everything was finished by 1:00 A.M.

Major Hanrahan went to 9th Army Headquarters the day before yesterday to settle about moving into town. He was directed to move us into a building assigned by the 2nd Division. Dave went along to look it over and did not like its proximity to the railroad, which could easily be a target for bombers. However, situated as we are in the midst of artillery, we are by no means immune here to a stray bomb or, more important, artillery fire. Thus, too, the railroad is not operative.

We did not know how to interpret the move into buildings. There can be only two reasons. One, cold weather and second, a long stay. Rumor has it that a push is coming shortly, so we can't quite figure it out. Incidentally, when Major Hanrahan told Shamboro about the proximity of the new hospital to the railroad yard, Shamboro said it was tough luck. He also said that, if the front line should move back, to get out the best way possible.

Saturday, October 7, 1944

Dearest Ginny,

This is just a brief note to say I love you and to let you know that all is well. We are in the process of moving, and I am sitting outside our new home while the men get things straightened out. I suppose it will not be so bad, but I think the pine forest is better and probably healthier. We will probably all get colds by moving indoors. Perhaps we will not be here long.

Fortunately, today has also been warm and sunny, and lugging our stuff around actually made me sweat. I am in the sun now without a field jacket. The local people say that there is a stretch of good weather about this time of the year—a sort of Indian summer.

Last night we heard bombers for 25 minutes continuously heading east. It was a beautiful clear night, but we could not see them—they must have been very high and in great strength.

During the day planes are overhead in varying numbers, but I have never as yet seen a German plane.

Sometimes at night planes are supposed to be German because of their motor sound, but I have my doubts about this method of identification. It is thought that if they are enemy planes, they are observing and, therefore, we are very careful about the blackout, and this is a great nuisance. There is apparently little to fear from bombing, as there has been none in this area for several weeks now.

We still have had only one patient, and this is an indication of the activity on this front.

Much love and many kisses, H

Sunday, October 8, 1944
1:30 P.M.

Dearest Ginny,

We are now rather nicely situated in a large house in Saint-Vith that is too small to be on any but the largest maps of Belgium. The house reminds me of one on Eutaw Place, in that it has high ceilings, is brick, and has no cupboards or bathrooms, except those put in as an afterthought.

Four of us—Carlson, Yost, and Gene Bennett—are roommates in the third-floor room about twice the size of an ordinary bathroom. Two cots go end to end on each side of the room, and there is a corridor down the middle about three feet in width.

Our duffel goes under the bed, and a clothesline goes over the cot for towels and the like. The hospital itself is on the first and second floors and is not bad. So far, no additional patients and, therefore, there has been nothing for the surgical teams.

Love, H

October 8, 1944
11:00 P.M.

Dearest Ginny,

After writing my letter to you yesterday, who should walk in but Lieutenant Colonel Gay. The Colonel had very little to say. All teams are now out, leaving none at headquarters. The Colonel is spending his time visiting around to see how things are going.

He ran into someone who told him that Major Margaret Craighill [Medical Corps Consultant for Women's Health and Welfare in the War Department Office of the Surgeon General and a friend of the Joneses] was coming over here to look things over from the female point of view. He wanted to know if you were still interested in coming over, but he had a notion that you would end up in a dispensary in Paris, so I said, "No, thank you."

Best love and oodles of kisses, H

10 *October 1944*
3:00 *P.M.*

Dearest Ginny,

Well, we finally have had some work to do in our new location [Saint-Vith]. We went on at 8:00 A.M. and there were two small cases waiting for us—a gunshot wound of the thigh and a wound to the finger, which had a fractured proximal phalanx.

Ordinarily, we do not take any cases except chest and abdomen, but because of the peculiarities of the setup here, we are taking everything. I am just as glad, as it sort of keeps us functioning. Colonel Gay said that none of the teams are working much now, so that our situation here is, therefore, a general expression of the quietness of the front.

I had sent a message back to send up from Paris my electric razor, which was in the Val-A-Pak back there, but when the Colonel came up, he brought the whole thing. It is just as well, as the books I brought over were in it, and if we do much orthopedics, it will be nice to have something to refer to.

Howard Jost asked a native in town how much snow they had and, to his surprise, received the answer that three feet by Christmas was the normal amount. With the gentle hills hereabout, we should get in some skiing.

Gene Bennett and I amused ourselves yesterday by reading some pamphlets left behind by the German Army. I do not think they were written by a German schooled in classical grammar, but they are interesting, and I hope that it is possible to keep at it, as there is a chance that at least I might learn some German. It is too bad that we do not have more opportunity to talk to the natives, but, for one thing, that is not allowed, even here in Belgium.

Love, H

Diary Entry: 10 October 1944
[Saint-Vith, 53rd Field Hospital, 3rd Platoon]

We are nicely settled in this apartment house at Saint-Vith. Yost, Bennett, Carlson, and I have a small room on the third floor. Very little work; this morning we had only three small cases.

The three cases operated on at Saint-Vith were more like typical evacuation-hospital cases than those expected at a field hospital adjacent to a division clearing company. We probably got them because we were not busy. We could provide some of the wounded definitive therapy without the further delay that would have been required to transport them farther back to the evac hospital.

The first patient P. L., Serial No. 4813328, was struck by a shell fragment at 5:50 P.M. 9 October. We operated on him at 9:50 A.M 10 October, 16 hours later and 10 miles from the front.

The second patient, J. O., 35918466, was wounded at 3:25 A.M. on the 10th, and we operated on him at 10:30 A.M., 7 hours and 5 minutes later.

The third patient, W. C., 37489917, was wounded at 4:50 P.M. 10 October and operated on at 9:00 P.M., 4 hours and 10 minutes later.

All three soldiers had superficial wounds to the extremities. We treated the wounds by cutting out dead tissue and sprinkling sulfanilamide on them and covering them with Vaseline gauze and a dry bandage. All these patients did very well.

Diary Entry: 10 October 1944
[Saint-Vith, 53rd Field Hospital, 3rd Platoon]

Dave had two abdominal explorations in his 24-hour shift, both negative. Col. Gay came in Sunday evening and spent the night. He was in a swing around the circuit, so to speak, to see how things were going.

Dave and I were glad to see him, as we had been talking of going to Paris to see him, as we were not having much to do. The

Col. said that no 9th Army unit had any more cases than we had, and he did not know the status of the teams with the 3rd Army. He was on his way to see them. It simply means that very little is in progress at the moment, but we (David and I) decided the thing to do for the present was to sit tight.

Gay told us of a scheme someone thought up (probably Col. Kidd, CO of the 4th Auxiliary Surgical Group) to send us (the 5th) back to the UK and replace us with the 4th, which had some teams in France.

General Hawley [chief surgeon, European Theater of Operations] apparently had about decided to do this when our Col. got word of it and wrote a letter to him stating that we had 50-odd teams in the field. The letter was accepted and the plan is temporarily off. It would have been a much-less-desirable appointment and is the one the 4th now has.

Kidd probably suggested it because he heard that we were having trouble with personnel and thought it would be an opportunity to get the 4th on this side of the Channel. One can't blame him, as they left San Antonio September 1943 (almost a year before we did), and we beat them to France.

Oddly enough, we were relieved at Plouay by a team from the 4th. It must make them boil to know that we have beaten them into action after staying in San Antonio almost a year after they left.

We have had word that distinguished visitors may drop in tomorrow. It could be General George Catlett, Marshall U.S. Army chief of staff, who is in the ETO at the moment.

Since moving into Saint-Vith, the teams have lived apart from the men of the 53rd, and we have had the feeling that they are not quite as cordial, for some reason. We are planning a little party tomorrow night to try to keep things going smoothly.

Wednesday 11 October 1944

Dearest Ginny,

Today the town was alive with MPs, and Gene Bennett and I were uptown when the visitors were expected. But it got so cold that we came back without knowing who the visitors were. We did not get to see them, but we were told that in the party there were sixteen stars in all, so there was plenty of rank.

The enclosed invasion money is used interchangeably with that issued by the Germans and by the French before 1940. Each franc is worth two American cents. There are also ten-franc and twenty-franc notes. From 50 francs up, they are the size of an American dollar. As far as I know, this money is backed by nothing except the fact that the Army financial department will give up American dollars for them at the above rate. These, of course, are no good in Belgium, and we will be paid in Belgian francs.

Love as always, H

Diary Entry: 16 October 1944
[Tongeren, Belgium, 53rd Field Hospital, 3rd Platoon]

Out of a clear sky we found that we were to leave Saint-Vith after all things suggested that we were likely holing up for the winter. On the 13th of October (Friday), Bennett, Yost, Carlson, and I decided to go over to the 1st Platoon at Bastogne for a visit.

We were fortunate in having attached to us five ambulances from the 580th Ambulance Company. Lt. Ryan was very happy to take us for the ride himself.

We left Saint-Vith at 10:00 A.M. on slippery roads. As a matter of fact, at one small hill, we slid off the road and hit a culvert, but no damage was done to the ambulance or us; Lt. Ryan, who was driving, was going very slowly. At any rate, we reached Bastogne in time for lunch and ate at the VIII Corps Headquarters Officers Mess.

We also shopped around town. I was looking especially for a German dictionary, but could find none. I bought a life of Pasteur in French and some short poems by La Fontaine and a small French dictionary. Then went to the 1st Platoon just outside of Bastogne and, upon walking onto the field, met Major Bartunek, who said that they were moving out in an hour. Already most of the tents were down.

No one knows where he is going. I saw Bill Boukalik and his team. Mac and his team had been to Arlon (1st Army) and happened to find out that the 1st Platoon was moving and were told to come back immediately, arriving about the same time we did.

Also, I saw Col. Bishop (surgeon, VIII Corps), who asked me to tell Hanrahan to pack up and be ready to move out first thing the 14th of October 1944. A few minutes later, he came over and gave me a penciled note to Hanrahan with the same information. No one seemed to know where we were going.

We just packed up, and around 8:00 A.M. 14 October 14 trucks from the 107th Evac Hospital came in to move us out. We did not get off until 2:00 P.M. By 6:00 P.M. we had gone only 60 miles and were about 5 miles north of Liège toward Tongeren. At this point, we came to the tail end of the 2nd Platoon, which was just ahead of us.

We were all supposed to meet a contact man at this point, but contact was not made. At 4:30 P.M. the 2nd platoon had halted and sent a man ahead. At any rate, we waited until about 10:00 P.M., when we pulled off the road into an open field into bivouac for the night.

The next day it was evident that we had parked on the front lawn of a château. It became apparent that headquarters of the 53rd had received orders to stay there, and the trucks were unloaded and sent back.

About 9:00 A.M. Gene Bennett and I walked up to the château and, just at that entrance, met a gentleman who proved to be the Count William de Grune, the name of the place being Château Hammel. The count spoke English well and said he was surprised to see troops in the field when he awoke. He invited the officers into the house and asked us if we would like to have some fresh vegetables. The upshot of it was that some of us—i.e., Bill Falor, Gene Bennett, Carlson, and I—moved into the château. Tomorrow, we expect to leave.

COUNT DE GRUNE was very hospitable. Each of the four of us who moved into the château for however long we were going to stay on the estate had a separate room with a four-poster double bed. The château dated from the seventeenth century, and so did the beds. At five feet eleven inches I had to sleep sideways with my knees bent to fit; the people of the seventeenth century were shorter.

The count invited us for breakfast, after which we strolled in his kitchen garden, where family retainers were weeding the vegetables. We commented that he seemed to be so calm and carrying on life as usual, despite the war swirling around him.

He said that we Americans were very impatient and overly concerned. He pointed out that, after all, the château had been there for more than three hundred years, and war parties had been through that part of the country many times.

The Germans came through in 1940, and they now had gone through the other way, just a little while before we arrived. One got used to it and had to get used to it.

Château Hammel was about ten miles from Fort Eben Emael, a Belgian fort that was an anchor of the Belgian defense line. The fort had been considered impregnable. That gave great comfort to the Belgians and the French, because the fort supposedly protected them against a German invasion of France through Belgium, which is the way Kaiser Wilhelm invaded both countries in World War I.

Fort Eben Emael was constructed after World War I, and it probably was impregnable against a World War I—style invasion. But Eben Emael fell quickly during the German invasion in 1940, because it had inadequate protection from airborne assault. Glider troops landed atop the fort and put a new kind of explosive against the cupolas and casements, subsequently overwhelming the fort's defenders.

After talking with the count and discovering that we had no orders to go anywhere, we drove in one of the command cars to Eben Emael. The count assured us that the fort was open and we could stroll through.

And so it was. The underground fort itself was surrounded by pillboxes and guns, so that a land attack would have been costly to the attackers. When the airborne Germans landed on the fort's roof, they landed on the grass sod covering the installation.

The inside of the fort resembled a beehive. We had a free stroll through the miles of underground passageways that led to the gun emplacements. In addition to anchoring the center of the Albert Canal defense system, the fort's guns were said by the members of the Belgian underground to control the city of Aachen.

This particular bit of information may have been a bit of exaggeration, because Aachen is about twenty miles as the shell flies from the fort. The maximum range of the guns, according to the information available, was about twelve miles.

France was also thought to be protected by the fort, because the adjacent Albert Canal was believed to be a barrier to approaching troops from Germany through Belgium. But with technology militarily available in 1940, the canal was easily crossed and the fort captured by the German glider troops.

THE MOVE FROM Brittany to Saint-Vith, which my team reached on 3 October, conformed to the movement of the Ninth Army from coastal Brittany to the line of battle to the east. Ninth Army, consisting at that time of only VIII Corps, was inserted into the line between First Army to the north and Third Army to the south. Ninth Army Headquarters was in Luxembourg.

The unexpected shift on 14 October from Saint-Vith to Nuth, Netherlands, where we arrived on the seventeenth, accompanied withdrawal from between the First and the Third Armies and its reinsertion north of First Army adjacent to the British.

Most of this transfer occurred on paper. Ninth Army Headquarters moved to Maastricht and took over the zone. Troops of XIX Corps and VII Corps, both of which had previously belonged to First Army, stayed in place. No real wholesale troop movement occurred; only units such as the 5th Aux moved. All 5th Aux teams assigned to Ninth Army when we were in Le Vésinet shifted from where we were (in our case, Saint-Vith) to support the repositioned Ninth. In that shuffle, my Team 3 drew Nuth, near the German border.

This move turned out to be extremely fortunate for Team 3. In

December, the strong mechanized German forces unexpectedly counterattacked the advancing Allied forces, inaugurating the bloody Battle of the Bulge.

The German counterattack's first objective was Saint-Vith. Many U.S. Army medical personnel in that town were captured and taken to Germany. But the 3rd Auxiliary Surgical Group teams there escaped. Who knows what would have happened to Team 3 if the First and Ninth Armies had not been shuffled.

The memoirs of General (later, President) Dwight David Eisenhower, then Supreme Commander, Allied Expeditionary Force, and General of the Army Omar Bradley barely mention the Ninth Army redeployment. But historian Stephen Ambrose reports in *Citizen Soldiers* that Field Marshal Bernard Montgomery, commanding general of operation MARKET GARDEN in September 1944, looked for scapegoats to blame for the operation's failure.

Much of the failure was attributed to lack of support by General Courtney Hodges's First Army, immediately to the south of Montgomery's forces. It takes scant imagination to conclude that Eisenhower and Bradley considered it politic and in the best interest of the Allied cause to place Simpson next to Montgomery—there would be no scores to settle.

I SAW GENERAL Simpson after the war in Baltimore, at the Johns Hopkins Hospital, where his wife was a patient of Dr. Richard TeLinde. He wasn't disposed to discuss it when I asked why the shift had been made; he simply shrugged his shoulders. At that time, all of the principals— Eisenhower, Bradley, and Montgomery—were still alive.

But in one of our conversations, the general asked me about our commanding officer, Lieutenant Colonel Gay. Gay remained a lieutenant colonel throughout the war, even though the Table of Organization called for a colonel in the post he occupied. Simpson told me that he had received from a member of the 5th Auxiliary Surgical Group a letter complaining that our commanding officer had not been promoted.

Did I know why Gay had not been promoted? Simpson said he always approved recommendations for promotion of anybody in Ninth Army, but that Colonel Shamboro (surgeon, Ninth Army) had never recommended Gay for promotion to full colonel.

I replied that I didn't know any details, which was true, but I did know that Gay never seemed to have anything good to say about the medical section of Ninth Army in general and about Shamboro in particular. I had never heard Colonel Shamboro speak about Gay, but Shamboro clearly never felt moved to recommend Gay for promotion.

All members of the 5th Aux were very loyal to Gay. We admired him, and we were disappointed that he did not get the promotion that all of us agreed he deserved.

Gay was always very good to those under his command. Most of us received our promotions as soon as we had served the minimal amount of time in grade.

Gay also was generous in handing out awards. Of course, all promotion and award recommendations had to go to Shamboro's desk for approval before General Simpson himself approved them. It's entirely possible that Shamboro judged that Gay exhibited insufficient selectivity in his recommendations for promotions and awards.

And although he commanded the 5th Aux, Gay was superseded and not even consulted by Ninth Army in regard to medical and technical matters. Lieutenant Colonel Gordon Smith, the affable and capable surgical consultant, judged the surgical skills of personnel and decided on placements for whatever assignments were available; that was the role of "consultants" throughout the army.

There were consultants in the War Department Surgeon General's Office back in Washington. Harvey Stone was a consultant there, and it was through him that I got into an auxiliary surgical group.

The consultant to the European Theater of Operations was Elliott Cutler, Harvard professor of surgery. Gordon Smith was Ninth Army's consultant. Consultants brought to the regular army their knowledge of the medical skills of personnel and advised their commands who should go where. Their mission was to get round pegs into round holes.

The consultants also were charged with alerting the army medical community to advances in medical science and effective procedures. The consultant system seemed to work pretty well. To its credit, the army realized that its regular army medical personnel needed consultants' guidance.

The consultants' personnel-assignment role and higher commands' tactical assignments of teams in response to the changing battlefield sharply limited the authority of auxiliary surgical groups' commanding officers.

I often wondered whether, instead of being a consultant, Lieutenant Colonel Smith should have been the commanding officer of the 5th Aux, because he was the officer making the medical-personnel-assignment decisions.

Shamboro, who could have recommended Gay for promotion, may have thought, despite the specification in the Table of Organization, that our auxiliary surgical group didn't require a colonel as CO. But every other auxiliary surgical group had a chicken colonel, which leads me back to the view that something between Shamboro and Gay—mutual hostility, lack of confidence—blocked promotion.

I did not discuss the relationship of auxiliary surgical groups to the army's surgical consultants with General Simpson; I did not think of it at the time. Nevertheless, I was fascinated that General Simpson brought up the Gay-promotion issue a few years after the war.

THE SHUFFLING OF First and Ninth Armies took place when action on the Western Front was quieting down. Allied forces had halted at the German border because of inadequate supplies of ammunition and gasoline.

When the supply shortage ended in early October, the Allies attempted to penetrate the German border and its Siegfried Line in the Aachen area despite wretched weather. The Siegfried Line was fiercely defended. The Allies suffered heavy losses of men and materiel.

Aachen appeared to be of minor military significance, but its capture was a blow to German morale. Allied armies in Western Europe now stood firmly on German soil. They closed the ring around Aachen on 16 October, when patrols of XIX Corps and XVII Corps met to the east of it.

The 29th Division, which in Brittany had been part of VIII Corps, was at this time an element of XIX Corps and involved in attacking Aachen from the north. The 116th Infantry of the 29th fought in the area of Würselen. The Germans battled desperately against the closing of the Aachen ring, trying unsuccessfully to overrun a roadblock on the Aachen-Würselen highway.

When we relieved the 3rd Aux in Nuth, some battlefield casualties came in. After the surrounded German troops in Aachen surrendered on 22 October, we saw fewer casualties.

We were in action at Nuth from 17 October until 8 November. I performed twenty-two operations; we never had more than about three cases a day. Thirteen of our casualties were from the 29th Division, two from the 102nd Division (which went into the line on 26 October as part of XIII Corps), other U.S. soldiers from miscellaneous units, and one German POW. Of my twenty-two cases, the first seventeen were brought in 29 October. Over the next few days, we had six cases, which arrived at irregular intervals.

The enlisted ranks account for the majority of casualties. Eleven of the wounded brought to us were privates. Except for two officers, the remainder was enlisted personnel above the grade of private.

Diary Entry: 18 October 1944
[Nuth, Netherlands, 53rd Field Hospital, 3rd Platoon]

Yesterday we moved from Château Hammel through Tongeren to Nuth, Holland, and set up there in a school, relieving the 49th Field Hospital. The distance was about 29 miles.

We are back of the 29th Division, which is now part of XIX Corps of 1st Army. How to explain the presence of 9th Army troops (i.e., us) in back of the 1st Army troops, I do not know. We arrived about 1:00 P.M., and by the time the 49th moved out and we in, it was 8:00 P.M.

The 49th had been receiving about four to six patients per day and were very sorry to have to leave, as the hospital is set up in a Catholic school and the teams (from the 3rd Army) are living in a room. When we finally got set up, Hanrahan thought that all of us could live in the one room, so 13 of us (officers) are crowded in a room about 18 feet square.

----

18 October 1944
6:30 P.M.

Dearest Ginny,

This time we can say that we are in Nuth, Holland and in action. After getting in late yesterday, by the flip of a coin, I went on duty from 8:00 P.M. to 8:00 A.M. and will continue through the week, and if we are still here, Dave and I will shift back. I slept until 1:30 this morning, and then they awoke me, and we did two cases from then until 8:00 A.M.

One was a traumatic diaphragmatic hernia with the stomach in the thorax and also the omentum, which in turn was eviscerated through a wound in the thoracic wall. It was easy to replace the viscera through a large thoractomy incision, and I shall now never have the slightest hesitation about trying to repair such a hernia in civilian practice, for I think I now know how to see almost any part of the diaphragm, not only because of this case, but others.

Then through an incision we found the jejunum [the middle part of the small intestine] severed just at Treitz ligament [a suspending ligament just at the beginning of the jejunum], and it was necessary and surprisingly easy to mobilize the third part of the duodenum [the first section of the small intestine between the stomach and the jejunum] through the mesocolon [the structure attaching the colon to the body] in order to get room for an anastomosis.

When we left our last château, the count gave us each several postcard photos of the place. I slept in the French King's Room in which a French king stayed when he visited here. The château itself dates from the 1200s and, of course, has been modernized. I found after writing you that the

*water around it was in fact a moat at one time, and a quarter of it has been
filled in.*

All my love, H

Diary Entry: 25 September–24 October 1944
[Nuth, 53rd Field Hospital, 3rd Platoon]

Dave and I have been alternating once every 24 hours prior to coming here, but it was apparent that we would be busy enough to use a 12-hour shift. Dave and I tossed a coin, and I lost. Dave chose the 8:00 A.M. to 8:00 P.M. shift.

The work we have done is recorded in the casebook. Our living conditions are good, and we have been inside. But working at night means sleeping in the daytime, and that does not work well with so many personnel in such a small place.

It turns out that a good many troops formerly belonging to the 1st Army have been transferred to the Ninth Army. The 29th Division, for example, has been transferred to the Ninth Army. About the 22nd of October, at 12:00 noon, the 9th Army was supposed to take over this sector. It was reported that German planes dropped leaflets welcoming General Simpson (commanding general, 9th Army). However, I have not seen one of the pamphlets, and it may be only a rumor.

Lt. Col. Smith, 9th Army consultant in surgery, was through this afternoon to see how we were getting along. He talked for an hour or so, but he had little to offer.

Dave told him that Bill Rote (his assistant) was ready to take a team, and I told him Howard Yost (my assistant) was also about ready. He knows that the 5th Aux headquarters was at Tongeren on the Count de Grune's lawn. If this is so, there should be work in a day or two.

We talked about reactions from blood. It seems that it is the general impression that we are having more reactions from American blood than from other blood. Smith says that it is the opinion of the blood bank that the blood is really OK, but the trouble is in dirty tubing. Today we had two severe reactions, and it is true that one of them was from English blood and one from American blood.

There were also two reactions from glucose, and the lab will be more careful in washing out the tubing. But without running water, this is difficult.

Compared with the situation outside of Saint-Vith, we have not been near the artillery, but we can hear the bombing in the not-too-great distance. Every once in a while, as tonight, the Germans come over with a few planes and go after the artillery with bombs. Tonight they made two separate attacks, the second time dropping a bomb near enough to rattle the windows and break a few loose bits of plaster off the ceiling. The antiaircraft fire was quite sharp.

We have never gotten any casualties from these raids, but each time we expect some, as we do tonight. While at Tongeren, we heard a flying bomb land, which the count estimated to be 6-to-7 kilometers away. The flying bomb explodes with two explosions, one while in the air, and this apparently knocks it down, and then another explosion near or on the ground.

No one seems to know exactly how far the front line is from here. Our patients are from the other side of the border, but no town name appears on the tags. The tags say "Europe" or "Germany."

We have put up with living 13 in a room as long as possible, and our team is moving into a pyramidal tent that has been pitched for us. Thus, I no longer have to put up with the blaring radio.

Diary Entry: 30 October 1944
[Nuth, 53rd Field Hospital, 3rd Platoon]

Since moving into the tent, things are quieter and better. The day before yesterday I took Dave's surgical truck and went over to Maastricht to see our headquarters, which had just arrived. Very little news.

Things have livened up around here. The artillery has been very loud all day. A battery must have just set up outside of town. Last night we had six artillery alerts, and the bombing woke me up several times.

Single German planes came over and dropped bombs on many installations. As far as I know, there are only two things around here to interest them—a railroad, which is operating and is located some half mile from us, and our ammunition dump, which is along the track. We have no cause to worry here if they hit the target. It is the missiles that might blow us up.

Today Bob Ewing came over to get Bill Rote.

---

2 November 1944

Dearest Ginny,

I did not get to write yesterday, as all of us (the team) drove over to headquarters at Maastricht and were therefore gone all day and last night. We were tired and went to bed in anticipation of work late that night. However, there was nothing again, making eight straight nights without a case. Things are quiet indeed. Perhaps the calm before the storm.

We have had some rearrangement of the teams here. Bill Rote, Dave's assistant, left, as I mentioned, to take a team of his own and was replaced by Joe Ketay, who is a shock man here without a whole team.

Howard Yost, my assistant, got a team yesterday, and we brought back Kenneth Tanner, a new boy in the outfit. He graduated from Harvard and was a nine-month surgical intern at Johns Hopkins, ending the first of January 1944. He is from North Carolina and, I believe, he will work out very satisfactorily.

We also got a second shock team, with Lt. Henry Cohen in charge, so that we now have two surgical and two shock teams. While at headquarters I got my old radio from Colonel Gay, and it seemed to work as poorly as it did in San Antonio. It still clicks on and off, but it is better than none, for sure, as we moved into the tent and we otherwise had no radio.

The commanding officer of this outfit is no ball of fire, but he is a harmless sort of a guy who was in general practice in South Carolina before the war. He has been in the Army four years and does not really have much fire to go out and get things done—he waits until someone tells him to do something before he does. In short, he has little initiative.

At any rate, Dave decided to kill a bottle of Scotch, which he did, and then told off the major in no uncertain terms what he thought about him. This all took place about 1:00 A.M. in the schoolroom, so that, fortunately, I missed it and heard about it only this morning.

It must have been bad though, for early this morning the major (Hanrahan) came out to the tent and wanted to know what we thought of the hospital, etc., etc., and all in all it was a most unhappy situation.

However, Dave and the major later had a conference and must have straightened things out, for everything seems to have quieted down, and strange to say, I believe the major is better for it. It is all an expression of inactivity for Dave, as he also does not do well to do nothing. I am sure Louise must have a terrible time with him.

The news seems to be better, and it now appears that Antwerp, Belgium, will soon be open to Allied shipping.

Much love to you and the family, H

Friday, 3 November 1944

Dearest Ginny,

Last night we had a case about 9:00 P.M., and the new assistant worked out very well. He had not first-assisted before and, of course, was not entirely at home, but with a little practice he will be all right.

The patient had what the assassinated Governor Huey Long of Louisiana is supposed to have died of: a hole in both the anterior and posterior wall of the stomach. In Huey's case, they are supposed to have not looked at the posterior wall and, consequently, he did not do so well.

The news seems to be good. I bet Carlson and Bennett each ten marks that this part of the war would be over by the first of January, but everybody here seems to be preparing for a long winter.

The other day, while at headquarters, at nearby Maastricht, we went to the clothing store, and I bought two pairs of combat boots. You remember those with the high tops in place of the leggings? They have the advantage of not having to worry with leggings, and this is some help in getting up, especially at night.

The radio has been noisy, and I took it over to a Signal Corps shop nearby. There I ran into a Sergeant Moore from Baltimore, and, for that reason, I think he is going to try to fix it.

As usual and always, my love, H

4 November 1944

Dearest Ginny,

Your letter mentioned the color picture of the ovarian tumor. I am so glad that you are keeping on with these things, for you are certainly thinking for the both of us. Although it may take us years, we should have the best collection of images of ovarian tumors in the world.

Today I stopped in at an evacuation hospital to see Charley Burbank and his team and ran into Tom Ambler. He is with the Pikesville outfit and has been for two years (artillery attached to the 29th Division). I don't know that we had heard about that.

At any rate, he seemed well. He came in on D+4 [four days after D-Day] and seems to have had a good time. I saw him only for a few minutes, as he had brought in a patient, but he is coming up to see me soon.

I have not been able to weigh in until today and found that I weighed 180 with clothes and 176 stripped. We went over to take a bath this morning at the mine and they found a scale. I think I had better lay off carbohydrates.

While in town today I managed to get a transformer to convert the 220 volts to 110, and the radio works much better. In fact, it works all right, so that tonight we had good music and could get the news, which seemed somewhat better.

We had no case again last night, and I am glad, as it was cold and rainy.

My love as always, H

5 November 1944

Dearest Ginny,

The village priest came in about 7:00 P.M. and stayed until just after 10:30. This priest I find very interesting and not as "Catholic" as the Catholic clergy at home. I really believe that it is the Irish in the American clergy that is so troubling to us. And, in thinking about it, perhaps it is the Irish Catholics who are so different.

Did I tell you that Mac is coming into headquarters and giving up his team? I do not know just what is behind it, but the Colonel has had to use someone else to do his job as executive, and it may be that the Army wanted it.

Also, it has been interesting that, professionally, he sort of sweat it out, in that he had a great deal of trouble with some of his cases, which left him open to criticism. I am not sure that this had anything to do with the new arrangement, but I feel sure that it has made Mac more than ready to go back to the administrative position that he had.

We have continued to be quiet and are now down to about 10 patients from a normal 100 and an average of 30.

Love to all, H

Monday 6 November 1944
10:30 P.M.

Dearest Ginny,

We have been talking about shock and its physiological background. We must know more about the normal vascular system in order to make sense in conversation. In other words, we need a book on physiology to let us know the mechanism of transmission of the pulse wave.

Is it simply the head of pressure in the fluid? Or do the vessel walls play a part in the lightning-like peristaltic wave under nervous control? It would be nice to have an adequate library, for we see shock such as is never seen in civilian practice, and I am sure the problem is a long way from being solved.

We had a bad case early this morning. The retroperitoneal [behind the peritoneum] part of the duodenum was badly lacerated, and I am not sure that we got it back together again the right way. The wounded soldier was badly shocked from copious amounts of bile-stained fluid in the peritoneum [the transparent serous membrane lining the abdominal cavity], and I am rather surprised that he seemed better tonight than at noon. We are having but very few casualties, and these are from sort of accidental situations, so to speak.

I love you, always, H

7 November 1944
(Election Day)

My dearest Ginny,

This is a peculiar presidential election day, to say the least. News of the campaign has been completely withheld. Only the briefest news comments in Stars and Stripes. Not a single speech of Dewey or the President has been published.

It is not possible, therefore, to judge the possibilities of winning for Dewey. Betting odds were quoted in Stars and Stripes substantially in favor of the President, so it appears that the election will be no closer than the last one.

Incidentally, while staying with the count, whose sister I asked you to write to, we found that he was much interested in the election and wanted to know who will oppose the President now that Republican Wendell L. Willkie was dead.

He had not so much as heard of [New York Governor Thomas E.] Dewey, the 1944 Republican presidential candidate] and, of course, had no conception of what a presidential campaign was all about.

If you get a reply from the vicountess, let me know, and I shall relay the message to the count, if feasible.

Today has been a sharp, cold day. Typical fall. The leaves are about off the trees, and it reminds me of a good football day, except that it threatened rain. It has not been nearly cold enough to freeze, but there has been much rain and dampness. It makes the first moment of sitting on the homemade latrine seat a terrible shock.

Speaking of the latrine and such things reminds me that I have become quite a coffee drinker, with the result that I keep an empty plasma can beside my bed. Each morning, not only I, but also all my tentmates, empty the can as part of the morning routine.

We have a convalescent ward where patients who are well on the way to recovery are sent. One patient there is OK, except that he has not been able to void in the 10 days since he was operated on. Two or three days ago, we moved another convalescent patient, who was five days postoperative, next to him, and now neither one of them can void. How do you figure that out?

Last night Gene Bennett, Elmer Carlson, and Kenneth Tanner went to the priest's house to supper. They came home with several Dutch expressions, and one of them was Ik hou van jou. I have known for a long time that Ik hou van jou, because it means, I love you.

As always, H

EXPERIENCE AT NUTH conformed very much to the army medical plan, in that we saw the nontransportable wounded.

Among the twenty-two casualties that I personally operated on, three had very troublesome and serious thoracoabdominal wounds; nine had abdominal wounds only, five had chest wounds, five others were so seriously wounded that they could not be moved. Four of the last five casualties had lost the most part of a leg, so that it was necessary to reamputate in each case.

The first patient upon whom I operated, J. R., a tech sergeant from the 115th infantry of the 29th Division, Serial No. 35035748, had a penetrating wound of the abdomen. We had the benefit of an X-ray of all these patients. In the tech sergeant's case, the X-ray showed a fragment of metal still in the abdomen, so the patient had only one external wound.

The fragment had penetrated the entire thickness of the liver and caused considerable bleeding. The missile then had made a single hole in the transverse colon and lodged within the colon, suggesting that it was almost spent when it hit J. R.

The U.S. Army auxiliary surgical group teams were guided by *The Manual of Therapy*. This manual—prepared by the army's medical consultants—was supplemented by bulletins reporting advances in battlefield medical knowledge and techniques. We also had frequent visits from our Ninth Army medical consultant, who did his best to keep us up to speed on late developments.

The tech sergeant upon whom I operated was a lucky man. I had learned from a recent medical bulletin not to close a penetrating wound of the *large* bowel. The bulletin instructed us to exteriorize the wounded bowel—in effect, leaving the patient with a colostomy through the holes in the colon. Experience had shown that closing wounds in the large bowel led to peritonitis in a big percentage of cases.

I performed the exteriorization operation on the tech sergeant, and I was very happy that he did very well during the whole ten days he was at the field hospital, before being evacuated to the general hospital, then at Liège.

THE SECOND MAN upon whom I operated at Nuth was also from the 115th Regiment of the 29th Division. He received a shell fragment about 8 PM 17 October. I operated on him at 5:30 AM on the eighteenth.

He had a penetrating wound of the chest. The X-rays showed what seemed to be his stomach lodged in the thoracic cavity. He had received five units of plasma and three units of blood in the triage tent before the operation, but his blood pressure was extremely low when he entered the operating room.

We opened his chest and found that a missile had made a large incision in the diaphragm and that the greater part of his stomach and omentum were in the thoracic cavity. I returned the abdominal contents to the abdomen with little difficulty and closed the diaphragmatic defect through the thoracic cavity.

I then necessarily opened the abdomen to inspect things there and found a large amount of blood in the peritoneal cavity. There was active bleeding from the Treitz ligament, which I controlled with a clamp and ligature. I resectioned twelve inches of the jejunum and did an end-to-end anastomosis from the duodenum to the upper part of the jejunum. The splenic flexure of the large intestine had been penetrated, and in accordance with Army policy, I exteriorized the intestine.

This very seriously wounded soldier was in shock when the operation began at 5:30 AM. We never could get his blood pressure above sixty. He died at 5:00 PM of irreversible shock. He received three thousand cc of blood and ten units of plasma within three and a half hours, which should have been sufficient to save his life. This was the second time a patient of mine had died of shock. To my deepest regret, he would not be the last.

THE ARMY HAD established an efficient lifesaving blood service. Our surgical teams always had as much blood as we could use. The blood was fresh. Each bottle bore a label stating when and where the blood had been drawn.

We had blood from the United Kingdom and the United States. We received it within a week of its being drawn. The army's policy was to always use O-group blood—there was never any cross-matching. O-group blood was then believed to be suitable for anyone. But we discovered that some subtypes of mismatch occur even with the O-universal-donor blood.

Our team may have seen one or two mismatches. But we never were able to determine whether a bad reaction of a patient was from the blood or from dirty tubing, as we were compelled to wash and reuse tubing and could not be sure that the tubing was as clean as it should have been.

We could not save all wounded brought to us. But we were able to save many.

I am thinking of patient M. K., a twenty-year-old from the 116th Infantry of the 29th Division, Serial No. 32921444, who was wounded by shellfire at 2 PM 19 October. The litter bearers got to him six hours later. They administered five units of plasma before he reached the field hospital at 11 PM.

M. K. had a penetrating wound of the left lower quadrant of his torso and a very tense abdomen, obviously from peritonitis, but his blood pressure was normal. We operated on him at 1:00 AM on 20 October, eleven hours after he was hit.

There were nine holes in the small bowel, with extensive bowel-content contamination of the peritoneal cavity. I closed these holes and dropped five grams of sulfanilamide powder into the peritoneal cavity, closing my incision one and a half hours after making it. During the operation, M. K. received two units of plasma and five hundred cc of blood.

The patient recovered beautifully, with absolutely no distention of the abdomen. When he was evacuated to the general hospital at Liège, he was doing fine. How gratifying that he and several other patients treated by our team recovered as well as he.

IN ADDITION TO the terribly troubling deaths from irreversible shock, we had other patients who died from munitions blasts.

For example, Private C. F., from Company A of the 125th Cavalry, was felled by an enemy mine. He had a penetrating wound of the right buttock as well as an abdominal wound. The buttock wound was cleaned up. The wound in the colon—too low to exteriorize—was closed with a proximal colostomy.

He also had a suprapubic cystotomy, and we saw that the two ureteral openings in the bladder were spurting clear urine. All of these wounds were tidied up in what seemed to be a satisfactory manner.

C. F. received five hundred cc of blood and eleven units of plasma during the three-hour operation, yet he did not promptly recover from the surgery. His blood pressure gradually decreased, despite additional transfusions of plasma, and he died. We attributed his and other such deaths to "blast," which probably caused particularly severe lung damage, because patients exhibited considerable, inexplicable pulmonary edema.

In short, the three soldiers with thoracoabdominal wounds upon whom I operated at Nuth were transferred in good condition. Five of the nine casualties with abdominal wounds died. One of the five casualties with thoracic wounds died; one of the four casualties with amputations died. A third of severely wounded men admitted to our field-hospital platoon adjacent to the clearing company died. Two-thirds were saved by front-line surgery.

Saint-Vith, Belgium, September 1944.

Nuth, Holland, October 1944. The 53rd Field Hospital,
3rd Platoon teams (except nurses).

Nuth, Holland, October or November 1944. A volleyball game outside the schoolhouse used as a field hospital.

Nuth, Holland, October 1944. Left to right: Tech 4 Vernon Frentzel, Tech 5 Lee McNitt, Captain Elmer Carlson, Lieutenant Alice Ridzon, Lieutenant Kenneth Tanner, and Captain Howard Jones.

Chapter 4

Letters from Home
1-15 October 1944

*I*N THE UNITED STATES, WAR PRODUCTION WAS AT its height. Shipyard workers built cargo ships in seventeen days, bombers in thirteen. In a single year, Americans at home contributed eighteen million tons of scrap metal and seven million tons of waste paper to the war effort.

Sunday, October 1, 1944

Dearest,

Just a wee note to say I love you and that B almost sat up today. I have been going over Willie's book of snapshots and I believe I can almost duplicate the book for B. It is nice to see the book, as there are pictures of Papa there.

I suppose Ess told you that Eunice [a first cousin living in India] is coming home, and from the letter, her husband is also. I do wish we could have that family reunion about January 1, but I find it is definitely out.

I do hope you are billeted in houses and not sleeping in meadows in the cold and rain and snow. My love is with you always, dear, and my thoughts are constantly about you.

With love and kisses, Ginny

THIS NEXT LETTER, to Joe Redline, who was a medical administrative officer of the 5th Auxiliary Surgical Group, was in response to my request to send some three-way stopcocks, which we did not have and which were very useful.

Baltimore, Maryland

Dear Joe,

Howard wrote asking me to send some three-way stopcocks. I have put one in each of three of his letters and am enclosing one to you. As I know that you will probably receive the mail before he does, could you be on the lookout for his letters marked "Medical Supplies" and, if possible, see that they reach him at once.

Howard's letters are most enthusiastic, and I know that the experience must be most valuable. However, I do hope it won't be too long, as waiting at home is a heartbreaking job. But, then, I am never good at waiting.

Give my regards to the Colonel and Bob Ewing and any of the other friends at home.

Sincerely yours, Georgeanna Jones

Tuesday, October 3, 1944
12:30 P.M.

Dearest Honey Bunny,

Missed my letter last night, as Mr. Powers [our minister] came and was so late in leaving. Hugh, his son has been assigned as a battalion surgeon and, of course, is quite upset, as is his father.

As yet we have no help, but B loves coming to work and Mother and Father are really lovely with Willie. He is getting much easier to look after also, as he plays in one spot and reads books indefinitely. He has a bad case of insomnia, though, and this A.M. woke up at 4:30, and at 7:00 he was still awake. I had taken him to the "toidy" twice and sung "Bye-Bye Baby Bunting" three times. The last time he called for a book, and that fixed him. He went to sleep and didn't wake up until 9:15.

I am wondering about the picturesque part of France and hope that now you are not too exposed, as I'm afraid the weather is very bad. I received your letter of the 25th today, which I think is excellent. I was afraid that you had not received any packages, but perhaps some will come to you shortly. Also, things in letters should arrive.

As I read your letter, I realize more and more that we have a wealth of happiness in our life and love together, that small details of life don't really matter. How fortunate I am to have you. Do take care of yourself for us.

Best love, Ginny

P.S. Phoebe Robinson Jacobson is pregnant.

Tuesday, October 3, 1944
11:30 P.M.

Dearest,

My day has been brightened and my disposition sweetened by your letters. I do not realize how much I depend upon them or how insidiously not hearing from you affects me until I hear from you, and then, suddenly, the sun is again shining. Also, it makes being here worthwhile when I can send you things. I loved rustling around for the stopcocks. I am sending four in all.

I have been asked to speak at the University of Maryland OB/GYN ward rounds next Thursday and really feel quite out of order, but think I will give them our figures of normal endocrine values. I still feel lost without your support and advice.

Well, Phil, who had just lent the Joneses his vehicle, came up and got the car today, so I am without. I really shouldn't bother to get another, as it is too strenuous to struggle with the gas and tires, besides paying outrageous prices. I am trying to get along without you, but it is almost impossible. I only hope you are not too exposed to the weather.

The babies continue to be cute and sweet. My constant regret is that you can't share them. Perhaps when we are on an even tenor again, we will have to have two more just for you.

All my love, Ginny

Thursday, October 5, 1944

Dearest Honey Bunny,

Today a maid came! She is very good and will be here until Saturday, at least, as I am not going to pay her until then. It takes a great weight off my mind to have her, but I'll probably have to go into private practice to afford her.

We have been having great trouble with Howard's sleep habits. I'm afraid he is a poor sleeper. From his point of view, I think it well, but from mine, difficult. He can now get out of the crib at will and has refused to nap. Today he did nap, but it is now 9:45 P.M., and he is raising Cain. He has been up twice already. I'm afraid we will just have to cut out the nap entirely. He is calling out "Doganna."

I hope by this time some of your packages have arrived. Frank Connoly was up today and was very embarrassed about not paying what he contracted for our car. I assured him it was satisfactory. He had a very interesting section of a nodule from a tube, which was removed from a woman with a simple serous cystadenoma [adenoidal cyst]. It was a mesonephroma and, I believe, a benign type of adenoma.

Every day and every way I love you more and more.

All my love, Ginny

Friday night, October 6, 1944

Dearest Honey Bunny,

Your letter written on the 15th arrived today. I seem to be getting them in reverse order. I gather you were working nights and sleeping days. How do you make out sleeping in the daylight? Do you need your eyeshade?

We are really making out quite well now. Betty Beecham [a hospital secretary] takes me and brings me. The maid is wonderful, and life's complexities seemed to be solved, at least temporarily. My real problem now is Willie's sleeping habits, which have suddenly gone haywire.

That, I suppose, is the fascinating thing about children. You never know what they will be doing next. Tonight it was only 10 o'clock when he went to sleep. Perhaps I had better cut his nap entirely and let him sleep from seven to seven, but I don't think I will.

I am very eager to know about your work and hope that the morning will bring more mail. How wonderful when we can sit down together and go over these letters.

Another thing that I noticed—Mother and Father and I are now alone, and you have no idea how much less the strain is. Family should never be combined if it can be avoided, and help should never be a part of the family! Remind me of that if you need to in the future.

Every night I put myself to sleep by going over a special part of our life together—a trip or adventure. We do have some beautiful memories.

All my love, Ginny

Saturday, October 7, 1944

Dearest Howie,

Just a wee note to really send you on the way—stopcock. I hope when it arrives, the fighting will have ceased and there will be no further need for it. But I am afraid that is a vain hope.

Henry Bennett [a Howard Jones classmate] is back on rotation. As yet he has not come east, but we expect him soon. Dr. Mackie from Australia was here and told us about him. He said that the Australian group had about 500 or 600 patients in a 4,000-bed hospital. They expect to be moved to the Philippines as soon as possible.

I hope you can tell by my letters that I am better adjusted than before. Please don't worry about us. We are all fine, and Papa will have a very well-behaved little family to come home to—I hope.

But because I am better adjusted doesn't mean I miss you less. Sometimes it comes over me in a sudden way, and I get panicky thinking of the possibility of a two-year separation. But we hope it won't be that long.

All my love, Ginny

Sunday, October 8, 1944
3:15 P.M.

Dearest Howie,

It is now Sunday afternoon—the first really nice, clear day we have had in almost two weeks. Willie is napping and B is in her carriage beside me, just trying to make up her mind to go to sleep. This seems my opportunity for a really nice long chat.

Yesterday we, Ess and I, took Willie to have his voice recorded for his Christmas present to you. It was really fun, and I think you can tell a little from the record what a picnic we had. He was fine for the first side, but we made the mistake of playing it before doing the second side, and it scared him.

I had brought raisins to try and make him count, but he would do nothing but sit and silently gobble the raisins. The last sentence of that side is very spontaneous: "I don't like it up here!"

We were three flights up in an attic studio over Krantz Music Store. When I played it over, I didn't know whether it was a good idea to send it or not, because I sat down and cried like a baby. But I guess you will not be so silly, and it really is very funny—if Papa were not so far away.

On the way back to the car we stopped to have Willie's hair cut, and they really snatched him bald. And anyone would have recognized him as a member of the 5th back at Ft. Sam about the 13th of July. I must take his picture and send it.

But his haircuts are unlucky, as we had just 3 minutes of parking time, and, sure enough, there was a cop writing a ticket for us. You see, it really takes a man in the household.

When we arrived home Willie carried the paper in and began to read—"Germans, Germans, Germans," ad infinitum. I couldn't believe my ears.

This morning he and I played catch like we were crazy, and in the middle he stopped short, looked up into my face, and said, "Oh, Mommie—having fun." I left him for a few minutes and came back to find him in B's carriage with their book, showing her the choo-choos. He was practically mashing her flat, but she loved it.

B really sat up yesterday, but in the most peculiar way I have ever heard. She sat on her knees. She now eats bananas and bacon for breakfast. Last night we had one of our thunderstorms and then a lovely gentle rain, and I thought, really, at these times I miss Howard most. It reminded me of our honeymoon cottage.

Today was beautiful, and I thought today surely I miss Howard most. It reminds me of our lovely hiking trip on the Skyline Drive—really our last vacation together alone. And so it goes. But these thoughts, although they ache in a way, still they are also very comforting.

The news again looks better, and perhaps we can still hope for an end this winter.

All my love, Ginny

Sunday, October 8, 1944
9:15 P.M.

Dearest Honey Bunny,

Everyone was so shocked and grieved about the unexpected death of Wendell— "God moves in a most mysterious way." It is hard for us to see the picture from such a close view. We are more and more impressed by Tom Dewey, but I'm afraid he has no chance.

The Orioles have been doing remarkably well. They are tied with the Kentucky Cardinals for first place in the Little World Series. Everyone in Baltimore is ball minded. Tomorrow they play the first game in Baltimore, and they expect to have 60,000. I'm sorry you aren't here to go with me. I haven't the heart to go alone, but would very much love to see the game.

Never forget for a moment that you are constantly in my thoughts and prayers. Now I shall be writing to many other people, but it is so much fun to write to you that I am writing a second letter today.

All my love, Ginny

Tuesday, October 10, 1944
9:00 A.M.

Dearest Honey Bunny,

I missed you especially last night, because I listened to the ball game and really fell asleep, much to my surprise. But, of course, knowing me, you would have expected it. The Orioles lost, but it was a close 5 to 4 and very exciting at first. I do wish you could be here to enjoy it with me. I am going to send you a clipping. They make front-page headlines almost every day now.

Yesterday I received your letter written on the 16th, the first one after you went on active duty, I believe. I did figure you had been at Brest. How interesting that you were with the 29th Infantry Division.

Best love from Mama, Willie, and B,

> *Wednesday, October 11, 1944*
> *10:00 P.M.*

Dearest Honey,

Today was a really wonderful one, as I received four letters—no sequence, but they filled in the gaps for me, so that now I can picture more or less what you were doing. For the time being, at least I have a less-uneasy feeling about you. I do not understand if, when you speak of "we," you mean just your team, or are three teams together in a truck? In other words, is Bill Falor with you? I take it he is not.

The package from Paris sounds very attractive. I feel much the same about Christmas presents as you do. Let us celebrate our Christmases when we meet again, and let us pray that it will not be too long.

The Orioles are going to win the Series. Everyone is very enthusiastic.

Postwar plans are very indefinite for me, but I do think about them a great deal. I'm still waiting to hear about Dartmouth. If we could arrange such a setup, I really think that would be ideal, but otherwise some less-drastic shift in our Baltimore setup could be arranged. This would be, to me, the most satisfactory arrangement, rather than a complete change from Baltimore.

I have been wondering about a car. I may have a chance to buy one from an intern—a 1942 Hudson with 16,000 miles. The price is somewhere around $1,600. This is not ideal and is really rather steep, but I'm afraid prices will not be dropping anytime soon. Let me know what you think. I don't need one now, but I'm thinking about the future.

Well, I must close and rehearse for my speech at the University of Maryland tomorrow.

My dear, I continue to miss you miserably, but how wonderful when we are together again.

All my love, Ginny

Sunday, October 15, 1944
12:15 P.M.

Dearest,

First—about postwar planning. Of course, I can't help but do it. It's such a pleasure. But I have felt guilty every time, because I thought you didn't want me to.

My ideas aren't really specific, except on certain points. I don't want any nanny or housekeeper in the house to live; no one to take meals with us. I want us completely alone.

If we should take over your mother's house, always providing we stay in Baltimore, I think we could work things out very nicely for a while, but I wouldn't want to stay indefinitely, as I think a house in town is more suitable for us.

If the children go to school in the country, I think that is sufficient—St. Paul's, perhaps, or Friends for both! Of course, if we could get a professorship in a university town, that would be ideal. I also want enough garden space to grow flowers for the house. Above all else, I want time for both of us to work together.

All my love, Ginny

Chapter 5

To the Roer
9 November–29 December 1944

U.S. THIRD ARMY TROOPS CROSSED THE MOSELLE
River in a drive to capture the German city of Metz the day
before I wrote Georgeanna from a comfortable schoolhouse in
Heerleen, Netherlands. The U.S. presidential election had ended three
days before—the voters having continued Roosevelt in the White
House for an unprecedented fourth term.

---

10 November 1944

Dearest Ginny,

*Quite unexpectedly, we have moved again or at least are in the process. At
the moment I am staying with Bill Falor at Heerleen while our outfit moves. This
is a good arrangement, as it gets me out of the mess of moving while giving me a
chance to see what others are doing.*

*Bill is located in a nice school building with central heat, and they have a nice
clubroom where I now am trying to write while nine other people are playing
bridge, etc., etc. My stuff, including bedroll, is being taken care of by Gene
Bennett, and I hope when I get to our new location that it will all be there.*

You ask in your last letter if we still have our nurses. We do—mine, Alice Ridzon, has worked out very well. At first she circulated and the sergeant scrubbed, but recently she has been scrubbing, and it has worked out better.

The enlisted man just needs more experience at passing instruments. He keeps too interested in watching the instrument table and does not keep up with the operation, so that he holds you up by not having needles threaded, etc.

I have just about decided to scrub both the nurse and the sergeant, using the latter on retractors, which keep incisions open. Up to now we have been getting along without a retractor man, and that has been difficult. This arrangement will leave us with only one man, a corporal, for circulating, but I think it will work out all right.

It is possible that there may be a gap in letter-writing after this, as this will go from here and succeeding ones from our own unit, and that may take a few days to get the mail functioning.

All my love, H

AT THE CONCLUSION of the patient flow at Nuth, we had been told to go to Eygelshoven, Germany, into bivouac to await further assignment. It was during this inactive time that I went over to Heerleen to see Bill Falor.

During this quiet time for us, there was considerable shuffling of the troops. For instance, on 9 November, the 7th Armored Division, which had been with the British Second Army, joined the XIII Corps of Ninth Army. This movement suggested future action.

Then on 11 November the British XXX Corps took a position on the south flank of the British army, including the region formerly held by the American XIII Corps southwest of Geilenkirchen, Germany.

The British XXX Corps immediately to the north of Ninth Army took over the territory as far south as the Wurm River in Netherlands.

We bivouacked at Eygelshoven on 9 November. I took the truck to nearby Heerleen to Bill Falor, but his surgical team wasn't busy. On this first visit to Heerleen I learned that Bill had answered a knock on the door of the schoolhouse, where the hospital was set up, and received a very tall Dutch gentleman who introduced himself as Dr. Gerard Lubbers and his wife.

Lubbers explained that he was director of the midwifery hospital, which was on the low hill adjacent the schoolhouse. He had come over to welcome the Americans and to express thanks for our liberating Holland. He would be glad to do anything he could for the liberators.

Bill couldn't think of anything, but Lubbers asked if the Americans would like hot showers. The midwifery school had its own well and thus its own water supply, which the village lacked.

His school also had its own powerhouse, so it had hot water. This was a special boon for the surgical team, and several members did go up to the Lubberses for a hot bath. The Lubberses became lifelong friends of Bill and me and, later, our wives as well.

While we were at Heerleen, we were invited a couple of times to the Lubberses' house, where we took hot showers and played bridge in the evenings, as well as dined on fare other than canned rations.

Gerard Lubbers later retired from the midwifery school and practiced medicine in The Hague. Georgeanna and I visited the Lubberses there, and they visited us in the States. The back-and-forth visits continued until Gerard's death in the late '90s.

---

14 November 1944

Dearest Ginny,

The last few days developed quite differently than I expected. When I last wrote three or four days ago I was with Bill Falor and expected to go on to join my own unit. No sooner had I mailed that letter, Mac came to get me and take me back to headquarters. Very little of the mountain of equipment that we brought over has been used, and an attempt was made to revise the needed equipment inventory.

Bill Boukalik was there, and he, Mac, and I went over the material and made a recommendation for revision. I then went on, stopping overnight at Bill Falor's again in Heerleen. I stayed there for one day, as he was still not in operation.

In the meantime, the colonel comes around yesterday and takes me back to headquarters, because Col. Shambora (Col. William Shambora, chief surgeon of the Ninth Army) had asked the Colonel to get the equipment ready in its original form, so my recommendation for revision never got any farther than our own unit. Now I shall go straight to my own hospital, if it goes into operation, so that I am losing nothing by jumping around this way.

One of the main attractions at Bill Falor's hospital is that it is located a stone's throw from the largest school for midwives in Holland. You will remember that a large percentage of women in the Netherlands are delivered at home by midwives. The national government runs three large schools for them. It is apparently a very thorough course, taking three years to complete.

Bill had made the acquaintance of the director of the school, a Dr. Lubbers, who is a charming man with a charming family. There is no midwifery school quite like the school in Heerleen in America.

The hospital is a teaching one and admits only ward patients, and, therefore, the entire staff is full-time. The buildings and equipment are modern and superb and do not at all compare to the county-hospital-type of thing that we have. The thick rugs in the offices and the marble operating room seem to belong to Park Avenue, New York, rather than the city hospital in Baltimore.

Dr. Lubbers, therefore, has a self-contained clinic in which he is czar. He lives in a very large house on the grounds and wants for nothing.

Of course he knows Dr. de Snoo, who is still living at present, but suffering from hypertension. He referred to him as the leading ob/gyn man in Holland, but said that, at the beginning of the war, de Snoo was thought to be sympathetic to the Germans.

With all my love, H

15 November 1944

Dearest Ginny,

The big news today is that about 10 letters arrived, and the package of hors d'oeuvres. I immediately devoured the bottle of olives and the sardines. It somehow made me a bit sad, and I might have cried had I not always been in the presence of a dozen other people.

I also apparently have missed a few letters, as Joe Redline said he got a stopcock and sent it on with three letters addressed to me, all pregnant. He also sent on your letter to him, which he appreciated and enjoyed, and which contained a stopcock.

Plans change hourly, and it now appears if I might go to a new hospital as "an experienced team." They like to send a team with some previous experience to a new unit. This is still uncertain.

I intended to tell you yesterday more about the doctor in charge of the midwifery school, as I saw him do two operations.

One was a hysterectomy for endometrial hyperplasia and a small (2 cm) ovarian cyst in a woman of 40, and the other an ovarian tumor in a girl of 26.

We talked at length about functional bleeding, and he knows nothing of hormones. Treats some cases of bleeding with estrin, with equivocal results, of course. Finds much bleeding in young girls from normal endometrium and thinks this is much more common during the months of March and November and, therefore (I am not quite sure why it is), treats them with Vitamin C. Never uses X-ray for therapy and prefers hysterectomy if radical treatment is necessary. He also does a supravaginal hysterectomy and has never seen a case of carcinoma of the left-behind cervical stump. Says he is constantly amazed at the reports of such from America.

Please send me one of your reprints on treatment with progesterone. I think he would be interested in it. I may get a chance to see him again.

Love, H

AFTER VISITING IN Heerleen, I drove the truck over to nearby Maastricht, to the 5th Auxiliary Surgical Group headquarters. While I was there, our offensive to cross the Roer River really began.

We heard that Bill Falor was deluged with casualties at Heerleen. Our commanding officer dispatched me to Heerleen in a sort of unofficial capacity to help out.

I was there 17 and 18 November, operating on thirteen men. After leaving on the eighteenth, I went over to Niewenhagen, where we were assigned to the 3rd Platoon of the 53rd Field Hospital in support of the offensive across the Roer.

Of the thirteen casualties upon whom I operated at Heerleen, five bore abdominal wounds; six, chest wounds; one, a thoracoabdominal wound; one required an amputation just below the shoulder, his arm having been traumatically amputated more or less in the elbow region.

Two of the five with abdominal wounds died. The six with chest wounds did well, as did the thoracoabdominal casualty and the amputation case.

SERGEANT L. B., Serial No. 38537514, presented a special challenge. He was in shock at the time he entered the receiving ward, and we could not get him out of shock.

Wounded in the abdomen, he had received three thousand cc of blood and five units of plasma, but his blood pressure never rose to normal; it had gotten up to about one hundred when we took him into the operating room, believing him to be bleeding internally. We judged that he would not do better.

After anesthesia and before opening the abdomen his blood pressure had fallen to eighty systolic. We found a tremendous amount of blood in the abdomen; his blood pressure and pulse were almost unobtainable as we opened the abdomen.

There was bleeding from a large vessel retroperitoneally, which we thought was the inferior vena cava (one of two large blood vessels conveying blood to the right atrium of the heart). We stopped the bleeding with clamps. But we were unable to adequately explore the damage, and the patient died on the operating table.

We did not know whether we should continue to give blood in supporting measures to raise the patient's blood pressure to normal before beginning the operation, or whether we might have a better possibility of saving his life by operating while he was still in shock, in hope that we could stop the bleeding and the patient would recover.

My experience as a gynecologist dealing with ruptured ectopic pregnancies (an ectopic pregnancy is the abnormal deposit and subsequent development of the fertilized ovum outside the uterus, as in a fallopian tube) argued for the latter course. Even though such patients were in shock, their pressure would almost immediately improve if we could get in and stop the bleeding from the ectopic. We applied this technique to the wounded from the battlefield. Sometimes it saved their lives.

PATIENT L. J., Serial No. 37584314, a private from Company L of the 120th Infantry, was wounded at 9:00 AM on 17 November by American artillery. He had lain in the rain all day. We operated on him until 1:30 AM 18 November.

He had a wound in the thorax, with a left pneumothorax, and a perforation of the large colon at the splenic flexure, plus numerous other smaller wounds.

We took care of the chest wound and did a colostomy through a midline incision. Despite his ordeal, the patient did quite well. How gratifying to him and us.

WE ALSO SAVED PFC E. H., Serial No. 35249368, from Company I of the 29th Division, 115th Infantry. Hit by rifle fire about 1 PM 17 November, he received three units of plasma at the battalion aid station.

By the time he had gone through the regimental collecting company and the division clearing company and was admitted to the field hospital, his blood pressure was 150/80. He received five hundred cc of additional blood in the receiving tent at the field hospital.

He was wounded in the left chest; X-ray showed much blood in the chest. We removed about five hundred cc of blood and closed the entrance and exit wounds.

The missile had traveled behind the spinal column and fractured the posterior spinous process, which we could feel through his skin in back. At the end of the procedure, the patient's blood pressure was 110/60. He was evacuated in good condition.

AT 7 AM ON 18 November, I operated on Staff Sergeant C. W., Serial No. 39847346, from the 41st Armored Regiment. He had a penetrating abdominal wound. Upon cutting open the abdomen, we found a piece of the liver about the size of a fist absolutely free in the peritoneal cavity, having been severed from the liver by the passage of the bullet.

The sergeant also had a hole directly through the gall bladder, with a lot of bile in the peritoneal cavity and a hematoma at least the size of a fist in the region of the right kidney, where the bullet exited.

We tidied the abdomen and put a T-tube in the gall bladder. We brought out the tube through the entrance of the wound. The patient did amazingly well and was evacuated to the general hospital at Liège.

Having concluded our treatment of thirteen patients on 18 November, our team was immediately transported to Niewenhagen. We had been assigned as an extra team because casualties were flowing in—the crossing of the Roer had begun two days before.

---

18 November 1944

Dearest Ginny,

The briefest note.

I have been very busy for 24 hours. Went to work at 2:00 P.M. yesterday and operated until 8:00 A.M., doing 13 cases. Slept for two hours, got up, transferred from one platoon of the 53rd Field Hospital to another, having just arrived at Niewenhagen to act as relief for the two teams now here.

This platoon is the one to which I was attached day before yesterday (where Dave is), but I am now officially attached to another hospital not yet in operation, and I am simply here on detached service for a day or two while work is heavy and before we set up.

I am going to bed right now and sleep until Dave needs relief.

The new platoon will be a good move, as I shall be the senior team leader and, therefore, in effect the chief of surgical service. It will make life a little more interesting.

It is now 4:30 P.M., and I am going to get a bit of chow and go to bed. Probably get up about midnight and work through the night.

All my love, H

ON 16 NOVEMBER, 2,807 U.S. and British warplanes dropped more than ten thousand tons of bombs on German forces near Aachen in support of the U.S. First and Ninth armies, which initiated the drive toward the Roer River.

Operation QUEEN was launched to clear the plain between the Wurm River and the Roer. When the battle began, we were assigned to Niewenhagen to back up the U.S. 84th Division, which, after a few days, we learned was attached to XXX Corps of the British army. The 84th's mission was to protect the left flank of Ninth Army's XIX Corps, whose mission was to cross the Roer at Jülich.

At the center was the familiar 29th Division, spearheading the attack toward Jülich. The attack stalled near Sierksdorf and Berthelsdorf, very near the line of departure.

The attacking force made scant progress all along the line. The 30th Division bogged down at Würselen, while the First Army's VIII Corps was slow to start toward its objectives, Düren and Cologne, to secure the First's crossing.

But by 18 November, the 84th Division had surrounded Geilenkirchen on three sides. Meanwhile, the 29th Division had penetrated the outer defenses of Jülich. From 19 November to 21 November, the 84th Division, still attached to the British XXX Corps, worked its way up to Wurm.

The going was very tough. By 22 November the Allies realized that the Germans were feeding fresh troops into the line west of the Roer; the enemy had been expected to fall back to defend the Roer line.

The 29th and 30th Divisions continued to be heavily engaged, as was the 85th Division on the left flank, which on 22 November took Mahogany Hill east of Prummern. On 23 November progress was so slow that the decision was made to switch to the defensive, and the flow of casualties essentially halted.

While we were at Niewenhagen, from 17 November to 4 December, I personally operated on fifty-two casualties. Thirty-two of the fifty-two operations were performed by 24 November. Then there were few casualties for five days.

On 29 November XIII Corps resumed the drive toward the Roer without artillery, in an attempt to take ground by surprise. The flow of casualties resumed. The lineup remained the same, as far as we were concerned, in support of the 84th Division under the command of the British to the left of XIII Corps.

The Germans fiercely resisted the advance to the Roer. By 4 December XIII Corps had overcome all resistance west of the Roer, except for two strongholds, at which point the offensive was suspended.

On 3 December the commander of the 116th Regiment of the 29th Division, which had battled so hard to take Jülich, was replaced in an effort to improve the regiment's performance. But the new commander reported on 7 December that any attempt to take Jülich with the 116th Regiment would fail, because of heavy losses already sustained. The 116th was replaced by the 115th, which took Jülich within the next few days.

IN NIEWENHAGEN WE set up in a schoolhouse that had suffered considerable damage that the engineers repaired in a reasonably satisfactory way. The building's spaces housed receiving wards, an operating unit and postoperative wards.

The surgical teams were billeted in town houses damaged little or not at all. Our team drew a house a block away from the hospital—a row house (Hoogstraat 109) occupied by the B. H. Logister-Hanssen family—an aged Dutch couple and Pierre, their adult son.

The family slept on the second floor, as it usually did. The ground floor consisted of a living room and the entrance hall, which continued back to the small dining room and kitchen. We settled into the living room, where we put up cots to accommodate the team.

We came and went at very odd hours and, of course, ate at the mess provided by the field hospital in the battered school.

The family seemed to warm to us after a few days. When we came in, the husband would always invite us to have a glass of schnapps before going to bed. We always accepted his kind offer, although we were often dead tired. We always enjoyed sitting with the old gentleman, even though he couldn't speak a word of English and we couldn't speak a word of Dutch.

———————————

20 November 1944

Dearest Ginny,

Things have quieted down here. We are still busy, but today we went on a 12-hour shift, and we were lucky enough to get on from 8:00 A.M. to 8:00 P.M. It is now about 9:00 P.M., and I have a chance to sit down and write a letter. I am still with Dave on a temporary basis, until my own unit sets up. We are going to stay here until called out.

Niewenhagen is a very nice town and the officers are billeted with families in town. Our team is together, and just now we are sitting around the dining-room table and writing letters.

The family consists of father, mother, and a grown son, all of whom are here. They are friendly and speak of the Americans as liberators, as do many of the Dutch. It must be hard for them to figure out why we should bother to come so far to chase the Germans out of their country.

After getting up to headquarters the other day, I found the three-way stopcocks waiting. They have been a pleasure to use after missing them so much.

In fact, it has been difficult to hang on to them. Miss Ridzon takes them home with her at night, so that they will not be misplaced. It was a good idea to send one to Joe, as he got them out in a hurry, although at that moment we were not in action.

Love and many kisses, H

21 November 1944

Dearest Ginny,

Since last night we have not been very busy. This morning, when we came on at 8:00 A.M., there was but one patient in the shock ward, and he was ready, and we did him early this afternoon.

It is now 5:30 P.M. and just about dark. I have just finished eating supper, have washed my mess gear, and am sitting in one corner of the schoolroom that we use as an operating theater. It is a square room about 24 feet on the side, and there are two tables arranged so that two teams can work at once.

Schoolbooks are piled in the corner and, every now and again, one of the sisters, to whom the school belongs, will walk up and down the hall or stick her head in the door, trying to keep track of the paraphernalia of the school that they probably spent so much time and trouble to accumulate.

The building is one story and consists of seven large rooms along a single corridor. It is of recent construction and undamaged by the war, so that the furnace works, and the village electrical system continues to function. We have wired the rooms with our own system hooked to the generator, in case the village system should fail.

The one case we had today has up to now been most amazing. The soldier was injured about 5:00 P.M. yesterday, and by the close of the operation at 3:00 P.M. today he had received the equivalent of 23,500 cc blood transfusions.

This is the most we have given anyone to date. Seventeen of the 23 were plasma and six were whole blood.

The patient had one of those terrible extremity wounds that do so poorly with the least motion. The left leg had to be amputated just below the knee, and the right thigh was shot away almost to the bone over an area one-foot square. Also, he had a fractured right radius.

Our team worked like a clock, and we turned him out in good time. His blood pressure was 96/50 at the end, which is good, considering our usual cases. If he gets well, it will be a real triumph of teamwork, because everyone worked like dogs on him.

As you can guess, I am more and more pleased with the team. The two enlisted men are hard workers and nice boys. The nurse is good and gets along with everyone very well. The new assistant and the anesthetist improve daily, and last but not least, I feel that I am getting better.

I did not realize how rusty I was at Brest, but now I feel that I am almost back to prewar facility. There will probably be a long lapse after the war is over, but I shall be happy to start on that at any time.

I also have today been realizing how lucky I really am. First and always, to have you. How did I ever manage that? But, then, relative to others, I have come out well in the Army.

Fletcher Wright is the other officer now here with Dave (he relieved me). He has been transferred from the 4th Aux and, of course, knows Mason Knox and Doug Stone. Mason is an assistant and, because of absence of training, will remain such. Doug has a team but will probably remain a captain because he has a major who is his assistant here. I have been very lucky with my promotions which come as quickly as the law allows each time, and with my team. The good Lord is good to me and to us, and we should always be thankful therefore.

As I am writing this letter, the other team has started an abdominal case on a civilian who was shot, and there is another case in the ward for us to do before we get off at eight.

With all my love and kisses, H

22 November 1944

Dearest Ginny,

Once again we have not had a very strenuous day. Three cases and perhaps one more before we go off at 8:00.

It is now just after chow, and I am sitting in the operating room while Fletcher Wright is about to start an abdominal case. He is the other team chief, who, as I mentioned yesterday, has come in here to relieve me when we leave to go to our new hospital.

I find that he went to Charlottesville with Bill Sturgis, in the same class, I believe. He has been practicing in Petersburg, Virginia, and reminds me for all the world of Harry Talmadge. He is a nice-enough guy, but has the same sort of nebulous approach to things.

My new pay-data card arrived today, and I find that the promotion to major was good for a pay raise of $91 a month—not to be sneezed at. It will probably take a couple of months to get the allotment straightened out.

I do not have your letters here, but I remember one about postwar planning, with which I agree. If there is any way to work out a plan that I shall also work with you during the day, I would like that too.

It is not only that I feel that I do not want to ever again let you out of my sight, but it is that I think that we would work together so beautifully.

As I have said before, I cannot think of a happier being than one who is working with the one he loves. I have no specific idea of how it can be done, but perhaps we will get an idea.

Love to all, H

Friday 24 November 1944

Dearest Ginny,

Since I last wrote we have been very, very busy and had to send for a fourth team, so that we could work two tables for 24 hours, 12-hour shifts. The tables arrived last night, and until then we were working longer than 12 hours for a day or two. That is not good, if for no other reason than I did not get a chance to write.

We have made good friends with the family with whom we live, and they have had little things for us to eat from time to time—apples, pears, some meat—of which they seem to have ample, as they butcher their own hogs—and coffee, which we bring them from the mess.

The other day we took home a loaf of GI bread and some butter. They had not seen any white bread since before the war, and when we toasted it over the coal range, they were amazed, as they had never heard of toast. They were very much impressed and seemed to enjoy it. Their bread, of course, does not lend itself to toasting.

The other day we all took a bath in their portable bathtub, just about big enough to sit in, but very fine when one needs a bath as badly as I did. After bathing, I put on the new ODs [olive-drab work uniforms] from home and felt very dressed up. I found the note that you put in the pocket over three months ago.

I have had some remarkable cases here. A beautiful traumatic diaphragmatic hernia caused by a rifle bullet that went through the chest and slit the diaphragm for about 10 cm, allowing the spleen and half of the stomach to slip into the pleural cavity. No perforation.

We opened the pleura wide through the 9th rib on the left and very easily repaired the thing. They are quite easy to do. That approach is superb for the spleen and cardiac end of the stomach, and I intend to use it in civilian practice for stomachs (the cardiac end). It is now 24 hours postoperative and the patient is fine.

I also did something today I have never seen work before. Patient in very poor condition. Holes everywhere. Near the end of the operation, after having his blood pressure 80/? for the entire two-hour operation, I pulled on the stomach to sew up two holes there—and his heart stopped. Blood pressure, 0.

Carlson kept breathing for him with the machine, and I massaged the heart through the diaphragm and gave him adrenalin intracardiac. To my surprise, after about five minutes, his heart started to beat again. That was four hours ago, and he is still pumping away. He will probably not make it.

Incidentally, the boy with the 23 blood transfusions within a few hours is OK, and I think he will be all right. To date, I have done 74 cases, including the six at Brest. Do take care.

All my love, H

Sunday 26 November 1944

Dearest Ginny,

This afternoon we went up into the church tower in the village from which we could look over the countryside for about 10 miles in all directions. It is beautiful Dutch rolling landscape with coalmines identified only by the mound of discarded dirt dug out to get at the coal.

We could see toward a recently captured city—Aachen—but everything seemed quiet and peaceful today. As we came out of church the organist was there and asked us to look at the organ. Then he played for us a toccata from Bach and Asa's death from the "Per Gynt Suite."

As I have said before, the Dutch are really friendly toward us and go out of their way to be nice. The Germans do seem to have carried many things away. The organist showed us the place in the tower where three church bells had formerly been, but now the tower is empty, because the Germans took the bells away.

Love, H

November 29, 1944
5:35 P.M.

Dearest Ginny,

Up to the present time, I have not had a surgical truck or PROCO [Provisional Operation Continent] unit myself, but today they brought a truck up from headquarters. Tomorrow, if there are still no patients, we will give it a going-over to be sure it is OK. It will be rather nice, as it will help the transportation problem on moves.

All the cases we have done here who survived the operation have done well. I evacuated the diaphragmatic hernia today. He did very well indeed. Another boy who had an ether convulsion on the table is getting along well. It is some compensation for being away from you to see the boys get along.

Love, H

1 December 1944

Dearest Ginny,

This evening we had dinner at home; i.e., we ate with the Logisters, which is the name of the people with whom we are staying.

We brought home some of that awful meat-and-vegetable stew and a can of carrots, and they supplied the potatoes, which seem to be in abundance here.

They also supplied some home-preserved peaches for dessert, and I think they enjoyed the dinner as much we did, for it was good to eat off plates and drink out of cups for a change.

With all my love, H

Sunday 3 December 1944
2:00 A.M.

Dearest Ginny,

Although it is technically Sunday, it is still Saturday for me, as we went on at 8:00 P.M. So far we have done only two cases, and no one is left in the shock ward, so that we may go to bed shortly and try to sleep the rest of the night.

It is really not such a good idea, because then you can't sleep during the day and have to be up the next night, and, as you can imagine, I get pretty glassy-eyed.

From what I read in Stars and Stripes, *tobacco seems to be hard to get in the States. But if it is possible, I would like you to get a box of cigars and send them to the colonel with a little note saying they were promotion cigars—Lt. Col. E. D. Gay. The cigars would be appropriate here, more than in the States, as they are hard to come by.*

With all my love, H

THE WOUNDED MEN brought to us at Niewenhagen in support of the 84th Division were, of course, severely wounded and nontransportable. Of the fifty-two cases I handled, thirty-one were from the 84th Division, six were prisoners of war, seven were from the 82nd Airborne Division, and the rest were from other units attached to those divisions.

Mainly the cases were very similar to those with which we had had experience at Nuth. But some were very, very odd.

B. T., FROM THE 334th Regiment of the 84th Division, sustained a penetrating wound in the left flank at 3 PM 18 November. We did not get to operate on him until twenty-four hours later. We found a through-and-through wound of the descending colon. We exteriorized the wounded intestine—pulled it through an opening in the abdomen—as the manual instructed.

During the course of the operation, the patient experienced an ether convulsion. We proceeded with the operation as well as we could while the patient spasmed on the table, until we controlled the convulsion by administering twenty cc of 2.5 percent Pentathol. The whole operation took forty-five minutes.

The patient's temperature hovered at 103 degrees for a day or two. But his abdomen was soft (indicating absence of gas), the colostomy functioned well, and his convalescence was mercifully uneventful. Ether convulsions during operations were infrequent, but we saw them, and we were never sure what caused them.

We were amazed at how often soldiers shot through the abdomen essentially had no damage inside the abdomen.

H. L., SERIAL No. 36599795, from the 84th Division, was wounded about 5 PM 20 November. He was brought to the aid station at 1 AM 21 November.

He had received eleven units of plasma by 7:20 AM, when he arrived at the 53rd Field Hospital without pulse or blood pressure. We administered two thousand cc of blood by 9:45 AM. His blood pressure was 110/80 and his pulse 80. We administered four more units of plasma and five hundred cc of blood and began operating on him at 12:45 PM.

H. L. had a terrible compound fracture of the right tibia and fibula, with extensive soft-tissue damage and a cold foot and leg. He had two perforating wounds of the right thigh, excessive lacerations of the left thigh, and a transverse lacerating wound of the abdominal wall.

He was anesthetized. I first explored the abdomen and found that the missile had severed both vertical abdominal muscles just below the rib. It also had slit transversely the posterior rectus (vertical) fascia. But the inside of the abdomen was undamaged. The missile had made a clean incision, and the omentum had prevented the contents of the abdomen from pouring out.

We closed the incision and debrided the abdominal wounds, but we had to amputate the right leg. Despite his wounds, necessitating transfusions of large volumes of blood and plasma, H. L. survived well. We calculated that we administered 9,250 cc of plasma and blood at the field hospital, in addition to the transfusions he had gotten before we got him. H. L. was in very good condition when he was evacuated on 25 November to the 15th General Hospital in Liège.

WE HAD A CASE in Niewenhagen similar to one at Nuth, in which the missile slit the diaphragm in a way that the stomach and the spleen were thrust into the pleural cavity of one of the patient's lungs.

The wounded man, S. C., Serial No. 0331223, was a second lieutenant from Company H of the 105th Infantry. I operated on him late at night on 22 November. I opened his chest through a left posterior incision, finding a four-inch slit in the diaphragm.

The stomach was undamaged. There was a crease along the spleen, which was bleeding a little, but I did not have to remove the spleen.

I reduced the hernia and repaired the diaphragm with interrupted black-silk sutures and closed the incision—the lieutenant did not need a drainage tube. There were no postoperative complications, and the patient recovered well.

We asked many of our mended patients how things were going at the front. They always expressed concern. In the advance to the Roer, the fighting was hard, progress was slow, and the battle often bewildering.

FOR INSTANCE, SOLDIER H. C., Serial No. 38356096, from the 335th Infantry of the 84th Division, was wounded in the left chest at 9 AM 29 November. The Germans picked him up, and he spent six hours in a German army aid station. Despite his chest wound, he could walk. He escaped the Germans amid the confusion of fighting near the aid station. He walked three miles to an 84th Division aid station.

When we saw him at our field hospital, we noted, of course, the penetrating wound in the chest. The wound was not a sucking one, so the infantryman had been able to breathe reasonably well, even with a fair amount of blood in the chest cavity. We patched him up, and he recovered well.

All in all, our patients in Niewenhagen seemed to fare better than the casualties upon whom we had operated at Nuth. Of the seven casualties with thoracoabdominal wounds that my team treated at Niewenhagen, two died. Of the seventeen casualties with abdominal wounds, one died. Of the nineteen casualties with chest wounds, one died. Which is to say, of fifty-two wounded treated by the team, four died—a mortality rate among severely wounded men of less than 8 percent and a survival rate of 92 percent.

I was never quite sure why a greater percentage of wounded survived at Niewenhagen than at Nuth. Perhaps we were closer to the front at Niewenhagen and, because the front did not move very rapidly, the time between wounding and definitive treatment was shorter. Be that as it may, we were pleased that so many survived.

---

5 December 1944

Dearest Ginny,

We really did move yesterday from Niewenhagen, Netherlands, to Übach, Germany, as anticipated, but a very short distance, and we are now in Germany; but unless I were told, it would be difficult to tell Germany from the Netherlands by looking at the landscape, which, of course, is exactly like that of nearby Holland, which we just left.

The border was quite unimpressive. The Germans seem to have annexed Holland into the Reich, with the result that there must have been little customs inspection and the like.

Übach is a beaten-up small town. There is a little stream and a wooden sign saying that Dutch civilians could not be admitted—and that was all. Only our one team moved in the surgical truck.

The new hospital unit had already moved up yesterday, and things were still a mess. We are in a former school that was pretty well shot up by shellfire when the armies passed through. We are living in the same building as the hospital and spent yesterday clearing out about two feet of rubble from the floor, so that we could move in. As I look around the room, I see only three small mounds. I don't know where the mess came from, but it just seems to accumulate.

All windows are blown out, of course, as they are always the first to go. This was easily solved at the same time we solved the blackout, for we took the linoleum off the floor and tacked it up at the windows. We are very fortunate, in that the frames still work and we are able to open the windows during the day and after putting out the lights before going to bed.

Our first evening here was marked by eating pâté de foie gras, which one of the men had received in a package from home. The team already here was headed by one Henry Swann [who later was professor of surgery at the University of Colorado in Denver] who supplied the pâté and coffee. We ate in his blackout room lighted by an oil lantern picked up somewhere. We ourselves had only a candle for light, as the building has not yet been wired. At the present time, the Signal Corps is stringing the wires, and tonight we will have electric lights as well as the radio.

I love you as always, H

> *Thursday 7 December 1944*
> *(Pearl Harbor Day)*

My darling Ginny,

From your remarks I take it that the blouse from Paris has finally arrived. I have not received a letter telling me this. I hope that it fits. I was afraid when I bought it that it might be too large, but thought that it perhaps could be altered, if necessary.

You remember that we got to Paris eight days after the Germans left and went shopping soon after that, so that we were, in fact, among the first American troops there and had an opportunity to buy some of the few things still there.

I am sure that it is almost impossible to get anything there now. As a matter of fact, when we got to Paris, the Americans were still quite a curiosity. The 3rd Army did not bother to stop.

We have gotten straightened out pretty well here. We now have electric lights in the room and the same old radio you and I had in San Antonio. It is blaring loudly. It still clicks on and off, but mostly on, and after being on for an hour or two it does not fade off. We never had it on long enough in San Antonio to really get it warmed up.

Love as always, H

P.S. Still no patients in this location.

Dearest Ginny,

I have an idea. I have enjoyed looking at your new picture so much today that it would be nice to have a leather folder about 5 x 7 inches, so that I could prop it up with your picture in it.

There is usually a place to put up such a folder—a box top, duffel bag, or the like. Right now, your little picture is propped up on the kitchen cabinet, which we are using as a bureau. I would be very happy to carry around this additional bit of baggage.

This is, beyond a doubt, the dirtiest place in which we have lived. The three of us—Ken, Elmer, and I—are living in a room that was formerly a combination kitchen-dining room at the school. The central heating plant is, of course, not working, so we have a GI coal stove in one corner. This makes for tremendous dust and dirt. There is a coalmine in the same town Übach, so we do not want for fuel. But like all the mines in this region, it gives soft coal. Our clothes are sooty and dusty, and the worst of it is that from here on out we will probably have to do our own laundry again.

This afternoon, as we still have had no serious patients, I took a walk around this town. It was the first time I have left the hospital since we got here.

There is not a single house or building that was not damaged. Most of the civilians fled before the battle, but a few hundred apparently weathered the storm and are now living in patched-together houses.

Some of them are working during the day in the hospital, scrubbing the floor, washing the walls, and cleaning up the debris, having been sentenced to do so by the military government for a minor violation of a curfew, off-limits regulations, or the like. They are paid for the work—how much I do not know.

The streets contain mostly muddy soldiers who are back from the front for a rest or who belong here. The streets are unbelievably muddy and a maze of telephone wires strung by the Signal Corps. There is scarcely a glass window in the town.

All is quiet now, but this is the first place we have been that has been actually fought over. Previous to this, we simply walked in after the Germans left.

Love to all the family, H

Saturday 9 December 1944

My dearest Ginny,

Things have continued to be slow here. We have not had a single patient in our new location and outfit. The Roer River has been so full of water that no attempt to cross has been made, as has been said in the papers.

They have given me a little job that will occupy me a bit. This unit mislaid some equipment, and now, as a disinterested officer, I must investigate the thing and discover the facts. It takes me back to a little desk work, but I have no cause to complain.

Love, H

10 December 1944
Sunday, 10 P.M.

My darling Ginny,

Today we had off, as we are supposed to go on duty at night. Therefore, we went over to our last place [Niewenhagen] to see Gene Bennett and the others and pick up some laundry we left with our landlady, who did it for us.

They are not having any work either, and the hospital is almost clear of patients. All of mine left, except the one I did the last night.

He is doing well. He had a bad hand wound, and it was betwixt and between whether to take the hand off. To our great surprise, today the hand was warm, and the patient had sensation in the ulnar-nerve distribution, so that I believe it was worth the extra trouble to try to fix it up.

One of our troubles in working so far forward is that we do not get a chance to see the result of some of these things, so that, if presented the same problem, we cannot use our previous experience.

It would be helpful to be able to spend some time in a general hospital, or even a general hospital in the zone of the interior. Follow-ups are important in just about all fields, although we are certainly interested in a field that requires more time than any other. There are such things as follow-up cards, but our Army surgical consultant says that they are seldom answered. However, I want to get hold of some and try them out.

Love, H

Tuesday 12 December 1944
6:30 P.M.

My dearest Ginny,

Today I had to go over to our headquarters in Maastricht, which is still not far away even though we have moved forward toward the front little by little. I drove our surgical truck over, getting it lubricated and the oil changed while there.

Sounds like civilian days, doesn't it? Same motor-maintenance trouble, except that it does not cost the driver anything to drive in and say, "Change the oil."

I went over in regard to the property difficulties of this hospital, as I mentioned in the previous letter, and it was a very successful day, in that I think that my work with it is over. I am making certain recommendations, and I have only to fear that somehow I might be involved in carrying them out. But I doubt it, as it is really their baby.

I saw the Colonel and several others, all of whom asked after you, particularly Al Eskin.

Mac has taken Charley Burbank's team, while Charley is home on a leave because his wife had a subarachnoid hemorrhage, as I think I mentioned before. Mac is not very satisfied back in headquarters as executive officer. He would rather operate. We have not done a case for about ten days now.

With my love as always, H

15 December 1944
11:34 A.M.

Dearest Ginny,

I have not written a letter since two days ago, and that makes me unhappier than almost anything else could in the ETO.

It also serves to bring out one of the amazing things about living: We have not been busy. In fact, we have not seen a single patient here in this new location now for about two weeks. You would think that, under such circumstances, time would hang heavy on our hands and one could be alone. But as a matter of fact, with 14 officers here someone always has an idea of doing this or that, with the result that there is constant milling around.

Yesterday, for example, I went over to the headquarters of this hospital (about six miles away) to finish up the survey of its property losses. I arrived back here about 2 P.M. and Ken and Elmer were hepped up about going over to our last place and outfit to see Gene Bennett and get Elmer's field jacket, which he had left behind. So we get into the truck and drive over there and bring Gene back here to spend the night.

This took up the evening, and, as a matter of fact, we talked about very little until 1:00 A.M. As usual, I was glassy-eyed long before that, and so could scarcely more than get myself to bed.

It is hard to figure out just what is going to happen on this front. Since getting up to the Roer River, there has been no activity, as one can gather from the communiqués. There have been rumors to cover almost every possible course of events, but I have long since been convinced that my bet in regard to the end of the war by the first of the year is lost. I am glad it was only 10 gilders ($3.00).

In a footnote to your letter of the 11th of November, you asked if the work was depressing. In general, it is not. By the time we get to see the patients, they have had their clothes cut off in the receiving ward and have, in most instances, been X-rayed, and we, therefore, are concerned only with the professional side of the case. Since we receive only chest and abdominal wounds, the patients who are badly mauled about the head do not come here.

We do get the very bad casualties who cannot go to the evacs, and we have the greatest respect for such wounds, as the men are very sick and do not stand movement of any kind. In fact, the last one we had was operated on without ever moving him for any kind of cleanup—an amputation of both legs, and the medical result was very satisfactory. No infection and no increase in shock.

So you see, we become engrossed in the professional care of the wounded and do not often stop to consider other things. The men themselves seldom try to talk about their injuries or the why and wherefore of the war.

Every now and then one of them asks a question that is beyond my powers to answer, and I have an incomplete feeling, not only in my own mind, but also, I am sure, in the mind of the questioner.

Recently we had three men brought in together, all serious cases. By chance, two of them, after operation, were put side by side in the ward.

About three days after the operation, I came onto the ward alone and stopped for several minutes beside the bed of one of them, trying to think of something to do, or we were otherwise going to lose him.

As I stood there, the second boy asks how his buddy is getting along. I had to say that he was very sick, and I was quite concerned. Then the second boy said that I must think of something, because, as the sergeant, he had ordered the youngster to go forward, and he thought that it was his fault that he had been injured.

What could I do? The next morning the youngster did die, and that was the day I left to come here. When we visited back there the other day, I found, to my great surprise, that about three days later the sergeant had also died, and when I left, he was doing very well. I believe that the death of the youngster killed both of them. So we do have our tragedy. But in general we do not often have time to think about these matters.

Actually, one thing bothers me about those who die. I am never concerned about the superprofessional aspects of losing a patient as far as the patient himself is concerned, but I never cease to think of his family at home, whose tragedy it really is. For them, I can try to do a little more for the patient himself.

The only other half-serious thought I sometimes have is when I watch them carry in a newly wounded man and I have nothing to do except to wait for him to get ready. I wonder by what power can one man persuade another to expose himself to battlefield dangers? Of course, I cannot satisfactorily answer the question. So many factors are involved.

But as I have already said, these things do not greatly concern us, and the more-interesting professional problems are ever crying to be answered.

We do know so little about these things we include under shock. It is more than striking that often it is possible to put a man back together mechanically, but he just won't run. There is something wrong with the physiology.

It is too bad not to have a complete library available, for many times someone knows the answer to things that are problems to us.

I think I mentioned that I was very pleased with the team, and that I myself have improved. This makes the whole thing a little more worthwhile, for I now have the greatest confidence in trying to explore anything in the chest and abdomen.

It was surprising to find out the improvements since Brest and to realize how rusty some 13 months away from surgery had left me. We have had nothing now for two weeks, but I do not mind.

It would be so much easier with you here. As a matter of fact, if and when things get over, and if it is being done, you must plan to come over here, for I cannot wait to return home.

Love to all, H

Saturday 16 December 1944
9:30 A.M.

My dearest Ginny,

While at the other platoon, we had a visit from Elliott Cutler, and I have been meaning to mention it. You know he is the chief surgical consultant to the ETO, as Dr. Finney was in the last war.

He is quite a lively fellow and made rounds seeing the patients one by one. He undoubtedly got a good notion of the care the men were getting. He had many interesting things to say and answered some questions that we have had presented to us.

For example, he thought that it was unnecessary to sew together the two arms of the colostomy, because the Medical Corps found that, in closing them, it was necessary to free the two arms from each other. I was glad to hear this, because it was the rare one of mine that got sewed anyway, although I know that the Manual of Therapy calls for sewing the arms together.

He also said that there had been some high fever following the intravenous method of sulfa therapy, and that there had been some pulmonary edema from too much fluid.

We have seen the latter in two cases. It is very, very difficult to differentiate this from so-called "blast" injury to the lung. In fact, I know of no way, and neither did he.

Traveling around or having visitors is very important in medicine, and I am so glad that you are going to be host to the travel club. You must be very, very good, and so spare no time or trouble in preparing things just so for them, even if it means missing a letter or two to Papa.

This letter will probably reach you around the first of the year, which to me is a very special time. For the first time in 14 years, I shall have to get along without you. But it will be just getting along, for there is nothing I do or ever hope to do that is more than half-complete without you.

Love, H

ON 16 DECEMBER, when I wrote to Georgeanna's father, the Germans began the Battle of the Bulge counteroffensive in the Ardennes. Hitler had shifted—in total secrecy—twenty-four divisions from the Eastern Front to the Western Front. These well-armored, well-equipped, and well-trained divisions' mission was to punch a hole through the advancing Allied line and capture the North Sea port of Antwerp, thus severing the closest Allied supply pipeline.

---

16 December 1944

Dr. J. K. B. E. Seegar
325 Hawthorne Road
Baltimore 10, Maryland

Dear Dr. Seegar,

This V-mail is to send you a word of greeting and appreciation on my birthday. I am glad you were so successful 34 years ago.

When I walked into a platoon of this hospital, it was astonishing to have the platoon commander say that he had heard I was coming and wondered if I was Dr. Seegar's son-in-law.

It was Jim McClintock, who was at St. Agnes Hospital for a few years, until about 1941. He sends his very best regards. I trust that this finds you well, as I have managed to remain.

Sincerely, Howard

SOMETIMES OUR PATIENTS had extremely long incisions that had to be sewed up. With the needle holder, an ordinary needle, and the average length of catgut that we had, the sewing consumed too much time.

Before going into the army I used a Bloodgood needle during operations. It is a very large handheld needle that enables surgeons to sew quickly. No Bloodgood needles were among the equipment provided auxiliary surgical groups or other surgical units.

So I asked Georgeanna to please mail me a half-dozen Bloodgood needles, if she could acquire them. I repeated the request in two or three consecutive letters, because I was never certain that my letters were going to get through. About six weeks later, I got one letter, then two consecutive letters, each containing a half-dozen Bloodgood needles.

I used them extensively; I could then quickly sew up an abdominal wound from the rib cage to the pubic bone. Because the Bloodgoods saved time, lives perhaps were saved that otherwise would have been lost.

---

18 December 1944

Dearest Ginny,

I am especially lucky again, for six letters have arrived in the last two days. Several were dated for the 1st part of November, when something went wrong with the airmail, so that I was able to catch up with some things like Smitty not to be operated on, your not having a car, and the like.

The letter with Bloodgood needles has never come, but I presume will be along one of these days.

We still sit here with nothing to do. It is discouraging, but good if it means that we are not having heavy losses. I hope the ammunition shortage is really not holding us up, but it could be, I guess.

My love to the family, H

21 December 1944

Dearest Ginny,

You are undoubtedly worried at the war news, and so are we. But at this spot at the moment, we have not been affected in any way. We have had no work and no patients.

Yesterday I played bridge from just after lunch until suppertime. Last night we had a real treat. A local outfit in town sent a truck into Brussels for some Coca-Cola and beer for Christmas, and they gave us several cans of Coca-Cola.

The stuff really tasted good after not having any since England, where I remembered having one bottle. Several packages from wives and sweethearts have arrived, and we had quite a party with fruitcakes, sardines, etc. I do hope that the hors d'oeuvres that you have on the way are delayed a little, as there is plenty over Christmastime.

Love, H

The midwifery school at Heerleen, Netherlands. The schoolhouse used as a field hospital is in the center along the diagonal road. The Lubbers house is within the complex, slightly to the right of the center of the photo. A 105-mm artillery battery was positioned in the open field between the midwifery school and the building used as a hospital.

Niewenhagen, Netherlands, November-December 1944. Pierre Logister, an amateur photographer and son of the family, in whose home we were billeted.

Chapter 6

Letters from Home
16 November-22 December 1944

*T*HESE LETTERS FROM GEORGEANNA WERE WRITTEN before and during the mighty Nazi counteroffensive to seize and hold the port of Antwerp.

The surprise attack and swift German advance shocked Allied soldiers and civilians alike.

Quickly named the Battle of the Bulge, because of the "bulge" the Germans abruptly created in the Allied line, the horrific clash of arms spread dread and gloom on the home front as well as the Western Front Allied troops previously fighting their way ever deeper into Germany.

Georgeanna's late-December letters record her fear for Howard's safety.

November 16, 1944
11:00 P.M.

Dearest Papa,

No letter today, and we received news that the great winter offensive has begun with Simpson's Ninth Army playing a major part. I do so hope and pray almost every waking minute that you are safe.

Did I tell you that Dr. Rich stopped me in the hall to tell me how much he had enjoyed reading (he is on publishing staff of the JHH Bull) our chorionic gonadotrophin paper? He said it was a masterful piece of work, and he had learned a great deal. I was very pleased and think it will be a nice Christmas gift for you.

All my love, Ginny

Friday, November 17, 1944

My darling,

What a lovely day! My Christmas present arrived today, and it is scrumptious. It fits perfectly, and I hope I won't be tempted to buy a whole new outfit to glorify it. I was really surprised too, as of course I believed Papa as usual. All this and $100 too!

Also, I have been counting my blessings since your last four letters. I don't have to mention the positive things, not the least of which is a husband who writes every day, but consider the things I don't have to worry about—a husband who gets drunk and tells off everyone or whose professional ability is questionable.

Really, I have to worry about your health, safety, and happiness (I'm not too concerned over nurses and such, although I am of a jealous disposition).

Seriously, I was distressed to hear about Mac, as I don't see why that wouldn't do something to him personally for life.

How nice to run into Tom Ambler! I was always very fond of him, and I hope you will get to see more of him. The MacKendrick boys are no longer with the 29th, having been transferred before D-Day.

I do hope your mail and packages have begun to arrive. It is very discouraging to feel that you are not hearing from home.

Things in the lab are progressing. I do have trouble with the resident Dave Cheek. He is very scornful of women, and not interested in endocrinology, and therefore treats my cases promiscuously and does not refer any. But perhaps I can circumvent him. He has just taken over since Pat left.

I imagine it is difficult for you to maintain a proper weight on your diet, and probably no exercise.

All my love as usual, Ginny

Sunday, November 19, 1944
9:45 P.M.

Dearest Honey Bunny,

Yesterday I missed writing, so today I seem to have so much to say that I hardly know where to begin.

First, how good the war news looks! I only trust we are not being prematurely optimistic. If only this drive could finish the business. The 9th Army is certainly prominently featured. I trust you are well and safe and not too busy.

Yesterday my day started early at 6:00 A.M. with Willie, and then rounds at 8:00 A.M., in the lab until 12:00, then printed pictures till 1:00, and so home to find Willie's beret waiting.

He loves it and looks adorable in it. He insisted on wearing it for lunch, and then made everyone else try it on. He really acted almost as silly over it as Mama did over her blouse. I put him to bed and fed B at 2:00 P.M., let her play until 4:00, at which time I got him up and put her to bed.

Willie and I then went out to play. We saw Henrietta Buck across the street and played row-the-boat, then walked to the store and carried Mrs. Ebling's packages home for her. Had our supper, fed B at 7:00 o'clock (she sleeps until then), dried dishes, sterilized bottles and made formula, read to Willie, played horsy on the bed, bathed both children and gave them thin Percomorph oil, and so to bed at 8:30, but Willie doesn't go to sleep before 9:00 P.M. Then I listened to the first five minutes of Gabriel Heatter, straightened the children's and my clothes, took a bath, and so to bed.

Willie, by the way, has been going through a phase of wetting again in the last two days. They tell me all children do so, so I'm not worried but am amazed. Last night, I had to take him in bed with me at 6:00 A.M. because he drenched his bed.

He went to Sunday school, I to church. I heard the sermon, "How to Develop Faith," which was good also, and consisted of brief advice about how to work on it. The music was beautiful, and I do wish you could have been there to enjoy it with me. They have a quartet.

This afternoon I finally took B to see Lou Whiting, and he says her feet are perfectly all right, not to worry about them a bit—so that's that!

The Perkins family drove out with me, and we had a very lovely visit. They were, of course, interested in hearing all about you and thought that the children were wonderful.

B is quite sentimental (she sleeps after her lunch in her carriage on the porch). Willie ate a supper for a pile driver, and we practically had to pick him up to keep him awake.

Darling, I am so praying this war will end by Christmas. It has been a dreary four months away from you, and I dread to think of too many more.

My love, Ginny

> Monday, November 20, 1944
> 9:30 P.M.
> (B's 7th-month birthday)

Dearest Honey Bunny,

Mary Virginia Vogt (a woman doctor from Tennessee whom we once had a double date with years ago) came in to see me today. She also married her date, and he is in the Engineers and has recently returned from Alaska. She wants my formula for becoming pregnant. I started to say, "Well, after all, Papa was 50% responsible." She sends her regards.

In the lab now. We are getting together the data on the Zenopus test, and it looks quite good; not 98% to 100%, as Weisman claims, but better than the Friedman.

The Female Club of OB/GYNs is being entertained by the clinic in February, and Eleanor and I are to occupy the afternoon symposium! Endocrinology! I trust they will be impressed

I had a very nice note from Ann Falor, who says she is now down in Salem. The baby is apparently lovely and doing nicely, as are she and Beth.

How is Bill, and what is he doing? I would have been more worried about him than Mac, which shows you can't tell by looks always. Has Bill Boukalik been well since his earlier problem, kidney stones?

I am fine, as are the babies, but Father is really not too well. I don't know how much physically and how much depressed. Ess is also having flutters again,

*but as far as I can determine, is mainly nervous. We all miss you badly and do
hope you are well, reasonably happy, and will return soon.*

Best love, Ginny

*P.S. Darling, do tell me sometime, honestly: Is the work depressing and are the
results such that you lose track of the depressing angle?*

Tuesday, November 21, 1944

Dearest Honey Bunny,

*Today, two letters—both old, but nevertheless nice—Oct. 24-26. In the one
you tell me about moving into the tent from your crowded room and of the case with
shrapnel in the ventricle. In the other, you tell about Dave coming with the mail.*

*It is too bad that the letters have no sequence, as I'm sure they don't make sense.
Let me repeat some important things in this letter, in case you have missed other letters.*

*I have received both money orders, and all the gifts have arrived. My blouse
is beautiful and fits perfectly. Honey, I am having a "winter white" jumper made
to wear with it.*

*I have bought one hundred shares of Remington Arms at $775 and took
this money from the checking account, as I had over $3,000 in it and thought
that if we wanted to buy a car at some time, we could sell some U.S. Bonds.*

*I am thinking of buying $1,000 of government bonds also, as it seems to me
$1,000 is enough for the checking account, especially as the government bonds are
so readily convertible. Is this logical?*

*I also had to exchange the Atlantic City Bonds for a new issue. It cost us
$29.80. Now I can't tell how to record this in capital transfer, but I put it all
down and hope you can do it when you come home. Understand, I do it my way,
and keep track of the capital, but I'm sure it's not quite the way that you should
do it.*

*Jerry Galvin came in today on his way out. He is with the 130th Evacuation
Hospital and hopes to get to see you. He had no air mattress, so I called Betty
Schilpp, and she is giving him Allen's, and he is very pleased.*

*Dr. Brady asked me to take the diagnostic clinic today, but I told him he'd
have to speak to Dr. TeLinde. I'm afraid he won't want me to do it, but it would
just about double my salary.*

I am praying constantly that this present drive will prove successful in a great hurry and that you will soon be here. It is sad to think of our last Thanksgiving and our present one without Papa.

All my love, Mama

Wednesday, November 22, 1944

My darling,

Tomorrow will be Thanksgiving, and I dread to think of it without Papa. I shall think of our many happy horseback rides together and of the time it snowed and sleeted and we really got lost, and these thoughts will sustain me.

But I am so worried about you now. All reports say fighting is fiercer on the Ninth Army front, and rockets are being used, and all in all, I'm frantic. There was a report in the paper today of the shelling of the 45th Field Hospital, and that has not made things easier.

I must close and get some sleep. I hope and pray that your Thanksgiving will be as pleasant as mine, and that God will keep you safe for us.

All my love, Ginny

Thanksgiving, November 23, 1944
11:00 P.M.

My dearest Honey,

Yesterday I wrote one of those letters I would like to snatch back, but really, last night was one of my panic nights. My imagination ran riot and I had pictured the most drastic things.

I pray for your safety, strength, and composure under trying circumstances, and I hope that my love will lend you support. This is all that I can do, but how little it seems to me at times. Yet it is really great, I suppose. Above all, I would desire to be with you, but I know it was impossible, so I am trying to adjust myself to it.

We had a very nice day. Willie, Mary, and I went to the 11:00 o'clock service, and who should we meet but Donnie and Jimmy; so we had quite a reunion, and the children thoroughly enjoyed themselves. Willie leaned across me in the midst of the service and said in his little bell-like voice, "Bessie's home and B's home too."

Then they stacked and unstacked the prayer books and hymnals. Jimmy fell down, cried. Willie fell down, cried. Jimmy ate a cookie. Willie again remarked to the congregation in general, "What's that Jimmy's eating?"—so Willie had to have one, but he really was very good and was still as a mouse while the organ played.

Never forget, my dear, that I love you more than words or deeds can tell. I do hope that you are not having too bad a time of it.

All my love, Ginny

November 24, 1944

My dear,

I trust that when you receive this, war will have reached its logical conclusion, and you will be free to visit as you please, but most of all to return to me.

Today at lunch, someone said, "How will Howard ever find life exciting enough after chest surgery?" I said that I was sure that life with Mama would offer excitement enough, and I promise it will.

All my love, Ginny

Saturday, November 25, 1944
9:30 A.M.

Dearest Honey Bunny,

Yesterday, still no mail. I am now twenty days behind on the news and so anxious to hear about after the 12th, when the drive by the Ninth Army toward the Roer River began. I talked to Louise last night, and she had a letter from Dave dated November 8, so that is three days better than mine. Louise is moving to Belair, which I think is very sensible with winter coming on.

Papa, I can't think of anything funny to tell you, and everything I am doing seems too trivial in contrast to what you are experiencing. I can only say I love you, I love you, and I hope that this at least won't seem too remote or unreal.

With all my love, Ginny

Saturday, November 25, 1944
11:30 P.M.

My darling,

Tonight the news is still of slow progress and fierce fighting, especially in the area of the Ninth Army. How I pray that you are safe and well.

Carrington Owen came home with me today, and we have had a delightful day. She was quite captivated by B and thinks she is inordinately smart. Of course, I think so too, but I don't say it out loud.

We took Willie to the barber to have a haircut (down on Roland Ave. near Hampton), and he was an angel. Climbed right up into the chair and sat like a little man. The barber said, "Well, you tell his daddy that he's a real man." It is a GI cut, too.

We dressed him in a little red-and-dark-blue snowsuit, which Jane sent from Hagerstown, and put his French beret on, and he was adorable. If the sun is out tomorrow, I will take a colored picture for you. If you have a chance to send some more berets, perhaps a little larger, do so, for he'll outgrow this one this winter.

My favorite after-dinner pastime is figuring out just how and when I will next see you. It is a lot of fun trying to picture where it will take place, but it is so wonderful, it is hard to imagine.

All my love, Ginny

Sunday, November 26, 1944
11:00 P.M.

Dearest Honey Bunny,

We have had a really very nice Sunday, except I have been constantly worried about Papa and so unhappy about the tragedies you must be immersed in.

Willie went to "Sunny cool" in his new outfit and Papa's beret, and I took two colored pictures. I hope they are good. He has been very cute all day, but is certainly a hot flower. He doesn't like cold weather and refuses to go outside.

Have I told you that the "Onward Christian Soldiers" hymn is his favorite? And he can sing it. He told me this morning, "We will go to Fort Sam when Papa comes home from France." Fort Sam is his idea of home and stability, apparently, and it was a mighty nice place at that, wasn't it?

Here's hoping for a large batch of letters in the A.M.

All my love, Mama

Wednesday, November 29, 1944
10:30 A.M.

Dearest Honey Bunny,

Last evening, Jane and I had supper with Kay Gibbs and Leoda Darner, and stayed to play bridge, which made it quite late when it was "and so to bed."

We had a really very pleasant evening, but I find that such social activities make me miss you all the more. The constant pressure of the three absent husbands was really amazing.

Willie has been especially sweet recently. He is a very affectionate child, which I think fortunate, as I believe such people are usually outgoing and happy. He knows all the picture postcards you sent and can brief some of the stories. Ess and Ruth spent yesterday afternoon with him and were delighted.

This morning he was playing paperboy. He had Mother fold three newspapers for him, and he came to me and said, "I have three newspapers." No one had told him the number, so I believe he can really count, to an extent.

He now has a cute way of saying, "Bess is out in the kitchen" (or any other fact). I think, uh-huh. He talks with his hands a great deal, and he came to me yesterday with a peg, saying, "Don't break it, and don't throw it up in the air," all the while shaking his finger at me.

Yesterday he did some little things, and Ruth said, "What do you think you are?" He said, "I'm a playtoy." He meant "playboy," as Father often calls him that.

I do hope that you are safe and well and that before long there will be some break.

All my love, Ginny

Thursday, November 30, 1944

Dearest Honey Bunny,

Yesterday we had quite a rat race, as Kitten was sick. We do have such a nice setup, and the work is so interesting that it is too bad not to be able to enjoy it to the full—but all of the zest is gone without you.

I sometimes stop to analyze just how I miss you most, and I can't, because each way seems the most important at the moment. As I go about my work, there are constantly things I think of to ask you, tell you, or laugh about with you, and that it is your companionship I miss.

But so often, it is just the physical presence of you that I long for, the touch of your hand and feel of your sleeves, the sound of your voice, and the sight of your smile—all of these things are acutely with me, and it seems impossible that you aren't just across town.

Willie now reads aloud to B, holding the book before him and making a wonderful pretense. He is very sweet and thoughtful, and this A.M. at breakfast, insisted on passing the bread to everyone, saying, "Have a piece."

Yesterday, while waiting for father at St. Agnes, he tried hard to make the acquaintance of a little girl in the next car. He showed "girl" to her and finally took a book over, but she apparently was very shy. Got along better, however, with Mary Louise Muse, who goes about the house calling for "How" now.

B has become very loud recently and is especially vocal, talking or crying when people eat in her presence without offering her anything.

I pray constantly for your safety and health and a speedy return.

All my love, Ginny

Friday, December 1, 1944
10:30 P.M.

Dearest Honey Bunny Major,

How nice to have two letters from you yesterday and one today, and how nice for you to have your majority. I learned about it from Joe Redline again, and I am going to write and thank him for his cute letter.

I wonder if you are now at your new location. I also want to say, if visiting Bill Falor keeps you from writing to me, you just have to give up visiting Bill (joke, Papa).

I was most interested in hearing about your team setup. It is nice for the nurses to be along, and I am sure a good scrub nurse is a great help.

Yesterday Wislocki talked on the histochemistry of the placenta, and it was very interesting, and we agreed with him, in part at least.

Kitten Foote and Eleanor Delfs and I then had dinner together at the Hopkins Club. The family took Willie to the Dunlaps, and he had a wonderful time.

I do hope you are safe and well. Don't let the bladder get the best of you. How is your digestion? I also hope your vitamin pills will not have to be renewed, but the news about the war is that progress is still very slow.

All my love, Ginny

Saturday, December 2, 1944
11:00 P.M.

My darling,

At last I am alone in the living room for my hour with you. The children have been in bed about an hour, Smitty is upstairs, Mary and Jane are visiting, and Mrs. Ebling and Mother and Father have gone to the theater to celebrate their 35th wedding anniversary.

I have gone over the eight letters, which arrived this week (for the 85th time), and am trying not to miss you too unbearably. Today's letter, November 20, says you are still with Dave and have been very active. From the news, I presume you have continued to be busy also.

You don't know how wonderful I think it is that you find time to write, even though you are, I know, exhausted. I am glad you are billeted with a Dutch family and hope you are comfortable. I was very pleased to hear that the stopcocks are appreciated. I don't know when anything has given me more satisfaction than sending them.

I suppose by now you know that I don't have a car, and I don't really need one. I thought that if we got caught short when you come home, we could always buy your mother's.

Again, may I say how pleased I was to hear of your majority, especially as it gives your mother so much satisfaction. You know that these things don't mean so much to me, because I know that if rank went with ability you would be a four-star general. However, I am sure it gives you a certain satisfaction and makes me feel easier about the maid, if I need one. Also, I do want to wear the earrings with the major's insignia.

Last night before going to sleep, I was thinking over our Christmases, the first in which you sent me roses and a Spanish hat, and I was too shy even to let you kiss me (although I wanted to); the second, when you brought me gloves and we went dancing that night.

The third was when we went to the hospital together, had dinner at home, and went back for the evening, and you gave me the twin sweaters. We went to the State movie theater and then back up to our little room on the 5th floor. The next year we sat on our couch and you gave me the watch, and I cried. I was so surprised and pleased.

Next year, the gift with a promise of things to come—my beautiful fitted bag (and how I have enjoyed it and the trips that it has helped us with).

Our second married Christmas, with my beautiful fur coat. I am enjoying it now, for it has begun to get cold.

Our first, with my three surprises. I have got my bed jacket put aside for the day when Papa will hold my book again for me. The coat will be worn out, I am afraid, and the pen, of course, lost.

Our third, with Willie and the photographs; our fourth, at Fort Sam, with our house and family and my glasses from Mexico. And this year, my beautiful blouse (I'll have the lovely white skirt made to wear with it by Christmas), and may we never spend another Christmas apart. But the memory of our previous ones will console me.

All my love, Mama

Monday, December 4, 1944
10:30 P.M.

Dearest Honey Bunny,

I am really wrapped up tonight, as it's quite cold, and "I am feezin' (freezing), as Willie says. How I do need Papa, for all sorts of reasons.

Today I received your letters of November 18 and 22; the first word from you about your new rank. How stupid of me not to send insignia as soon as I learned of the promotion. I will send some off tomorrow.

I was delighted that the ODs arrived, as I suppose you can use them always. You must indeed have been frightfully busy, and it makes my heart sink to think of the dreadful number of casualties now and in the future.

I do hope that you are safe. The mere possibility that you are in danger really incapacitates me.

Your idea of postwar planning for our life together is one of the sweetest I could ever dream of, and it must certainly be worked out in some way.

I am pleased that your new job promises to be even more interesting, but I do hope it will not be more dangerous. I also hope you will take care of that cold. Joe Sadusk came home with gruesome stories of pneumonia.

Both B and Willie, I am sure, would approve of the tent idea, and I know I would.

Betty called today to say that Allen arrived Sunday. She is going up at 2:00 P.M. and returning Wednesday, because the grandmothers couldn't manage after two days. So, of course, I said bring them here and we will take them Thursday and Friday.

I think it will be quite a picnic. In return, Betty is going to do my Christmas shopping in New York for me—neat, eh?

Have I told you that Willie can whistle and shoot marbles? Mr. Schilpp was much impressed when he saw him this evening. Both Mr. and Mrs. Schilpp send regards.

All my love, Ginny

Tuesday, December 5, 1944
11:00 P.M.

Dearest Honey Bunny,

Your letter of November 21 arrived today. You have no idea, I keep repeating, how much it means to me to get these daily letters. When you move and there is a lapse, I am frantic.

This letter was especially interesting, in that it describes your operating-room setup and tells about the casualty who received 23 transfusions, so to speak. The shock seen in peripheral injuries is indeed interesting.

I was delighted to hear your enthusiasm for your team. I am sure this means a great deal to you, as it is really, of course, a tribute to you.

I am frequently amused and pleased to notice that our ideas cross in the mail. I am not a mystic, and I do not believe in psychic transmission. But I do think it indicates a deep congeniality. My letter in praise of Thanksgiving and my many blessings must have been within the week of yours.

I am even more absent-minded than before, as now I spend every idle moment thinking of you. I even have trouble collecting my urine specimens to analyze for pregnanediol.

We are running the effect of Vitamin E on a normal cycle. Today I walked into the john with my bottle, placed it on the top, sat down, and let fly, all because of you.

You would have laughed to see us (the laboratory force en masse) buying your insignia today. I called all the stores I could think of, and none carry them, so Herbert, Kitten, and I left at 4:45 P.M. in Betty Schilpp's car and toured Baltimore Street. Kitten says you should find her a nice husband after that, and seeing some of the stores she traveled, I agree.

I will probably not write tomorrow, as I have the Schilpps coming. So until later.

All my love, Ginny

Thursday, December 7, 1944
3:30 P.M.

Dearest Honey Bunny,

"Pearl Harbor Day!" This time last year we must have been in Mexico, and the year before we were at Myrtle's. How far away that seems now. This time next year, where will we be? If I could only think we will be together, I wouldn't care.

Your letter of November 24 arrived today. I am constantly amazed at your ability to write such interesting letters and under such difficult circumstances. I am so glad you enjoyed the hors d'oeuvres. There is another package on the way, and in another few weeks, I will mail another. As Ess has already mailed you one or two, I believe this should take care of the situation.

I will attend to your major insignia as rapidly as possible. Please don't apologize for asking me to do things for you. Darling, it is my greatest pleasure.

Smitty was never operated upon, as no one would positively say that it would have any effect upon the colitis, and also because she is so much better simply on an antifat diet. You will have to do the operation when you come home.

All my love, Ginny

Monday, December 11, 1944

Dearest Honey Bunny,

My letter yesterday just didn't develop. I was too depressed to write sensibly. But today I received two letters, and everything looks much brighter. Also, we have roundabout, but very reliable, news that King will be here within the next three weeks.

Then I had a letter from Juanita Ross, and she had a lovely sentence—she said Weldon was away 1½ years, which, while she was living through the time, seemed interminable, but once he was home again, the whole thing telescoped, so that it seemed that he had never been away. This, I am sure, is true—and I live for that day.

At the laboratory we are getting interesting figures on our habitual aborters and on the experimental hypothyroids. I suppose we will have quite a volume in ten more years.

It's slow work. But when patients come into my office, as one did today, and look longingly at the folder with your two pictures and, tucked into each lower corner, a picture of each baby and say how they envy me, I know that my lot is not so hard, and the day will come when we are side by side.

Did I tell you the disappointing news about Dartmouth? They do not plan to have a four-year medical-school course—too bad—but there may be others.

I am most excited about a picture in the offing. Have you received my letters requesting one or two? Or maybe you have received none.

The wool socks I will pack in an hors d'oeuvres box, as I guess they will arrive just as rapidly that way. Hope they are satisfactory.

From the news, I suppose your front is still quiet. I still hope for something sudden and spectacular in the way of a German crackup. I suppose it's foolish, but it helps my morale.

This should reach you close to the anniversary of our first date. Do you remember what fun we had, what a lovely day it was, and how Elizabeth Ender fell off the horse?

Do you also remember how I called you "Allen" when I said good-bye? I was embarrassed, but you passed it so sweetly that you at once put me at ease. I knew you were something quite special, even then, and I have grown to know it more so each year.

Tonight I miss you for a very special reason—along with the usual one—to put drops up my nose. Every time I do it, I have a feeling of satisfaction of how pleased you would be.

All my love, and come home soon, Ginny

Tuesday, December 12, 1945
9:30 P.M.

Dearest,

Your picture arrived today. I love it! It is by far the best you have ever had taken, and I am so pleased that you will send the negative. Your friend, Pierre Logister, is not only talented, but an angel (I mean something with wings, not corners). Do you think I could send him anything via you in the way of photographic supplies?

We spent the day having resident trouble. The house staff comes to me to go to Dr. TeLinde, which is a little difficult. It is too bad Dr. Telinde does not give up his enormous private practice and retire to run the clinic properly. I can't imagine a nicer life, can you? I don't know what he is going to do with his many problems. He is such a splendid teacher and executive, it's too bad to see his talents go to waste.

Our present house staff is almost impossible; e.g., upper staff, D—C—, resident, who is completely unreliable; R—S—, an older man, who was in practice in Washington 10 years and made money hand over fist doing very poor obstetrical care; to G—W—, an Army discharge, I believe for psychiatric reasons. All of them are so peculiar. None are Hopkins-trained people who know our methods or philosophy.

The interns are very nice and mostly good, but they are being taught all wrong.

GYN/OB Journal Club starts again next week, and perhaps I will get a time just to chat with the professor; but the main trouble is he just doesn't have the time.

Both children now have colds. Poor little B just doesn't know what to make of it. It's her first illness (not that she is really ill).

Do impose upon the Dutchman again. I can use any number of such photographs.

All my love, Ginny

Wednesday, December 13, 1944
11:30 P.M.

My darling,

Your Christmas card arrived today with the negative. I shall enjoy playing with it no end. Every time I look at it, it makes me smile, as I can almost hear you giggle. Ess is especially pleased to have a picture with a major's insignia.

I received a very nice Christmas note from Tom Auld. He is now CO of a small medical unit and says life is not too unpleasant, but certainly not exciting. Willie now insists upon holding his glass in one hand, to the consternation of the entire family. His favorite expression is "How about it?"

I often wonder, and halfway fear, that things at home must seem far off and very unreal when you are in the midst of such carnage, but letters from you, like I received today, are most reassuring. How fortunate I am to have such a husband.

You said in your letter today that you did not need to go away to appreciate me, and that is certainly true from your actions. Just today, at lunch (before your letter arrived), Eleanor said Marion Sadusky had said that the war was a blessing for their household, as it had matured Joe so. I said I had no such compensation, as you needed no improvement.

Eleanor, of course, dutifully agreed.

Today was my dispensary day, and so I spent the morning seeing patients and teaching interns. This afternoon I read in the library and did a D&C at 4:00. There is some current discussion on the service about the so-called Meigs Syndrome. They think they have one on the medical service.

I was interested in hearing about your surgical truck. Do tell me more about it and how it works.

How nice for you to be treated as family or guest in the Dutch household. If you could just have a few such experiences and then come home.

We are still excited about the prospect of King's arrival. This cheers me no end, as it makes me realize that sooner or later this period of waiting must terminate. I just can't wait three years, however, or even one and a half. If the prospects look that long, something must be done about it.

All my love, Ginny

Friday, December 15, 1944
7:15

My dearest,

Yesterday I missed my letter again, as it was one of those nights. I just rolled into bed unconscious. Somehow with you those nights are a real lark. But without you, they are just a waste of time.

Today the V-mail of November 29 arrived. It said, as I had judged, that you were busy again. I guess that you are, at this time of my writing, again busy after another lull.

The political news continues to stink, but I refuse to think about it. We can worry about those problems together in the postwar era.

Today the printer's proof of our pregnanediol-chorionic-gonadotropin paper arrived, and we were very pleased with its appearance. I am afraid the reprints will be too late for Christmas.

We continue to be tremendously excited and pleased over the prospect of having King home. I am planning our meeting all over again, as Jane plans hers. I can't decide whether to wear my hair long or short or whether to wear clothes you know or a new outfit. Right now, I lean toward the old familiar things.

At one time I thought of being very efficient and learning how to do everything on schedule, so that I would be a super something when you come home. But I have decided against that too, as I am afraid it changes my personality, and I figure you must have liked it as it was. What changes are made, I will let you direct. I long for the day you return, my dear.

All my love, Ginny

Saturday, December 16, 1944
10:00 P.M.

Dearest Honey Bunny,

Today your letter of December 3 arrived. You have not yet moved, I take it, and I am glad.

You must know by now that Smitty's back and really working quite nicely.

If I ever find a proper girl, I would like to have her, but it is almost impossible to locate a really satisfactory one.

I think I can get the cigars without too much difficulty. I am sorry to hear that the Colonel has never received his promotion.

Lib is coming home for New Year's, and everyone is hoping King might make it also, but I am afraid that is a bit optimistic.

I spend a great deal of effort in postwar planning, but without you it is difficult. Perhaps we will have a few months before they muster you out.

All my love, Ginny

Sunday, December 17, 1944
9:45 P.M.

Dearest Honey Bunny,

Well, it looks as if you will lose your New Year's bet, and right now I am very pessimistic about the prospects for the year of 1945. But who knows? And regardless of what breaks, we are still fortunate in our love for each other.

You asked for a box of cigars, and we were fortunate enough to have a friend in the right place. Boxes of cigars have not been available for over six months, they tell me, but Father procured a box. I don't know what kind they are, but they are supposed to be good. I will get them off to the Colonel in the A.M.

I have finished all my essential Christmas shopping, but still have lots of odds and ends. I wish you were here to meet me and have dinner downtown, although I don't think you enjoyed that Christmas escapade as I did.

I keep going over some way for our postwar activities. The best would be for you to have a professorship in some nice medical school and I could be your research assistant.

Barring that, I suppose if Dr. B retires and you reign supreme at the Kelly Clinic, I might do much the same. I could also talk to the difficult patients. If you go into practice for yourself, perhaps I could be your anesthetist. All pipe dreams, but fascinating ones.

My other pipe dreams are concerned with how Willie and I can get to Papa, but they, at this point at least, seem very important.

We just heard that the 9th Army is being attacked by tanks and infantry.

They also said that the situation is now under control. Paratroopers were also dropped, and air support has been given. I pray that you are safe.

All my love, Ginny

P.S. Someday, when you have a chance, tell me how many letters of mine are missing.

Monday, December 18, 1944
9:45

Dearest Papa,

Today your two letters of December 3 and 5 arrived. You had just moved into Germany, as I had expected, and right now, with the present news of German counterattacks, I am unhappy. I can't believe, however, that fate would be so unkind as to deprive me of such a wonderful husband.

The letters contained snaps of you and the team, and again it makes me realize just how badly I resent not being with you. I dislike the nurses terribly for being able to be so near Papa and share the same experiences. I feel much the same toward Ken Tanner. It's just not right.

I saw Dr. Stone today, and he asked to be remembered to you. It's the first time I've seen him since I've been back. He had little to say, except that he still thought the surgical group was the only place for surgeons in this war.

I told him you were very pleased and did not tell him you have your majority, as it will come out sooner or later anyway. He really did better by you than by his son. I am sure you have the best CO.

Willie is now much interested in plumbing and goes around telling everyone, "Water goes down the hole, down the pipe, into the cellar, into the drain, and under the street—I can see it."

B is as cute as can be, even though there is very little to say for her. I am afraid her hair is going to be straight like mine, but I got along, so I'm not too worried.

Discoveries at the laboratory are slow, but it is really my salvation. I should be like poor Martha in Phipps Psychiatric Clinic, if it weren't for my work. Did I ever tell you that she has gotten worse, not better, and may be in the institution for a year (and her husband permanently stationed in this country)? I could scream at such people.

Also, did I tell you, or have you seen in the *AMA journal*, that Weldon Ross was given the Distinguished Service Medal for some invention he made for making flying at high altitude easier?

Also, Willard Goodwin received the Soldier's Medal for rescuing a drowning nurse in New Zealand. The catch to this one is that his wife says he had no business swimming in New Zealand with the nurse in the first place, and as far as she is concerned, he needed to bring the medal home. You see, all we wives have a time with the little green god. But you know, dear, I trust you implicitly and can't help envying anyone near you.

With all my love, Mama

Tuesday, December 19, 1944
9:30

Dearest Honey Bunny,

The news is still very upsetting. I don't dare think of it. I guess it will be several days until we know exactly what will take place, but I am feeling very pessimistic. If only I could be with you and know exactly where you are and what is going on.

I spent the afternoon showing Dr. Grady from Portugal the laboratory. This also depressed me, as he showed what the poor Europeans expect of us, and I am sure we have no idea or ability of fulfilling the same.

He seems very discouraged about European prospects, especially if peace does not come in the very near future. He certainly was hard on the Germans, and I hope he is not right about everything. But the papers are saying that the Germans are killing all prisoners.

I, of course, asked him about traveling in France now. I am still considering some scheme to get to see you.

I am trying to get up some kind of Christmas spirit, but unless King gets home suddenly, I am afraid it will be very dreary. Jane really expects him at any time.

Tonight while Willie was playing around, the tune "Jingle Bells" was playing on the radio. He immediately recognized it.

R.G. Swing on the radio has just said that the northern front is stabilized—

I pray so. If only this would be the last German struggle and the war would be all over.

It makes me ache to know that I will not hear from you at this time for at least two weeks. But tomorrow I may have a letter and will feel better. Your letters are my constant source of courage.

All my love, Ginny

Wednesday, December 20, 1944
9:30 P.M.

My darling,

The news continues bad, but thank heavens the 9th Army section seems to be holding. All of this seems so unreal that I can't believe it is happening to me and us. I keep thinking I will wake up and find you there, because you are my greatest reality.

It is difficult for me to write the petty trivialities which are occupying my time, and yet I know that is what I should do.

I had a very full dispensary today and a very satisfactory one, except that POWs are now housecleaning the hospital, and I really hated to see them. It brought the war constantly to my attention (as if I weren't thinking about it, regardless).

This afternoon I finally did most of my Christmas shopping. Earrings and a slip for Ruth, a medical caduceus and small black dress bag for Ess, a sweater for Mary, beads for Donnie, slip for Libby, books for Father, milk-glass china for Jane, and a woolen scarf for Mother. Books for most of the children we know, and I still have Betty Schilpp. Perhaps I will give her war stamps.

Eleanor was frantically doing her shopping at the same time. We are a pair. She is leaving for home tomorrow evening. Did I ever tell you that her sister's husband is moving to Argentina and that Eleanor may take two months off and help her sister move the three children down this spring?

No mail has come through yet. That really makes only 15 days, but it seems forever when you are holding your breath, and that's how I feel between letters. It is a peculiar feeling to go through the motions of living and really not be living at all. My life without you is time past, but not counted.

All my love, Ginny

Thursday, December 21, 1944
10:15 P.M.

Dearest,

What black news! I keep telling myself that the 9th Army front is still stable and that you were at least not in the first melee, taken by surprise, and so totally mauled, and finally that you have a truck which you can move with rapidly, if necessary.

I am so hoping every hour to hear that the lines have been stabilized and that the German retreat has begun. If only they don't swing back of your lines.

Of course, when you receive this, it will be over, and we will know what has come of the great German counterattack. But then, you realize I write what I think at the moment, so that you will be in touch with my life as much as possible.

It is hard to go about the daily routine normally when every moment you are wondering about what is going on a thousand miles away, and everyone asks, "Where is Howard now?" Dr. TeLinde was most encouraging, but it is easy to be optimistic when you are not truly interested.

Louise Monahan called from Aberdeen today, frantic because she has not heard from Dave in a month. I can only tell her I had had mail to December 10 and that at that time all was well.

Your mail of December 9 and 10 arrived with pictures of the group and news of your job investigation. Also, about your trip back to see Gene Bennett and the man whose hand was healing.

Willie was awfully cute today. Looking at the funny paper, he saw a picture of a baby sliding down the banister. His eyes fairly shown, and he said, "I can do that [a true member of the Jones family]. Can you do that, Bess?"

Mother was a little astonished and said, "You better go show it to Mama." He came running to me with it, repeating the whole procedure. He then raced to the hall to try it, but unfortunately he was a little too small to make it. His favorite pastime is playing diving board. He climbs on the arm of the sofa and catapults onto the sofa—fine for the springs, etc.

Darling, you asked in your letter today why you always save the last paragraph to say you love me. You always save the best for last, and I love it. I live only for the day of your return, and the joy of life is gone without you to share it.

All my love, and do come home to me soon and
safe and well, Ginny

Friday, December 22, 1944
11:00 P.M.

My darling,

Tonight I feel slightly easier about your position. There seems to be good reason to believe that the Russian winter offensive has begun and also that there has been no further German penetration. Of course, there is the ever-present dread of the V-bombs. I must rely on my prayers to keep you safe from them.

It seems as if we might have a white Christmas. But although I would usually rejoice, I am sad thinking of the handicap such weather means in Europe. Today, while I was shopping like mad, one of those candid men took my picture. I am going to send for it and forward it to you just to give you some amusement. I am sure it's a dilly.

I have decided against buying a car, as you no doubt know by now. I have a ride to and from work and really very little time for other diversion, so I don't miss it. If we get stuck without one, I suppose we can always buy your mother's, as she frequently bemoans having one.

It doesn't seem possible that I could love you more, but somehow I do. I think about you so much and about our life together that somehow I seem to understand you and love you even better than I did.

With all my love, Ginny

Chapter 7

Back to Belgium and Netherlands
19 December 1944-7 February 1945

*T*HEY ALSO SERVE WHO ONLY STAND AND WAIT. BUT much to our regret, the 5th Auxiliary Surgical Group's role during the Battle of the Bulge was to remain in reserve until called upon. The 5th Aux waited first in Bocholz, Netherlands, and then in Wellen, Belgium.

On 24 December 1944, when I wrote a Christmas Eve letter to Georgeanna, American and British army groups were fiercely battling the German armies trying to roll back the Allied offensive and capture Bastogne, Belgium.

The U.S. Army had stored an abundance of fuel at Bastogne— fuel that the German armored divisions absolutely needed if they were to reach the North Sea Port of Antwerp, Belgium.

Improving weather enabled previously grounded Allied aircraft to drop supplies the day before to the besieged U.S. Army units at Bastogne. The Germans failed to capture Bastogne and never reached Antwerp. The bold German thrust by cutting the Allies' supply pipeline at Antwerp was stopped.

---

24 December 1944
Christmas Eve

My dearest Ginny,

Christmas Eve, and what a Christmas! How well I remember the one of 13 years ago when I burned a hole in the back of my coat while trimming the tree in the hall. Tonight we are having a little celebration to the sound of bombers going high overhead—our bombers, I am glad to say.

We have moved. We are now back in Bocholz, Holland. This time we are not even set up to work, but are in bivouac again in a school building with running water and electric lights, for a change. At the moment, we are not involved in the tremendous battle going on. We are in reserve and not yet committed.

Today has been beautiful. For the first time in many days, there has not been a cloud in the sky, and the planes have been out in great strength. It has been cold. The ground is frozen solid and, of course, I could think of how nice it would be for us to be on a trip somewhere. It is very similar to the one good day we had skiing at Lake Placid, only a little colder.

After arriving here, the weather was so nice that I got my bedroll apart and put the contents out in the sun to air. Airing was not before needed, but I found some mold between the air mattress and the comforter part of the sleeping bag. I think I got it out well enough.

It has now been several days without mail, but I suppose we will get none until the German attack is straightened out. I hope the Germans have not captured any of your letters.

Love, H

Christmas Day 1944

Dearest Ginny,

All things considered, this has been a nice Christmas day. Yesterday, when we got here (Wellen), everyone was a bit tired. But last night everyone slept well. We had not done any work at the last place, but the anxiety of the general situation made everyone restless and sometimes sleepless, but not me, so the outfit as a whole was a bit tired out.

This is a quiet town not very far from the war, but they have not seen much of it. That is, there have not been many soldiers here, and all the windows are still intact, and I have not seen a single bomb or shell mark. We are in a Catholic school in bivouac, as I said.

Last night the nurses all put on Class-A uniforms and had a party of sorts, dancing to the radio, etc. I felt rather sorry for the lot of them, as they tried so hard to make things lively, and they succeeded in a measure. But I thought that most of the men, including me, got very glassy-eyed too soon for the girls. They actually are in an unfortunate position, but we do have three very eligible bachelors, and that keeps them interested.

By the way, it is beginning to appear as if we have a budding romance on our team. Alice and Ken seem to be together much more than they need, for all practical purposes.

Today we had breakfast at 9:30 and a good turkey dinner at 2:30. We had turkey, cranberry sauce, sweet potatoes, dressing, and pineapple pie. This morning at 10:30, four of us went to the village church to High Mass. It reminded me, of course, of the times we used to go to St. Agnes for Christmas Eve Mass. This afternoon at 4:00 P.M., the girls sponsored an organization party at which Santa (Nick Codik) gave each a Red Cross gift.

Love, H

———————

THE GERMAN ARMY'S westward drive toward Antwerp reached a standstill on 26 December, and U.S. armored units broke through the encirclement of Bastogne, bringing strength and relief to the embattled defenders.

———————

26 December 1944

My darling Ginny,

It is again a nice day—beautiful, in fact—crystal clear and cold and one that would be nice to be out in with you. It is one of those rare days when vapor trails from the planes are visible entirely across the sky, and there are many of them.

Each plane leaves a track of two streaks—one for the tip of each wing, I think. They are sort of life-sized tracks in fresh snow. The area is so clear that the tracks remain for hours and gradually spread out and dissipate.

So many planes have been in the sky that by yesterday afternoon there was a thin cloud covering the zenith, a cloud made by vapor tracks. I saw a dogfight so far away that the planes were invisible, but we could see the tracks crossing and crisscrossing and crisscrossing and hear the .50-caliber-machine-gun fire through the quiet, cold air.

The truck from headquarters was around today, and I heard that Mac had been transferred to the 105th Evacuation Hospital as chief of the surgical service. I think it suits Mac, because he will now be able to do his surgery as he wants to. That suits the Colonel, as he can now get himself an executive officer who will content himself with administrative duties.

All my love, H

27 December 1944

Dearest Ginny,

It is good to see security measures tightened up. Although we had to go but a short distance, we were stopped three times and had to give the password and identify ourselves.

It is not sufficient to have your papers in order, but the guard also asked questions that only Americans can be expected to know and to answer, like, "Who is The Voice?" or "What happened to Daisy Mae on Sadie Hawkins Day?"

We have seen nothing of parachutists or the Fifth Column, but as you can read in the papers, the Jerries have tried to make use of the same sort of tactics as in 1940, in order to create as much confusion as possible within our forces.

While we were back in Germany, it was difficult for us to get out of bed in the morning because we were able to open a window and did, with the result that the room was very, very cold.

Then, all of a sudden, Ken began getting up first thing, shutting the window, and starting the fire. After this happened three or four times, we found out that he had got his inspiration and strength from reading Henry Link's book, The Return to Religion.

In turn then, each of us has read it. It is a good book. It does not strike me as a particularly religious book in the ordinary sense of the word. It is more of a book in applied psychology, with emphasis on the possibilities of religion's helping people who are not well-adjusted.

Of particular interest to me was the chapter, "Children Are Made." He maintains that the best way to teach children the difference between right and wrong is if it is agreed that a supernatural power carries more authority than parents can muster.

About this I am not too sure, but he then defines personality as the ability to subordinate one's own desires, so that one is pleasing to the other, and then goes on to say the strategic time to teach children to subordinate their inappropriate impulses to higher values is when they are too young to understand, but not too young to accept.

This seems to me that it might be right. I cannot tell whether this has any application to our family, but I thought it was interesting. You might find it so.

There is also a chapter on "Love and Marriage," but he says what we already know. There is no question about the fact that the smartest thing I ever did was marrying you. Nothing else approaches it.

Love and kisses to all of our little family, H

28 December 1944

Dearest Ginny,

Recently I went back to Germany to visit the Siegfried Line fortifications. As far as the eye could see, there was a line of so-called dragon's teeth, just as shown in the movies.

Nearby, and about 200 yards inside the line, there are numerous pillboxes that are actually bunkers for guns, probably 88mm. The idea was for the tanks to be halted by the dragon's teeth, and then have the 88s take a crack at them. This particular area was never used.

The pillboxes have been blown up by our engineers to prevent their possible future use, but the dragon's teeth have been untouched. The whole thing is now deserted—a monument to the past. It gives me the same sensation as visiting other deserted places, like the Algonquin Hotel at Saranac Lake, for instance.

The present fighting in Saint-Vith and Bastogne is very real to me. We went to Bastogne for several days directly from Brest, and we were in Saint-Vith when I wrote to you about the beautiful pine forest.

I hope to go back there someday. I know the place must be leveled. I feel so sorry for Saint-Vith, for it belonged to Germany before 1914. It should never have been given to Belgium by the Versailles Treaty. It is another example of a minority that created such trouble.

Love to all, H

Diary Entry: 3 January 1945
[Wellen, 48th Field Hospital, 3rd Platoon]

I have not written anything in this book for two months, because I thought by the time I got home this narrative would not be very interesting to you. However, I have just reviewed some of it and find that it helps me recall some instances, so I might take up the task again for you and for me. I want to write here only those things that I cannot write in a letter.

When it became apparent at Nuth that we were moving into bivouac at Eygelshoven, I went over to the 2nd Platoon at Heerleen to stay a day or two with Bill Falor and watch him work. As a matter of fact, the flow of casualties was very slow, and I saw only a case or two. It was during this time that we visited the midwifery school I wrote about.

At that time I went into headquarters at Maastricht for a day or so to keep my finger in the pie and found that my team was to be transferred to the 3rd Platoon of the 48th Field Hospital. We were also to be given the surgical truck that Fritz Joachim had at the 100th Evacuation Hospital at Tongeren, Belgium, so that each platoon of the 48th and 53rd would have such a truck. Fletcher Wright, who was at the 48th, was to come over to the 53rd.

While in headquarters, the Col. asked me to stay a day or so, as we were in bivouac, so that Bill Boukalik and I could go over the PROCO outfits. After talking over the equipment lists of these outfits, we decided that a much-more-workable list could be made if numerous items were eliminated. It amounted to a recommendation that all expendable material be eliminated and only nonexpendable equipment, such as suction machines, anesthesia machines, autoclaves, generators, and the like be kept.

This was equipment that we had found usable in a field hospital. We had discovered that the problems for which the PROCO units were designed never arrived. However, field hospitals were designed to run only one operating table, and with PROCO equipment, two tables could be operated at once. This was the basis of our recommendation.

We advised omitting the expendable items, because they were duplicated in the field hospital and, if not used, would be lost to all concerned, because they were packed in wooden boxes, subject to getting moldy, wet, and ruined. We recommended the surgical trucks be left as constituted, for although they had expendable items, they were good housekeeping units, and the expendable items would be preserved, even if not used for some time.

Prior to this, the Col. had tried to turn in the PROCO units, as they had caused headquarters considerable worry in transporting and keeping the material together, inasmuch as equipment not being used and not stored under lock and key tends to get lost or stolen.

As a result of trying to turn them in, Col. Shambora became interested, and between Col. Gay and Shambora, a demonstration of the PROCO and the surgical truck was arranged while Bill Boukalik and I happened to be going over the problem to make a recommendation.

Bill Boukalik, with very little assistance on my part, pitched all the tents and set up the equipment. Col. Shambora and many from the surgeon's office came over. The equipment looked very nice when set up.

However, Col. Shambora had previously made up his mind anyway and insisted that all PROCO units and surgical trucks be made ready for immediate use. How? We did not think he was quite clear on it, but the general idea was to use them as operating rooms (which they were) to follow a rapidly moving column, like an armored division, a column moving faster than a field hospital could.

It did not make much sense to Bill Boukalik and me who had worked with most of these units and with field hospitals, but this was the decision.

NONE OF THIS had seemed to make much sense to us, because the PROCO units, or surgical trucks, if they did follow an armored division, had no facilities for hospitalizing the postoperative patients. This was the function of the field hospital, which itself lacked surgeons; surgical teams from the auxiliary surgical groups supplied the function. In general, this seemed to work pretty well.

The MASH (Mobile Army Surgical Hospital) unit of the Korean War seemed to be what Shambora was thinking of. He later became a general in the War Department Surgeon General's Office in Washington, and it is entirely possible that he is the person who dreamed up the MASH unit, a concept that didn't quite congeal in the European Theater of Operations.

In the morning we had written our recommendation to modify the PROCO to contain only a few items. At noon we had the exhibit and then went home and tore up the recommendation. That is the way the army often runs.

I had planned to stay a day or two longer and help bring the PROCOS up to snuff, as directed by Colonel Shambora. However, on 16 November, the Allied offensive toward the Roer River started, and word arrived at headquarters that Bill Falor and Bill Fuqua were swamped at Heerleen (2nd Platoon, 53rd Field Hospital). Lieutenant Colonel Friege (assistant surgeon, Ninth Army) had ordered Humphries and another team from Tongeren (48th Field Hospital in bivouac) to help out.

However, it was apparent that it would be late night by the time they got there. Falor and Fuqua had been working thirty straight hours by this time. I suggested to Colonel Gay that he give me a voco (vocal command) to get my team from nearby Eygelshoven, in view of the fact that we were due to go to Tongeren to the 3rd Platoon of the 48th Field Hospital anyway. This he granted.

I immediately set out in a one-and-a-half-ton truck. This was the

17th of November, and I heard from Lieutenant Colonel Smith that morning that while he was in the Surgeon's Office he had seen the order with my promotion to major. By 2:00 PM the team was at Heerleen. We went to work immediately and worked until 8:00 AM the next day (18 November), doing thirteen cases.

Late that night (17-18 November) the two other teams arrived and, on the eighteenth, we were ordered by Colonel Gay to go to the 3rd Platoon of the 53rd Field Hospital (which we had just left) at Niewenhagen to help with the work they had.

We were very busy for about ten days. When we first arrived at Niewenhagen, there was much heavy artillery around the town, and we became quite used to the big guns. You heard a bang and, about one second later, felt and heard a severe blast, which was the muzzle blast that fairly shook the building.

We stayed at Niewenhagen for about two weeks as a third team, and there we heard from Colonel Gay, who had come for a visit in December, that the 3rd Platoon of the 48th Field Hospital was that day setting up at Übach. We were to go over there (eight miles or so) on 4 December. Things had gradually quieted down at the 53rd Field Hospital, as the Ninth Army had by that time reached the Roer River. A lull of a few days was expected before the river was crossed in strength.

AT HEERLEEN WE had had patients from the 29th Division, some from the 30th Division. At Niewenhagen we had principally the 84th Division, with some from the 102nd Division.

While at Niewenhagen, Sergeant Bolanger brought up Fritz Joachim's surgical truck, which we were to have at the 48th Field Hospital, 3rd platoon. Our team therefore traveled to Übach in that truck and an ambulance, but we found that we could put our duffel and all six of us in the truck if three rode in front.

I had described in a letter our trip to Übach. Life there was quiet, except at the time of the opening of the German counteroffensive. On that day we had several Jerry planes over and a lot of antiaircraft fire.

It was here that I saw my first German plane by day. I heard many at night, and some antiaircraft fire. But on Sunday, 17 December we saw several two-engine bombers at about three thousand feet picking their way through antiaircraft fire, each reminding me of a halfback running a broken field. Most of the antiaircraft bursts were behind the plane. The day was so noisy that I suggested we sleep downstairs, but Ken and Elmer did not feel like moving; so we went to bed as usual, about 10:30 PM.

At 12:30 AM, I was awakened by a tremendous explosion and could hear a plane disappearing in the distance. I realized at once that the explosion was a bomb. But I was not at all frightened, because it seemed to me that the bombing was over. Elmer and Ken had both been awake. They had heard the plane coming, as well as the other bombs in the stick and then the whistle and the explosion.

The concussion knocked off most of the blackout curtains in our room and, without hesitation, we went down to one of the wards to finish out the night.

We found most of the blackout material knocked off on the east side of the building. Fortunately, all the glass had previously been blown out. We guessed that the bombs had fallen about 100 yards from us.

Our latrines were in three pyramidal tents about twenty yards from one of the entrances to the school. The next morning one of the men looked out the window and reported seeing only two pyramidal tents, so we reasoned the third must be around the corner out of sight, because we thought that the bomb could not have been that close.

We were wrong. The bomb had made a direct hit on the enlisted men's latrine. The tent was shredded into pieces spread over the nearby tree like tinsel on a Christmas tree. The four holes of the latrine were not to be found. Instead, there was a crater ten by five feet. No one received as much as a scratch.

We all moved down to the cellar and stayed there until we left Übach.

From the opening of the German offensive until our departure from Übach, artillery shelling filled days and nights with noise. En route from Übach to Bocholtz, our team rode in the truck, but not in convoy, because convoys were considered fat targets.

We moved from Bocholtz to Wellen on 29 December, and we stopped by headquarters in Maastricht on the way. That was when the Colonel Gay asked me about joining the Evac Hospital. So after arriving at Wellen, I returned to headquarters on the thirtieth and stayed until New Year's Day. During this time, I talked to Mac, who had by now been a few days in his new job as chief of surgery at the 105th Evac Hospital. I also traveled to Valkenburg to the 91st Evacuation Hospital to talk to Stewart Welch, chief of surgery. He advised me to take the job.

SO I HAD the opportunity to become chief of surgery at an evacuation hospital. Medical personnel were often shifted. The 5th Aux at first had few personnel qualified to be chiefs of general-surgery teams.

The quality of the 5th Aux teams gradually improved. My diary note of 24 October records that I successfully recommended that my own assistant, Howard Yost, become a team chief. Lieutenant Kenneth Tanner of North Carolina, a Harvard graduate who had had a nine-month internship on the Johns Hopkins surgical service, replaced Yost. Ken stayed as Team 3 surgical assistant until the end of the European war. He was a very competent—though at first inexperienced—assistant. He was also very pleasant, easy to get along with, and a great asset to the team.

There were also "advancement" opportunities for team chiefs, usually to status of chief surgeon at an evacuation hospital, a slot calling for a full colonel. Our 5th Aux executive officer, Lieutenant Colonel McIntyre, who had been a surgical teammate of mine at our first stop in Brittany, became chief of surgery at the 105th Evacuation Hospital.

Around New Year's Day, during a lull at Wellen, I received word of an expected chief-of-surgery vacancy at an evacuation hospital.

Even though the possibility of promotion to full colonel seemed attractive at the time, the chief surgeon at an evacuation hospital bore a heavy load of administrative responsibilities, and the cases at the hospital were quite different from those seen, at the field hospital. Patching up severely wounded fighting men near the battleground was of far greater importance to me; I decided to try to remain

chief of Team 3 in the 5th Auxiliary Surgical Group and to be content
as a major.

———————————

1 January 1945

Dearest Ginny,

*I have spent the last few days in and around headquarters visiting an evac or
two, trying to make up my mind about the evac-hospital possibility. It is a very
difficult decision, because it may involve more than the immediate war situation,
that is, it might make it likely that I will go to the Pacific, and so on.*

*For the moment, they have delayed making a change that might send me to
an evacuation hospital, so the decision does not have to be made right now. It may
be best if the whole thing falls through.*

*This is hastily written, standing in the mailroom while they are sorting a few
first-class letters that arrived today and while other people are talking to each
other and me. But this is the only place available right now.*

*Even so, I have constantly in mind that this day of all days in the year is our
day, and more important to me than any other day, and you are more important
to me than anything else in the world. We shall make this day one of holiday and
thanksgiving for all the good that has happened to you and me together.*

Love, H

2 January 1945

Dearest Ginny,

*It is too bad that you have had any anxiety about me since the German
offensive started. As a matter of fact, we have been in reserve the entire time, and
I have spent a great deal of time playing bridge. As you know, we have moved,
and while I was occupied with the evac-hospital proposition, we moved again. We
are now in Belgium, but not in the fight.*

*To recapitulate the evac-hospital situation: The other day Colonel Gay told
me that it was anticipated that a chief of surgery for an evacuation hospital
would be relieved in the near future, and he had advance information that he
would be asked to supply a candidate for this job. He consulted with Mac, who
suggested Bill Boukalik and me, in that order.*

Mac, you know, has such a similar job, as I previously mentioned. Bill Boukalik turned it down, but he also said, of course, that if the Colonel thought it was the best for the service, etc., he would take it. It was then that he approached me. I don't know what to do and have not decided, as the decision to change the chief has not been finally made. As I see it, things line up as follows:

For (1) An opportunity to organize a large surgical service (450 beds) and use the little flair I have for executive work; (2) The opportunity for promotion. This does not mean anything to me or to you, and it is more potential than real, for it will be a year before this takes place. Besides, I feel, in spite of recent events that this part of the war will be over by then. However, it might mean something to others who do not know anything about it. Nothing succeeds like success.

Against:

(1) The danger of failure. The change is being made because the surgical service is not running satisfactorily enough to suit the Army authorities, while the hospital CO apparently is satisfied. This means a situation requiring diplomacy of a very delicate sort and a situation in which it will be hard to be right.

> *If I failed, either due to my own fault or someone else's, I would be out of the 5th Aux without friends at court. I hope to get a more definite promise of the Army headquarters' opinion on this point before coming to a decision. I might be able to get a promise from headquarters to support me to the point of changing other men on the staff, if necessary.*

(2) I would not be able to do as much operating as before, but actually, I have done nothing here for a month, and chiefs of service at other hospitals tell me that, from their point of view, the service is what you make it. Our man who is chief of service at a hospital and has been through Africa has done about 700 chest cases and seen another 700. He also feels that the breadth of cases at an evac hospital gives a broader view of war surgery. All in all, this point is equivocal, and I do not think it is of much importance.

How to evaluate:

What will happen to the evac, as compared to the 5th Aux, at the end of the war? No one knows, but a good many people think that both will be sent to the Orient by way of the U.S., for refitting as necessary.

Do write me what you think, because the opening for a chief of surgery may come through at any time, as Mac's change was in the file for about two months. I have not had a chance to talk to Bill Falor or Boukalik about it. Apparently, the post will not be offered to anyone else in the 5th if neither Bill nor I want it, although one of us may have to take it.

We do nothing. It is very difficult to occupy myself with anything that amounts to anything. It is easy to say that it is, because we live in a large room with eight others, and one's attention is devoted to just living and getting along with each other. But, more particularly, it is due to the fact that when you want to do something, your roommates want you to do something else, or they play the radio loudly, or want the lights out, or a thousand and one things that do not give you an hour alone without being disturbed.

Really, of course, the trouble is none of these things. The problem is that Papa does not have enough of what it takes. Just as at home, it was easy for me to take it easy when I should have been doing something more important. This is why I want to change our routine at home somehow, to see if it might be possible to somehow detour me away from my innate inertia. If anything can help me, Mama can.

All my love, H

Diary Entry: 2 January 1945
[Wellen]

While I was at Valkenburg, Germany, on a visit, Elmer Carlsen walked in. He had chased me over the country, because I had gone off with several fifths of Scotch whiskey in the back of the surgical truck, and he was afraid I would not be back until tomorrow.

However, I had planned to return, and so he stayed with me. When we got back to headquarters (at Maastricht) the Col. and Mac insisted that we stay until the first, as the 105th Evac Hospital was having a party that night. We sent the Scotch back to Wellen by the mail truck just then leaving.

That night the party was going full swing. About 11:00 o'clock, I got hot and took my field jacket upstairs and was looking out the window of the 4th floor with Joe Redline at some antiaircraft fire at planes apparently trying to bomb the bridges over the Maas. Things had quieted down when, suddenly, I heard the whistle of a bomb, fell away from the window, and heard a tremendous explosion, all at once. Joe fell on top of me.

We were both all right. Every window in the north side of the building was broken, and several people undoubtedly would have been cut by flying glass, except that almost everyone, except Joe and me, were at the moment at the dance. We were saved because the windows were open and the glass did not break. It did blow the door to the room off the hinges, and it did other damage nearby.

There was very little sleep that night, as the Jerries were active. Two other times that night I heard diving planes, whistling bombs, and explosions, but none near enough to break anything in the building.

The bomb had hit about 20 yards outside the window. Two bombs had really fallen, but one was a dud. The bomb-disposal squad said it was a 500-pounder. If they had both exploded, we would have had more than six personnel slightly injured by flying glass. The next morning, Jerries were out in strength, and we were afraid to go back to Wellen until the afternoon. But we saw no planes. When we did we found that there had been some antipersonnel bombs at Wellen on New Year's Eve.

---

3 January 1945
4:00 P.M.

My dearest Ginny,

In the letter to your mother and father I wrote today, I mentioned about taking a bath in a child's tub. I did not mention that we are using children's toilets, and outside ones at that.

It is quite a feat to use a pot a foot off the ground and only 5" in diameter, especially if it is in a subzero breeze coming up from below and a sprinkling of rain to keep things moist. I have learned to admire the genius of the person who invented the modern bathroom.

Love to all the little family, H

4 January 1945

Dearest Ginny,

In your letter of November 16 you mentioned that Dr. Rich [Arnold Rice Rich, professor of pathology at Johns Hopkins] stopped you and complimented you on the pregnancy chorionic gonadotropin paper. I am anxious to get the reprint. Is it on the way? This paper by Georgeanna proved that chorionic gonadotropin arose from the chorion rather than from the pituitary, as had been previously thought.

We continue to be in bivouac farther from the front than I have been in a long time. Our front is simply not active.

Love, H

5 January 1945

Dearest Ginny,

Today we have had a beautiful, clear day, as we had at Christmastime. The planes were out in force. They could be seen at about 25,000 feet only by their vapor trails. Four trails for a four-engine bomber, two for two.

Today they reminded me of boats leaving wakes in a blue lake. At one time I counted 90 four-engine bombers in the air at one time. They go in gentle arcs, first this way and that, apparently to throw off the German radar as to the point of attack.

They also drop "clutter" to jam the radar. This clutter is tin-foil-backed heavy paper that deflects the radar beams as well as enemy planes and so confuse the whole thing. These are the most warlike things we have seen.

You have mentioned Buzz bombs from time to time, but actually, we have seen less than a half dozen the whole war, and those going high overhead.

Today I mailed a small package containing a lace centerpiece and a chair headset. I do not think they are pieces of great handwork, but they were made by the sisters here at the convent and will serve as souvenirs. One of them appears to have been used. These little cards were also made by the sisters. I do not know what you will do with them, but I think they are nice.

My love as always, H

6 January 1945

Dearest Ginny,

Today I visited the Chapel of the Convent. Without a doubt, it is the most beautiful church of its size I have ever seen.

In the first place, it was scrupulously clean. The nuns must go over it daily with scrub-brushes, and there is no musty dirt, so common in churches.

I know so little about architecture that I am not able to name it, but it is a high-arched church and most interesting, and the thing that makes it unusual is that it is highly colored with enamel colors and pastels. This does not sound good, but it was done with great good taste.

In one corner of the chapel, there is the usual manger scene so common in Catholic churches. This was beautifully done, with a most unusual use of mirrors. There is no doubt that these people have a widespread talent for artistic things.

Today I went into a Tongeren and bought Willy two berets and a pair of sabots. These sabots are exactly as every child here wears. The sisters wear them about the convent when they are working.

The town interested me. Three months ago we were at bivouac very near there, and the shops of the town were almost devoid of goods. Today, however, the shops were full. Where did the goods come from? I don't know, but most likely they were brought from places near the front, like Liège.

I will get these things off in a day or two, when an opportunity comes along.

As these weeks go into months, I scarcely know what to hope for. All my hopes and thoughts are channeled one way, and that is through you. I cannot think about anything that does not involve the one I love.

I knew this before, but the separation has made my love stand out above the other things in life so much that there is simply no comparison between it and other things. How fortunate for me to have this, because it gives some hope and purpose to a world about one which seems to have no destination or a purpose.

Love, H

P.S. I believe I mentioned once before that I hoped you would be able to find a book on European history. I would enjoy it.

Tuesday, January 9, 1945

Dearest Ginny,

Here I am back "home" again after a day or two at headquarters. The result of a roundtable talk with the Colonel, Bill Boukalik, and me was, as I said yesterday, nothing. It is my opinion now that no change will be made in the near future, and perhaps never. There has not been enough volume of work to make it necessary for Colonel Smith to come to a decision. This is perhaps the happiest resolution for all concerned.

Recently I had an opportunity to visit the Church of St. Servatius at Maastricht. It is the most interesting of all the cathedrals I have ever visited, perhaps because we were shown through it by one of the priests who spoke good English.

Parts of the church date from AD 600, and it was rebuilt in 1100 and added to from time to time until about 1400 or 1500. No additions have been made since then.

As with all these old churches, it is interesting to trace the connection of church and state. For example, there is an Emperor's Hall, where ecclesiastical crimes were tried by the emperor, who at one time was Charlemagne, whose empire was ruled from Aachen. The most interesting thing was that it looked for all the world like a stage set for "Lucia di Lammermoor." For the first time, I saw the real McCoy on the stage, and movies have done a good job. I expected to see Lord Bucklaw at any moment.

The news is good tonight. It appears as if the Bulge will be reduced very shortly.

With love and kisses, H

10 January 1945

Dearest Ginny,

The enclosed *Mitteilengen* is of interest for two reasons: In the first place, because of its contents, and in the second, because I picked it up in a former Nazi headquarters in Saint-Vith, which has recently been in the news.

This Mitteilengen is intended as source material for officers in leading discussions of their troops about war aims and the like. The substance it contains is the part I have marked with the pen. It is not worth reading the whole thing.

I found it in a book about Pasteur I bought in Bastogne. I came across it today while straightening things out a bit.

I mean to constantly repeat my love, H

11 January 1945

My dearest Ginny,

Today has been, without a doubt, the coldest day we have had. This morning I put on my regular woolen clothes, then a field jacket, then my combat pants and combat coat (like a ski suit), then my rubber galoshes, then my field overcoat, then my wool cap, then, with hood all buttoned up over the helmet and gloves, I drove in an open jeep into Tongeren, about 15 kilometers away.

The countryside was as beautiful as the prettiest part of the path at New Germany, Maryland. A bit chilly, yes, but good. I went to get my tortoise-shell glasses fixed. An arm had broken off. The glasses will be ready tomorrow. While there, I bought some small doilies, which I put in the box with the berets and sabots, and which I finally got off today.

The boarding school at which we are staying started today after the Christmas holiday. It is a real convent school. There is one Belgian male teacher of French who is giving an evening course in conversational French, beginning tomorrow. I do not have many hopes for it, but I am going.

We had a very chilly night last night. Just right for two in a sleeping bag.

Love, H

12 January 1945

My dearest Ginny,

It is now 10:15 A.M. and very quiet in here. Most unusual. The radio is not going, and there is only one other officer writing a letter.

This business of several people living in a single room is a small problem which becomes large when there is no work to do. The only thing that bothers me in particular is the radio playing *fortissimo* for prolonged periods. We have a MAC [Medical Administrative Corps] officer who is a juvenile and insists on jive at 50 yards when everyone else wants to read or write or simply not listen to the thing.

Aside from this, I think I get along very well with myself and do not annoy the others too much.

It is very interesting to watch the others become irritated at trivial things. It is easy to understand how one wants the stove door open when the other wants it closed. How someone is ready for bed when two or three others still want to play cards. How someone wants to keep the light on and write letters while everyone else is ready to go to bed.

One of the biggest problems to me, and somewhat of an annoyance (but not bad), is trying to do what I want to when I want to. I start to write a letter, and Elmer suggests that we take a walk. We come back from the walk, and after finishing the letter, there is that one who will want to play bridge when I would rather read—and so it goes.

I can find time to do very little each day, and that is why I wanted the French-conversation class to get started, so that for an hour each day we will be separate and not disturbed. This will probably sound to you as if I am bored and, of course, I am, but not more so than just being away from you would make me. I do not think being at war without you is any more difficult than being away anywhere without you.

I do not know how I got started on that tack, but it will perhaps give you an idea of what life "resting" is and what I think about. It does not give an idea, though, of what I think about, because a good part of that concerns being and working with the girl (or are you a woman?) I love. During this period of the war, you are for me what Pasteur referred to when he wrote, "Heureux celui qui parle." You are for me the ideal and, therefore, I am "heureux"—i.e., as happy as possible away from that ideal.

Love, H

13 January 1945

My dearest Ginny,

We have had a quiet day, and tonight several of us are invited to go to the home of the village doctor. The others have been and say he is an interesting country doctor.

The catch: all conversation is in French. I can understand fairly well, but am tongue tied when trying to speak.

Love and kisses, H

17 January 1945

Dearest Ginny,

Last night we went to our French lesson for 2½ hours, until I could not say anything to suit "the Professor." He is a young boy, about 24 or 25, who is the son of a Belgian Army officer and who had been sick for some time.

In the city he found life very difficult, because every time there was an air raid, it took four people to carry him down in the cellar, and so he came out here in the country.

In the meantime, he has apparently recovered, for he now teaches French in the convent school. Most of the children are from the Flemish part of Belgium and must be taught French, as all well-educated Belgians must be.

I was anxious to keep the class small, but we had to invite the others— but they are dropping out one by one, as expected, and so, if we stay here long enough, it will get down to a good size, and we might make some progress.

When I asked him how much we should pay him for his trouble, he said that he was the son of a Belgian Army officer and, therefore, did not expect any remuneration. He had apparently taken a Hippocratic oath for French teachers.

Recently we had an opportunity to visit an advance-fighter airstrip near Tongeren. We were looking for some friends of one of the platoon officers and arrived just as the fliers were leaving on a mission. It was to be over the Bulge and against targets of opportunity; that is, they were to fly over a given area and shoot at any enemy transport on the roads or at any installation or group concentration.

We happened to be outside the briefing room as they streamed out in a very matter-of-fact way, as if off for a joyride. No goodbyes were said, no remarks of any kind. I did hear one boy say to another who was climbing in a ship, "Well, take it easy"—that was all.

The planes, which were fighter models, did carry bombs under the wings, as I believe the German planes do. We saw them take off, circle around, and disappear.

We heard later that the mission was considered a success. All bombs were dropped. Four planes were shot up, but no pilot was injured.

Love to you and our little family, H

19 January 1945

My dearest Ginny,

Today I had to go over into headquarters at Maastricht, along with most of the officers from this platoon, to an "orientation" lecture, as they called it. It was very interesting, in that it had to do with, among other things, problems which might arise with the cessation of hostilities. Problems that explain why no one will be able to go home until probably several months after the fighting stops.

Of course, everyone knows these things but rather hopes against hope that somehow things will shape up, so that staying on will not be necessary.

Other questions were discussed, such as the problem of units who do not have much to do.

The other problem discussed was the support of the home front. It is just impossible to explain a labor-union strike to a soldier, even those who have been workers before.

The whole meeting was, I think, the result of the fact that the morale of the Army at the present time is not as good as it might be, and this is the result of expectation of victory back in the September days, when things were going so well. I do not know whose fault this is, but I would guess that a good many individuals high up were fooled.

Love, H

24 January 1945

Dearest Ginny,

Elmer and I got back "home" this afternoon after a very satisfactory visit with the Bills—Falor and Boukalik.

A weekend in the ETO is as necessary for me as one at home. It gives you a chance to reevaluate yourself in the light of what others are doing and thinking.

I believe I mentioned that Bill Falor is analyzing his cases and reproducing the X-rays of his cases using captured equipment. Bill Boukalik continues his very careful and excellent clinical work, but, of course, does not have the professional point of view that Bill Falor has.

The only important change in the professional care was that dictated by the extreme cold weather. Postoperative morbidity has increased, due in large measure, it is thought, not only to upper respiratory infections, but also due to a general "lower resistance" of the men resulting from difficult living conditions in extreme cold and manifesting itself by every physical complication known to man.

Our journey took us through Aachen for the first time and the countryside east of there.

Aachen must have been a very nice city. Most of the houses in what seemed to be the residential district are of the better type of Eutaw Place homes and probably built at the same time. The large downtown hotels and stores are of the most modern construction. The streets are wide, and many of them had central parks, à la Eutaw Place, only wider, according to the European fashion. There are, of course, some old, narrow streets.

The destruction is tremendous. Aachen is a large city, and nowhere is there an undamaged structure. Whole blocks are of the Saint-Lô style, with nothing left but a pile of rubble in what was once the cellar. But there are areas where the buildings are relatively intact, so that the roof is on and the walls are standing. The doors may be on, but the windows have long since disappeared. We are said to have fired 300,000 105-mm shells into the city.

In addition to this, many of the buildings, particularly in the residential areas, show pockmarks of small-arms fire, where the infantry cleared out the city block by block.

The debris has been cleared from the main streets, so that traffic is flowing easily. But other side streets are so filled with rubble that you can tell where they are only by the absence of what was once a wall.

The countryside east of Aachen is vacationlike—gentle, rolling, like Western Maryland, but the trees are all pine, apparently planted, but beautiful, as their branches are covered with snow, and similar to the Ardennes that I told you about when we were at Saint-Vith.

It looks like good skiing country, and I am told that there is a place in Aachen that rents skis. But I don't think skiing would be any fun without a chance for a Georgeanna.

The Russian news is outstanding. The Soviet Army had reached the Oder River, 24 miles west of the then-German city of Breslau (now the Polish city of Wroclaw) and were advancing in Latvia and Czechoslovakia.

This war could be over shortly, for now the Germans must be losing important manufacturing areas. After all, Germany is only as big as Texas. Be prepared to jump on the first boat to bring wives to the Army of Occupation.

Love, H

25 January 1945

Dearest Ginny,

The other day one of the sisters fell and hurt her ankle. It appeared to be a fracture, but with simple strapping it is getting better . . . . so now I am not sure.

What I started to say was that this morning she gave me a "souvenir" of Belgium, which I am sending home as a specimen of something or other. It is the damndest-looking pincushion you ever saw, but I appreciated the thought behind it and thought you would like to see how they spell Jones in French (actually, it was spelled "Johnes").

Our French teacher has gone home, and so we have not had a lesson for the last two days. But we are due to resume tomorrow.

The Count de Grune has offered to get a Belgian couple to come to America as maid and man, but I do not think that it is possible to get them in. When the war ends, we may find out what rules are applicable.

With all my love, H

27 January 1945

Dearest Ginny,

Recently I had a chance to spend about two hours at Fort Eben Emael. You will remember that this is the Belgian fort that was supposed to be the anchor of the Belgian Albert Canal defense system. It was taken the first day of the war, and the newspapers at home carried stories of a new nerve gas used by the Germans, etc., etc.

It is indeed a remarkable fort, and to see it one would think that it was quite impregnable. It is not a fort at all, in the sense of an area surrounded by wall, like we ordinarily think of a fort.

It is really a hill through which the canal is cut. The hill is then burrowed by 16 kilometers of corridors leading to gun turrets.

The gun turrets are the only things that extend above the ground. Living quarters, supplies, hospital, everything, are along the corridors, sometimes 100 meters from the crest of the hill. It is absolutely safe from the largest bombs.

The Albert Canal defense system was by no means a pushover on paper. The canal itself is about 100 feet wide and has very high banks; perhaps 100 feet high along most of the way. There are fixed defenses along the whole length, of which Eben Emael is the largest and strongest. It is easy to see how the French, relying on this defensive system, did not continue the Maginot Line along the Belgian border.

The whole canal and forts have been built since World War I—i.e., between 1932 and 1936—and are probably unique military establishments, in that the canal, while conceived for defense, has also been a great waterway for the whole country, connecting Liège with the sea at Antwerp. The canal is now the principal route for getting food to Liège, although there are many barges sunk in the canal.

Therefore, the investment was not entirely lost in the early morning of the 10th of May 1940. The area of the fort is 80 hectares—i.e., 900 meters on a side. The perimeter was protected by pillboxes with machine guns pointing out.

No one could approach the fort, except in the face of very heavy machine-gun fire. There were no antiaircraft guns, and once inside the ring of pillboxes, it is impossible to cover the hill itself with machine-gun fire. The heavy guns cannot be depressed to cover the hill.

The solution to the problem was . . . obvious to the Germans. They dropped paratroopers from planes that could not be fired on and dropped them within the pillbox perimeter. They could then safely approach the heavy guns with heavy charges of dynamite and blow a crack in the turret and then drop explosives through the crack. We saw the spot where the first turret was blown—really the spot where the German victory in the West began.

The Belgian commander surrendered after three hours, so that there is some reason to believe that treason let the Germans in. The Belgian commander had been changed only 24 hours before the attack. All the men in the fort are, of course, prisoners in Germany, so that the truth may not be known for some time.

The place is now deserted. The Germans had a factory in the 16 kilometers of corridors safe from Allied bombs, but now about 30 members of the Belgian "armee blanche"—Belgian underground—act as guards and caretakers.

About 100 yards from the entrance to the fort, there is a stream with a sluiceway that turns a water wheel to a mill probably 100 years old. A strange contrast of old and new and, by its undamaged presence, proof that not much of a fight took place in the early morning.

The lighting system, of course, did not work, and we were guided through the maze of corridors. So we picked our way in inky blackness with a single flashlight.

It is doubtful that the fort will ever assume its prewar importance, for it is a relic of the Maginot philosophy at the time of a new type of warfare.

I did not expect this to take so long, and I hope it has not been tedious. I know it is much more interesting to see than to hear about.

I do not write much to anyone but you and hope you keep everyone informed. I just can't get much stimulation to write. Writing to you is easy, and I love to do it. Kiss my little boy and girl for me. I know I should hardly know them when I return home.

Love, H

29 January 1945

My dearest Ginny,

I am pleased with the progress we are making in the French class. I can now read the stuff very nearly as fast as English, but when I open my mouth to try to say something, very little comes out. Still, if we stay here much longer, fluency might be possible.

Tomorrow we may get a chance to put our French to some practical use, as Elmer and I are going to Brussels for a 24-hour sightseeing visit. We have tried to figure out a way to get a ride, but have not succeeded, and so we are going to thumb a ride, as it is too bad to be so close and not get there.

Hitchhiking is very easy over here, especially for field-grade officers. They say Brussels is a beautiful city and undamaged. It is like other European cities with many historical places, and we were well-primed tonight by our guide.

My love as always, H

31 January 1945

My dearest Ginny,

In your letter written the 17th of December, you spoke about postwar planning and mentioned three possibilities: (1) a professorship, (2) both of us at the Kelly Clinic, (3) private practice with you as anesthetist. I have been wanting for some time to put down in a letter to you what I had in mind, so that I could clarify it for myself and let you know what I am thinking.

When I say that it is my fondest dream to bring together our work and our love, I do not necessarily mean in the practice of medicine.

I used to realize in the days at the Kelly Clinic, and have had the same feeling emphasized in war surgery, that applying knowledge is good, but leaves one unsatisfied. We treat cancer with X-rays, radium, and surgery, but most of the patients die. We operate upon a soldier and get him together mechanically, but cannot keep him going.

It would be more satisfying to me to figure out how to do one new thing in medicine than to apply existing knowledge to 1,000 people.

There are many people to do the latter. I am talking about something important; not a triviality, not a new clamp, or the results of a study of 1,000 cervices, but something with which we can say, do this and that and this person will be cured. Otherwise, he won't be.

I do not have to sell you on this. You know it. You spoke about the women who come to you in order to get pregnant, how they envy your aid, and how you know you must try to help them. How much better it is to learn how to remove one cause of sterility than remove 1,000 fibroids.

Now, what to do about it, and what is our field? There is, I am sure, some way to work it out. It means, of course, that we must have a laboratory, and then, I must have time to work therein.

If you could apply a new technique to the cancer problem, that might be promising. Does the electron microscope have any application there? Do any of the newer concepts of immunity have an application to the growth of neoplasms? What about endocrinology? Could I fit there?

Somehow I believe that if we had a really good idea, and a place, and presented the idea to, say, Blalock [chairman of the Johns Hopkins surgery department], he would provide the means. But this is ahead of the story. What we need is a good idea and the working out would follow as a matter of course.

How could I get the time and stay at the Kelly Clinic? That depends, it seems to me, on how good an idea we get. It may be that I should work there in the mornings and in the lab in the afternoons.

You should not be required to participate in the humdrum part of the practice of medicine to help us make a living. There should be no need for you to talk to the "difficult patients." If I could earn enough for us by working half a day, it would be a pleasure to me to do it.

Does any of this make sense when applied to the realities of the things we will have to face? I have just received the letter from you and find that it expresses in part what I mean. But it does not include the tremendous power in he combination that you and I have.

I just cannot seem to say it. It is the working out through you of my own selfish dreams of accomplishment. For the first time, I see how something might be expressed in music that cannot be spoken or read.

Two themes—one yours, one mine, working in and out and finally brought together in final orchestra with a power that just has to give birth, not only to our family, but also to ideas and work. That could not possibly exist without the union of the two forces.

Now, the thing that is lacking is the idea. How much easier to come down to earth with this if you were here or I were there, where there is access to things. I keep my eyes open, but the language is such a barrier and the universities at such a low ebb that I expect very little.

The best might be for you to come over here if the opportunity presents itself after the war; then we could look around here and talk and dream before going home.

All my love to you and ours, H

5 February 1945

Dearest Ginny,

Today I left here full of expectation, but tonight I am a little disappointed. The fiancée of our French teacher is an artist of some merit—that is, I have seen some of her sketches and drawings and think them quite good. She offered to do a pastel of me and, today, I "sat."

She worked for about four hours while I read. The result is of a rather serious Papa, more serious than I usually am, but perhaps no more serious than when I am reading. The drawing is not finished, and I go again tomorrow to sit, so that it may be better when it is finished. I had planned not to say anything about it until it came, but I thought I had better warn you about it, so that you would not be surprised and too disappointed at the same time. The artist is only about 20 years old and has not had too much formal training, so you cannot expect too much.

The house, like all houses over here, was cold. There is practically no coal or fuel of any kind. The family dug up some coal and made a fire in the stove in the room, so that it got a little warm. I was a little bit cold, but every now and then the girl or her mother or someone else would pop in and ask if it was too warm, and could they please open the window? These people have been used to having it cold.

They had me to lunch, and we had some good tomato soup, some stew made out of some kind of meat that we ordinarily would not look cross-eyed at, and always boiled potatoes—the steady diet of these Europeans, whose food is so scarce.

The family was most kind, and I had to speak French, which limited the conversation to the essentials. All in all, a good day, and I go back tomorrow to have the portrait finished.

On returning here, I found that we would probably be moving again in the near future. Where, I do not know, of course, but there is a general feeling of great confidence in future operations on this front.

Love, H

5 February 1945
11:45 A.M.

Darling Ginny,

In your letter of the 8th of January you asked if Eleanor [Delfs, M.D., of Hopkins] might be assigned to the group. It would be difficult, I think.

Separate officers come to an ETO pool en masse, from which they are assigned to 12th Army Group, then 9th Army, then 5th Aux. In other words, it would require arranging all along the way.

Margaret Craighill might be able to arrange some directive from Washington, but it seems to be doubtful, because theater officers do not look kindly to such directions, figuring that Washington does not know the local situation.

You told me about the arrhenoblastoma Kodacrome and the possibility of using the pregnanediol-assay method for a pregnancy test. I love to hear about these things, as it keeps me in touch with you.

I am distressed that you have to do such things as go to the box factory to get and bag the shavings for the rat colony, but it is a source of satisfaction to me to realize that if such is necessary you don't mind doing it.

I carry with me a constant feeling of incompleteness and yearning that can only be resolved when we are together again.

Love, H

7 February 1945
10:00 A.M.

My dearest Ginny,

Today I went back at 9:30 to have the pastel finished [it was necessary to go to Hasselt for this], and the girl, Yvonne Roose, and her father, who was her teacher, were not satisfied. And so today she started over, this time in charcoal, and after my sitting for about seven hours, the picture was finished. She had to finish it today, for tomorrow we move. It is better than the other one, but I think shows the hurry. It is very serious. Perhaps you will like it.

I enjoyed very much meeting the family. The father is an engraver, the only one in Limberg who has a multicolor lithography machine. His specialty is labels, and he has some very beautiful ones.

We have not been able to pay our French teacher, and I would like you to send me a couple of books to give him; American history for one, perhaps American literature for another.

Love, H

THE EVENTS RELATED in the diary and in the letters written at Wellen do not adequately describe the Allies' luck at the Battle of the Bulge. In their memoirs, both General Eisenhower, the Supreme

Allied Commander, and General Bradley, commander of 12th Army Group, say that they were completely surprised by the German counteroffensive of 16 December 1944. I have previously noted that we set up in Saint-Vith in early October, in support of the winter offensive to clear the Germans in front of the Roer River in order to cross the Roer and push on to the Rhine River.

All of this happened immediately after the 5th Aux moved east from Brittany. But in the October transposition of the Ninth and First Armies, the 5th Aux teams followed the Ninth Army and, therefore, we left Saint-Vith for Nuth, well to the north and out of harm's way when the Battle of the Bulge began 16 December. Saint-Vith was an early objective of the German offensive, and had we stayed, goodness knows what would have happened to us.

On 8 December, we moved to Übach, closer to the front, in support of the continuing winter offensive to clear the approaches to the Roer. But the front was quiet, and we received no casualties.

During the night of 16-17 December, German bombers massed for the counteroffensive by German armored forces through the Ardennes scored the direct nighttime hit on the enlisted men's latrine just outside our window in the schoolhouse we occupied.

That first night we also heard the loud rumble of tanks of the 7th Armored Division as they passed through Übach. Eisenhower himself had ordered the 7th Armored transferred to XII Corps of the First Army. Saint-Vith defended until forced to withdraw on 23 December. The 7th Armored's stand seriously slowed the German advance. The 7th Armored retook Saint-Vith on 23 January, exactly one month after its forced withdrawal.

The German counteroffensive benefited from an extraordinary quantity of resources. Four German armies were employed: the Fifth Panzer, the Sixth SS Panzer (the latter under the command of General Josef "Sepp" Dietrich, who had proved such a bold warrior in the 1940 *Blitzkreig* in France); the Fifteenth German Army on the north flank, the Seventh German Army on the south flank.

Field Marshal Walther Model, commander of Army Group B, was tactical German commander. But Commander in Chief West, Field Marshal Gerd von Rundstedt, had overall responsibility.

On 16 December 36, German Divisions, with six hundred tanks, thrust forward. The tanks were new, recently fabricated in the Ruhr Valley industrial center—many of the divisions had been refitted with new arms from the same Ruhr industries. That the concentration of the vast German force of two hundred fifty thousand men went undetected constituted a major failure of Allied intelligence.

THE PORT CITY of Antwerp was the main objective of the German counteroffensive. The Belgian port had opened to Allied sea traffic on 28 November and had become the main entry point for supplies for the Allied armies on the extended front, supplanting the long overland haul from the French port of Cherbourg.

Had the German offensive succeeded, the British Expeditionary Force to the north, including the U.S. Ninth Army (which encompassed the 5th Aux), would have been severed from supplies, with likely disastrous consequences for the Allied cause.

The Allies could well have been compelled to withdraw as many men and as much materiel as possible across the English Channel to Britain, as the British had been compelled to do at Dunkirk.

On 19 December, the principal Allied commanders, excepting Field Marshal Montgomery, met at Verdun. They decided to halt the drive to the Roer and concentrate forces on eliminating the salient (the "Bulge") in the Ardennes.

On that same day, the 101st Airborne Division arrived at Bastogne from Reims, France, where it had been in Supreme Headquarters, Allied Expeditionary Force reserve. It had been refitting after its ill-fated MARKET GARDEN attack across the lower Rhine River in September.

On 20 December, Ninth Army was transferred to the 21st Army Group, because of possible difficulty of communication between the Ninth, headquartered at Maastricht, and the 12th Army Group, headquartered in Luxembourg. The 5th Aux thus came under Field Marshal Montgomery. We were not aware of the switch at the time, because orders still flowed through Ninth Army from Maastricht (Ninth Army headquarters was not required to move at any time during the Battle of the Bulge).

The 48th Field Hospital's 3rd Platoon, with its attached 5th Aux teams, was ordered out of Übach on Christmas Eve. We were to go into bivouac at Bocholtz.

BECAUSE EVENTS WERE confused at that time, the 5th Aux got permission from the commanding officer of the 48th Field Hospital Platoon to go alone in our surgical trucks. It seemed reasonable to us that convoys would be more likely to be attacked from the air than a single truck bearing a big Red Cross on its roof. So our team traveled alone to Bocholtz in our surgical truck.

We stayed there but a few days before being ordered on 29 December to Wellen, where we remained safe in the little schoolhouse.

We celebrated a delayed Christmas dinner with turkey and most of the customary trimmings. The U.S. Army always made a special effort to ensure everybody a turkey dinner on Christmas, but the German counteroffensive disrupted the schedule. Nonetheless, the Army managed to get the turkey feast to us several days later.

We felt quite secure in Wellen, away from the murderous events reported on the radio. Wellen is not far from Hasselt, where Montgomery, who had not been at the 19 December Verdun meeting, met with Eisenhower on 28 December (the day before we arrived in the town).

Wellen was then a village on a winding one-lane macadam highway between Tongeren and Hasselt. Tongeren itself was on the main highway, at that time a two-lane macadam road between Liège and Brussels.

WE HAD BEEN a few days in the Wellen schoolhouse when we were surprised by a knock on the door by two nuns outside. The callers explained they were from the nunnery across the very narrow street from the schoolhouse. They welcomed us to Belgium and thanked us for liberating their country.

We ourselves had liberated nothing, but we accepted the nuns' offerings gracefully. The good sisters spoke English quite well. They invited us to come over to the nunnery at an appointed time to shower—a most-welcome invitation to members of an invading army.

Three or four of us accepted the offer immediately. Next day we appeared at the door at the agreed-upon hour. The nuns showed us in and escorted us to the bath facilities. Not all of us showered. The nuns had had not noted that the nunnery itself had no heat and no hot water; our showers were measured in seconds, rather than minutes. But the water both cleaned and stimulated us.

Three or four of us took three or four showers each during our month in the schoolhouse. We were the only ones to brave the cold nunnery and the cold shower. But the exercise seemed worthwhile after returning to the warmth of the schoolhouse.

At the nunnery we met a young man—perhaps in his early twenties—who had been in the Belgian army, but taught French at the school. He also served as the handyman and building engineer who fixed things at the convent. He lived in Hasselt—about ten kilometers away—and commuted by bicycle. He appeared three or four times a week to teach and to check on the nuns and make needed repairs.

He was a pleasant fellow. We invited him over for GI food, and he eventually invited Bill Falor and me to Hasselt to visit him and his girlfriend. He told us she was an artist and would make a drawing of each of us. So we got an army truck and drove with him to Hasselt, which was nearby. He took us to his girlfriend's family home.

Her parents were printers. Their specialty was wine labels. They seemed to make a good living from the wine-label niche in the printing trade.

The young man's girlfriend had a studio room, which was in the printing plant. She did charcoal drawings of Bill and me. We traveled three or four times to her studio, so she could complete the portraits. She made two of me. They were very good. They hang in our Colorado condominium.

A HALF CENTURY later, on a trip to Europe, I experienced a sort of *déjà vu* in response to the name of Tongeren, which was not far from Wellen. Also in the vicinity was Château Hammel, where we had bivouacked on the Count de Grune's lawn in September 1944.

At that time, we had visited Tongeren, and now we were back again, and the *déjà vu* sensation seized me again, because there in the square was a small statue of Ambiorix—king of one of the tribes of the Belgae. I remembered Ambiorix and Tongeren from Caesar's *Gallic Wars*—required reading in Latin in the educational climate of the early twentieth century.

I had coffee in the square in Tongeren some fifty years later. I was delighted that Ambiorix was not only still there, but he also had been refurbished and looked great. I also revisited Wellen. I was surprised and delighted to find the schoolhouse exactly as I remembered it. I stepped inside and discovered—in the room that a score of 5th Aux officers occupied in January 1945—a class of youngsters who looked to be ten-year-olds.

We interrupted the class, of course. I was pleased that the teacher spoke enough English to understand me when I explained that I had spent January 1945 in the room and was eager to see the building again. She graciously received us and showed us through the school. What a joy!

But the nunnery, I was shocked to discover, was gone, the building demolished. I was surprised at the smallness of the building's footprint. The lot had been converted into a charming public park with benches. I attributed the disappearance of the nunnery to a change in the culture after World War II. Nunneries had gone out of fashion. I gathered from talking to passersby that the nunnery was long gone and the public park had been in place for years.

BACK IN 1945, as the Battle of the Bulge raged (and as I recounted earlier), Bill Falor and I had passed through Tongeren, which is on the road between Bocholtz and Wellen. The new Allied airfield at Tongeren had been immediately beside the highway.

Although the ground was heavily covered with snow on that long-ago day, endless streams of fighters were taking off and landing. The fighters were pounding the Germans in the Bulge.

Bad weather had grounded all aircraft during the initial phases of the battle. But on that day, the sun was out, the skies were clear, and the airport bustled with activity. Warplanes essential to stopping the German advance were doing their job.

Ninth Army was on the defensive during the initial strategy of German counteroffensive. At one point its forces had been reduced from sixteen divisions to two. The shrinkage of divisions explained the surplus Ninth Army medical-support units, many of which were safely in bivouac and living in relative comfort, as we were at Wellen.

First Army, which bore the brunt of the German offensive, ably managed without medical reinforcements from Ninth Army. But First Army had received additional divisions from Ninth Army and contained many more soldiers than normal. As far as I know, Ninth Army medical units were never called to support Allied units fighting in the Battle of the Bulge.

Colonel William Shambora (left), Ninth Army surgeon, with Lieutenant Colonel Elmer Gay, commanding officer, 5th Auxiliary Surgical Group. No love was lost between these two.

Übach, Germany, December 1944. The schoolhouse used as a field hospital. Note the tents just outside the schoolhouse. These tents sheltered latrines. One of these tents took a direct bomb hit on the night of 17 December.

"Latrinite Emerges in Greatest Strength Since D-Day"—
Stars & Stripes. Annihilation of the Enlisted Men's Latrine.
Übach, Germany, Dec. 17, 1944

A sketch of the missing latrine by Ernest Craig, who later
became professor of medicine at the University of North
Carolina, Chapel Hill, North Carolina.

Two sketches made in Belgium, Hasselt, in February 1945
by Yvonne Roose, one a pastel and one a charcoal. Her
father was not satisfied with the pastel and insisted that
she repeat it in charcoal.

Chapter 8

Letters from Home
23 December 1944-7 February 1945

O N THE DAY GEORGEANNA WROTE THE LETTER below, she had not heard the news that clearing weather had for the first time enabled Allied warplanes to strike back at the German Army and SS Panzer Units rushing toward Antwerp in the Battle of the Bulge.

While Allied transport aircraft dropped supplies to the 101st Airborne Division surrounded in Bastogne, Allied warplanes bombed the exposed Germans. The last-ditch German counteroffensive on the Western Front had produced bleak news reports in the United States.

Saturday, December 23, 1944
10:00 P.M.

My darling,

Once again I think the news sounds very ominous. I am so worried about you that Christmas is really a great strain on me.

Today your lovely orchid arrived, and I adore it. Such outward signs of your affection are really very nice, for it is a pleasure occasionally to display to all the world the little warm feeling that I carry with me personally always. The certainty of your love is the orchid that really matters to me. I shall wear it to church tomorrow and on Christmas with affection.

We had a tragedy on the service yesterday. The resident (woman) in medicine at Baltimore City Hospital died following a criminal abortion by T. She was under Dr. TeLinde's care.

Uncle Stanley, in a letter to Ess, said that he was spending the summer in South America. Eunice and her husband are coming here sometime in January. I pray for your safety constantly.

All my love, Ginny

> *Sunday, December 24, 1944*
> *11:00 P.M. (Christmas Eve)*

My dearest,

Today I feel that we have really received a Christmas present, as the indications are that the German counterattack has really been pulled up and the 9th Army still holds. Please, God, this will speed the end of the war and your return to me. We are still wondering where Hitler is.

All day I have been missing you terribly, as I always do when I have a pleasant day. Everyone in church admired your lovely orchid and, again, I repeat, it is nice occasionally to flaunt your husband's devotion so that all the world may see, although my knowledge is so sure, I really do not need such tangible evidence.

I am afraid I shall not have my skirt finished to wear with my beautiful blouse tomorrow, but I hope to wear it up to Myrtle's Wednesday. I am going to get the girls to take some pictures of me in it for you.

The twins came over at 6:00 to supper and helped trim the tree. I thought of the time you burned a hole in your coat. This year, we have the tree on the sun porch and expect to have a dreadful time with Howard. He still insists, "Gonna knock it down."

All of the pleasant activities lose their meaning without you, Papa. May we never have to put in another Christmas without you.

All my love, Mama

Monday, December 25, 1944
11:00 P.M.

Dearest Honey Bunny,

We have spent a really very nice Christmas—our best gift brought over the radio in the form of good war news, if only it continues.

We managed to get Howard to finish breakfast before going into the living room, where his stocking was hung. Mother had the mantel decorated with greenery, choir angels, and reindeer, and he just stood and looked.

Then he exclaimed about every item. "Oh, look, angels! Oh, look, reindeer!"

Finally, we persuaded him to open his stocking. There was a horn—which was difficult to blow, fortunately—candy, apples, oranges, boats, and his scrapbook.

Then B opened her stocking. A teething ring, rattle, and scrapbook. She thoroughly enjoyed it.

After this, we told Howard to look on the sun porch, and he was thrilled with the tree. Again exclaimed about each item—balls, lights, tinsel, etc. His presents were piled below, and a xylophone, which your mother gave him, at once caught his fancy.

It took him at least an hour to open everything. We gave him a pounding toy, which pleased him no end. You hammer a peg on the top and another shoots out the end. The Perkinses gave him a whole fleet of boats, and it took him a solid hour to take his bath tonight, as each boat had to be washed. Donnie sent him a two-pistol holster, and he shot things up for a short time.

He also received a number of nice books. Ruth gave him a dictionary. Edith Sutherland Drake (did I tell you they all wanted to be remembered to you?) gave him a lovely wooden puzzle set of Old Mother Hubbard. Rob and Dar Robinson sent him a lovely book called Who Is God? *Mother and Father gave him a wonderful big wheelbarrow, and he carries his dolls and toys around in it all day.*

Mommie was very lucky too. First, she wore her beautiful orchid, then she got enough lingerie to last another two years and two beautiful blouses, besides the one Papa sent. A very lovely blue one from Father and Mother and a white one that Smitty made. She also made B some adorable slips and Howard the cutest set of beanbags. Lib sent us a beautiful Charleston etching.

I was quite overcome with it all. If I could just snuggle in with Papa now, it would be the end of a perfect day. It is that sense of companionship and sharing of pleasures and sorrows that are so wonderful—and what I miss so. Letter writing does help so much, but it's not the real McCoy.

Please get the job over and come home. We miss you terribly.

All my love, Ginny

Tuesday, December 26, 1944
10:00 P.M.

Dearest Honey Bunny,

In a few minutes I will hear the latest news, and I am almost afraid to hear it. I haven't the faintest idea where you might be now, as I think perhaps you may have been moved. I hope not, in a way. I now feel that the so-called good news was put out just for Christmas Day.

Today I have missed you terribly, physically and mentally. Life without you is motion to be gone through, with nothing more.

Rob and Dar stopped at the hospital today and called me. Rob wrote me a very sweet note the other day when the German offensive began. They both are terribly worried about you, and I have promised to keep them closely in touch. Phoebe Robinson continues to do nicely.

Well, the news is no better or worse, apparently. This surprise is very difficult, but I still go on planning for the day when Papa comes marching home. I now have laid aside a gown and robe, and I am still contemplating something in black chiffon.

I met Tom Chambers in the hall today, and he stopped me and asked all about you. Said he was keeping his fingers crossed for me. He's very sweet. He also said Lehman Guyton had written him November 15 and that Guyton had been in Holland. He should be somewhere close to you.

Letter from Ann Falor today. She said she was having a breast abscess. Poor thing—she certainly has trouble with her pregnancies. She also said that Bill Boukalik didn't tell Wanda anything. She didn't go into it, but I judge that Wanda is quite a worrier.

Do take care of yourself and don't stop loving me even when you are busy.

All my love, Ginny

Thursday, December 28, 1944
10:00 A.M.

Dearest Honey Bunny,

This morning I received your letter dated December 18. It was a great relief to me, as apparently you know nothing about the drive of the 16th. I presume that shortly after this you must have become acquainted with the facts, but at least you weren't in the first surprise encounter. I am sure you must be busy now, and I hope and pray you are safe and well.

I don't know myself how much your letters mean to me until there has been a lapse of a few days. Then when letters arrive again, I realize just what they do for my morale. You are constantly with me.

All my love, Ginny

Thursday, December 28, 1944
10:00 P.M.

Dearest Honey Bunny,

I am still a new woman, having heard from you this morning, December 28. I presume there may be an interruption in the mail, but at least I have this.

The biggest news I have is rather tragic. Frank Kendall died suddenly—an esophageal varicocele, I believe. I hate that for Dorothy. They were so congenial and had such a short time together. Such things make me a little panicky about us.

Still no word from King, and I am beginning to believe that he might really be on his way home. Did your mother tell you that Eunice and Ken are now supposed to be here in the middle of January? Dar and Rob heard that Ken was coming by himself, but that doesn't seem to be correct. Wouldn't it be funny if they came on the same boat?

Darling, when you come home, I do hope, for more reasons than one, that it's by the East Coast, as I just couldn't stand to wait for the time that would pass before I would see you if you landed on the West Coast. That will be an anniversary to end all anniversaries.

I shiver to think of the field hospital with the 1st Army being overrun by

Germans. I do hope this is the Germans' last gasp. The news seems so much better, if only it can continue.

I can't wait to really show you how much I love you. How will you get in practice for all those hugs and kisses and so forth?

All my love, Ginny

P.S. Someday when you have a chance I would like to know approximately how many letters of mine you are missing.

Saturday, December 30, 1944
10:00 P.M. (Your birthday)

My darling,

Your Christmas cards to the babies from Holland arrived today. They are sweet, and Howard enjoys them, as usual. B would like to eat hers—her usual reaction to every stimulus. I am hoping for more mail, as Sylvia Siegleman had a letter dated December 19.

And may I wish you many happy returns of the day—all with me. We did have fun last year, and there will come a day again.

Willie and I had a very nice walk this afternoon and watched all the children sledding. Unfortunately, he has no sled and our sleds are all broken. If it looks as if we will have as much snow as now for some time I think I will buy one, even if it is only a wooden-runner one.

Today for the first time, as I was preparing to go out, Willie said, "Don't go out, Mama. Don't bother. Stay home with me." His language really astounds everyone, and he seems to be up to it physically.

He does have a hernia, however. I have thought so for several weeks now, but haven't said so, because I wasn't sure. It's a femoral one and quite definite now.

I don't think there is anything to be done about it and don't want you to worry. But I do think you should know everything. You know I don't keep anything from you, and I believe you do the same for me. It's a very sorry lover who can't stand bad news.

I know this will arrive probably in time for Valentine's Day, but you know that today I had a very special thought and, if possible, more requests than ever.

I'm not sure it's possible. I wish you were here to go ice-skating and do other things.

All my love, Ginny

January 1, 1945

My darling,

Today 12 years ago we had our first date. It was a far different day in many ways than today. It has blown, sleeted, and rained practically all day, and the roads and sidewalks are a sheet of ice. Perhaps in view of our sentimental history, a horseback trip through the Smokies would be the most fitting first-vacation focus.

We have had a very pleasant day. Lib arrived at 8:00 A.M., looking very well and happy. She was charmed with the children. Howard is indeed lovely with people.

Jane arrived at 4:00 P.M., also looking radiant. The fact that King is coming home shines all over her. She is collecting her trousseau pieces together and even planning how much linen, cooking ware, etc., she will need for an apartment. I am trying to persuade her to go easy for, although I hope they won't send him out of the country again, you never can tell.

She is planning to spend the first week with him here, then the second week in NYC, and the third week at her home.

It's wonderful just to have someone talk of reunion. It makes ours seem more real.

All my love, Ginny

January 2, 1945

My dearest,

Two letters dated December 16 arrived today—the V-mail to Father and your sweet New Year's letter to me. It was interesting to hear about Jim McClintock, and Father sends regards, and also Tom Hughes. I was also interested in your description of Cutler.

I will mail the glasses' case as soon as possible. You have mentioned no Christmas *packages, so I am afraid they have not arrived, and with the news as uncertain as it is, I am afraid that they will be much delayed.*

I am terribly worried about you, of course, and pray that you are not in danger as grave as I sometimes picture. The news continues to look ominous to me.

All my love, Ginny

Wednesday, January 3, 1945
11:30 P.M.

Dearest,

The war news seems somewhat better today, and I received two letters, December 21 and 23, so I feel quite relieved. I shall, of course, retain that funny little dull achy feeling in the precordium until I once again have you to snuggle against. Temporarily at least, the great anxiety has gone. I am afraid that you never have and never will receive your Christmas packages. Have any of the group?

The allotment is still $240 for January. Also, your mother tells me that John Young advised her to sell two shares of Wheeling Steel at a profit and buy two of Washington Transit. She did sell the former and has not yet bought the Washington Transit. I heard of it only by accident, as she did not seek my advice. I told her I would feel more comfortable about it if I looked it up, and I will do so before she concludes the transaction.

We had a very lovely tea for Lib today—about 50 people. Willie had the time of his life. I was combing my short locks and said, "Willie, I look like a Hottentot." He said, "No, a baboon."

I asked him where in the world he had heard about that, and he said, "Baboon sits on the cover of the book." Very complimentary, eh?

He was so excited that he could hardly stay still a minute, and every once in a while he would dash into the dining room and snatch a piece of fruitcake. I believe he ate 10 pieces, much to Dr. Bowe's amusement.

B also did herself proud. She wore little shoes for the first time and looked adorable. She giggles and laughs at people, so that they are all captivated by her. She is just overcome with mirth, and draws up her shoulders and laughs all over. Both of them were very attractive, and I am sure you would have been proud of them.

I know there were lots and lots of things I had to say. One was that

Layman Guyton is with a field hospital of the 5th Armored Division in the 1st Army. You may probably run into him.

The other thing I had to say was, probably, I love you, I love you, I love you in a number of different ways, but right now it's 12:00 midnight and I love you so much.

Love, Ginny

Friday, January 5, 1945
11:30 P.M.

My darling,

Two lovely Christmas and Christmas Eve letters today. It is so wonderful to have mail and, from your letters, I am afraid you have had none for such a long time now. I am terribly disappointed, as I had so counted on your receiving my Christmas card and letter.

Again, I remark about how frequently our thoughts cross. Our school and intern days also have been with me very much in the past month. They were indeed very sweet, and I, too, count every hour spent apart as wasted.

How interesting that in just our active courtship I can remember only two quarrels, and the cause of one of them escapes me. But I do remember sitting icily apart in Hurd Hall, and then you meeting me in the corridor and being so sweet and considerate and asking me to go home with you that I completely forgot and forget to this day the cause of my irritation. I am sure you have probably forgotten it, but I can still remember that your arms that evening felt even more comfortable than before.

I was so interested in hearing the details of your Christmas Day. All day I was trying to picture yours. It was nice for you to have a Christmas Eve party, and I, too, from a distance, feel sorry for the nurses. But I will not have you feeling sorry for them. I feel much sorrier for myself. I wondered just from the pictures if your nurse and assistant wouldn't be interested in each other. They both are very nice looking and must be nice.

I shall take your suggestion about old pictures, as I am sure I will enjoy looking at them. May we soon be taking new ones together again.

All my love, Ginny

January 7, 1945
12:00 noon

Dearest,

Yesterday was a full day, and I will describe it in detail in the evening letter. I received your letter of December 26 and was so relieved that you are well. The description of the air battle was interesting, but I hope you will not see any other air battle any closer. I am distressed that you are not receiving mail, but hope the service has improved by now.

Monday I am going to see John Young about the portfolio, as you advised. I am provoked that he has sold your mother's Wheeling Steel (2 shares) in exchange for the Washington Transit. Neither he nor your mother said a word about it until it was over. However, I think I will see about the possibility of selling Washington Transit soon again, as I don't consider the transit company good security.

Don't worry about these things. I am going to see that it doesn't happen again.

All my love, Ginny

Monday, January 8, 1945
10:30 P.M.

Dearest Honey Bunny,

How good to have some better news, but now there are rumors of gas warfare. Always something to worry about, but most of all, I do not actually worry about your safety, but just grieve about our separation. I do wish there were some way for me to be with you, but that, I am sure, is impossible.

Do you think it would be at all possible to have Eleanor assigned to the group? She is very much interested.

In the past few days we have been playing with a new pregnancy test based on our pregnanediol-assay method. I don't think it will turn out to be very significant, but it is an easy procedure, and we are thinking of discussing it as the most talked-of recent test for pregnancy, along with frogs, at the travel club meeting on the 26th of February.

I located a glasses' case for you that may be a trifle smaller than yours, but was the only thing close in town. I will mail it with a small notebook. I called John, and he said he would have a list of securities ready for me Wednesday.

Our arrhenoblastoma Kodachromes are very beautiful, so we have really made a start, at least, on the OTs (ovarian tumors). Eleanor thinks I should have them ready to publish when the war is over, as there will no doubt be a clear demand for such things by people who are brushing up.

All my love, Ginny

Wednesday, January 10, 1945
1:30 P.M.

My dearest,

Yesterday was pretty hectic in the laboratory, as we had to go to the box factory ourselves to get shavings for the animal cages. We finally found a factory that was not using the shavings for fuel. Then, we boxed them ourselves, and carted them off in the rear trunk of Eleanor's car.

I didn't get home until somewhere around 7:00, and when I put the babies to bed I somehow went to sleep myself and didn't wake up until 11:00, at which time I tore off my clothes and dived under the covers. (Sounds familiar, eh?)

The two students also arrived, and we had a lovely time with them. They are most enthusiastic, and I should really accomplish something. We are frantically working up everything in the lab for the Travel Club. I hope we can make it practical enough to be interesting.

Joe Sadusk was in yesterday, and I hate him. He wanted to know what you were planning to do after the war. Said so many men had changed their minds and plans, as they found that, before being in the Army, they had never really lived. Is that so? Or is that as bad hooey as it sounds? He is comfortably sitting before a big desk in Washington.

No mail today. Yesterday an old one, but a letter, and how I devour your letters. Your mother's Christmas letter arrived today. I got John Young's list and am mailing it separately, so that it will travel faster.

The children were very cute tonight. Willie was in B's pen and said, "Isn't she a darling? I'm a darling too, and I'm my big brother."

Tonight in his crib he asked me to talk to him about himself. "What am I?" That stumped me, but I said, "You're Mama's little boy, and Papa's little boy, and B's big brother."

That seemed to satisfy him. Then he wanted to talk about going across the big ocean to Papa in Holland. He wanted to know if we would have a horse there, and he was charmed by the idea of a bicycle and skates. He frequently mentions Papa casually, but this is the first time in over a month that he has talked about you in detail. Perhaps he has not forgotten as much as I was afraid he had.

I am busy working on your Valentine and hope it arrives in time. But if it doesn't, don't forget you have a Valentine—that is me.

All my love, Ginny

Thursday, January 11, 1945
11:30 P.M.

Dearest Howie,

I have just finished reading the chapter on "Children Are Made." I think it is excellent, and I agree with it almost entirely. The difficulty to me is in teaching the development of skills.

I think the teaching of right and wrong should certainly be done before the child can really reason, and I do hope you will be home to help me with these things. Also, consideration of others and others' interests is a difficult thing to develop. I am anxious to read the whole book, and I believe it is something Lib would enjoy.

I keep hoping that your next letter will say the mail has come through. I have the feeling that I am throwing my letters down the drain when I put them in the box these days, and although I do enjoy writing, I feel much more in rapport when I know you are receiving the letters I write and we can chat about things.

I am working on my paper for the visiting firemen, and also on the income tax, which is foul.

I mailed the copy of the portfolio, and I trust it arrives.

Did you know it has been a year since I came home for the first time? Why, I will never know and never cease to regret. If only we could see some end in sight, I promise you, I will never let you out of my sight again.

The reprints of your article arrived. Would you like one?

All my love, Ginny

Friday, January 12, 1945
9:30 P.M.

Dearest Honey Bunny,

No letter today, so I am rereading your very lovely one of December 27.

I was so tired yesterday that I am afraid my letter was not very coherent. I have always believed that children should be sent to Sunday school and taught Christian ethics and teachings at a very early age. I think that such things can be more easily discarded, if the person chooses to do so, than they can be acquired in later life. And to me, these teachings and ethics are quite worthwhile.

It is unquestionably true that it is easier to teach right from wrong to a child by the use of the Bible and its stories. God to a child is very real, if you remember. This teaching, I think, has to be done very carefully and not too didactically, otherwise the establishment of understanding and reasoning will make the beliefs look childish. As I have so frequently said before, I hope that before long you will be home to help me with this guidance.

I was very much impressed by the idea of planned pleasure. You represent the peak of this to me. It seems to me that I can look back on our vacations and find not a moment wasted—the entire time filled to the utmost with fun. I hope that this capacity can be acquired by our son and daughter.

I have also read the chapter on love and marriage tonight. It scares me occasionally, because I, too, feel that nothing can be said to improve ours.

This sounds entirely too complacent (like the article I read yesterday on the frog test—the author said no improvement can be made over this test). However, I don't feel at all sorry or complacent about our marriage, just always constantly amazed at how really wonderful it is to love and to be loved so greatly.

It is very stimulating to me to read a book that I know you have been reading (although not as pleasant as when I can read it with you and stay warm while you hold it for me). I wish you could do it more often.

Today I saw a letter written by a soldier in which he said, "The thing I miss most is the lack of discussion about important issues concerning us now and in the postwar world. The average soldier wishes to quietly avoid the issues until after the war and then see what the world presents him with."

I hope this isn't true, but I suppose it is next to impossible to hear news, and I can see that many things would seem trivial in the face of the appalling personal tragedies you are constantly facing.

I think that the average American soldier is and should be deeply interested in the final peace conference.

With all my love, Ginny

> *Saturday, January 13, 1945*
> *9:30 P.M.*

My darling,

Today I received your V-mail letter of December 29. I am writing a V-mail tonight also, as you seem to think they come through better. Your airmails have always arrived in better time than any other mail, so far. I do hope that all of your mail has caught up with you by now. Your last letter must have been back in November.

I was still interested to hear of your opportunity at the evacuation hospital. I think, regardless of what you have by this time decided to do, that it was a very nice compliment for the Colonel to ask you.

I know, of course, that such a decision is extremely difficult, and I only wish, too, that I could be with you to hear firsthand the pros and cons. However, I am sure that whatever you decide will be correct. Let us pray that the hand of Providence, which has so well directed our lives, will not desert us.

I almost hesitate to venture a thought on the subject, as I feel sure you will have made your decision long ere it was written. However, perhaps for future reference, I would like to say that I believe, as I am sure you do, that the most important thing in the Army is the people with whom and under whom you work. This, I believe, should be the first consideration, as long as professional work can be disregarded (in view of the fact that we know that would not be exchanged ever for a less-desirable place).

If you are not happy, regardless of the scope, it is not worth it, and surely happiness in the Army largely depends upon your CO rank, which, as you know, means nothing to me, and I believe that it should be the least consideration.

Of course, if it is, it will be a deciding factor if the war continues at this rate, unless the new Russian offensive is really a good one and underway.

I feel like I have been reading a continued story with your letters—something I am always disposed to do, as I always read the last chapter first, but now I have no choice: I must simply await the next installment and hope that it is not lost in the mail.

The other day, Myrtle wanted to know if you save my letters also. She couldn't imagine what you'd do with a stack of them. I said I only hope you were receiving them to make a stack.

In the V-mail I will tell you about the children, but in this one I will send lots of kisses, as you can't send enclosures in V-mail.

All my love, Ginny

January 13, 1945
(V-mail)

My dearest,

It seems to me that it has been some time since I outlined "my day." I like you to know the most minute details of my life, for I like you to think of me concretely and specifically.

At 7:00 Willie wakes up and calls for me. I bring him into my bed (this morning he called, "Mommie, you like to have me in your bed?"), where he stays fairly quiet until 7:45, at which time we arise.

He eats breakfast in his robe and slippers. I come upstairs and get B at 8:30, and then off to the hospital at 8:45.

Home again at 5:00, and recently I have been taking Willie out on his sled (Mary fixed the broken one) until 6:00, when we come in to eat, get B up at 7:00 and feed her, then play and read to Willie until 8:00. Then upstairs with both babies and both in the tub.

Both get cod-liver oil. B goes to bed and Howard has a story, then to bed. He plays "yoo-hoo" with me in my room and "peekaboo" with B, until about 9:30 some nights, so then to sleep. Recently, he sleeps through the night, so I am getting more rest, but he is occasionally awake at 4:30. We all miss Papa and talk of going over the big ocean to see him.

All my love, Ginny

Sunday, January 14, 1945
11:00 P.M.

My darling,

You keep emphasizing V-mail, so here goes: although I find it hard to be cuddly with V-mail, somehow I always feel cuddly and cozy when I am writing to you. Yesterday, in reference to the possibility of a new assignment, I emphasized happiness, but I neglected to consider ambition and that, after all, contributes to happiness.

Perhaps if you were chief of surgery your work might reach the attention of the U.S. Army Surgeon General and you would be brought home to teach.

By the way, what happened to the last chief surgeon? I somehow feel that you will accept this place and am exhilarated by it, for I feel it would bring you a step closer to home (I am relying upon our special Providence).

King writes asking me to help Jane arrange their three-week leave. She wants to go to New York City.

It set me thinking about us again. I don't think we would consider New York City. Somehow my thoughts keep going back to Jack Hoff's place in the Great Smokies. But then I think you prefer the White Mountains, and I have never been there, so that's a good possibility.

I took Willie to a birthday party this P.M., and he had a wonderful time for a two-year-old. I think he mixes very well.

With all my love, Ginny

NEXT DAY, 15 January, Washington ordered a nationwide dim-out to conserve scarce fuel.

January 17, 1945
11:30 P.M.

My darling,

Today I received two wonderful letters, and let me say before I forget it, the fourth postal money order. This makes the list complete to date. I am sorry I don't have the serial numbers, as they are deposited.

The first letter since way back from December 15, but a lovely seven-page one. It describes more about the type of work you have done and what you thought of it.

I love to get your thoughts and reactions on these things, as it makes me feel nearer to you. Just as I try to keep you posted with mine. But as they are mostly about you, I am afraid they must bore you.

I know you must find living with a number of other people extremely difficult. Being billeted alone would be so much more pleasant, but I suppose that in Germany, as I hope you will not be ere long, that is not feasible.

Your letter of January 2 also arrived, in which you detailed the matter of an evac hospital more clearly. It seems to me that you have made a very clear and adequate summation of the situation.

The two points that still seem uppermost to me are, first, I feel that the latitude (i.e., freedom from any Army routine and unpleasantness) in the auxiliary surgical group is very valuable, and that perhaps it might even offer a quicker trip home.

Also, I personally would prefer the type of surgery that you do and feel that you would probably get more; second, ambition tells me that if there is a reasonable chance of succeeding and being happy in the surroundings, you should take the place at the evac hospital, for as you say, "Nothing succeeds like success." It is a step up in the eyes of the Army, is it not?

Again—may I say?—exert the most care possible in making your decisions, so that you will be happy. Providence, I am sure, will again guide us.

The Russian offensive still looks good, and I am trying not to get my hopes too high.

Today was a gorgeous, sparkling one, with snow still heavy on the trees. Willie and I had a wonderful time trying to shovel the car out, but finally gave up.

I had a splendid dispensary, with all kinds of interesting meno—and metrorrhagia. The boys are so dumb they send everything to me, even carcinoma.

I also act as a mother-confessor, and they weep on my shoulder. Poor little Dr. Meek told me today he thought he would end up a chronic alcoholic if he had to go to the Navy at this point. He wanted to know about the Maryland General Hospital. I told him to take it, as anything that would give him a difference was worth doing.

Our paperwork is progressing apace, and the thyroid experiment is, I am afraid, equivocal.

All my love, Ginny

January 19, 1945
5:30 P.M.

Dearest Honey Bunny,

The news continues to be good, and I would be most optimistic, except, with you away, it is difficult under the best circumstances. If only things would suddenly break, and perhaps they will.

My day today was occupied largely in the morning by dispensary patients. As I have said before, I have built up quite a practice and, although I try to limit them to Wednesday, it just doesn't work out that way. Once I get down there, the boys call me for consultations, which are fun, but time consuming.

My thyroid experiments seem to demonstrate again that experimental animals—e.g., rats and guinea pigs—are not suitable in investigating the thyroid function and reproduction. In other words, absence of thyroid function has no bearing on reproductive function. This is certainly not true in the human.

We heard today that little Bill Maltby, the son of Father's best friend, was killed December 10. Such things do bring the tragedies of war too close for comfort.

Did I ever tell you how much I love you and how wonderful it is even to be able to think about you and recall our life together? Remind me to do it some time.

All my love, Ginny

Saturday, January 20, 1945
9:00 P.M.

Dearest Honey Bunny,

Still no mail today. My last news of you was January 2. I do hope for more Monday.

I have two addresses for you. One, Margaret Gey's brother, who has apparently been trailing you since arriving in France. He is Sgt. Karl Kondelka, 115th Infantry, Hq Co., 29th Division (message center). Then Buddy Seegar has just left the country. He is with the headquarters of the 71st Infantry Division (A.P.O. #360).

Today following rounds at 8:00 A.M. I devoted the morning to writing. I wish I could help you on your shock-death problem.

Came home in time to put Willie to nap and give B her lunch. I then got two cartons of cigarettes off to Elmer. Jane's father got them for me, and I hope they reach him.

Mary helped me take some colored pictures of B and some of me, and then Willie and I played until suppertime. We played amusement park (his own idea). He purchased tickets and furnished the amusement. Mostly I was a camel, and he rode. I lay on the floor with my knees for the hump. You can imagine I really got a workout. My only rest was when I'd make him get off and go buy another ticket.

There are always so many things I want to tell you about throughout the day, and I can't think of them when I start to write. Just think, when I see you I will probably be speechless.

I have often wondered about your exercise. Is it lacking, as mine is? I do miss that greatly and hope we will be able to take up badminton again.

I expect to spend tomorrow bookkeeping. Horrible thought.

My darling, I live only for the day when we can take up our lives together once again. Without you, I am desolate.

All my love, Ginny

P.S. Let me say again, I received four postal money orders. Have also mailed the glasses case.

January 22, 1945
11:30 P.M.

Dearest Honey Bunny,

Today your sweet V-mail of January 1. How true our spiritual oneness is, and what a pity our physical oneness must be so interrupted. But with the war news so good, perhaps we shall once more be tracking and packing the mountains together before we think. I was going over the pictures of some of our fishing trips the other day, and it is certainly true that there is a mighty good spot even in the Chesapeake.

Let me recapitulate about the evac hospital. I feel that if the personnel setup is such that you think you would be personally happy, you should accept. If the CO or the other officers were inferior in ability or unpleasant in personality, I would go very slowly.

This I say because happiness means everything in the Army, and if I thought you were unhappy in your surroundings, I couldn't stand it. It seems to me that it is a promotion and, therefore, should be accepted, if possible. If you have too many doubts (and you are very good at sizing up a situation), I certainly wouldn't take the job, if I could avoid it.

Yesterday I did the 1944 bookkeeping and, although I am not quite finished,

I am sure we don't have a deficit. I will send you the figures for checking when I finally get them arranged. I don't seem to have as much expense for insurance as I expected, so I must check it.

Somehow there is no incentive to go to bed when you are not here, but I bet I will wear the springs out when you get here.

Good night my love, Ginny

January 25, 1945
11:30 P.M.

Dearest,

Today your letter arrived with enclosures to Jane and Lib. Still no definite news of the evac. The news today says the 9th Army is poised for a strike. I wonder if that means you are again set up for action?

You asked about Lib. She was here January 1-7 and is very well. She is, I believe, as happy as she can be. I intend to review with her, Return to Religion. *I don't actually believe it will do her any good, but she needs it. She is completely self-centered. It is sad, as it is impossible for her to do anything about it, as she can't understand the situation.*

I am amused at your description of the toilet facilities in the girls' convent. It makes me pause for thought, as most of my postwar vacation plans call for the great outdoors. Perhaps you will enjoy more highly civilized rest, such as Sky Top. The children and family remain well.

All my love, Ginny

Saturday, January 27, 1945
9:30 P.M.

Dearest Sweetie Pie,

Thursday night we had the first Gyn Journal Club, and next month they want me to give the "Recent Advances in GYN Endocrinology over the Past Five Years." As I have been doing much the same thing with the students, it shouldn't be too difficult. Everyone, especially Dr. Richardson, asks about you.

Ridge Trimble is back on furlough, and I think looks fine. Everyone, of course, says how ghastly he looks. People certainly do like to cry the blues. Tom Brown was back for 30 days, and Mrs. Tom is now pregnant. Pretty lucky, I would say.

I expect to hear from Donnie again tomorrow, as Joe reported to me today. They have been at his brother's in Washington, as they also have a baby Jimmie's age and are also expecting another one.

It must have been pretty hectic, especially as Donnie and Jane are not too congenial. How lucky we are, Papa, to have had such an ideally happy time before you left. I hardly remember the few moments of heartaches, but recall only our great happiness in being together.

You mentioned in your last letter my stated jealousy of the nurses, darling. It might have been even more accurate to say I am jealous of Ken. It is always the person who is closest to you and helping you that I envy. You know I trust you implicitly, but I also know how attractive you are. Most other men by comparison are cripples and defectives.

I love you always and forever and forever, Ginny

> *Tuesday, January 30, 1945*
> *10:30 P.M. (our President's birthday)*

My darling,

No mail today, so I am incomplete, but my two from yesterday are quite a comfort. The news continues good and, if I could only think that you might be home soon after the close of the war in ETO, I would feel greatly encouraged. I wonder if the meeting of the Big Three is in Moscow. "The Big Three"— Britain's Prime Minister Winston S. Churchill, President Roosevelt, and Soviet Union dictator Joseph Stalin—met in February at Yalta, in the Crimea, to determine the future of the postwar world. Decisions made there set the stage for the Cold War.

From all reports, the snow on your front must be terrific. What a pity not to be able to enjoy it.

Dr. TeLinde now wants me to present the results from the xenopus test to the Baltimore City Medical Society in March. I'm not enthusiastic about the paper, but find that most people are very fascinated by it.

B continues to grow apace. Stands alone occasionally and, I am afraid, is rapidly growing tired of her pen. Willie is really adorable. He is now very much interested in his A. A. Milne book, which your patient sent him. He loves songs and poems, but he is really too busy riding the duck or playing garbage man to sit still long.

Don't forget to remember how much I love you and miss you, and I look forward to the wonderful day when we are again together.

All my love, Ginny

> Thursday, February 1, 1945
> 11:45 P.M.

My darling,

Today your lovely letter of January 15 was received. I take it that you have finally received the insignia and Kodachrome. Many people did not think the Kodachrome good, but I thought you would like the idea.

I am so pleased that you could take some French classes, and I trust you will be able to take German ones also. I am presuming that you have moved by now.

We have been so thrilled by the news that we have been unable to get to bed. Between the Russians and MacArthur, we feel very encouraged. Drew Pearson digressed a little to discuss the scandal at Walter Reed Army Hospital—he says the hospital is not well run.

I have gotten your electrical equipment together and will mail it tomorrow. Also, tonight, I helped Mary pack a box of cakes for you. I am afraid I am not very good at it, and I am anxiously awaiting news of the box I packed for you before. If you can get the candies out of the tin cocoa box, I think you are good.

Did you know that Dick Shackelford is a Lt. Col. in Italy? Also, Brown Dunning is finally engaged. Don't know the lucky girl.

Do continue to outline your daily routine occasionally. I always enjoy hearing intimate details of your life. Even such practical details as what you eat and how many clothes you wear fascinate me. Are your corns better? Do your shoes fit better? Do you ever find anyone to play chess with you?

More and more I appreciate what you do.

All my love, Ginny

February 2, 1945
11:00 P.M. (V-mail)

Darling,

No letter today, so I am doing some postwar planning. I see no solution to our problem but for you to be a professor somewhere. That will solve everything, because I could then work with you every minute. I must hurry with the OTs, as I think that publication will be very good for you. Isn't there something in the ETO you could report?

That is one of the minor discouragements in my work. I feel that I am not really building for our future. Indirectly, perhaps, but I want something very close to your interest right now.

I long for you in every phase of my existence, and your absence makes every moment of our life together more meaningful.

All my love, Ginny

Saturday, February 3, 1945

Darling,

Your letter of January 9 arrived today, containing the fifth money order (22661) for $70. The allotment came through this month as $240, but I presume from what you say that it will be changed in the next month.

You say buy anything we need, and I will try to do so; it is difficult to buy anything really worth having. I am considering two chests of drawers for the children, a 35mm camera for you, if I can locate one, and some upholstering of the furniture we have. Also, I will keep my eye out for a car, but finding cars for sale is really impossible. Without you, dear, my desires are very limited.

I see in the Wall Street magazine that Armour & Company is going to put out a new bond at 4½%, with 30-year maturity. Sounds good to me, and I thought I would get John to look at it.

The war news continues good, and I am still counting on our little angel to do something spectacular for us.

All my love, Ginny

February 4, 1945
9:00 P.M. (V-mail)

My darling,

It hardly seems possible that being away from someone can really hurt, but it does. Every once in a while the funny little pain in my left chest gets just too unbearable, and I really believe I miss you most when I am trying to do something interesting.

I've been at the laboratory all afternoon, trying to analyze our habitual abortion cases, and they certainly are interesting—if you were only here to discuss it.

All my love, Ginny

Tuesday, February 6, 1945
11:00 P.M.

Dearest Honey Bunny,

I have just climbed out of a nice hot tub and into bed, and how I do wish you were here. How long it has been since we took a bath together, and how long will it be before we do it again? I was thinking tonight of the showers we took at our cottage on the river, and how sure we were that some night we would have visitors while at it. I do hope we never lose our vacationing habit.

No mail today, but it just means that I must be piling up loads somewhere, as I am already 10 behind, up to January 23. Every newscast we hear says that action is expected on the 9th Army front, but none so far. I suppose, therefore, that you are still not busy.

The ballet is here this weekend, and I am trying to work up enough energy to go. I really am anxious to see it, and I am afraid I am already too late to get tickets.

How are you fixed for reading material? Do you get to see any medical journals? Do you have any medical meetings? How wonderful when you are here and we can discuss our problems. I surely need you.

All my love, Ginny

February 7, 1945
6:00 P.M. (V-mail)

My darling,

No mail today, but the two little lace pieces arrived. They are very sweet and, as they say, the best kind of souvenirs.

I was unable to get ballet tickets, but compromised on the Baltimore Symphony. I am wearing your red blouse and wishing you were here. Now that Donnie is back in town, perhaps I will get around more. I will have some encouragement and company.

Willie has been asking very frequently to see the colored pictures on the screen. He enjoys every one and takes great pleasure in the "Sort Sam" pictures. He insists upon calling the picture of him as a baby "B."

Papa is constantly in our hearts and thoughts, and also on our tongues.

All our love, Mama

Chapter 9

Across the Roer and Up to the Rhine
8 February 8-25 March 1945

*W*E SET UP IN BAESWEILER ON 8 MARCH IN preparation for the offensive to finally cross the Roer and head up to the Rhine. Except for Übach, which we considered a false start, this was the first time we had set up for action within Germany.

We were prepared to receive casualties on 8 February. The Roer crossing was scheduled for 10 February, but the Germans blew the sluice gates in the Roer Dam, so that crossing had to be postponed until the river level and current subsided.

The crossing then was rescheduled for 23 February. Casualties trickled in during the first few days. I had but five cases from the eighth until the twenty-second. Most of these were in the first days, when I had one a day. Henry Swann, who was my partner and with whom I alternated at twenty-four-hour intervals, had about an equal number.

These first casualties were from the familiar 84th Division. All regiments were represented—the 333rd, 334th, and 335th. The big push began on the rescheduled day. Casualties started coming in. This time they were from the 102nd, which we had backed at Nuth.

We were all extremely busy from the twenty-third until we completed our last case on 1 March. During these six days I operated on five-to-seven casualties daily. Considering the severity of the wounds and the time we took to repair each wounded man, the caseload was very heavy. We operated about three hours on each casualty.

HAVING THE AUXILIARY surgical group take care of the nontransportable wounded, who were shuttled to the battlefield surgical team from the division clearing company, worked well. The interval between wounding and definitive care was relatively short.

In the early days at Baesweiler, when we got a case or two a day, the average seemed to be about four hours from wounding to operating table. Of the eight patients upon whom I operated on 23 February, the shortest interval was three and a half hours and the longest was nine and a half hours. The nine-and-half-hour time-lapse was the exception; others were between four and five hours.

As the front moved forward, transporting the wounded to us took longer. For example, on the very last day, when I had operated on two wounded men, we did not receive one patient until eight and a half hours after wounding and the other patient until passage of twelve and a half hours.

Four of the casualties had thoracoabdominal wounds, seventeen had abdominal wounds, ten had chest wounds, and eleven were severely wounded in arms or legs or both, which led to four amputations.

The mortality rate at our field hospital was low, probably because of the short intervals between wounding and definitive therapy— and maybe because we continually became better trained at treating the wounded, learning as we went along.

Among the four thoracoabdominal patients, two died. Of the seventeen abdominal cases, two died. One of ten chest cases died. Of the eleven men requiring amputations, one died; he succumbed following the operation.

With six deaths out of forty-two patients, the mortality rate was 14 percent. The overall Army statistics for severely wounded treated by auxiliary surgical teams was 17 percent. Some of the cases at Baesweiler were especially interesting medically.

PATIENT C. E., Serial No. 34968686, of the 107th Infantry of the 102nd Division, was brought in with three perforations to the sigmoid colon. The perforations were closed without great difficulty. The soldier had had two units of blood and four units of plasma throughout the operation.

C. E. also had a fractured hip and a fractured arm. We thought that these fractures explained his low blood pressure more than his abdominal injuries. Following the operation, however, the patient passed only a few drops of urine, which were a clear cherry red. The urine contained very few red blood cells, but gave a strongly positive Benzedrine reaction. His blood pressure steadily rose, rising well above normal (140/80 was the highest I recorded). His circulating blood became increasingly watery—somewhat cherry color.

He undoubtedly had blockage of the kidney tubules, because he could not void any urine; he died a few days after the operation. We never knew whether this was attributable to a toxic reaction to the blood, hemolysis (the destruction of red corpuscles with liberation of hemoglobin into surrounding fluid), or his very extensive trauma, particularly his hip and leg fractures. He did not respond to treatment in the way the average soldier with abdominal wounds did.

WE ALSO HAD irreversible shock cases at Baesweiler. One patient—whom I remember vividly as I write this a half century later—was T. C., Serial No. 36898202, wounded on the morning of 23 February and operated on several hours later at 6 AM 24 February.

His bowel was damaged severely. I resected five feet of jejunum (the middle part of the small intestine) and joined the ends together. Two holes in his stomach were closed, and I did a transverse colostomy because of injury to the transverse colon. The patient died an hour after the operation, never having recovered from shock. I noted:

This was a patient who was never in condition for operation. At the end of three units of blood and four units of plasma, the blood pressure was 90/?. To have given more fluid was to invite pulmonary edema, to do nothing was to have him die. So we operated in the hope that the profound shock was due to hemorrhage, which could be controlled. In my experience, under such circumstances, if hemorrhage cannot be arrested, operation is useless. The profound shock here was due to gross soiling of the peritoneum from the complete contents of the jejunum near Treitz ligament, so that the entire intestinal stream was diverted into the peritoneum. This is associated with very severe shock.

IF YOU CAN arrest hemorrhage when a patient is in shock, the patient recovers. For example, H. L., Serial No. 36561271, from the 548th Antiaircraft Artillery, was in profound shock when he was admitted at 10:25 PM 24 February. He had had two units of plasma before admission. His blood pressure rose from 50/? to 118/60 at the time of operation, and we thought that we should operate on him, given this recovery.

We had to do a circular amputation of the left arm. Exploration of the abdomen showed that his spleen was severely damaged, requiring a splenectomy. Holes in the small bowel were sutured, as were perforations in the stomach.

Despite the severe, extensive damage to his body, the patient's blood pressure, which had come up to normal prior to operation, was stable throughout the procedure, thanks to the continuing administration of blood and plasma.

H. L. did surprisingly well. When we departed Baesweiler on 2 March, he was one of the patients being prepared for evacuation to Liège. He was near death when brought in, according to the note I made. I also wrote, "I am sorry we do not have a more accurate account of his fluid."

PATIENT J. W., SERIAL No. 34163185, also recovered remarkably well, considering the devastation wreaked upon him. J. W.'s external genitalia were savagely lacerated. That the continuity of the urethra had been disturbed seemed certain. J. W. also had an abdominal wound contaminated by much foreign matter and a very hard abdomen.

I closed fourteen perforations of small bowel, opened the bladder and passed a catheter from above and through the laceration into the penis. I passed a second catheter from below. In this way, I identified two urethras—the continuity of the urethra had indeed been interrupted—and performed an end-to-end anastomosis, leaving in place an indwelling catheter. The patient received one unit of blood and one unit of plasma before the operation and two units of blood during the procedure. His blood pressure was 70/40 when the operation ended. Next day his pressure was normal. He was evacuated to Liège in pretty good shape. I believe he did well over the long term.

PATIENT A. S., a seventeen-year-old German civilian, was the only wounded female upon whom I operated in Europe. Looking back, I am amazed that we did not have to take care of more wounded civilians. Civilians seemed to have disappeared—gotten out of the way somehow.

The young woman brought to us had been shot through the abdomen at 6 PM 27 February. I operated on her from 12:45 AM to 1:40 AM on 28 February. She had liver wounds that were pulled together gently. We measured five hundred cc of blood in the abdomen, but the bleeding from the liver seemed to be controlled by cautery, so we put some cigarette drains one-inch soft tubing with a gauze inside that vital organ.

Her stomach and large bowel and small bowel were undamaged. We administered five hundred cc of blood while operating. A full recovery seemed assured when she and the wounded soldiers were evacuated to the general hospital in Liège.

The surgical cases and outcomes at Baesweiler were consistent with what the U.S. Army had expected. Everything worked as well as possible, given the miserable circumstances in which we worked.

Of the forty-two wounded upon whom I operated while in Baesweiler, exactly half of them were from the 102nd Division. Six cases were from the 84th Division. Four were German prisoners of war. And the 17-year-old was a civilian. I failed to record the Army units of five of the patients. Some casualties were from attached units—engineers, aircraft, and field-artillery units.

BY 1 MARCH, Operation GRENADA (code name of the Ninth Army assault by XIII and XIX Corps across the Roer) was clearly going well, and the flow of casualties at Baesweiler had essentially stopped.

I received orders to take Team 3 closer to the Rhine. My partner at Baesweiler, Henry Swann, was to stay behind to look after the postoperative patients who filled the wards of the 48th Field Hospital's 3rd Platoon. I was directed to find the 3rd Platoon of the 63rd Field Hospital, said to be near Hostert, where casualties were expected from the mop-up operations east of the Roer and west of the Rhine.

It seemed to be the general experience that casualties became light after a defensive line was broken and motorized units were free to roam the countryside. As Ninth Army crossed the Roer at Linnich, and units such as Task Force Church roamed the countryside, the 63rd Field Hospital's 3rd Platoon operated upon few casualties.

After 1 March, the 48th Field Hospital's 3rd Platoon, which was back at Baesweiler, had no further casualties, and this probably explains why it was the first unit picked to cross the Rhine. We were elated on 14 March to leave the confused 63rd, which we had been with at Hostert and were now on its way to Krefeld, and return to the hospital unit picked to be the first across the Rhine.

Operation GRENADA ended on 6 March, although the Germans still held a small bridgehead at Wesel. On 6 March, the Germans abandoned the bridgehead and blew up the bridge, dispelling any possibility of seizing an intact span.

Diary Entry: 1 March 1945, Hostert, Germany
[63rd Field Hospital, 3rd Platoon]

Our stay at Wellen was marked by a trip to Brussels that I have written Georgeanna about. After the Bulge had been reduced, it was expected that the offensive over the Roer would be mounted soon. The 9th Army had been reduced to about two divisions (102nd and 29th) during the latter part of December. But toward the end of January we noticed passing through Tongeren elements of familiar divisions—84th, 30th, and others—and it seemed likely that the original plan of crossing the Roer would be put into operation.

At any rate, we (3rd Platoon of the 48th Field Hospital) finally received orders to set up at Baesweiler and were assigned to back the 102nd Division. We had had them at Nuth, soon after they came into the line.

Baesweiler was crawling with troops and artillery. The engineers fixed up the school building we occupied for a hospital and went to a great deal of trouble to put a small pane of glass in the beaverboard they placed over the generous windows. The insertion of the glass proved to be in vain; the glass had to be boarded up, because the 8-inch guns nearby broke all the glass and blew in many of the beaverboard sheets covering the windows.

The blast from the guns was terrific. It is a most remarkable experience to feel the blast a split second before hearing it. If that were not the case, one would be scared to death. These guns fired sporadically. But as they fired the time for the assault-crossing came closer, a few minutes of barrage almost every night.

The crossing had apparently been set for about the 10th of February, for on that day I think all troops of the 21st Army group were read a message (Order of the Day) from Field Marshal Montgomery, saying, in essence, that the final push was here, etc., etc. The message was peculiar, in a sense, because it likened the coming fight to a boxing match in which one fighter (Germany) was pitted against two opponents (Russia and the Western Allies) and was, I thought, apologetic for having to strike a man while he was tottering from one opponent (Russia). The message went on to say it was OK and to go in and give him hell even though he was already groggy.

At any rate, the sluice gates of the Roer River Dam were blown by the Germans and the crossing had to be delayed. Apparently the 78th division was to take the dam before the gates were blown. Incidentally, this operation started as a 9th Army project, but was switched to the 1st Army in the midst of it. When the report was written up, the 1st Army got credit.

I started to tell about the blast from the 8-inch guns. It is the only sound you can see coming. You are sitting quietly in the room when suddenly you saw the blackout curtain blown in, followed in a split second by an ear-splitting noise. The visible evidence of the sound wave also gives you a chance to brace for the crack.

As time went along and the river receded, it became more and more evident that the crossing would not be delayed long. One thing, enemy air was much more persistent. Nightly, while we were at Baesweiler, Bed Check Charley would come over and look around, but drop no bomb, and would not be fired on for fear of giving away ack-ack positions.

Since being at Baesweiler we have had an occasional case. The crossing was postponed from time to time, as indicated by information from Lt. Col. Feinstein. (Med Bat CO, 102nd Division), and the Jerries would drop mortars, artillery, and the like on what they supposed to be troop concentrations.

On the 12th of February, they gave us particular attention. A patient was wounded by mortar shell, resulting in a traumatic amputation of the leg below the knee. We did a circular amputation just above the knee, and as the operation started, we heard the planes and the bombs and very heavy antiaircraft fire.

As a bomb would fall, I would involuntarily duck below the table, all the while cutting way at the leg. The bombs fell about 300 yards away and so did us no real damage. The bombing did bring the war home, because an ambulance driver of an attached ambulance company was brought in dead a few minutes after the raid.

Jerry had dropped flares, and John Hill and George Coe were watching from our cellar home and thought that one of them had landed on the hospital roof. As soon as the planes left, they came running over, and I met them in the hall. George was as white as a sheet, as he thought the hospital would catch on fire. It did not, and examination the next morning did not reveal any scratch on the roof, so probably the flare had floated down beyond the roof.

In our ignorance, we did not worry about the flare. The patient was the only one not scared.

It is dangerous to go outside when antiaircraft fire is heavy, because what goes up must come down. The one patient we had had at Übach was hit by a piece of flak and died of a massive hemorrhage when a pneumothorax [a pocket of air in the chest] was released.

One day at suppertime, a few days before the crossing was really made, there was very heavy fire. Some members of the team went outside, but I went to the window and I could see a dogfight.

At that distance it is impossible to distinguish friend from foe. After a few moments, a plane began to smoke and then seemed to elude two pursuers. You do not know whether to be glad or sorry.

However, the smoking plane started a long straight dive from our right to left a mile away and, as the planes went by, the high fin of the Messerschmidt and the unmistakable silhouettes of the P-51s were apparent. The German crashed in flames about a mile away. It was interesting to watch the P-51s pull up as soon as the 50-caliber-machine-gun fire opened on the Jerry as he approached the ground. In view of the way the tracers lagged behind the diving plane, I cannot blame them.

On Washington's birthday we got word that at 3:00 A.M. the next day the crossing would be made. Where the information came from I do not know, but everyone seemed to know. That night we had a poker game, but went to bed early, as I thought we would get casualties early.

At 2:45 A.M. the barrage opened. For 45 minutes the roar of the guns was unbelievable. It woke us all, of course. Henry Swann was on nights, but at 6:00 A.M. I was awakened with the information that we already had a backlog of six wounded. Did I think we had better start to work then? I did.

We worked from then until 8:00 A.M. the next morning. Henry worked until midnight. The pace was rapid for about five days. The division surgeon had estimated that we would have 40 admissions in the first 24 hours. The actual count was 37. Lt. Col. Gordon Smith (surgical consultant of the 9th Army) spent the night with us.

THE FOLLOWING LETTERS to Georgeanna from Baesweiler reveal how we lived and some of my thoughts at the time.

---

9 February 1945
6:00 P.M.

Dearest Ginny,

We have spent the day getting ready. This consisted of getting the spacious windows blacked out, putting a GI potbellied stove in each room, as the heating system is shot, sweeping the floors, then setting up the hospital. The only thing I have to worry about is the OR.

Things had been packed so long in the wet that a good many of the dressings, etc., were molding, and, of course, everything had to be resterilized.

This particular platoon takes too long to set up. It is due to inexperience, as the unit has never functioned as a field hospital. The setup at Übach was the first time, but, actually, we had no patients. I am holding my breath to see what will happen if we get a rush, as happened at the 53rd at Niewenhagen.

I am taking the night shift because Henry Swann (the other team) has a bad head cold. Alice Ridzon (our nurse) also has a head cold, so things are a little doubtful. If we get busy, we may have to have additional help to fill in these spots.

The Colonel was by this afternoon and said that the box of cigars had arrived and asked me particularly to convey his thanks.

The town is your impression of what a war-torn town should look like. I have not seen much of it because I have been at the hospital and in our cellar, where we are living all day, but every house and building has been hit and, at best, is only partially inhabitable. Some, of course, are completely knocked down.

Outside of those that have been used by the troops are high piles of debris.

For instance, outside this school-annex building is a pile of broken benches, torn-up books, beds, mattresses, broken chinaware, as there was evidently an apartment for teachers, as is the custom in a good many German schools. There are great quantities of straw, source unknown, and in the building, broken children's toys and the middle of a piano perched precariously on its top and, of course, completely ruined by being thrown out of a third-story window.

Love, H

Saturday 10 February 1945
Germany

Dearest Ginny,

I am delighted to hear that Dr. TeLinde wants you to give the research paper about the xenopus [frog] test for pregnancy at the City Medical Society. I wish I could be there. Did you ever get any male frogs?

Last night we had our first patients since the 3rd of December. The first came about 10:30 and the other immediately after. The first had perforations of the large bowel and a liver injury. The second had a ruptured spleen and a perforated eyeball.

I am glad to have had the spleen, because I have never had occasion to remove one and have always been uncertain how I would go about it, although I had read up on it on several occasions, as I saw that sooner or later one would come along. It was a great relief to know that it was easy to do, and I shall no longer be apprehensive.

The eye was interesting. I am afraid the patient will be blind, but I did a flap operation with a pair of manicuring scissors and tweezers which belonged to a nurse. We had eye instruments, but at 4:00 in the morning no one could seem to find them.

I am glad we had only the two cases, as they were a dry run, and I found a few bugs that were straightened out today. For instance, who washes the instruments after use, and the need for another light in OR and more electrical outlets for the suction and OR lights, and adjustment of the techniques for taking a lateral abdomen and chest picture—all things that come with handling of patients for the first time.

The men of the hospital all worked willingly and felt that they were on the spot, as I noticed several of them had big beads of perspiration on their foreheads in spite of its being generally cool.

Colonel Smith, the Army consultant, was through today and looked things over. He usually has a pearl to drop, and today he talked about sodium balance, feeling that a good many patients were getting too much with saline, plasma, etc., etc. He is undoubtedly right.

I find that the cellar where we live is a dirty place. My hands are constantly black, and I find dust sprays on our beds and belongings, especially when the big guns start banging away. However, it is warm and dry and much better than it could be.

The enclosed photograph was given me by the father of the girl who did the charcoal. He is very proud of her and reminded me of your father. I have not yet mailed the sketch itself, as I have not found a suitable mailing tube.

With all my love and kisses, H

11 February 1945
5:30 P.M.

Dearest Ginny,

Our electric lights are kaput, and I am writing this by candlelight in our cellar. This is a coalmine area, and today we got a power line from the generator at the mine, and the lights have gone out several times. For some reason, the Germans apparently did not destroy one of the generators when they left. Unusual, as they are pretty good at the scorched-earth technique.

The weather continues to be miserable. It has warmed up considerably, and all the snow has disappeared, but yesterday and today it has rained on and off all day. The result is a quagmire.

We have a pretty good path from our living quarters, 100 yards to the hospital, except for across the road, which is a soup. The worst of it is that a place appears to be more or less solid, only to find on trying it with your foot that you are up to your ankles or worse. The 100 yards are especially cute at night—these nights without moon or light.

You asked if I think the adrenals play a part in shock as we see it. I have not the slightest idea. As far as I know, a good controlled series of shock cases has *not been tabulated with the hormones. It was my impression that adrenal changes at autopsy in shock patients were the result of shock. Is this wrong? I don't know.*

I have just heard a strange sound. This town is ruined by the fighting. There is really no good building, no stores, and no utilities. But a short distance away there is a small church with only a few holes in the wall. I have just heard beautiful church bells. The belfry is apparently undamaged, and the handful of civilians left must have church services, about the only form of assembly for them.

The bells are completely out of setting, but beautiful, and seem to emphasize once again the strange contrast of war. We have noticed again and again that when war comes by, be it France, Belgium or Germany, that the civilians carry on with their daily tasks, which they have done for years in spite of a crumbling world about them. There is nothing else to do, and it must be their salvation in misery.

Love and kisses, H

Tuesday 13 February 1945
7:00 P.M.

Dearest Ginny,

We had one case last night—a messy one, in that it took four hours to do. The patient was in profound shock—no pulse or blood pressure—but came back very nicely with four pints of blood.

He had received a quarter of a grain of morphine and within an hour had received a second quarter. What happens is that he gets no relief from the first quarter, because he has no circulation, so someone gives him a second shot.

He comes out of shock and the whole half grain hits him; then he won't breathe, and because he won't breathe, Elmer can't get him to go to sleep, and his belly wall was as hard as a rock and his intestines out all over the place. It is a situation we see not infrequently, and drives me to drink, because it takes so long to give the anesthesia. Elmer never was a speed merchant, and Colonel Winters at Brooke is the same sort, with the result that I wish he were faster. I don't think that Winters turns out practical anesthesiologists. I like someone like Griff Davis who had he patient ready in ten minutes—or else.

The case was a lieutenant of infantry who had a bad arm. The brachial artery, among other things, was severed, and I tried to anastomose it. The joint leaked like a sieve, and I gave it up and cut off the arm, as we had been working a while and I did not want to jeopardize the wounded officer's life for a procedure that would have produced a poor arm had it worked.

This morning the lieutenant was fine, and he said he had had a look at his arm and knew that he would lose it. I asked him what bothered him most, and he asked if someone had noticed that he had a ring on his finger and could someone look it up? As a matter of fact, we had noticed the ring and had taken it off and saved it.

With all my love and kisses, H

14 February 1945
4:00 P.M.

Dearest Ginny,

Valentine's Day. I hope the little collar I sent got there. It is a poor substitute for an adequate expression of love, and I should much rather put my arm around your neck than any collar, but c'est la guerre.

I have noticed a few articles recording the use of intravenous fluorescein in studying the circulation in various things like pedicle grafts, pinch grafts, burns, etc. Would this have any application in studying the endometrial circulation in the menstrual cycle?

It could be applied to a clinical study of skin epithelium. I don't know what it would show, but as I think of it, very much is not known about the circulation through neoplasm. Incidentally, I certainly do not know much.

Today has been clear, warm, and sunny. Chastain, a field-hospital officer, and I took a walk around the town. The mud is as bad as ever, and I did quite a job on my trousers. We went up the belfry with the three bells I mentioned. The church has one shell hole through the tower and one through the body of the church. Otherwise, it is in fairly good shape.

The houses in town are for the most part ruined. GIs are living in a good many, but others have furniture, dishes, and broken canned foods spread over everything. In a few, we saw clothes still hanging in the cupboards. Most of the inhabitants were miners, and the houses are all alike and apparently built by the mine or government. The doctor's house, now ruined but still showing a sign, and is better than the rest and stands alone rather than as a duplex, as are most houses in town. Tonight we are having Rhapsody in Blue. *I saw the movie once but wanted to see it again.*

All my love, H

15 February 1945

My dearest Ginny,

Last night I saw Rhapsody in Blue *again. I saw it when I visited Bill Boukalik at Stolberg and liked it so much that I sat through it again. The music is, of course, all of Gershwin's best, beautifully done, and Oscar Levant is entertaining being himself.*

The thing that struck me was the unhappiness of the genius. Gershwin's life was incomplete because he was so self-content that he did not really love anyone. I now realize as I never realized before that unless someone, i.e., me, can love someone else, i.e., you, he cannot be truly happy.

Gershwin was, I suppose, a genius and had an obsession to write music. I am sure that most geniuses have this obsession in their field, but they must be unhappy. Take Dr. Kelly, for example.

I am glad we are not geniuses, and I guess everyone who is not decides he or she would rather be happy. I suppose this is not really right, but the thought occurred to me just now that one had to have one or the other. A lot of people are neither, and the Curies must have been happy. How could they have missed?

No business again last night. All patients doing well. We have a German woman to do our laundry, which helps.

Love as always, H

16 February 1945
7:45 P.M.

My darling Ginny,

I had a chance to examine the big gun pictured on the cover of the January 1 edition of Life. *The picture was taken in August at Saint-Malo. We went over to the gun with Alice one day, and it was explained to us in detail.*

We have long since found out that if we want to see anything or get anyplace where we otherwise might not be wanted, we simply take Alice along and always get the best.

The GIs usually whistle and shout at her, but she does not seem to mind and is our ticket to anything we want to see.

You would make a much more satisfactory ticket, but that is another subject.

As always, love and kisses, H

> *18 February 1945*
> *10:00 A.M.*

Dearest Ginny,

You asked about the food and vitamins. The food is in general all right. We all have been so well-supplied from home for Christmas that if any meal is not palatable we have something in our quarters to nibble on. Almost always at night before going to bed we have toast over the fire and a spread of sardines or anchovies and the like. All in all, quite adequate. My vitamins now stand at one month's supply. Perhaps it would be well to send a bottle sometime.

Too bad about the rats and guinea pigs being no good for thyroid function in reproduction. I suppose monkeys are out and probably not suitable anyway.

We are now on day shift and had one patient—a member of the medical battalion who has the Bronze Star and the Silver Star for gallantry in action. He evacuated 40 wounded by driving a jeep through heavy fire into a recently captured town and leading some ambulances out over the route he had used to get in.

He is a very popular and important man, because within an hour of his being brought in, everybody and his grandmother was in to see him, from the colonel commanding the battalion down.

The irony of it all is that he was accidentally shot by an MP who was demonstrating a weapon to the soldiers. Of course, it was not loaded, he thought. The wound was a through-and-through one of the chest, and I am glad to say I believe he will be OK

It is now 2:30 P.M. Actually, he was OK, but we aspirated 700 cc of blood from his chest and he was able to breathe much better. We are having a dreary rainy day, and I am overcome with sleep.

All my love, H

Monday 19 February 1945

Dearest Ginny,

You asked if there is something in the ETO I could report. I have had this in mind, but have not accumulated enough clinical material to make it worthwhile.

As I mentioned in a previous letter, I am coming to the conclusion that clinical reports, while necessary, are not completely satisfying. They deal with superficials. We must deal with fundamentals, and in our postwar world I hope we can get at a big problem and peg away at it. At least, I feel that way now.

I do want to finish the ovarian tumors though, because I feel we know as much about them as anyone and because I feel a little obliged to Dr. TeLinde to finish them up after he made the secretary available to us.

As I read the yearbook and periodicals, I keep constantly in mind my desires and hopes. I am on the lookout for some idea—some new approach to the cancer business. I know that you will have a good idea. Our reading matter is adequate, in that there are some journals available and, of course, the reference part is nil. We have a library of medical books at the hospital that is adequate for ordinary things.

I do keep a record book of my cases. A page to each case. History of where and how injured, condition on admission, treatment, operation, and results. Some records are more complete than others, and, of course, some cases much more interesting than others. I have also a sort of diary, really not a diary, but a continuous letter to you containing things I cannot write to you now, such as our location, units, moves, etc. I write in this about once each month, so it is not very complete.

The boys last night had three patients, but nothing all day today. The papers say that we are ready for a drive through here, and if so, I expect we will be busy then. We are ready, and it will certainly help to get this war over and me home.

All my love, H

20 February 1945
7:00 P.M.

My darling Ginny,

This morning we went over and had a shower, and I put on clean clothes. This is more of a procedure than it sounds, and it takes about two hours to do.

The shower place is some three miles from here in a town not so beaten up as this and sporting a coalmine that has the usual abundant shower facilities found in European mines. The mine itself is defunct, as the retreating Germans destroyed or removed most of the important machinery. The office building which has the shower is the only one of the series of buildings which has been cleared of debris, and we are using that for the 10 shower stalls and an equal number of bathtubs reserved for officers.

We dress in a common room adjoining the shower room, and the attendant, a German who apparently had the same job when the mine was functioning, brings you clogs, also left over from the Germans. The water is abundant and hot, but the showerheads are partially stopped up, so that in some stalls they have been knocked off and you bathe very satisfactorily under a hoselike stream of water.

I usually take along clean clothes and wash my hair. Our laundry here is being done by some German civilians and is quite satisfactory. My ODs are gradually shrinking, like everyone else's, and one of these days I will have to break down and get a pair. There is now an officers' sales store in Maastricht.

All my love, H

21 February 1945
5:45 P.M.

Dearest Ginny,

We have had another quiet day, although they just brought in a patient to the shock ward. Today Colonels Gay and Smith, the Army consultants, dropped in and brought Bill Falor. They were here until lunch and made ward rounds and saw our eight patients.

Bill is the same as ever and looks very well. He has gained a little weight, and I have also, but I have not actually weighed.

I just have looked at our patient, and he has a traumatic amputation of the right leg and a broken left leg. We ordinarily do not get these cases, but there is a tourniquet around the leg, and he is in mild shock, so he obviously should not be transported any farther. We recently had two cases, each of which received 10 bottles of blood. One died the next day without having passed any urine, and the kidneys were very heavily filled with hemoglobin.

We had a similar case at Niewenhagen, so it seems that when you get into the region of 10 bottles of blood, it is not without danger of hemoglobin deposits in the tubules, even though there is no indication of a mismatched transfusion reaction. The moral, of course, is to get by with as little blood as compatible with life. Col. Smith was talking about Rh factor, but said he knew nothing about it, and that was obvious. What relation would the Rh antigens have to transfusions?

All my love, H

> *22 February 1945*
> *1:30 P.M.*
> *Washington's Birthday*

Dearest Ginny,

Near here is a little church. It is the church that contains the bells I have mentioned before. Since I wrote that day, I have been over to the church and found that they do not in fact have any services there; it is much too beaten up. But the belfry is relatively intact and contains three large bells, each three feet in diameter across the bottom. It is possible to ring them by pulling the clapper, and today I heard them. Some GI was no doubt playing.

The church is beaten up, as I said. It was called, oddly enough, Friedenskirche— Peace Church. But the most interesting thing is a quotation on the inside wall in large German script taken from Von Mackensen who was, I believe, chief of staff of the German Army during part of World War I. It says in free translation, "A thorough background in Christianity is necessary for the German youth so that they may better endure the hardships of bearing weapons against the enemies of the Fatherland."

I suppose we rationalize our Christianity to fit in with the war, but I have never before heard it said that the better the Christian, the better the soldier. You can really make most people believe anything, if you go about it properly.

I thought you might like some notion about our hospital. The clearing company is on the first floor, we have the second, and the clearing company lives on the third. We live in the cellar of an annex, as previously mentioned.

Patients come upstairs and into the shock ward. When they are in condition, the shock man sends them to X-ray, from which they may go directly to the OR or back to the shock ward. If we get busy, those who are not in immediate need of operation can be sent to the preoperative ward, which has not yet been used (they go to the postoperative ward).

The setup in this place is very satisfactory, except that central supply is too far from the OR. This is minor. It is a good help to have a reliable and experienced man in the shock ward, as he can then do the triage for which I am responsible. It is timesaving to have him say that this patient is next, or that one, and have some confidence that such is the case.

Jean Bennett was the ideal, much better than the boy we now have. I think I could get Jean back, but if I did, everyone would know I was responsible, and so I would rather not.

You are constantly in my thoughts.

Love, H

24 February 1945

Dearest Ginny,

Everything here is under control. I am sitting in the OR, waiting for Elmer to get our next case to sleep—a bad perforation of the abdomen.

We started to work at 6:00 A.M. yesterday and operated until 8:00 A.M. this morning. It is now 8:00 P.M., and we are beginning over with cases today, having slept from 8:15 to 4:00 P.M. You see, we are a bit busy, but everything seems to be going well, and wounded Germans are beginning to come in, which is always a good sign.

Colonel Smith spent the night here last night. He made Bill Boukalik take the evac hospital, but there is another one on tap. In the showdown, I don't believe that there is really a choice, which scares me. I really do not want it.

Love as always, H

26 February 1945
6:15 P.M.

Dearest Ginny,

Still going strong, getting about 4-6 hours sleep. Things quieted down this afternoon, and I sort of took a bath and put on clean clothes, and I feel fine and am ready to go. Received five letters from you yesterday, including one with the pictures taken, I think, on New Year's Day at Lake Roland.

The news seems to be very good, and the noise and the battle have moved away from us. I wish I had time to write more details, because it has been very interesting, and I have been free of a head cold at that.

Love, H

27 February 1945

Dearest Ginny,

Things have quieted down here. It is now about 11:00 P.M. There are two cases in the shock ward, but neither is ready to do. One is a German, of whom we have had many, and the other is a Chinaman who is also an American.

The news continues to be very good, and from the stories the wounded tell, things seem to be going very well. We were very busy last night, but we spent most of the night on Krauts. We have only the two surgical teams here now, so things are very tight. I guess I did not say that we had an extra team for a few days, but actually they were of little help because they were so slow.

I have had several interesting thoracoabdominal wounds and three spleens in all, all doing OK so far. It is a remarkable thing that, with our team having gained a little experience, sick patients who would have died a few months ago seem to get along OK, and for no discernible reason.

I think we have two more patients now, and I must go and take a look at them.

Love, as always, H

28 February 1945
(Really the 1st of March)

Dearest Ginny,

It is now 20 minutes after midnight, and I have just finished what I hope is our last case at this stop. We are now too far from the battle to get any but overflow casualties. I hope in a few minutes to go to bed and sleep through the night.

The last case was another spleen, which is the fourth one, all with thoracic wounds and holes in the diaphragm.

You are responsible for perhaps saving the life of a few of these poor fellows. After you work for 24 hours straight, it is easy to fall asleep anywhere. But more than once I would think of something that needed doing and being tired would almost decide to let it go in the hopes that the ward man would have checked to see if the catheter was draining or a chest needed tapping.

And then I would remember that somewhere each of these men had someone who was waiting for him to come safely home, just as you want for me. And then it would be easy to tend to the slightest detail, if I but thought of it. For to do less would not be doing what you would want someone to do for me.

I am writing this letter in another room in our cellar, formerly occupied by another unit. The others are asleep in our own cellar, and I got a candle and am writing by candlelight. As I held the candle high to see where I was, I noticed on the shelf, Abundant Living, *by Uncle Stanley [Howard's father's brother and a Methodist minister]. It is a brand-new book, evidently sent to one of the former occupants of this cellar who could not carry it. I am going to take it with me, as I have never read it.*

The weather continues to be warm and generally good. I think this is favorable to our side. I do not know how long we will stay here, but not long, I presume. The other day it was necessary to send the surgical truck on ahead with another team. I will probably never catch up with it again, and I am very sorry, as it was a good catchall.

Love, H

Diary Entry: 5 March 1945, Krefeld
[63rd Field Hospital, 3rd Platoon]

Early one morning a general's aide appeared and asked if I would come and look at a patient about a block away. I agreed to do so. The patient was General Church, assistant commanding general of the 84th Division. He was hit in the town of Wegberg. His guard consisted of four men from the intelligence-and-reconnaissance platoon; they were in a separate car. His driver and aide were with the general.

General Church had small shell fragments in both legs—about eight in all. The wounds seemed clean. He was very anxious not to be hospitalized. He had no disability. I dressed the wounds with sulfa, gave him 20,000 units of penicillin, and sent him on his way.

On 27 February General Church had been given a task force (Task Force Church)—i.e., the 334th Infantry—motorized to exploit rapidly the American breakthrough across the Roer. Task Force Church was highly successful. It overran Boisheim on 1 March. The general had been wounded a couple of days before I saw him, presumably while leading his task force.

This platoon, to which we are assigned, is the poorest of any we have been with. The movement yesterday from Hostert to Krefeld was the most disorganized of any movement I have seen.

No one seemed to be in charge. The enlisted men spent their time running around on bicycles, motorbikes, and the like. The first shuttle left Hostert about 1430, and, when we arrived in Krefeld about 1930 the hospital was all confusion. I took over the OR and shock and had things straightened out in a few minutes. Col. Blank from the 1st Army was here about 8:30 P.M. and asked if we could open by 10:00 P.M., which we were able to do.

Capt. Hughes [medical administrative officer of 3rd Platoon] had the idea that the central-heating plant would be open in a day or so and did not put up any stoves. The colonel from First Army was here this afternoon and raised hell because the place was so cold. I had told Hughes [commander of 3rd Platoon] myself, at about 1800 hrs, that if the heat were not on, the stoves would have to go up in surgery.

The colonel looked me up a little later and said that he specifically authorized me to order the platoon commander to get those stoves up in an hour. Capt. Hughes was not here at the time.

It seemed like making a mountain out of a molehill, but it was exasperating, because I had already mentioned it. At any rate, it still took them about four hours to get them up. The platoon needs a new CO, a new MAC, and a new first sergeant.

Diary Entry: 7 March 1945, Krefeld
[63rd Field Hospital, 3rd Platoon]

Lt. Col. Burstein is CO of the Medical Battalion of the 84th Division. Major Day is CO of the clearing company of the same battalion. I have never told about the trip from Baesweiler to Hostert.

We got a note from Col. Gay on the 28th of February to be prepared to move at 1400 hrs on the 1st of March. Henry Swann was to stay at Baesweiler with the 48th to take care of the patients, and my team, with our two shock teams (Craig and Koesterer), was to go to the 3rd Platoon of the 63rd Field Hospital. We did not know who the second surgical team would be.

We worked the night of the 28th and went to bed about 7:30 A.M. At 1:00 P.M., Fritz Joachim and his team arrived at Baesweiler to join us. Soon afterwards a PROCO unit and a truck from headquarters armed with a note from Lt. Col. Anderson (executive officer, 5th Army Auxiliary Surgical Group) arrived, saying that I was the chief of surgery at the 63rd Field Hospital, 3rd Platoon, and to proceed with the convoy and join the 63rd at Wegberg.

We went to Linnich, Erkelenz, and Wegberg. We crossed the Roer at Linnich over our infantry-support bridge on March 1, just 7 days after the assault crossing. We later learned that it was on that day that Task Force Church had reached the Rhine.

The engineers were putting up a Bailey bridge across the Roer as we went across. Erkelenz was completely destroyed. Not many walls of buildings standing, just piles of rubble. Each badly destroyed town seemed more like the one before, but Erkelenz seemed worse.

We drove with the utmost caution to stay in the center of the road, because of the danger of mines on the edges. Even though the road shoulders are swept, one constantly hears of vehicles or individuals being blown to bits by getting off the road.

Upon arriving in Wegberg we learned from the MP directing traffic at the main rubble heap that about two hours before the 63rd

Platoon had moved up and Checkmate [the code name for the 84th Division] clearing company had also gone.

I felt sure that since we were going to support the 84th Division that we had supported at Niewenhagen I should know the lieutenant colonel commanding the medical battalion. About one hour before reaching Wegberg, I had asked Elmer [the lieutenant colonel's] name, because I wanted to know it when I saw him. I had seen him at Baesweiler and at that time had asked him his name to introduce him.

Not knowing quite what to do, we were standing in the rain and looking at the map with the MP when who should drive up but the lieutenant colonel in question (Burstein was his name).

I was very glad to see him, because he would undoubtedly know where his clearing company was, and also the location of the field hospital. He told us that it was toward the front, about five miles. "You can't miss it." He did not know the name of the town, but he said it was a large group of buildings on the right of the road with a huge red cross on the roof.

So down the road we went, two 1½-ton personnel carriers of the PROCO, one 1½-ton surgical truck with Fritz Joachim's team, and two 1½-ton personnel carriers with my team and two shock teams. We, of course, were uncertain if we were going correctly, and we saw no one and, of course, expected to come across some Jerries.

It was also here that General Church sustained the wounds in his leg that I saw later. However, after about two miles, we came to a line of vehicles, bumper-to-bumper: the 771st Tank Battalion, several battalions of field artillery, and others. The traffic jam stretched for miles. We drove on the left side of the road and passed the column, which was creeping along. We finally saw the group of buildings described by Col. Burstein and drove in.

The town was Hostert. It had taken us about four hours to drive the 30-odd miles. When we got there, we found that the Germans had left only the day before and a battalion aid station was only 500 yards away. At this point, as when we first arrived at Krefeld, where we now are, I thought we were the most advanced hospital unit. An unenviable situation. Here, as at Krefeld, the Germans could blow us off the map with artillery, if they wanted to.

While at Hostert at the insane asylum and in the cottages we saw perhaps a dozen German soldiers dead in their foxholes and ditches. The day we left there, a group of about eight German civilians from the asylum had a big wagon and gathered them up and buried them in back of the asylum. It seemed to be an organized search and was under the direction of the AMG (American Military Government), I presume. At least one GI body was in the woods nearby, and Col. Hughes notified Graves Registration, which came and got him.

The losses of the 84th Division give an idea of how an army maintains its manpower. The 84th first saw action at Geilenkirchen. It jumped off at the time of the Allied offensive on the 18th of November 1944. At the time, we were with the 3rd Platoon of the 53rd Field Hospital at Niewenhagen, supporting the division.

We were very busy for about two weeks. The division surgeon, Lt. Col. Jones, told me that their losses were heavier than at any other time, including the crossing of the Roer. This was due, first, to inexperience, because a new outfit often has a high casualty rate in its first big operation, and, secondly, to the fact that the Geilenkirchen operation was really a cracking of the Seigfried Line, which in that area consisted of numerous pillboxes. The division knocked out 78 such strongpoints.

The casualties admitted to the clearing station are revealing. From the 18th of November to date (March 1), they have admitted 15,000 cases—a whole division. They were not only 84th Division casualties, but they also came from attached or nearby units and the like.

The 84th has had roughly 6,900 casualties, consisting of 900 killed, 1,500 missing, and 4,500 wounded. Around half of the latter were returned to duty.

These figures were given me by Major Gebhart, executive officer of the battalion and, incidentally, an intern at Harriet Lane Home, Johns Hopkins Hospital, 1939-1940. The 5th Aux Headquarters is now at Viersen.

Col. Burstein is responsible for the following stories:

The clearing station had been in Krefeld about four days and the troops perhaps a day or two longer. In spite of nonfraternization regulations, four cases of gonorrhea occurred in the division.

Burstein also quotes the medical-battalion commanding officer of the 29th Division (104th Medical Battalion) as authority for the following story:

Eight men were sent out on combat patrol behind the enemy line. About four days later, one member of the patrol reported in for sick call, and a positive diagnosis of gonorrhea was made. It developed that, while behind the German lines, the soldier came upon a German civilian who in a few minutes presented him with Hitler's secret weapon. The soldier continued on his mission and returned to our line—and he could not speak a word of German!

There was a little feeling of being let down among the officers of the medical battalion. When Col. Jones left us at Hostert, he half-jokingly and half-seriously offered to bet that on the next night he would be on the east bank of the Rhine.

The Germans, of course, blew all the bridges. One gets the impression that the high command had an outside hope of seizing the Rhine Bridge intact and was prepared to continue the pursuit if such proved to be the case.

As things stand now, an assault crossing will be necessary. It is the Roer all over again on a large scale. We shall probably wait until the 1st and 3rd armies get close to the Rhine. Once again, as before the Roer, the 9th Army has had to wait for its flanks to come up before going over. Still no patient since arriving here.

ALLIED FORCES WERE moving rapidly toward the Rhine when I wrote the next letter.

---

1 March 1945
8:50 P.M.

Dearest Ginny,

After I wrote you last night I went to bed and was awakened at 2:30 A.M. because we had three patients. These took until 6:30, and then we got some early breakfast from the mess.

In the meantime we had received orders to move my team and the two shock teams, leaving the other surgical team at Baesweiler. So we went to bed at 7:15 and slept until 1:00 P.M., when we got up and were met by Fritz Joachim and his team, and we proceeded to our new hospital in Hostert, or where it was supposed to be.

When we got there we found a lone MP in the town who said that the hospital had moved in two hours before. So up the pike we go, finally finding our destination about 5:00 P.M. The numbers of vehicles and equipment on the road are beyond anything I have seen before.

Our hospital is a former insane asylum, and all the inmates have been moved to a single building while we are occupying two buildings. It is by far the most luxurious setup we have yet experienced. When war moves rapidly there are isolated battles for road junctions, etc., but the greatest part of the countryside escapes relatively undamaged.

We passed through some towns where destruction is absolute and complete. Saint-Lô is our measuring stick, and what we have seen today surpasses that in thoroughness, in that not a wall is standing. Fritz Joachim's team is working tonight, and so I shall go to bed between sheets, thanks to der Führer.

Love, H

2 March 1945
9:30 A.M.

Dearest Ginny,

It is again one of the contrasts of war that being for a while closest to what might be called "the front" we have had a quieter and, so far, not as busy a time as we had at other places. Last night I slept through, and the other team had no cases.

I am in the delicate situation of being outranked by the other team and yet designated as chief by special order. I, therefore, was rather inclined to say that I worked last night, but the others, especially the EMs, were pretty well tuckered out, and I asked Fritz Joachim to take nights at first. As it turned out, there was nothing to do. I must have been more tired than I thought, because I went to sleep at 10:30 and had to be waked up at 7:00 for breakfast.

This hospital contingent is fresh from the States and, until arriving here, had never had its equipment out of the boxes. You can imagine the confusion, but they are more than willing to take suggestions, and by 10:00 last night we could have received patients.

This is not record time, but enthusiasm made up for lack of experience. The operation room is much the largest we have had, with two tables side by side and plenty of room on all sides. These take up about half the space, and the rest of the room can be devoted to supply function.

This will be a grand opportunity to observe the effect of a long, as compared with a short, training program on the efficiency of a hospital unit. This outfit was trained at Fort Meade beginning in March, and officers were assigned just as the unit left for overseas. None of them had so much as seen field-hospital equipment until it was taken from the box here yesterday.

My prediction is that this method of putting the unit together will offer a shakedown of a few days and prove to be just as effective as a long-term training program. Furthermore, the personnel have nothing to unlearn, and that is a great boon.

Interesting things do happen. In the midst of great confusion, I saw a boy stringing up a wire in a room that was to be a ward. When I inquired what it was for, he said that the wire was to suspend sheets so that patients could use bedpans. In field hospitals one just does not worry about things like that.

During the same confusion the dentist was walking around worrying about putting up his dental chair, another unessential, for the dentists assigned to these units never have any work on casualties. They concern themselves with routine dental treatment of the men.

The news is unbelievably good. As I said yesterday, when we tried to find this outfit with our PROCO, which we now have in lieu of a truck, the hospital had already moved. I found out this morning that the Germans had left here only night before last, and the American battalion aid station was only 500 yards down the pike when the hospital arrived. By now I think the aid station is many miles away.

It is a beautiful, clear, cold, sunny day, and, of course, I cannot help but miss you.

All my love, H

P.S. *11:00 A.M. Still no patients. Things are straightening out.*

3 March 1945
10:00 A.M.

Dearest Ginny,

We now have a total of four patients, two of them POWs. This represents the caseload during 48 hours and indicates that casualties are very light, as they always are with a rapid advance. There were three units here together at this insane asylum, and yesterday morning two of them left, leaving us to rattle around in buildings much too large.

However, we soon heard that an evac hospital was moving in during the afternoon. At about 6:00 P.M. their trucks begin to arrive. It will be a very satisfactory setup for an evac. It shows how fast things are going—a battalion aid station 500 yards from here when we arrived and now an evac hospital. It would be reasonable to suppose that we will be moving when the evac opens for business, which I judge to be later today.

Bill Boukalik was through here yesterday afternoon. The changes in chiefs of surgery were never made in the two hospitals under consideration around the first of the year, but a new one arrived without a chief, and Bill was given the job.

When Col. Smith spent the night with us on the 23rd, he said that that day they had almost given me a new job, but had given it to Bill instead. Smith further said that there was still another hospital coming that might need a new chief and, if so, they might not ask but just give it to me.

Yesterday Bill said he was very unhappy about his new assignment, because he had turned it down in so many words during the January 1 period and no one said anything to him about it until 48 hours ago, which was three or four days after I knew it. I am a little bit panicky about it now, because I have decided I do not want it, because the end of war may be in sight, and a hospital fresh from the states may not go back so soon. I will certainly work on the Colonel in no uncertain terms when I see him.

When we arrived here two days ago the Germans had left only the night before, and the German doctors and the civilian employees of this asylum showed by action and expression that they were deeply disturbed and not a little bit worried about the procedure of taking over.

It did me good to see it, and I have no sorrow for any discomfort that they experienced. I am only afraid that it may be necessary to let all Germans experience this before they say uncle.

All my love, H

Sunday 4 March 1945
10:30 A.M.

Dearest Ginny,

We are all packed up waiting to go, but, as yet, no orders, so we may or may not be going. The evac hospital, which, as I mentioned before, moved in here yesterday, opened and received patients. I spent a few hours last evening just watching them and was much amused.

The outfit is an experienced one, having been through Africa, Sicily, and now the ETO. It is unquestionably a first-rate hospital, but they had the same troubles everyone else had.

In the midst of the operation, the lights went out, as happened to me the night before, when I was freeing up the splenic flexure. The suction tube got stopped up. The nurse put some Vaseline gauze on the Mayo stand and it was knocked on the floor. The EM dropped the iodine bottle on the floor and broke it as he was getting ready for the scrub-up, and, all in all, it was not impressive for an outfit in action two years.

They apologized, saying that they were not set up as yet, etc., etc., all of which was true. But it did me good, because we have the same troubles, due in part to ourselves, but probably more particularly by changing from hospital to hospital with new personnel and, at this step at least, not due to complete inexperience.

The equipment still has the paper on it; however, I still will be interested in comparing the results with the green outfit and with one with a long training program. I think the green boys will do as well, because the Army training program emphasizes the military, as compared with the professional medical, aspect of training.

The number of cases at the evac is by no means comparable to that at the field hospital. Most of the work last night, as always, I am sure, consisted of debridement of extremities and application of casts to broken extremities.

Incidentally, most of the patients were POWs. The method of handling the patients—i.e., the mechanics of preoperative X-ray, the treatment of shock—is exactly the same as in the field hospital, only on a larger scale.

One team usually runs two tables simultaneously. The surgeon will do one case alone while the assistant surgeon does another, and the anesthesiologist gives both anesthesias, usually Pentathol. For chests and bellies, of which I saw none, the teams come together as a unit. Their wards are arranged so that all chests and bellies are in one place, with a medical officer in charge of the ward.

The extremities go to one ward, and the operating surgeon is responsible for the postoperative care. Most of the latter are evacuated as soon as they recover from the anesthesia. They keep the chests and bellies 10 days, just as we do. The maxillofacial cases go to a single ward and are taken care of by maxillofacial men.

All in all, it is a good setup, but I become more and more pleased with my own lot and hope to high heaven that I am able to hang on.

All my love to our little family, H

P.S. Stewart Welch is chief of surgery at this hospital. He is an assistant professor of surgery at Albany.

Monday 5 March 1945
11:00 A.M.

Dearest Ginny,

Since writing yesterday we have spent almost our entire time providing ourselves with the necessities of existence. We had expected to leave the evac, and so had packed in order to be out of our room so that the evac personnel could move in.

Incidentally, the executive officer of the hospital was very unpleasant about wanting us to get out, as if the place really belonged to them. I enjoyed the little tilt I had with the gentleman, because I knew he would have to throw us out, and so I gave him a little straight talk, as I do now and again, and he left us alone.

The truth of the matter is that the medical group had assigned us the building first and then assigned the evac there, which meant that both of us should have shared the building until the proper people, i.e., the medical group, gave us orders to move on.

At any rate, it seems to me that the evac people took advantage of the inexperience of our platoon commander, Capt. Hughes, and the upshot of it was that we got orders, finally, to move yesterday, and we were, therefore, without a home.

Finally, Capt. Hughes scurried around and found some vacated houses about one half mile from the hospital, and the evac said that they would feed us, and we all moved to the houses where we now are.

These houses are quite nice. They are all duplexes with a generous space between. There was practically no fighting through here, so the houses are in good condition. However, the doughboys used the premises for billets and have thoroughly ransacked the place. Everything is pulled out of the drawers and cupboards.

There is evidence of a hasty retreat by the civilians where there is uneaten German food, half-prepared and one of the boys who had arrived early said that when they arrived the lights were still turned on and the radios playing. The electricity is now turned off, and the water, which was running at first, has now stopped. The village water supply has apparently been exhausted.

This settlement is not immediately adjacent to the town, which is some 4 kilometers away. It is in woods by itself. The houses have been constructed within the last five years and are very nice. The kitchen has a wood-stove and another in an alcove off the dining room, which the four of us have taken over for our quarters. This is very satisfactory, because we have a nice fire in the range and are able to cook up a little something to eat from time to time. We have had regular chow at the evac hospital.

Last night somebody dragged out a bottle of wine, but no one could produce a corkscrew, so Ken claimed that he could get the cork out by pounding the bottom of the bottle on a doorjamb. He did this with success until the cork was about out and with one final blow intended to complete the job. This he did by smashing the bottle and losing the wine all over the floor.

We had no lights, except a candle, and so we could not read, write, or play cards. Fritz Joachim told us the story of his trip to Baffin Island, Alaska, for the Army, and it is a great long yarn. He was there for some 15 months, during which time he received mail once by plane.

But the most interesting thing is that he had been in the Army about one week during the summer of 1941, at a time that was particularly hot. He got a teletype order directing him to report to Washington for further orders, and then followed a string of directions, as is the custom. Travel by train, etc., and ended up by saying, "Travel by dog team authorized."

He had no idea of what it was all about, as he had no previous knowledge. It turned out that an eight-man expedition was going to Baffin Island to make weather observations, and he was the doctor. All other members had been especially selected, but the Army had apparently taken his name out of a hat.

He learned to speak Eskimo and entertained us for an hour with his yarns. Incidentally, he uncovered an unusual skeleton with a humerus, three feet long, which he has found out since then is longer than almost any known skeleton. The skull was broad and flat and had no optic foramina. There was a groove around the outside of the skull, and the optic nerves apparently circled the head outside the skull and entered by the foramen magnum. He has mentioned it to people connected with museums, and it is likely that after the war someone will go after it.

Love, H

————————

WE OPERATED ON only one patient at Hostert, where we were with the 3rd Platoon of the 63rd Field Hospital. The patient was the first operated on at this platoon, which, as I have noted, was totally disorganized. He was a POW with a through-and-through abdominal wound. He had been wounded around midnight 1 March and was admitted at 3 PM 2 March.

He was in moderate shock, with a blood pressure of 90/60. His abdomen was tender. He had an entrance wound in the left flank and an exit wound posteriorly, apparently through the sacrum. He had had five hundred cc of blood before operation, which took place at 5:00 PM 2 March. He had a large retroperitoneal hematoma and, curiously enough, we could not find any intraperitoneal bowel damage.

Due to the course of the missile, we thought it advisable to inspect the descending colon, where we discovered a small retroperitoneal slit in the bowel. We exteriorized this portion of the bowel with a colostomy.

The POW had a lacerating wound of the scalp that I closed with a black silk suture. He seemed also to have a fractured skull, but probably only the outer table. He got along very well and was fine when we left him.

Also as noted previously, the 63rd Platoon was "pinched out" by an evac hospital at Hostert. On 5 March we were ordered to Krefeld, where our Team 3 stayed for a little over one week.

————————

Tuesday 6 March 1945
8:00 P.M.

Dearest Ginny,

We are now situated in by far the best quarters we have had since leaving Fort Sam Houston. As a matter of fact, the place reminds me somewhat of Fort Sam, because it is a German military post [Krefeld, Lemmenhof] of much the same order. It apparently was more of a school for officer candidates, they say, because the buildings are divided into mess halls, classrooms, and suites of rooms for living quarters, rather than large barracklike rooms.

The hospital has taken over two of the buildings, and we have oceans of room. Elmer, Ken, and I have set up in a room with running water—cold. There is a brick-tile stove built in the wall. The coal is thrown into the stove from the adjoining room. There is also central heating from a big central power plant, but this is not working, as most of the other buildings are unoccupied and there is no one to run it.

We have a bathroom adjoining, which has turned out to be a private bath, as the other two rooms it is designed to serve are not occupied. There is a fine bathtub and a water heater for a warm bath. Ken made a fire in it last night, but it would not burn, and after a while he discovered that the thing was leaking down into the firebox, causing the fire to be drowned. We found the leak this afternoon and spent four hours and a bar of solder fixing it, only to find that when the water was turned on, it leaked about as bad as it had before we started.

However, after cleaning the leaking area with gasoline, alcohol, and sulfuric acid, which were the three cleaning fluids available, and going over the area again with the iron, the leak quieted down, and we all were able to take a hot tub bath in a clean tub and put on clean clothes and now, of course, I am sleepy.

The hospital setup is the most spacious we have had, and the operating room is large but cold.

My first and only patient here was a general who, soon after the crossing, got mixed up in a pistol fight with some Germans and got a few fragments of automobile in his leg.

It seems that at one point in the fight a tank column and a battalion of infantry had gone ahead and been stopped. The general took off down the road to see what the trouble was. When two or three miles outside a small town, he suddenly realized that the guards in the vehicle in front of him were firing back toward his car, and looking up, he saw a German in a ditch beside him firing at his car. One of these shots hit the metal windshield wings and several splinters from this hit the occupant of the car.

All this was several days ago, and when I saw the general today, we took an X-ray and found only a tiny match-head-size piece of metal in the calf of the leg and advised doing nothing except give him penicillin. You can see that we have not been very busy.

Several others of these barracks have been taken over by the military government as billets for foreign nationals [the authorities] are rounding up. In one building they are putting all the Dutch; another, the Belgians; another, the French, in preparation for sending them back to their own countries.

These are people that the Germans brought in as laborers for German factories. They have been bringing them in to us by the truckload, with their scanty belongings. No provision is made to provide food from Army stores, and those that brought no food are probably hungry. Those in the barracks next to ours gathered outside tonight where we wash our mess gear and, as I walked to the door, they walked up to scoop the leavings from my mess kit. In a day or two they will probably be safely home.

In a town in which we stopped, we found a German newspaper which said that spearheads of the 1st Army and 9th Army had crossed the Roer, but had been surrounded and were being reduced. That same day, these people fled from their homes, leaving uneaten food on the table to escape the same spearheads.

I have spent most of the day taking care of the necessities of life, helping Ken fix the water heater, fixing the blackout to our room, arranging with the electricians to have a line from the generator put to the room, and seeing about having some heat in the wards and operating room until the central-heating plant gets going in the next day or two—all things that would become unimportant and would not be done at all if there was real work to do.

Much love, H

Wednesday 7 March 1945

Dearest Ginny,

When we left Baesweiler, where we lived in the cellar, we were very busy and left that field hospital behind and joined another. This going from one place to another is very interesting, and I enjoy it.

There is a great contrast between this platoon and the one we just left. The older one was rather GI. The commanding officer, John Hill, is a youngster—that is, about as old as I am—who is a recent fellow in proctology at the Mayo Clinic and who is a very nice man.

However, he is a terrible worrier and takes himself too seriously. He used to make rules about everything and post them on the bulletin board when, very often, if nothing were said or done things would straighten out.

For example, when we finally got into operation at Baesweiler, there was naturally a great deal of interest on the part of the enlisted men in the proceedings in the operating room.

At first, when we were not busy, several of them used to come to the OR during an operation, and their presence worried the life out of John. He finally put up a notice that no one could enter the OR, except those working there. Now this is a small point, but I feel sure that when you got busy and the boys had something to do, they would not come, and besides, they were not in the way in the first place. This just illustrates what I mean.

Here, on the other hand, things will be different. The CO is Captain Robert Hughes from Washington, D.C., who is older and a redheaded Irishman of the Hail-Fellow-Well-Met type. There are no rules here and everybody is for himself, so to speak.

I like this better, because at the other place there was always tension for fear of doing the wrong thing. We had gotten into the habit of keeping a certain amount of food in our quarters—things from home, but supplemented by bread, butter, coffee, sugar, and cream, all available at the platoon mess. John would have fits at any of us getting these things from the mess hall because, well, it just was not GI.

One of the first things he asked me when we joined them at Übach was that the surgical team be instructed to stay away from the mess hall. The practical solution turned out to be for our nurses to get things from the mess sergeant, who apparently concluded that the extra-food rule applied only to the males.

Here, things are much easier. Elmer made a trial case last night and asked the mess sergeant for a pound of butter, which was immediately delivered. He also gave me a can of milk for coffee in the room. Actually, as far as food consumed is concerned, I dare say it comes out even, for, in this way, many times we skip the GI meal if we do not like it and substitute rations from home.

Things are more or less Zone of the Interior here. As I mentioned before, this post reminds me of Fort Sam, and more so since I discovered a swimming pool *complete with water. It is a little too chilly to try, but if you were here, I dare say we would try it.*

To make it seem even more homelike, the colonel CO of the medical battalion came in yesterday morning and asked me if I wanted a car. Saying that I did, he took me down to his headquarters, where his soldiers had collected some captured vehicles—more than they knew what to do with. I now have a two-cylinder, small-size European car—sedan body with a sort of convertible top that rolls back to enjoy the view. It runs, but the battery needs charging, and it has a miss in the engine.

Frenzl and Mac (our enlisted men) are working on it this afternoon. Under the Army rules, captors of vehicles—i.e., me—can apply to the proper authority for permission to retain vehicles. If permission is granted, Regular Army serial numbers are issued. I doubt if we are given permission to keep it, but it would help solve our moving problem, which is great.

We are enjoying these things, but we are closer to the enemy than we have ever been before, but are, I would judge, immune to a counterthrust because of geography.

The American Military Government still is bringing in by the truckloads the displaced nationals and screening them with a view to sending them back home. I noticed today that a mess line had been set up, so they probably are no longer hungry. Yesterday one of the many people in here was a major, CO of a clearing company. It seems that the colonel of one of their regiments was wounded and had a partial severance of the ulnar nerve through a small wound, the major wanted to know what I knew about a Major Fred Gibe, who was with the 3rd Aux and who had seen the colonel in Belgium. I gave a good recommendation, and I believe they are going down to see him. We do not have a first-rate neurosurgical team.

Yesterday Ike Humphries's team left us so that Fritz Joachim and I are alone. We have had no cases here because the fighting is over for the moment.

I started to tell you about a little party we had last night. The field-hospital officers had within the last couple of days received their Christmas packages, because they had been on the move and are only recently from the States. They had a buffet, ETO style, after the movie.

When we arrived here, the bar in what must have been the officers club still had beer running from the tap, and in the cellar were about 400 bottles of wine, some of which was consumed last night.

When Ike Humphries left, he took about 50 bottles with him. It must have a very low alcoholic content, because no one seems to get pickled in spite of prodigious consumption. We could never have had such a get-together at the other platoon, because, well, the enlisted men could not have one, and they must not know that the officers could have a party, etc., etc.

Of course, the enlisted men cared little, because they do as they want anyhow, as I am convinced after being with several units. These little get-togethers are a good thing, I think, because it gets people together, especially the teams and the platoon officers, so that they get the feeling of being one team rather than two units working together.

My love as always, H

Friday 9 March 1945

Dearest Ginny,

This afternoon, Elmer, Ernest Craig (shock team), and I drove one of the PROCO trucks over to headquarters, which has moved to within 20 miles of here. Nothing new there. Not even a good rumor.

I was not sure how riding around in an enemy country would be, but, as a matter of fact, the population is quite subdued. They have been so recently occupied that I suppose this is to be expected.

There is so much talk of an expected German underground that I expected more display of hostility on the part of the civilians. None is in evidence yet.

In contrast to the country west of the Roer, most of the civilians are still in their towns, and we have seen some towns that are not destroyed. The $64,000 question is this: When the civilians who, after all, fought the war trickle back to their homes, are they more or less likely to want to fight again in 20 years if they find their homes destroyed? If the answer is that they are less likely to want to start something, the proper course of action in respect to German cities is horrible to contemplate.

The city [Krefeld] we are near was one of the frequent targets of the Strategic Air Force, and I must say that the mission was successful, as most of the city is destroyed, and that means there is no place for a rat to live. In the undestroyed cities, all inhabitants have brought out white flags. It is so uniform that it may be a requirement of the American Military Government.

I can only wish that you were here.

Love, H

10 March 1945

My darling Ginny,

Your remarks about Rh factor are interesting. We recently had a man with a large burn injury on whom I did a colostomy. He also had a fractured femur and humerus and was in profound shock on admission.

I did the colostomy the night he was injured, but did nothing to his arm and leg. He was given 1,000 cc of blood before the colostomy.

On the 4th day he was doing well, and we took him back and put on a hip spika and arm cast. He did not behave too well, and his blood pressure went out of sight while we were putting on the cast. His hemoglobin was 51% on the morning we did the cast, and so we gave him 500 cc of blood, after which he needed nothing more.

He must have had a massive hemolysis at the time of the last 500 cc of blood, as the little urine he passed was bright cherry red with few red blood cells, and he died four days later in uremia, having passed not a cc of urine during the last three days. The history would fit into Rh sensitivity, I suppose. Please answer the following:

1. How long does it take for sensitivity to develop?
2. Does sensitivity always develop if Rh-positive blood is given to an Rh-negative individual?
3. Is there a simple way to test for the Rh factor?

As I figure it, there is roughly a one-in-ten chance that any given patient will have a reaction if sensitivity develops immediately and if the patient gets more than one bottle of blood, which the patients almost all do. Eighty-five percent of 85% equals 72%, and 15% of 72% equals 10.8%.

Interestingly enough, this figure is somewhere in the neighborhood of the serious reactions we have had with blood in the last couple of months. Our gross mortality—that is, hospital mortality—for the last months was roughly 25%. My personal operative mortality is 15%, regardless of the cause of death.

Today reminds me of the Thanksgiving I built the bookcase. This morning I discovered a substantial wooden box that would make a good footlocker. The footlocker I brought over is still in England, I suppose. I had to put on hinges and *hasps and make a few alterations that I figured would take about an hour, but one thing led to another. The hinges had to be countersunk to work, the lid did not quite fit, etc., etc., until I had spent the entire day at carpentering. Had I known it was going to be so much trouble, I would never have begun. It illustrates the difficulties of living in the ETO.*

The displaced refugees continue to come and go. Individuals and families, but few small children. Yesterday one of the GI guards came over to the hospital and asked if a medical officer could come over to look at a woman who was moaning around, and he thought she must be going to have a baby.

Captain Cullen of the field hospital sauntered over, and his eyes almost popped out when he found the head on the perineum. He had taken nothing, and he so tied the cord with a piece of string and sent a boy back to the hospital, about 100 yards, for scissors and other things.

He used no anesthesia, no asepsis, no nothing, and today both the mother and baby are doing very well. The child was not a complete surprise to the family, and they had brought along with them some baby clothes, bottles, cans of milk, and the like. The refugee woman had been in labor since 5:00 A.M., and only at 1:00 P.M. did the family raise enough commotion for anything to be done about it.

Love, H

12 March 1945
2:30 P.M.

Dearest Ginny,

Yesterday I spent the day gallivanting. Elmer and I went. We took a PROCO truck and visited three evacs and headquarters, all of which are within a radius of 20 miles or so. We stayed overnight with Gene Bennett, who is unhappy at an evac, and then went to headquarters this morning to see if somehow the Colonel was not in a position to switch Gene back to us

You see, a shock team at an evac gets patients from the receiving ward where the triage is done. The shock team's problem is to treat shock and nothing else. In a field hospital, the shock ward is also the receiving and preoperative ward, so that the shock team also has the very important function of triage. In other words, Gene has more ability than he can use at the evac.

The Colonel also said that it was entirely possible that within a few days Colonel Smith would come to some decision on the chief for still another evac, and that he knew Smith had me in mind. For reasons which I have stated before, I have strongly decided that I am not interested and so told the Colonel, who said that he would do all he could to prevent it.

The number of people being handled by the American Military Government at the local staging area, or whatever it is called, is daily increasing; that is, the displaced people being sent home. Today we noticed a long line, and on close inspection found that they were passing through a spray of DDT for lice and other crawly and jumping insects. They say that the CO of the unit took a spray first to get things started, and from looking over the people, I would say also because he thought it was a good thing. At one civilian hospital, there were several cases of typhus in an isolation ward.

The Rhine crossing makes good news and cannot help but speed the end. If only we did not have the Japanese to finish off, things would be rosy indeed.

Love to all, H

13 March 1945

Dearest Ginny,

This morning I found Lehman Guyton in a small town about 5 miles from here. He looks thin. He does not have a job that is likely to offer him much in the way of surgical experience or advancement and so is, I suppose, one of the many unfortunates in the Army in this respect. It makes me consider myself all the more fortunate. He hopes to come up and spend the night with me. If I have a case, I will get him to help me with it.

Driving around the countryside this morning made me think that at least some of the civilians hereabout figure that the war is over for them, as they have begun reconstruction. We saw one farmer filling in the foxholes along the highway on his farm while a team was waiting to plow the field. Another farmer was rebuilding the corner of his house, which had been blown away. Many others are clearing away the rubble and debris that seem to accumulate even if there has been very little damage.

All my love as always, H

14 March 1945
8:00 P.M.

Dearest Ginny,

This afternoon Lehman came up to see us and planned to stay until this evening. But no sooner had he arrived here than our team got orders to return to Dülken to the 48th Field Hospital, 3rd Platoon, the platoon that we were with at Baesweiler west of the Roer.

The hospital had since moved, of course, and we were there in an hour. This move broke up Lehman's visit, but I had a nice chat with him. He is still trying or, rather, wants to get out of his outfit and do anything else. Tomorrow, therefore, he is going to stop by for me, and we will go over to Colonel Smith's to see if he has an opening in an evac or something that will suit Lehman's training and wishes.

It is doubtful that Smith will want to make a change from a tactical outfit, but he might. At any rate, Smith is the guy to see.

I was a little sorry to get sent back here, because, after all, they take themselves a little too seriously to suit me. Law and order are desirable, but you can make rules about trivial things, and this outfit will do it. We are in bivouac, so will not have any work until we move again.

All my love, H

Diary Entry: 17 March 1945, Dülken

Since being back at Dülken, we have been over to München-Gladbach on two occasions. The 9th Army Headquarters is here, as is the 5th Aux Headquarters. It is here that the Post Exchange officers store is located and here that Lt. Col. Smith (9th Army surgical consultant) is to be found.

Since we have come up to the Rhine, there have been many road patrols out. They stop all vehicles and usually ask only the password. The purpose: Round up German soldiers who may be traveling in civilian clothes and prevent travel by German civilians, which is forbidden by the American Military Government.

We apparently act and appear like Americans, for many times

we have been caught out without knowing the password and often end up by having a patrol tell us what it is. On one occasion, when the password was "raft," we were stopped and the soldier asked us for the high sign.

Generally, they simply say "password" or "what is the password," but "high sign" puzzled me, and with a shrug of the shoulders I looked bewildered at Elmer. After but a moment's hesitation, the soldier went on to answer his own question by saying, "High hat," and motioned us on.

As we left the one-sided monologue, I still did not know what it was all about. I think we get by so easily sometimes because I drive myself, and the guards are surprised to find two officers in the front seat.

Everyone is sending home "loot." There are guns, items taken from homes and public buildings, etc. There is a rigid rule against looting, but the dividing line between looting and taking the spoils of war is thin and hard to determine in many cases.

Interestingly enough, Lt. Col. Hogland, who is universally disliked by his own unit, recently read an order forbidding looting, and that very afternoon (the day we rejoined) brought in a large sack full of ancient firearms taken, he said, from the city hall and given to him by the AMG. They were all pistols and the like of three or four wars ago and, I suppose, were interesting to collectors of such items.

Many people are sending home captured enemy arms not needed or used by our Army. Henry Swann sent home an electric train found in the attic of the Gestapo chief. I have sent home nothing.

17 March 1945

Dearest Ginny,

We still sit in bivouac at Dülken. All three platoons are together, and this makes a large crowd of men and officers. Our team is fairly lucky, though, for the field hospital suggested that we get in the room with them—already 8 there—and we said that it would crowd them too much, and wasn't there some other place?

Yes, there was. The chaplain and another officer were living in a house down the street, and he might have room. So we went down the street, and there were two small rooms on the second floor, full of debris. This seemed better to me, so we cleaned out the two rooms, managed to squeeze three cots into one room, and we plan to use the second room for a living room. It is about 6 x 12 feet.

The other houses up and down the street are occupied by civilians who seem to have more than the usual number of children. It is a very sunny, springlike day, and the kids are out skipping rope, playing ball, and yelling as if they were not "conquered people." The war seems very far away.

This house belonged to one Herr Dorn, who has fled before the Army because he was a prominent Nazi. The chaplain said that Dorn had a bank book that indicated that he had a deposit of some 23 million marks which, at the current rate of 10 cents per mark, ain't hay. I want to look at this myself, because the house, while it has some good functions, is a small house in the middle of the block and seems to me more like the house of a $40-a-week proletarian.

At any rate, Herr Dorn seems to have had an attractive daughter, Tilde, who occupied the room we are now in. There are stacks of letters from various suitors and a pile of cards that must have accompanied flowers and candy.

We have set up a potbellied stove in the "sitting room" and have electric lights from a generator down the street. Our water is carried in 5-gallon cans, but we do sport a private latrine, which in prewar days we would call an "outhouse."

I spent the day rearranging things. My baggage now consists of a bedroll, cot, box, footlocker, one duffel bag, gas mask, musette bag, and pistol belt. Quite a load at that. We have one duffel bag full of basins, water cans, buckets, and necessary things for living. You see, we carry everything with us.

Love and kisses and everything, H

Saturday 17 March 1945
1:30 P.M.

Dearest Ginny,

Yesterday the early December mail, which was on a ship that had mechanical trouble, arrived at the front, and I got your letters of December 8, 9, and 10.

Today has been one of those days while we were at Baesweiler, which was the first time this platoon had received patients. I thought we did not do a good job taking care of the patients—the X-ray bogged down, the shock teams did not function well, and I was not too happy about it. That is why I was disappointed about coming back here.

The humorous thing about it is that the colonel of the hospital got the teams all together while we were away and made a little speech in which he said he was proud of the way things went in the first action, and particularly of the third platoon (the one at Baesweiler). Furthermore, the third platoon was commended by the division and corps commanders.

When the division commander was there, I think he was won over by the swept floors, which, of course, is important. The corps commander stopped and asked a patient how he was, and the patient selected a word to respond that gave the impression that he was being well taken care of. The patient said he was comfortable. Of such small things are good impressions made.

To do a better job we have got to have better shock teams, and I asked Colonel Gay, but he really has very little to do with the shifting of teams, and tomorrow I am going to see Colonel Smith and tell him we have got to have better teams or else not to expect too much.

Yesterday Lehman Guyton stopped by, and I took him up to see Colonel Smith. Guyton is anxious to get out of his present unit. Smith told him that in about two weeks he thought he might be able to make a change, if his CO would let him go, and this latter might be a hitch. At any rate, Lehman will feel better for the effort having been made.

This afternoon we are having a little professional meeting on blood, and I am going to make a little statement about Rh, although I know very little about it to say. I will describe a case which could very well be a reaction.

I never cease to dream of the day we shall again be side by side in facing the problems and happiness of the world.

All my love, H

17 March 1945
9:50 P.M.

My dearest Ginny,

You have asked me to tell you a little about my companions, and I thought tonight I would talk about Elmer, who is now about six feet from me, shuffling through his letters while he is making some cocoa on the stove in the next room.

Elmer is a string-saver. If you want anything, Elmer's got it. His bedroll is a hardware shop, with hammer, nails, screwdriver, pliers, etc., etc. He carried a small saw, until about a week ago, and gave it away because he never used it. Since then he and I have wanted it a couple of times.

It is very good to have someone like this on the team, especially if we have plenty of room while moving and especially for somebody like Ken, who is very improvident.

I fall between and collect some things, but not nearly to the extent Elmer does. He is about my age, actually a year or two older, and was in practice with an older man in Ontario, California—a general practice in OB/Pediatrics, assisting at operations when he referred a case, and perhaps giving the anesthetic.

He took the Army course in anesthesia at Brooke Hospital under Winter, and he is a capable, if slow, anesthetist. He never throws anything away, and he hates to pass up anything that is hard to get in the States.

Among his Christmas packages was a bottle of "hemo"[the name of a dry powder that, added to hot water, makes a terrible drink], which he does not particularly care for. But he has carried around that "hemo" until he is now trying to get somebody to drink it, and failing that, he has undertaken a campaign to drink some "hemo" each night until it is all gone. As a matter of fact, the cocoa he is brewing on the stove is "hemo," and I am going to help him with it tonight, because I am hungry, and we plan to finish up Mary's fruitcake.

Elmer has sent home more packages than anyone in the hospital, and by now his wife must have added a room to the house to accommodate the really awful oil paintings, bric-a-brac, etc., he has sent.

He has also sent his daughter, age 4, metal toys that he acquired because they are unavailable in the States. This may be a good reason, but it seems to me that our children really do not need these things.

Elmer is the provider of the household. He maintains a breadbox acquired from a German home. He provides bread, butter (when available), coffee, cream, and sugar. He tells Ken and me to swipe a can of cream or some sugar, or whatever, hot from the mess, but we never do, and poor Elmer finally gets it himself.

The "hemo" is now ready, and Alice and Ken have come in, and we are going to have a little private supper.

Love, H

Sunday 18 March 1945

Darling Ginny,

Your comment about our postwar plans is music to my ears. When it is all said and done, my ideas can be summed up in your words, "Really, it makes little difference to me what the work is; with you, anything would be interesting and productive."

Our essential problem, then, is the mechanics of it. Where do we work, for whom, and how do we support ourselves doing it? As I said before, this problem solves itself if we have a good idea for money, because experimental work can always be found for a suitable idea. I feel very strongly that the cancer field is sterile, except for a new idea involving a new technique or at least the application of a technique new to the cancer field.

I shall constantly have our future life in mind as I go our paths, and perhaps jointly we will get our idea.

The idea I have now is that I love you, H

21 March 1945
1:30 P.M.

Dearest Ginny,

All three platoons of this hospital are in bivouac here together in Dülken. There is very little to do, but we have a class in something at 10:00—military censorship this morning, for example. Ken, Alice, Elmer, and I have talked about playing bridge ever since we have been together, and tonight may be the night.

It is useless to plan ahead or depend too much on previously made plans, as someone is constantly thinking up some bright idea. It is essentially true that you should not figure on anything involving the nurses, because some artilleryman or infantryman will sweep in about 6:00 and take the nurses off. Alice will go in spite of a tentative engagement with Ken, like for this evening.

I privately accuse her of playing hard to get and being frequently indifferent, and this always brings forth a loud denial. But I cannot help but believe it is true. I tell her she is going to outsmart herself.

The romance between Ken and Alice, if you call it that, is hard to figure. Sometimes weeks go by and they seem not to pay too much attention to each other, as when we were at Wellen. And then everything changes, and, like now, Ken gets in regularly at 2:00 A.M.

We ask him in the morning where he has been, and he says at the officers club, which is probably true, because about one block down the street from the school where we are staying is an ex-tavern that has been taken over for a club. There is a billiard table, a small card table in one room, and in the other, a piano and bar with small tables.

We have Belgian beer about three nights a week. It is, I suppose, a typical German beer-drinking place and immediately identifies itself as not American, because the music piled up on the piano is Mozart, Beethoven, Wagner, and the like, rather than boogie-woogie. We often go to the club after the movie, and I often pass up the movie because the room is crowded.

The boys found a shoe factory, which was pretty well ruined by bombs, but which had several hides in good condition. These they took as spoils of war, and when we arrived, John Hill, George Coe, and Henry Swann and others were making billfolds, pistol holsters, letter cases, and the like.

They had also come upon captured guns and pistols of all descriptions and still are engaging in polishing, shining, and cleaning them. Most of these are being sent home as souvenirs or gifts. I am not interested in the guns, but if I had gotten here when there was some leather left I might have made something.

All my love, H

23 March 1945

Dearest Ginny,

The hospital advertised that it had a barber, and I thought I would try him out. As I sat in the chair, the barber got out a piece of Kleenex and put it around my neck. This was most unusual, as an old dirty towel is the best one can expect.

Then he would turn my head in a jerky sort of way, step away about three feet, come up with a decision, and come in a sweeping motion to snip off a lock here and there.

I immediately got the impression that he must have been something other than a professional barber in civilian life, and I was about to ask him when he said, "Um, you're the first major's hair I ever cut." The platoon commander is still a captain, and we were the first team assigned. It appeared a little bad for a good haircut, but I did not think it mattered and so stuck it out.

At the end, I found that I had slid way down in the chair, as if trying to get away from him. Actually, he did not do such a bad job. He was a farmer in civilian life and had just picked up barbering a few weeks before, as there was no one else to do it.

We have had a few officers in the 5th Aux take up barbering in the same way, but no one on our team, so that I usually catch a cut on the fly somewhere.

The papers speak of tremendous numbers of bombers being out, and I can believe it, as I do not think there has been a minute that a plane has not been in some part of the sky. We are still in bivouac.

Love and kisses, H

WE WERE FINALLY sent up to the 108th Evacuation Hospital at Kempen, where we operated on only two patients, both of them prisoners of war.

The first was Adolf Merroisch, who was wounded about 3:45 PM on 24 March. I got to him at 10:00 that same night. He had a penetrating wound of the abdomen with prolapse of the omentum.

Curiously enough, at laparotomy, which took only one hour, we could find no wound within the abdomen. A bullet simply made an incision in the abdominal wall without otherwise causing any damage. During operation, the patient had a mild ether convulsion, which was controlled by the Pentathol.

The other patient I operated on at Kempen was Karl Goofenbaker, a prisoner of war who was wounded about 3:15 PM 24 March and was admitted about 8:30 PM that same day. He had a penetrating wound of the left chest, which was sucking, and therefore he had considerable dyspnea.

As soon as the sucking wound was closed and the chest aspirated, the patient breathed normally, and he seemed to recover smoothly.

He was the last patient we operated on before crossing the Rhine. On this same day we were reassigned to the 48th Field Hospital, 3rd Platoon, for the crossing.

THE HIGH COMMAND did not seem to agree about the best strategic plan for crossing the Rhine. Montgomery had always thought that the war could be ended more quickly by crossing the Lower Rhine and going straight for Berlin across rather flat territory. His concept led Eisenhower to approve in September the ill-fated airborne MARKET GARDEN operation.

Despite that costly failure, Eisenhower clung to the idea of crossing the Lower Rhine. To do this he would have to divert a major portion of supply to the British. This meant that the 12th Army Group probably would have to go on the defensive and that there would be a single crossing of the Rhine.

General Omar Bradley explains in his memoir that he was very much opposed to this particular plan. He thought that it would be far better to cross, not only where Montgomery wanted, but also higher upriver, more or less in the region of Frankfurt, so that there would be a two-pronged attack across the Rhine. The two prongs would unite somewhere in the region of Paderborn.

That plan would effectively encircle the Ruhr Valley and its great industrial complex, which was supplying the tanks and guns used by the German army.

The dilemma was resolved, almost by chance, when units of the U.S. First Army seized the Ludendorff Bridge across the Rhine at Remagen, fourteen miles above Bonn. The bridgehead that the Allies established on the east bank of the Rhine led to the Autobahn from Frankfurt eastward and essentially sealed the commitment of Allied forces to the two-pronged encirclement of the industrial Ruhr.

Operation PLUNDER began on 23 March. PLUNDER was the code name for the assault crossing north of the Ruhr by the British, which occurred beside XXX Corps near Rees.

On 24 March, Ninth Army crossed at Wesel; the 30th Division— including all of its regiments (the 119th, the 117th, and the 120th abreast). XVIII Corps' First Allied Airborne Army, dropped the British Sixth Army and the U.S. airborne divisions east of the Rhine, north and northeast of Wesel.

Three teams from the 5th Aux rode gliders in this operation. The U.S. 13th Airborne Division could not be used because of a shortage of aircraft. The division most important to the 5th Aux was the 79th, which crossed at 3:00 AM on the twenty-fourth. The crossing regiments were the 315th, the 313th, and, later, the 314th. They cleared the town of Friedrichsfeld of remaining German soldiers that we were to occupy two days later.

Actually, the 48th Field Hospital, 3rd Platoon, with its attached auxiliary surgical groups—we among them—crossed the Rhine on 26 March. No shooting greeted us. Upriver from the pontoon bridge on which we crossed were riflemen in boats that slowly motored back and forth, their marksmen prepared to shoot any floating mine that might come down the river.

Baesweiler, Germany, February-March 1945. An eight-inch gun just beside our schoolhouse field hospital. One could hear and feel blasts from these guns.

Dülken, Germany, March 1945. "In Dülken everyone greets With Heil Hitler!"

Dülken Germany, March 1945. Checking out a German rifle. A dangerous thing to do, as left-behind enemy weapons were sometimes booby trapped.

Chapter 10

Letters from Home
8 February-22 March 22 1945

*I*N FEBRUARY 1945, PRESIDENT ROOSEVELT, BRITISH Prime Minister Winston Churchill, and Soviet dictator Joseph Stalin met in the Crimean resort city of Yalta for the Big Three Conference that essentially shaped the political and economic destiny of post-World War II Europe and, unhappily, set the stage for a half century of East-West Cold War.

And Allied armies cracked the Siegfreid Line.

On the home front, 3.5 million American women were working alongside men in defense factories. More than sixteen million Americans—overwhelmingly male, but also more than 270,000 women—were in uniform.

———————

February 8, 1945
10:30 P.M.

Dearest Honey Bunny,

Still no mail. Actually, it has only been four days, but it seems like a month. I have reread the poor little V-mail from January 23 until it is threadbare.

It is nice to know that you had an opportunity to sleep in a real bed for a change. I wonder if you will have insomnia when you get home from being "shut in"?

The news tonight says that the big northern offensive is really on. I wonder if somewhere over there you are on the move. Are you permitted to tell me how you move? Trucks, jeeps, staff car, train, on foot, etc.?

I am really very familiar with most of your surroundings, as I dream about them in detail almost every night. It doesn't take a Freud to help me figure that out. Everything is very distinct, except the people. You are the only dear one.

The symphony last night was very enjoyable. "Gaudiamus Igature" and Shostakovich's new symphony. The Russian composer's symphony is a real musical exercise for me and, therefore, very interesting. It was melodious only in spots, I thought.

I always do miss you so much, though, when I hear music. They had a very comical part on the xylophone that you would have loved.

Dr. Guidemia, our Portuguese friend, leaves tomorrow. He requested me to send you his address in Lisbon in case you should come there. He would be most charmed to meet you.

Rumor has it that all of #118 is to be rotated, and Jack Whitridge will be the first home. Poor Jean Stiffler is now worrying about getting Bill stationed close by. That would be very nice. Job, children, etc. If you were in Seattle, Washington, I'd be there.

Did I tell you poor Henry Bennett was slated to go out again with an evac, but had a recurrence of malaria and so escaped?

Here's hoping for more mail in the A.M. and the end of the war by the first of March.

With all my love, Ginny

Tuesday, February 13, 1945
9:00 P.M.

Dearest Honey Bunny,

Today the exquisite piece of Belgian lace arrived. I adore it and shall cherish it always. Mother says it will be perfect for a cap for B's wedding veil. A bit previous, eh?

Your letter of January 7 also arrived, in which you mentioned the possibility of a leave to Paris. I am still toying with the idea of taking British children back, if it is possible.

I suppose I would only do it if it seemed that you might have some time which we could spend together. It's a pleasant thought, even if nothing comes of it.

The conference of the Big Three has provoked a great deal of talk, and I hope more. I haven't as yet been over the newspaper, so I don't have a clear idea of the conclusions.

Willie has been highly excitable in the past few days. I don't know what gets into him. He hates to see me read a letter and today shrieked at the top of his lungs. I really believe he doesn't get enough exercise and trust that as the weather gets better and he gets out more he will be less explosive.

This Saturday we are planning to have Mr. and Mrs. Coler and the Boyles for tea. Mrs. Coler has called me on numerous occasions, and I have missed her practically every time, so I have decided I will just have to set a date.

Donnie hasn't heard from Joe since last Tuesday and presumes that he is now on the high seas. Did I tell you that Eleanor thinks Donnie may have a bicornuate uterus? That might account for her obstetrical difficulties. The Year Book of OB/GYN is out and your article is reviewed. I am certainly going to get our paper written this year to keep your name in print. Has anything of interest about which you might write turned up?

I hate to, but I am beginning to wonder about your summer uniforms. Do you use them in the ETO? If so, I am afraid I should be thinking of sending them by the time you get an answer back to this. I am still back a number of letters, so I hope for a landslide sometime soon.

The picture of B is not good, but I am sending it for what it's worth.

I was thinking today of our Mexican trip and how much we enjoyed it, even though it was rough in spots. How much we have in common, and how wonderful to have so much fun together.

Have I ever told you how nice it is to have a husband to whom you can really talk? But, then, there are so many wonderful things about you that I am sure I couldn't begin to tell you all.

Until we meet, all my love, Ginny

February 14, 1945
(Valentine's Day) 11:00 P.M.

My darling,

What a lovely Valentine's Day, the best I have ever had. Yesterday the exquisite Brussels lace arrived and a letter of January 7, and today two wonderful letters, February 2 and 7. This is indeed a remarkable time, and I feel ashamed of myself for feeling so sad last week. However, except for two V-mails, I had received no letters since yours of January 17, which I had received and responded to. As you say in your letter of February 2. The mail is surely freakish.

I hope the 600 colored WACs are good. I hear that they are to handle the mail. I received a letter from Elmer, dated January 29, in which he said my Christmas box had finally arrived. He sounded pretty homesick.

In your February 2 letter I was delighted to hear that you have had such nice trips to Brussels. It is indeed a beautiful capital, as I remember it. We stayed in the hotel on the plaza directly across from the train station.

The Belgians were celebrating their 100th anniversary when we were there and had fireworks in the plaza. How I would love to stroll through those beautiful streets with you and enjoy the numerous excellent pieces of sculpture.

I was also pleased to hear you had received some letters, and I also enjoyed hearing that you liked the pictures I labored over. B was cute on the Christmas film, wasn't she? I am anxiously awaiting more letters to hear the details of your trips.

Of course, the most exciting thing was to learn that I am to receive a charcoal portrait of Papa. I can hardly wait. I am interested in learning that you will move. I wonder if you have had any trouble with the floods caused by the breaking of the Roer dams.

I still do my best about the books for your French tutor. The weight is the most difficult thing.

I shall also pay the two bills you forwarded.

Today I took Willie out to stay with Ess and Ruth, and he enjoyed himself immensely. But he is so pleased to see B when he comes home that he is gratifying. He insists that she be put on the floor so she can "kramble" (scramble). He further told me, "I won't hurt her, I won't pick her up or love her too tight," all with gestures.

The news is good, but not nearly rapid enough for me. I grow more impatient *of every minute away from you. I miss you more, not less, and my greatest pleasure is planning for our postwar future together.*

All my love, Mama

Thursday, February 15, 1945
9:30 P.M.

My darling,

Today again a letter, old, January 20, but nonetheless lovely. You say that my letters are your greatest pleasure, and of course this is what I love to hear. I sometimes reread them and am a little ashamed of them, as I am sure they are not very amusing, and they seem to repeat "I love you" so often that it becomes monotonous, but it's true.

Willie was sick last night with a high fever and a beginning cold, so I stayed home and kept him in bed. This evening he was quite himself again. The climate is actually horrible for colds. I have had a sinus infection since early in December. B also has a runny nose, but does not seem sick.

I hope you have been as well as your letters indicate. Someday tell me about the people with whom you live. You practically never mention anyone specifically.

I have been missing you very acutely again, as I do every so often, and then it settles down to a dull ache. I have figured that, even if the war is over in several months, I think I would be lucky if you were to get home before Christmas. I just don't see how I can live through that. I hope the little guardian angel hasn't deserted us.

I am still excited over the prospect of receiving your charcoal portrait.

All my love, Ginny

Saturday, February 17, 1945

Dearest Poppy,

For "Poppy" you are to our son and heir. Willie insisted upon seeing the colored pictures again tonight, and you are there. "That's my Poppy." He reminds me of how much we liked magic-lantern pictures as children. If I put one in upside down, he says, "Don't bother, I like it that way."

He has a queer sense of humor. He now sings "Yankee Doodle," and when it comes to the macaroni, he always "calls it macatutti." Then, he nearly dies laughing and says, "I'm a funny boy."

You have a great deal to live up to, as everything is "when Poppy comes home." He is going to have a swimming pool, a dog, some sheep and wear only "diders." He still has an aversion to clothes. It's worth your life to keep shoes on him.

Your letters of January 11 and 14 arrived today. This has been a banner week, with a letter or so every day. You have had enough experience with winter to know what you think of the type of climate to live in.

Of course, a bedfellow would make the nights more attractive, even if we did have cold feet. I am awaiting eagerly the berets, sabots, and doilies. I will let you know about the doilies. I think everything you have sent has been excellently chosen and quite worthwhile.

This evening, after bedding the babies down, I went back and, on the way, I saw the Schilpps. It is Allen's birthday and they had spent the afternoon with the big Schilpps. Allen had just received your letter of December 5. He looks good. He has gained weight and looks years younger.

Betty also seems well, and the children were lovely. Bobby talks a little now. The difference between him and Willie is amazing in that respect. All send their love and said that they would write. Allen says his school is terrific and that he will be a full-fledged doc when he finishes. He is half through.

I finished the frog-test paper today and feel that it has a definite place, especially as we are sure Weisman is associated with the Paramount Aquarium and, therefore, his results are probably prejudiced.

Next week we will get the moles, chorios, and miscarriages together. They are really fascinating, but I am afraid they will require years-more work.

We are also working on a new Vitamin E method. Did I tell you I have an excellent 17-ketosteroid method? I would like to do something with Vitamin B also, but right now it is not practical. How sweet life would be if only you were here, and how tasteless life is without you.

All my love, Ginny

P.S. Don't forget to tell me a little about your companions occasionally.

February 19, 1945
10:30 P.M.

My darling Papa,

How fortunate I am to have such a wonderful husband. Today four letters and the sweet Valentine collar. In your January 19 letter you tell me about your "orientation" lecture and the fact that it might be several months after fighting stops before men get home. I hope you aren't trying to break an Army of Occupation [tour of duty] to me gently.

I find the pictures taken on Christmas Day very interesting, and I am sure they will be worthwhile in later years. I do like the picture of Yvonne Roose. She looks very nice and intelligent. I repeat—isn't it possible for you to find something of medical interest to report? I could do any shaping up of information for you if you would send the main material.

Your description of Aachen is also fascinating. Someday we may visit these areas ourselves; i.e., together. Your dear little "I love you" V-mail is also a treasure, and last but perhaps best is the letter of February 10—very good timing, I think.

I am glad in a way that you are back at work, although it increases my anxiety somewhat. I am sure you find it more stimulating and worthwhile. Your remarks about Col. Smith make him sound very sensible. Who is he when he's home?

I await your portrait anxiously. I will repeat that the exquisite piece of Brussels lace arrived some days ago, and it is quite the loveliest piece I have ever seen. Your taste, as usual, is superb.

Today at lunch we learned that Dr. Blalock is doing operations for the "Tetralogy of Fallot" [a serious congenital heart defect]. He now wants to do them on newborn infants. He anastomoses the innominate artery [carrying blood from the heart] and pulmonary vein.

I hate to think of your living in dirty cellars, but I suppose you are safer there. Hope the whole mess will soon be over. Radio news commentator Fulton Lewis says it's a matter of weeks and months at the most. Don't worry about my taking the first boat. I will be on the first plane.

Our remembrance of quarrels is interesting. I don't regard the St. Augustine affair as a quarrel. I was really ill that day and just didn't feel like traveling. As I said, I don't recall the cause of the other two affairs, only the making up.

How I would love to hear you sing "Kiss Me Again" or "Oh, Promise Me."
Do you remember that in the little Plymouth roadster?
Until we meet, my sweet, do take the best care of yourself.

All my love, Ginny

> Tuesday, February 20, 1945
> 11:00 P.M.

My dearest Honey Bunny,

I never cease to be amazed at people who say, "What can you find to write about every day?" I could write two letters and then find I had forgotten something I wanted to say.

No mail today, so I have reread the four from yesterday and two from Saturday. I have also played my favorite game of picking out the prize-winning letter for the month. The month of January being now almost complete, let me say again I think an occasional V-mail a good idea, although not too often. How quickly do mine come through? Shall I resume the custom of writing one every other day, or would one or two a week be sufficient? Can you read them after I write them?

Willie was really adorable today. I do wish you could be here to romp with him. He now stands on my shoulders and walks about the house. I can just make it. He will sit for hours if you tell stories, recite poetry, or read to him.

Tonight Mary was playing liar pretending to be somebody else, and he insisted on having the crib bars between them. Such shrieks you have never heard. He thought it was great sport. It was really rather almost too much. Finally, he ran out of the room, down the hall, and into the bathroom, with Mary right behind him. He slammed the door and said, "I don't like that funny kind of liar!"

B has had a little cold and last night got off to coughing. I am always afraid that when the children have colds they will aspirate something, so I went in, took her up, and gave her some cough medicine, and then took her to bed with me. You would adore her. She is so cuddly. She just snuggles right down and does no wiggling like Willie.

Ruth and Ess still have colds, but are better. I read your letters to them as usual.

Don't joke about my taking a boat over if you don't really mean it. I am seriously considering it. How much do you think we could afford to expend on such a luxury?

I love to hear about your work in detail and only hope you won't be too busy, for my own peace of mind. I am glad you are snug and warm, but it must be disconcerting to be dirty all the time. However, don't be foolhardy and move out of a safe place.

We have about completed our plans for the Travel Club, and I hope it will be interesting for them.

This year would have been ideal for skiing in Western Maryland. There has been snow since November. What fun to get caught in a drift at midnight.

Do take care of yourself, and God bless you.

All my love, Ginny

February 21, 1945
11:00 P.M. (V-mail)

My dearest Honey Bunny,

My weekly V-mail. Do let me know if it is worthwhile.

I am thinking more and more about the Army of Occupation. If the 9th Army should be it, would that mean that the 5th Auxiliary Surgical Group would automatically stay too? It would be foolish to keep such an outfit in occupied territory. But let that be as it may. I would like to see some kind of Army occupation, and soon.

We are all well, and I am thinking that this time last year we were anticipating home for a furlough. How short, but how sweet, that time seemed. Tomorrow will be George Washington's birthday, and it makes me think of the Grachur Club. What wonderful evenings we spent in the canoe, and how lovely to sleep in your arms.

I am eagerly awaiting the news of your new location. What a pity our system* is not too exact, as I frequently wonder when names of small villages are mentioned if you have been there. Do take care of yourself, and come home to us soon.

All my love, Ginny

*Before Howard went overseas, the Joneses purchased two copies of a world atlas. Howard would place a sheet of stationary on his atlas map and stick a pinhole in the sheet, literally pinpointing where he was in Europe. In the letter he provided a clue to the atlas page number. Georgeanna placed the pin-pricked letter on the same page in her atlas.

Thursday, February 22, 1945
11:00 P.M.

My darling,

Just a V-mail to say that I received your wonderful letter of February 5. It was indeed inspiring, and it sets a truly splendid goal for us. The contemplation of it even enables me to do better work, even though alone.

I shall write in detail later, but now I am learning exactly what I will want to say tomorrow to the Travel Club. Would that you were here to lend me courage.

The news continues good, and if only I could think that there was even a remote possibility of joining you overseas, I should indeed be happy.

Do take care of yourself, my dear. Your love constantly sustains me.

All my love, Ginny

Friday, February 23, 1945
10:00 P.M.

Dearest Honey Bunny,

Today I received your beautiful letter "On Letter Writing." I feel that it is a lovely little essay. I am sure that no sweetheart receives more beautiful letters than I, and I think this in itself is a tribute to our love.

You speak of our work together in the postwar era, and I am sure I know what you are thinking of. I, too, have always felt a sense of, not only incompleteness, but also lack of fulfillment, as if much better things, bigger things, could be accomplished with a really combined effort.

That is more than interest and consultation, which I think we have always had. But even small projects have seemed to move along swiftly and smoothly when working with you. I agree that the practical points are difficult to work out so far apart. There are things which appeal to me in both the fields of endocrinology and cancer. But I am so out of touch with the "thought" in the cancer field that I would really have to do a little meeting-going to catch up.

The electron microscope has certainly seemed like an excellent approach, but surely the people who own them must be getting the "in" on such things. There is one in Baltimore. With you as inspiration and help, I am sure that we could work at the physiology of female reproduction, and it would undoubtedly have some clinical significance—how much I am not sure. An accomplishment in the field of cancer would be more spectacular and perhaps more gratifying.

Do you really think that there will be any chance for me to come to Europe, and how about bringing Willie? I think I shall, if possible. Just the thought gives me goose pimples.

I gave my paper this afternoon and did very credibly, too, I believe. I was handicapped by not being enthusiastic about the problem. The men, however, were fascinated and crowded around to see the "toad," so I suppose it was news to a number of them. Two men especially asked to be remembered to you—Lou Scheffy and George Kosmak.

Dr. Scheffy does not look well, and I judged he is depressed by having his 18-year-old son in the Marines. He is very attractive and wanted to know of Dr. DeSnow. Howard Taylor was there and really was the most intelligent discusser of Eleanor's paper and mine. She gave the chorionic and pregnanediol data very nicely. How I miss you, but, then, never a month passes when I don't.

All my love, and God bless you, Ginny

Sunday, February 25, 1945
11:00 A.M.

My darling,

Yesterday your letter of February 13 arrived, the letter in which you describe your anesthetic troubles. How I wish I could be there, as I am sure I could at least learn to do it to suit.

The war news is so wonderful that I am almost beginning to pack up for that boat trip.

Willie is sitting on the floor at my feet and sorting pictures. He really plays very nicely, for the most part, but he is very excitable—prone to shriek with pleasure. However, I am sure this is natural for little boys. He has just astounded me by practically saying all of "Little Orphan Annie." He will listen for hours while Mother or Mary recite to him and will listen to me reading A. A. Milne indefinitely.

He is pretty good at manual skills. He can throw a ball fairly straight, take off and put on his trousers, and put together a jigsaw puzzle. He does need his papa, however, and I hope he will not be too much older before he has him again.

B has three upper teeth, and I am afraid that she is missing her two eyeteeth, like her mama. She is fast outgrowing her baby stage.

It is spring out today, and we hope to get out shortly for some nice air. My thoughts are with you constantly, and I am wondering how busy you have been with casualties from the push.

I was never able to find a history of Europe that I thought suitable for you, so asked Carolyn Jones to look in New York. She tells me she has sent a history of France and one of Holland. I hope they are suitable.

I wonder if this will find you in Cologne. I have still been unable to locate a camera for you. Your other requests are, I trust, up-to-date.

This time last year we were spending your precious furlough together. The two days before you arrived seemed endless. What will they seem when you are returning this time?

As you say, every GI loves his wife or every wife loves her husband, but I am sure that no two people ever loved as we do. The comments and remarks others make prove it.

Your letters are continuous inspiration to me, and I only regret that alone I do not seem to have the drive or time to accomplish all that I seem to dream of.

Now that the Travel Club meeting is behind me, I shall turn with renewed energy to other things. We have many good problems which need only a little elbow grease to start them rolling, such as Vitamin E and corpus luteum function. The OTs need secretarial work, mainly, and I am going to try to get at it again.

What would I do without the little communication with you every day? When your letters come through as well as they did last week, life does not seem so bad. I still dream of a vacation with you somewhere in the mountains—our home over there—who knows? But with you I am in heaven.

All my love, Ginny

Sunday evening, February 25, 1945

My darling,

We have had a very nice Sunday. This morning, Willie and I went walking, and this afternoon, we had a real "at home." Mrs. Perkins and Marie came out and were very pleased with the children. They were really very nice with them, but later, when the crowds gathered, Willie was quite hilarious. Mrs. Snyder (Professor Snyder's wife) and her daughter, Francine, were here.

They were interested in the fact that you had been in Holland. Mrs. Snyder is Van Hoff's daughter. The Boyles called with Jimmy, and then the fun began. The boys were really very cute together, but rather noisy. They tussled and chased and, all in all, had a marvelous time. The result was that Willie went to sleep over his supper at 7:30. Such activity is exactly what he needs, and I will try to see that he has more of it as the weather gets better.

Donnie hasn't heard from Joe as yet (it has been three weeks), but she does not know whether he went as an engineer or as an M.D. How do you figure that?

B now tries to feed herself. She takes the spoon after it is filled. Donnie says she has her full quota of teeth (or will have), so I feel relieved. She also says that Willie's hernia is an inguinal one, and I am sure she is right, as the ring is very easily palpable now.

Have you ever run across anyone who has seen Lehman Guyton? He is with the 3rd Armored Division with the 1st Army. He is in some sort of medical unit, but I am not so sure. What about Tom Ambler? I can't wait for letters dated after this push, and I can't wait for the push to gain more momentum. If it seems slow to us here, how must slower it must seem to you who are at hand and so closely interested.

How I long for the day when we can once more plan for our future and family together. Just about this time of year we would begin to plan vacations, like the one at Williamsburg, sometimes with children, sometimes just alone, but always lovely because we are together.

Tomorrow starts a new era of effort in the laboratory, and as I work, I shall subconsciously think of our future work, and us together.

Do take care of yourself for us, and God bless you.

All my love, Ginny

Monday, February 26, 1945
11:00 P.M.

Dearest Honey Bunny,

Without a doubt I am the most fortunate of all women. Five letters today! The two latest are ones of February 14 and 16.

Let me say again, in case you have not received the letter, that your sweet Valentine collar arrived, strange as it may seem, on the 16th. I love it, and all the more, of course, because it has been recently caressed by your hands. I am glad you liked the pictures and will try to send the folder at once. It is really very flattering to think you want it.

I shall forward the letter of thanks to the Becks. Did you ever receive the letter in which I said she sent B such an adorable swimsuit? Also, I take it you have never received the recording of Willie's voice made back in September. I would like to have another made, but he doesn't like the idea.

Both children have been unusually cute today. This A.M. I asked Willie to tell Smitty what Jimmy Wharton looked like. "He looks like Howard," he replied. I had to laugh, because he really does.

Then, I read him the poem about "Mary Jane, crying with all her might and main," and he said, "She's afraid of the pressure cooker, I guess. Yes she is." I do wish you could see his eyes as big as saucers and his gesticulations telling me about something.

Tonight he and B just laughed out loud at each other when I put them to bed. He called her, "Hear B talking." It became so hilarious, Smitty had to go in and quiet it down. I am so pleased that they adore each other and hope it continues, but with such a wonderful father, how could they help not be superior?

All my love, Ginny

Tuesday, February 27, 1945
11:30 P.M.

My darling,

I have just returned from Journal Club at Dr. Richardson's, where I was "the whole show." Unfortunately, Dr. TeLinde was not present, as his comments are always interesting to me. However, Dr. Richardson is also very astute, and we had quite a nice and lively discussion. How I wish you could have been there.

The whole evening was made for me by the three letters I found waiting for me tonight, January 29 and February 18 and 19. In one letter you say that you are recording your cases, but I know what you mean when you say that clinical reports will not satisfy.

I know this, my dear, but I was thinking of a means to an end. I am still thinking, of course, in terms of a professorship somewhere or at least "keeping in the public eye." It was just a passing thought. If it does not apply, disregard it.

The field which appeals to me greatly is cancer work in blood—leukemia, etc. Perhaps I know so little about them, but I shall think along and look at the recent literature.

Both babies are well and adorable as usual. Ess and Ruth are fine. They were hostesses at the club Sunday night and had just returned from a Catonsville party today when I talked to them. If they maintain their proper nutrition, I think they really are all right.

How wonderful to hear from you so regularly.

All my love, Ginny

Wednesday, February 28, 1945
11:30 P.M.

My darling,

Again three letters, January 12 and 26 and February 11. What an extremely fortunate wife I am. This makes 11 letters in three days, and such beautiful ones. You say they may sound silly and uninteresting. They are neither, and every word is fascinating, and each is read at least three times the day it arrives and many times thereafter.

I am impressed by your progress in French and do hope that you will continue to be able to use it. By now, however, you are probably using German, or is fraternizing still "verboten"?

Donnie had lunch with me, and we had a most enjoyable time talking over medical-school days. She is so starved for "medicine" that it is sad.

How fortunate I am to have an intelligent husband. Joe is very much opposed to her working, and she freely admits that she believes it is because he has an inferiority complex about her better training.

Dr. Everett was very complimentary this A.M. about the Journal Club meeting which I conducted last night. He said he enjoyed it more than any he had attended. Did I also tell you that Miss King said George Kosmak was very complimentary about my xenopus presentation?

Willie and B are both fine and—did I tell you?—B now calls the dog's name, "Spot." She also has four upper teeth. B and Willie continue to be adorable together. He calls to her, "Don't 'ky' (cry) B. I'm coming." I must take some pictures this weekend, as both children are growing rapidly.

I hope that by now you are out of the cellar and that the mud has dried. I keep wondering if you could be more specific about locations. I think I know where you are, but I am not sure.

How wonderful if the war would be over and we could visit the French Alps together this summer. I, too, like new things, but it would be nice to continue them with some of those things we do so well together.

All my love, Ginny

March 1, 1945
11:00 P.M.

Dearest Honey Bunny,

Four more letters today, making 15 in the past four days, the last being February 21—record time. Your graphic description of what you, as a GI, think brings us ever closer together, because as I am a GI, I so frequently think exactly the same thoughts. What a great day when these thoughts become a reality.

I am so glad to hear that the record arrived, and I hope you will be able to hear Willie someday. The backup and voice, as well as the laugh, are Mama.

The question of the Rh transfusion may be answered in this manner: No adverse effect can be expected unless the man has previously been transfused and sensitized.

It would be interesting to know the Rh quality of the patient's blood if he has been previously transfused. If Rh negative, the old blood administered should be Rh negative. People here wonder about the amount of citrate administered with 5,000 cc of blood. Would it not be sufficient to cause hemolysis? Statistics show 15 percent of the population to be Rh-negative.

George W. Corner III is back from Leyte. He is ill, having lost 40 lbs., and looks ghastly, but is now on the upswing. He says that the Luzon campaign was a great surprise, as everyone thought that the casualties would be many more, much heavier, and the campaign at least six months.

We are now considering some work in the laboratory which would prove whether the germinal epithelium of the ovary in the human continues to produce primordial follicles (e.g., germinal cells) after birth and, also, that the granulosa cells are not inactive. There is a very nice piece of work in the rat ovary, which indicates that the theca and, to a lesser extent, the interstitial cells, that is, the stroma, of the ovary produce estrogen and that the granulosa cells are merely the proliferative phase of the corpus luteum and physiologically inactive until they reach the corpus luteum phase. The difficulty is in locating a refracting microscope.

We have just listened to the President's speech, and I hope that he is not as ill a man as he sounds. I really believe the guy is good and that he can probably cope with the situation as well as anyone.

Buddy Seegar is somewhere in France, and I will send you his address in case things quiet down, and you can see each other. He is a Lt. Col. His Lt. Col. is supposed to come through at any time. This would give us a Col., Lt. Col, Major, and Captain, plus a Lt. J.G. in the family.

Receiving such lovely letters just makes me constantly want more, but most of all it makes me want you.

Until that day my dear, all my love, Ginny

Friday, March 2, 1945
11:00 P.M.

My darling,

What wonderful news tonight. We are so hoping that the push to the Rhine will end the German phase of the war. I am also praying that you are safe—I do hate those jeeps, trucks, etc., to say nothing of German rockets. It is getting harder and harder for me to wait to see you.

My constant strength is the thought of our postwar life together and remembrance of our past. This is why my two favorite letters are the one describing your ideas of our future together with the one describing your memory of our love together. Both give me goose pimples and chills up and down my spine. Here's to our reunion, dear, and may it be soon.

Willie is as cute as ever. I do wish you could see him. He saw a boy in a white coat and asked Ruth, "What's he got on?" She said, "A coat." But this did not suit him. Finally, he said, "He must work in a laboratory, I think." She fainted.

You know the little rhyme, "Ladybug, ladybug, fly away home. Your house is on fire, your children will burn?" He also changes this to your "tatoes will burn."

I am afraid he is ruined, for "children should be seen and not heard." We will never be able to keep him quiet. B is crawling around now, and he loves it. They are good company for one another.

All my love, Ginny

Sunday, March 4, 1945
2:30 P.M.—V-mail

My darling,

I missed writing yesterday because I attended the Women's Medical Society. Grant Ward spoke on carcinoma of the breast, and it was fun to hear about cancers again.

I helped him with his slides and kept thinking how much better you could have been in giving such a talk.

The old girls are really a group. A number of them look like scarecrows, but they are all really interesting people. It did my heart good.

Did I tell you that they (WFBR) asked me to talk on the "Women of the Week" program? Both Dr. TeLinde and I decided my work was a little too spectacular to lend itself well to radio, so I was spared that.

It is a beautiful day, and were you here, it would be ideal down on the Magothy River. I trust that the weather is as good where you are and that the insane Germans will finally decide it is time to stop sacrificing everything for their Führer.

All my love, Ginny

Sunday, March 4, 1945
10:00 P.M.

My darling,

We are so excited by the news. I so hope that it is true that the Rhine bridges have been gained. Of course, I know that I shouldn't count my chickens, but I do think it might be possible that I could see you perhaps within six months.

At one time, that would have seemed a terrifically long time, and it really does now, but to have some definite time in sight is a comfort. When you receive this, we will probably know.

Willie and B continue to grow apace. B is not satisfied very well in her pen now and has to be allowed to crawl about on the floor. This is also because Willie likes to have her do it, so Willie is really a comedian, and I do wish you could see him, as I am sure you would enjoy him too. He is fascinated by anything pertaining to animals. He will surely have to have a dog and at least a cat when he has his own home again.

He woke up last night (for the first time in ages) and was wide awake, and he began to tell me, "Lions eat bones like dogs. They have long tails. The butterflies mustn't come in the house. They are not mosquitoes, but they might sting you." When I remonstrated and said I didn't think butterflies would hurt you, he said, "Yes, I think they might. They have long things on front. I think they do."

Such rigmarole goes on indefinitely. He thinks of the strangest things. He now wants to know, "What is blood pressure? Like a pressure cooker?" He is still definitely afraid of the pressure cooker and will not let the family go near it, if he can help it. He stops everyone en route to the kitchen, saying, "Don't go out there, the pressure cooker's out there." He can now put his shoes on, as well as his trousers, under supervision, to be sure he gets the back and front straight and the right and left straight.

I keep thinking, as of course I have always done, but it is difficult to write about our postwar work. I can't tell you how glad I am that you want us to work together experimentally.

My ideas center on gyn problems always, and this is not too good, as it is limited if it is practically my only experience with cancer. I feel that perhaps some other branch would be more fertile, and I continue to toy with the idea of immunological factors, as I did in blood dyscrasias.

In the meantime we are going with endocrinology, and perhaps if you could be interested in it we might work from this field. With a little help and encouragement we could solve the problems of the human menstrual cycle, or did you think it was solved?

Really, it makes little difference to me. With you, anything would be interesting and productive.

Do take care of yourself and come home very soon, as life without you is wasted.

All my love, Ginny

> Monday, March 5, 1945
> 12:00 P.M.

My darling,

I have just returned home from dinner with the Joneses and the Don Cossack choir—an extremely enjoyable concert. But it again served to emphasize something I have noticed many times before. Work without you is without zest or inspiration, but play without you is heartbreaking. I would much prefer coming home to the children.

The Cossacks were excellent, and I do think we appreciate Russian music probably best of all.

The Joneses asked me to dinner especially to talk to Virginia (Brad's youngest daughter). She thinks she is interested in nursing or technical work. She is apparently quite a problem, as she has lacked discipline and supervision, as do many children of divorced parents, and has almost become a delinquent.

Brad is patiently trying to salvage her, if possible. I am afraid it will be difficult, as her mother tears down as rapidly as he builds. It is tragic, as she is most attractive and bright, and also, they say, the man has no interest in marrying her and she has no interest in giving him up. He is now in the Merchant Marine, and they hope he will locate in another port.

Your letter of February 9 arrived today, and I am still more discouraged about your surroundings. I trust that by now you are in a less-desolate spot. After being elated last night, I am again discouraged today. Those dumb Deutschmen can't call it quits.

You ask which is my room. I am in the room that was Mama's and where the furniture has always been. The children are in the room where Uncle Will was. They have been there since his death.

King writes more encouragingly about rotation. Perhaps when you receive this he will be home. All of this discourages me, as it will have been four months at least from the time it looked fairly definite that he would get home, and we have even begun to hope for us. But, darling, although I do become impatient, your wonderful letters and the thoughts of our life together and what we will do after the war make life really worth living after all. Having a husband like you and

*memories like ours and plans for the future like ours is far better than having any
other husband on the spot.*

You say some people have colds—I do hope you have kept well.

All my love, Ginny

P.S. The allotment came today and is $240.

*Tuesday, March 6, 1945
11:00 P.M.*

Dearest Honey Bunny,

*Today your letters of February 22 and 24 arrived. You were terribly busy,
but sounded well. I do hope that you will get enough rest and not be exposed to too
many upper respiratory infections. I am even more impatient with each day of this
senseless war. The only consolation with the passing of each day is that it brings
me closer to you.*

*We have another man with a chorioepithelioma [a very malignant tumor],
and perhaps a woman also. Things never happen singly. We spent the day frantically
doing pregnanediols, but we won't have them pipetted until this A.M., so we don't
know the answer.*

Did I tell you that Kosmak (editor of The American Journal of
Obstetrics and Gynecology) *was amazed at the number of moles we have
studied. If we get two more chorios, he will never believe us.*

*I am also getting my cases of amenorrhea and thyroid therapy together and
hope to have some information on blood cholesterol. It would be a nice group, as I
think it is going to mean something. But to me all of this means very little, for
Papa is not here to enjoy it with me.*

*Jim Plagge wrote that he had received a nice letter from you. He is a good
correspondent.*

*Just about this time of year we should be planning vacations. How about
spending it in Europe this spring? And I am not joking.*

All my love, Ginny

*P.S. I said in yesterday's letter that the allotment is still $240. Also, who-all is
with you now? I don't know the shock team.*

Wednesday, March 7, 1945

Dearest Honey Bunny,

The package with berets and sabots and also lovely, cheery lace doilies arrived today. All are excellent. The doilies are very nice indeed—handwoven linen thread. We shall keep them ourselves. Willie adores his sabot and beret. I look precious in the berets.

I also received letters of February 26 and 27. It is wonderful to hear so promptly and to have a husband who writes even when so busy.

I really do not let myself worry about you. You know that is my disposition, but, of course, especially when there is activity, it is a wonderful satisfaction to know everything is progressing.

I long to be with you and am so pleased that you are pleased with the way things are going. Of course, I know it is the best all-around surgical service, and probably the speediest.

It is interesting that Bill B. has no choice with the evac situation. I am sure that whatever turns up for you will be right, for our little angel won't desert us now.

Annabelle Brack really thinks that Dr. TeLinde is going to get Bozo out of the Army. What a shame it won't be someone with a little better disposition, and I don't think the Army will have improved him.

Willie answered the phone today. It happened to be Father, but they say he did it beautifully, "Dr. Seegar's residence," etc. In another year I will have him in the laboratory.

This didn't get finished or mailed, so it will be in addition to today's.

All my love, Ginny

Sunday, March 10, 1945
9:00 P.M.

My darling,

I missed writing yesterday and have felt something lacking ever since. My greatest satisfaction is my letter at the end of the day.

The Journal of the AMA *for this week, March 3, has in it an interesting article about cancer by Spencer. It embodies many of the principles which I believe to be true and which are too involved to write in a letter. It seems to me that the "inciting" factors in leukemias and lymphosarcomas have never been worked out, and the problem in doing so would also be closely related to immunity, etc. It is a difficult but rather challenging field.*

There is also a letter in the issue about the results of forward surgery in the British Army auxiliary surgical teams. Percent recovery for various wounds: 68% for penetrating wounds of the abdomen, 90% for nonpenetrating abdominal, 46% thoracoabdominal, 85% perforating chest wounds. I thought you might be interested and might read this before the AMA Journal arrives.

The war news continues to be good, and, if the bridgehead only holds, perhaps we can yet vacation in the Alps.

I am anxiously awaiting news, as I think perhaps you may have moved by now. I am sure you are as anxiously optimistic as I. Sometimes it seems as if I couldn't wait another minute to see you. I also wonder about what the evac situation is.

I have tickets for Aida April 2. You will be beside me every minute, but how I wish I could feel you.

Lib writes very nice letters from Charleston. I believe she is as happy as she has ever been.

We have just had a call from Jane who reported that a letter dated February 25th said King's replacements were in India. This means that he is perhaps on his way home now. I do hope this is true and that he won't be sent out of the country again.

Willie is getting to be such a boy. Tonight I had to go back to the lab to inject some rats and he went with me. He said, "Mama, go faster than the other cars." I told him we have to wait for Papa for speeding.

Donnie has heard from Joe, and he is in an infantry-replacement pool in France. He said he would write as often as possible, but, as they were moving, it was difficult. I didn't say that that never bothers Howard, but it was nice to think it.

Sometimes our love seems so perfect that it scares me. Were two people ever so blessed?

I love knowing the exact setup of your hospital and living quarters. All these things help me form more-exact mental pictures of you, of what you operate in, e.g., clothes. Have you or anyone else used the trucks for operating?

Tomorrow will be Sunday, and no mail. How will I endure?

All my love, Ginny

Monday, March 12, 1945
9:00 A.M.

Dearest Honey Bunny,

I went to a cocktail party given by Frances Snyder Jennings yesterday and came home counting my blessings again. The more I hear about other people's husbands, the better (if possible) I like my own, even 2,000 miles away. The same applies to my children.

Willie was out almost all day yesterday with me in the A.M. and with Ess and Ruth from 4 to 6. He had a delightful time. He kept telling Mary Jane, "What a pretty dress." I think we have a ladies' man on our hands. At the car barn this morning, he told everyone he met, "Mama's got to go inject some rats at the laboratory." This really amazed them.

The weather is so beautiful that it's just a heartache to be away from you. Please push it up and let's get together again.

All my love, Ginny

Tuesday, March 13, 1945
12:30 A.M.

Dearest Honey Bunny,

I have just finished the income tax, and I must write you to improve my disposition. It appalls me to think of making out yours when you come back. Perhaps it is a mistake to let it ride. I believe I will at least figure it.

The big news today is that King is actually on his way home. He left India March 5, but they said it might take 4-6 weeks before he arrives. This makes me wonder if he is coming by boat.

Also, I received your lovely letter of February 15. I do want to see the Rhapsody in Blue *movie if it ever comes to Baltimore again. I am sure I would enjoy it. Your remarks about geniuses are interesting, and I suppose unhappiness does supply some sort of a drive for some people, but it incapacitates me.*

You mention the Curies as being difficult, and I, of course, immediately think of the Brownings 19th Century English poets, Robert and Elizabeth Barrett Browning. It is only common sense to know that two thoroughly congenial, happy individuals can accomplish more than one unhappy soul, if there is the will to do it.

I believe that the creation of a family is really sufficient in itself to most couples, but as you so frequently say, this is physical, and the intellectual must also give birth, and I believe we both feel the urge.

Betty Schilpp called today with symptoms of cystitis. She doesn't seem to be too sick. Techniques are important in all things, and I am glad you are so skillful.

The news continues very good, and—who knows?—perhaps I shall see you before too long, although each day is an eon.

All my love, Ginny

March 16, 1945
10:00 A.M.

Dearest Honey Bunny,

Your letter of March 1 has just arrived, and I am a new woman. I am sitting on the side porch with Willie, and it is 90 degrees in the sun. The lilacs are budding, and the forsythia is in bloom. Lovely Grachur Club weather.

I was interested to hear that you had moved and relieved to know that your quarters were so luxurious. I am anxious to hear more details about the setup, e.g., who is in charge, etc. Also anxious to know how you felt about the last hospital in regard to efficiency, etc. I don't know any of the men with whom you are associated, so any description will be appreciated.

Willie now weighs 30 lbs. and has grown 1¾ inch since January 15, making him 3 feet 3 inches.

The rapid progress of war is encouraging, but makes me restless and even more impatient for the end. We are expecting King daily.

I am going to dress now and will go to the laboratory at noon. I love you and miss you with an infinite ache, which is nevertheless pleasant.

All my love, Ginny

Friday, March 16, 1945
10:30 P.M.

My darling,

It is amazing how my outlook on life has changed since the mail this morning.

I knew, of course, that you had moved, and thus the delay, and it is not that I worry about you, but I just simply miss you terribly, and now I hope I shall be talking to you everyday again, for a while at least. Perhaps the charcoal will even come someday soon.

Ess, Ruth, Willie, and I are going to Washington to see Phoebe's baby tomorrow. We will go by train and are awfully anxious to see them all. Willie, of course, is anticipating the trip no end.

He was heartbroken this afternoon because I thoughtlessly mailed the "letter to Papa" myself. That, he feels, is his special privilege. He remembered it again as he was going to sleep and began sobbing all over again. I finally comforted him by saying he could drop this one down the train chute.

After his "cod re oil" (cod-liver oil), Smitty always gives him a candy pill. Tonight he called for five. She brought him two, and he said, "Smitty, I want three more." I don't know whether it was an accident or whether he really can do arithmetic. Who does he take after? Not me.

The stories of the Ramagen bridgehead are indeed fabulous. I am sure much more exciting, even to you, who are on the spot and anxious to get on and get over with such things.

What a fascinating experience, in a way, you must be having (if it must be, one might as well see history in the making). I shall never cease to regret that the experiences could not be shared, but I must rely on you to share them. In retrospect, indeed, you do so beautifully in your letters.

I am glorying in Jane's anticipation of King's arrival, as it makes our reunion seem more real. May it be sooner than we can anticipate.

All my love, Ginny

Saturday, March 17, 1945
11:30 P.M.

Dearest Honey Bunny,

Your wonderful, nice, long, chatty letter of March 7 arrived today, and since it was the first I have received telling me of your new surroundings, I enjoyed it especially. I suppose I am missing perhaps four or five anyhow. It sounds like a marvelous place, and I hope you enjoy it, but not for so long, unless the 1st Army finishes out the war right here and now.

I am glad to hear of your parties, and I suppose it is a good idea to get together. But if it means you don't get to write to Mama, well, she just doesn't like it. I am anxious to ask Carol Jackson if she knows the field-hospital CO from Washington, DC.

I know that you have been in the swimming pool if the weather has been like it was here. For the past two days, we have sweltered.

We went to see the Robinsons today, and Willie had a royal good time. He loves a train, so it is a real pleasure to take him on one. He was a sensation, and when he saw the conductor, he literally shouted with excitement, "Here's the 'ductor! Here's the 'ductor!"

Then he called, "All aboard," and began, "New York, Philadelphia, Baltimore, Washington, St. Louis." The girl sitting next to me said, "Did he say St. Louis?" She couldn't get over that he had been there. I said, "Yes, and if this war isn't over soon, he is going to Europe too." He had some ginger ale—"ginger trail"—and said, "Oh, it's good and crispy."

B, aside from being just adorable, is really getting quite pretty, I think, and I don't believe I am prejudiced, as I have never thought so before. Willie is also a really hands-on child, and I am just sorry you can't be here to enjoy them both. They cause sensations wherever they go.

I will write more in detail tomorrow. But let me say, at the risk of being monotonous, never a day goes by that I don't recall some pleasant memory of our life and love together, and this keeps me moving onward to the time when we may again relive that life and love.

Always, Ginny

Sunday, March 18, 1945
11:15 A.M.

My darling,

I am sitting in the car before the Bon Secours Hospital and writing while Willie watches the children skip rope and ride bicycles. It is another beautiful day, and the temperature must be close to 85 degrees. We were distressed to hear that the Ramagen Bridge had fallen into the Rhine River, but hope it will not make any real difference.

Yesterday the Robinsons were chiefly concerned with the nurses' draft. They think that the Army takes nurses for the purpose of morale, mainly. Rob even went so far as to say that "good looks were the major requirement." I believe and hope that they are wrong here. I am a pacifist, but I do think they are unduly hard on the Army.

Father came out here, and we left for home. This P.M. at 2:00, Willie and I met Dr. and Mrs. Ralph Stephenson, late of Washington, D.C., and now assistant resident. They and their four children took us down to Gibson Island for the afternoon. They have a fabulous establishment, with a ballroom which they use for a playroom, replete with man-size sliding board and swings, seesaws, jungle gyms, etc.

Willie had a wonderful time. He is as large as their four-year-old and talks as well and twice as intelligently. The two-year-old, one can barely understand.

The Magothy was lovely and, of course, made me terribly homesick. I also have made some more contacts. A friend of King's was there who is secretary to Senator Thomas of Utah, who is chairman of the Military Affairs Committee. If I ever need a priority to get overseas, perhaps she can assist in furnishing it.

Interestingly, she is an acromegalic [the consequence of a tumor of the pituitary gland], arrested, they hope, and, of course, sterile. She was treated with X-ray.

I am intrigued by news of your car. I hope it works well, but don't go tooting around the countryside and get wrecked, please, dear. Can you keep it and bring it home?

I am afraid you have been idle for some time and do hope you are finding something interesting and worthwhile to occupy your time. It must be very difficult, as you are not allowed to fraternize with the Germans.

Everyone was interested in knowing Freddie Geib was with the 3rd Auxiliary. Most people I have seen were not aware of it before.

All my love until we meet, Ginny

Monday, March 19, 1945
9:45 P.M.

My darling,

Today I received another lovely long letter dated March 5. How very nice for you to have such comfortable quarters, and I do wish they would end this horrid war with you right there. These last days are certainly hard to bear.

Bozo Brack is back, and just the same as ever. I don't think he has matured a bit. It took him three weeks to come, and he says not to expect King for at least another week. It is really true that Dr. TeLinde is trying to have Bozo released. How lucky for him.

Bill Stiffler was in Santa Thomas prison when the Japs bombed it, and there were two people in his room. All were blown to bits except Bill, who had only a shrapnel wound in his thigh. He was, however, terribly shocked. He must be being saved for something very special.

I was delighted to see you had treated a general—all such contacts are, I am sure, valuable, even if it is only to give you inside information into the possibilities of me seeing you as soon as possible after the war.

We tried our phenylhydrazine reaction on the ovaries today and think it worked really very well. Now all we lack is a fluorescent microscope for photographic purposes. If we can work it out in the placenta also, it will make a nice contribution to our clinical work on the spontaneous abortion problem. Phenylhydrazine reacts with the sex steroids (alcohols or ketones) to form phenylhydrosone, you remember.

Our life seems so perfect to me that I dreaded anything in the way of a change, fearing it could be for the worse. I don't feel this way now and think that perhaps our separation has even crystallized certain things for us and will make our postwar life even more complete.

It came as a little bit of shock to me at first when I realized you were not happy in your work; e.g., the trip we took to look at an opportunity in North Carolina. I feel now that I was so happy that I was not observant enough of you.

For some time I have been afraid that the same situation might have existed in your home life. To a little extent, I would not have known that either. I considered you so much a part of me that I took your choice and attitudes for granted, perhaps. I hope I have learned to consider you individually.

It will be wonderful, as you have suggested, if we could have several quiet months to plan our work and domestic arrangements together. I would love to do it in Europe, mainly because it will also give me an opportunity to see the places where you have been. Also, we could perhaps see other places in Europe together.

Disregard most of this as ramblings, my dear. They are thoughts very badly expressed. But perhaps because you know me so well, you will know what I mean. But always, and most and above all, you know I love you, I love you, I love you again, Ginny

Tuesday, March 20, 1945
(B's 11th-month birthday)

My darling,

Just think, in another month B will be one year old. She is standing alone very nicely now and will be walking, I believe, before the month is out.

If only you could see her. I frequently think this as I watch both of the children. How much they have missed not to have you play with them and train them. But I am sure that it is even more important as they grow older, and surely you will be home before then.

Donnie just phoned, saying that Joe was waiting for a camera and if I knew where to get one. I told her I had been trying for six months, as have the girls on photography, but I had forgotten to ask Jane to look for one in Hagerstown. Joe had not received any mail as of March 11. Donnie cabled him because his letters were so disconsolate.

In two more weeks it will be Easter, and what a lovely one it promises to be. It would be ideal for our trip to Atlantic City. Bicycling on the boardwalk and riding on the beach. Perhaps dancing Saturday night and then the auction shops.

Isn't it queer that we really do enjoy the same things? I often hear people say, "I do it because my husband enjoys it." We really do things, I believe, because we both enjoy it. Perhaps you swim, especially in cold water, for my benefit, but once you are in, you give a good imitation of enjoying it at least.

Perhaps next year we can resume our Easter holidays. Do you think that Willie will be old enough to take?

Dorothy Cross Leighton (who graduated with me) came in to see Dr. TeLinde today about sterility and two miscarriages. He referred her to Eleanor and me. Do you remember her? I am sure you will say, "She couldn't pop an egg."

I saw in the Journal of the AMA that the Russians were using vague block to combat shock with 0.25% procaine HCL-50-80 cc injected slowly into the edge of the sternocleido mastoid muscle above the point where it crosses the external jugular vein. This is used effectively in conjunction with plasma, apparently.

From the British comes the thought that most of the operative shock difficulties in auxiliary surgical cases are due to the anesthesia. Cyclopropane and O_2 together is the anesthetic of choice, and N_2O and O_2 supplemented with very small amounts of ether is the second choice.

All these gems you are no doubt familiar with, but I write them just to let *you know I am thinking about your work. Also, everyone has had trouble with too much plasma. Overenthusiasm is frequently dangerous, eh?*

I see that the 9th Army is massed again, and perhaps before long you will have work to do again. I hope so, as I am sure it must be happier in a way to know that you are getting the war over.

You must come over soon, as I have quite a problem: I can't tell whether my tummy button is still ticklish. Try as I might, it won't tickle. I am afraid it will be so out of practice that I won't be able to cope with the situation.

All my love, Ginny

Wednesday, March 21, 1945
9:45 P.M.

Dearest Honey Bunny,

Your letter of March 9 arrived today. It is certainly good to get mail, and I am glad to hear that you have received at least two letters as late as February 25.

You speak of Willie's hernia, and I will repeat that he now wears a truss very nicely; "trust" he calls it. And I have seen no evidence of the hernia since he first put it on two weeks ago. This should at least forestall the necessity for an operation. I should look up the monograph you suggest.

Joe Wharton has now been assigned to the Headquarters, 13th Airborne Division Artillery, as regimental surgeon, APO 333. He is with a number of people he knows and is apparently quite happy. They are still "in training."

I am a little disturbed about your $64,000 question; that is, to prevent future wars, should houses be destroyed or otherwise? There is no problem, as its solution was given to us 1,945 years ago, but we have not yet learned the real truth, apparently. Surely the best way to prevent a fight permanently is to make a friend. That reservoir of good will, which Willkie spoke of, has always been our great asset, which we have not used and are fast losing.

I still think the Golden Rule is the only practical solution, but, of course, I know it will not be used, and don't think I feel this way for any love I bear the Germans. I don't.

It's pure self-preservation I am thinking of, and to me it's common sense that if you build up hatred and resentment, sooner or later a fight ensues.

We thought these are fairly cute pictures of the babies, and I am amazed at how little B has actually changed since her pictures back in October. Willie had just recovered from a GI upset and needs a haircut, but still in all, I think they are cute.

I love you more and more and miss you eternally and infinitely.

All my love, Ginny

Friday, March 22, 1945
11:30 P.M.

Dearest Honey Bunny,

Still no mail today, and I feel that it has been ages, although it's actually been only three days.

I have just returned from dinner with the Braddock Joneses and attending a book sale. I purchased two histories of Belgium and an old book of ballads for the price of $1.25. It was really fun.

This afternoon I talked to the interns on functional GYN conditions, and they acted as if they enjoyed it and asked intelligent questions. My next hurdle is the JHH Medical Society in Heard Hall. Dr. TeLinde told me months ago it was to be the Baltimore City Medical Society, but he was a little confused. If you were only here to advise and give me courage.

Our reprints are out today, and I will send you one tomorrow.

There was a rumor in the hospital that Ken Tanner had been killed. Fortunately, I didn't hear it until after it was disproved. How do you suppose that got started?

All the JHH units for India are home, except Mike Tilghman, who requested to stay, and Ed Kelley, who is touring the Western Front. Perhaps you will see him.

My fondest dream is to walk with you through some European garden spot where the war has not left its ugly scar and make love in some unconventional spot, as we used to love to do. May it become a reality soon.

All my love, Ginny

Chapter 11

Across the Rhine
26 March-4 April 1945

*W*ORLD WAR II IN EUROPE ENDED ABOUT A month after the diary entries below which summarized the historic ten days preceding the end of the war in Europe. Japan's surrender was five months away.

Diary Entry: 4 April, Dorsten
[48th Field Hospital, 3rd Platoon]

When we came to Friedrichfeld, it appeared to be a dangerous spot. We were the first hospital of the Ninth Army to cross the Rhine.

On the disposition of the hospitals for the Rhine crossing, which we all knew was coming, it was with mixed emotions that we discovered that we were not committed on the west bank. This meant that we would not get any casualties from the crossing, and if we were the first to cross, as it began to appear that we were, it seemed unlikely that we could be busy on the far bank.

Our experience on the Roer crossing had been that as soon as the crossing was made the breakthrough occurred and the chase to the Rhine produced no casualties. We spent our time chasing the 84th Division to Hostert and then to Krefeld, having to set up only to find that when we were ready the battle had moved so far away we were useless to the division.

Across the Rhine, however, the method of use of the field hospital was to be different. Prior to this a single platoon supported a single division. With fast-moving warfare the casualties are light and a single platoon moves so slowly that it is too large and cumbersome to support a single division.

To cure this, area support was to be tried. That is, a single platoon would support a corps or perhaps half a corps, and then a second platoon would leapfrog frequently.

We were, in fact, the first platoon over and supported not a single division or half-corps or a corps, but the whole 9th Army for 48 hours.

Fortunately, casualties were light, but supporting so many units we were very busy for about three days, during which time we had 67 admissions. We were physically set up near the 30th Division Clearing Station (105th Medical Battalion) at Friedrichfeld. We also received patients from the 79th, 35th, 17th Airborne, 8th Armored, and 75th divisions.

On the east bank the Ninth Army went to great trouble to get the 67th 1st Platoon Field Hospital in position to take care of the airborne division, which was to land on R-day. They sent three good teams—Sam Talmadge, Dave Monahan, and Bill Fuqua—along with three good shock teams—Gene Bennett, Clark, and Stevens. As far as I know, all other field-hospital platoons had the usual two teams. If anyone really knew that we were to be the only hospital for 48 hours, we should have had the third team.

At any rate, we started at 4:00 P.M. on the 26th. We were on days and Henry at nights, since at Baesweiler it was the other way around. The first night we had only enough casualties to keep one team busy, but beginning the next day casualties got a little ahead of us, and we were in need of another team. We put a call into Army for help, and as it turned out, it was slightly over 24 hours before we got a team.

We put in a call about noon on the 27th, and Tom Tighe got here about 6:00 P.M. on the 28th. In the meantime, other hospitals had come over and the 20th Field Hospital was in bivouac across the road, waiting to move after the 8th Armored Division. Col. Hogland, therefore, got hold of Howard Yost and Mitchell, who were with the 20th, and they came over, and each did a couple of cases, using our spare table until the 20th moved out that night.

For the night of the 27th, the 91st Evac, which had come into Dinslachen, furnished a team headed by Capt. Pierson. They worked all night and did six cases. The Col. also found Ike Humphries and his team, which came in about 5:00 P.M., but Ike's team had worked the two previous nights and was moving the next day, and Ike was not anxious to work unless absolutely necessary.

Besides that, the operating tent had but three tables, and three teams working at once was inefficient. So Ike went on back to his unit, also in bivouac down the road. By the time Tom Tighe got here, the work was over.

All these extra teams who dropped in for a case now and then were here unofficially and represented how you get help in an emergency, which not infrequently happened.

It does seem that headquarters could plan a little better. We had the chance to call for help and all during the first 24 hours. John Hill kept asking, "Shall I send for help?" But I had no way of knowing, because we had no idea how many casualties were expected or even how many divisions we were supporting.

In other words, we are in no position and are not familiar enough with the tactical situation to make an intelligent guess, whereas the corps surgeon should be able to do this, or the group CO, or the Army surgeon, but they are too far back to know what is going until 24 hours later. As it turned out, the casualties admitted to the 67th 1st, where preparations were so carefully made, were no heavier than here.

The first night we were here (D+2), we had an exciting time. Friedrichfeld is about three miles from the Rhine River, and the ack-ack was as thick as flies. The Germans, as soon as it got dark, made several passes at the bridges on the river.

I felt perfectly safe as far as bombs were concerned, because after all, we were two or three miles from the target. But the ack-ack was so heavy that we were all worried about falling flak, which is as fatal as any other cold steel.

We went to bed about 11:00 P.M. but were awakened every 15-30 minutes by the noise, which was terrific. On one occasion a plane in leaving the river came directly overhead, flying at about a few hundred feet, being followed all the while by flak. Three planes were shot down that night within sight of our area.

At 2:00 A.M. I got up, got a litter from the hospital, and went over about 80 yards into the basement of a bombed-out school building being used by the clearing station for sleeping quarters. After that, I slept fine all night, because there was absolutely no fear from the falling flak there. Things quieted down about this time, and those who remained behind also got some sleep. As far as we know, no sizable flak fragment fell in the area.

The next night I went to sleep in the basement, but the Germans apparently gave up all hope of destroying the bridges, because they did not come over. Since then they have come over only occasionally, and then in single planes of the bed-check-Charley type. About two nights ago, a piece of flak fired at one such plane fell through the supply tent and ripped a hole in it, scaring everyone but not injuring anyone. We seldom hear automatic fire now, and I have slept in the tent with the others.

At Friedrichfeld the evacuation plan seemed to work pretty well. We set up in tents and were extremely busy for four or five days. We had two casualties on the 26th of March and two on the 30th and the remainder in between.

In all, I personally did 21 cases there, which is about maximum for one person, considering the extent of the injuries. There was one thoracoabdominal wound, 12 abdominal wounds, 6 thoracic wounds, and 2 extremity wounds, both of which ended up in amputations.

Two of the abdominal cases and two of the thorax cases died, for an overall mortality of 4 out of 21, which is about average for these types of wounded.

Because of the fast-moving front, we operated on wounded from a number of military units. The two divisions that we supported mostly were the 79th and the 30th, but we had three wounded from the 8th Armored Division and wounded from a number of attached units at the Army level. There were three prisoners of war, one of whom died.

———————

AMONG THE SPECIAL cases: C. H., age nineteen, from the 30th Division, was wounded at 2 AM on 27 March. We began his anesthesia at 11 AM that same day. He had several penetrating wounds of the transverse colon in the region of the Treitz ligament and several wounds of the jejunum below the ligament. The jejunum was transected, which we all were hoping not to see, because such patients had very profound shock from the upper-intestinal contents.

We did an end-to-end jejunostomy and a colostomy at the hepatic and splenic flexures on each side of the abdomen. We had to do these as quickly as possible, because by the time we were finished he registered no blood pressure—none.

But the patient surprised us immediately after the operation: While we continued administering plasma and blood, his blood pressure came up and, much to our delight, he seemed to survive well, despite the transection of the jejunum and all of the shock usually accompanying that dreadful wound.

PFC J. N., AGE thirty-four, from the 120th Infantry, was wounded about noon 27 March. We started his operation at 3 PM. He was brought in with several loops of small bowel outside the abdomen. The wound had been covered by temporary dressings in the field. There was a slit in his diaphragm and his left lung, and his stomach had collapsed in the thoracic cavity. We were able to restore his organs to their proper positions. (I described this patient and his surgery in my Easter Sunday letter to Georgeanna).

———————

28 March 1945

Dearest Ginny,

It is now about 10:00 P.M., and we have been at it hard all day. Fortunately, we are on days, and so resting is a little bit better. This reminds me of Brest, in that we are in tents for the first time since then. It is rather nice for a change, especially since the weather is pretty good.

We had Army photographers around all day yesterday shooting a story of a patient through a field hospital. They took several photographs of two operations; watch the papers, as they may be published. Although they may have taken over 100 shots, they will probably use only one or two.

We had the pleasure of being the first hospital across the Rhine, and I, personally, did the first operation east of the Rhine with the 9th Army. There are many hospitals over now.

Love, Howard

31 March 1945

Dearest Ginny,

Our work is over—the battle has gone off and left us again, according to the now-familiar pattern—and I hope that I shall have an uninterrupted hour to write you about the events of the past week.

Our rush really ended yesterday. I looked forward to a letter to you then, but we had so much detail work in the ward, and so many visitors, that I just did not get a chance to write.

We were sitting in bivouac about 30 miles west of the Rhine. We had guessed from the scanty information we had and from putting two and two together that we would be the first field hospital across. This suggested to us that we would cross on D+2. The assault crossing was made on Saturday. On Sunday, while eating lunch while still in bivouac west of the Rhine, I was handed a field order to take my team and Henry Swann's to an evac hospital that was nearby.

When this news got around, everyone at the field hospital was much disappointed, as it seemed that the plan as we had figured it out had been changed. You see, this left the field hospital without any surgical teams, although the two shock teams were left behind. So Henry and I loaded ourselves on a truck and arrived at the evac hospital at 4:00 P.M.

This was my first experience at an evac. They had been busy, but by the time we arrived the rush was under control. It was agreed that we would work that night—i.e., Sunday—and Henry, days.

I thought then and there that we would probably work all night, get orders to move in the morning, and then have to work all that night, because it seemed to me that our move to the evac was a very temporary one to cover any emergency associated with the Rhine crossing, but which no longer really existed.

We went to work at 8:00 P.M., and, to my surprise, they gave us two very good cases, a chest and a belly. The latter had an ether convulsion on the table. At 12:00 I thought it would be a good idea to see what was going on. I called back to the field hospital on the phone and found that about 30 minutes after we had left the unit got orders to cross the Rhine early the next morning and that the Colonel had been in touch with Army and that we would be ordered in the morning to join them on the east bank.

It had worked out just as we had predicted. So I got approval to knock off and go to bed, which we did, and early the next morning we loaded ourselves on to another truck, drove forty miles, then got into an ambulance and drove again across the river to our field hospital near a small town only a few miles east of the river.

This was on Monday—i.e., D+2. We got here about 1:30 P.M., and the hospital was well on the way to being set up. We opened officially at 4:00 P.M. The first patient had arrived at 3:55, and I operated upon him soon after—the first operation east of the river.

The trip across was very impressive, and I shall never forget it. The whole thing gave the appearance of meticulous planning and execution. We crossed on a so-called treadway bridge; i.e., a pontoon bridge on rubber-inflated boats. There were landing craft running around on the river and the sandy shores, and the barrage balloons reminded me of Omaha Beach.

Antiaircraft guns were so thick you could see one by looking anywhere. MPs at every crossroad were thoroughly familiar with the roads already, and our little three-ambulance convoy found the spot without any trouble. From here we can easily see the barrage balloons at the crossing.

The tent setup is very satisfactory. I believe it is better than the building, because you do not have to model your hospital after the building, but rather as you like to have it.

We were very busy from the time we opened through Thursday night, during which time we had 67 admissions, practically all chests and abdomens. They have all done wonderfully well.

Yesterday I expected to spend my time writing you and catching up on the ward work, but visitors caught up with us. Early in the morning the division surgeon of the 30th Division came in and said he would like me to look at a tumor in the palm of the hand of General Hobbs, the division general. This took an hour. The general had a growth attached to the skin, but below it, and I am not sure what it is. It does not seem to be attached to the tendons.

In the afternoon Lt. Col. Gay came by and spent the night. This completely consumed all time. He made ward rounds with us and watched a trochar thoracotomy and a ligation of a femoral vein. We got to bed about midnight. To make things worse, I stumbled over a tent rope in the dark and turned my ankle. Ken put on an adhesive boot and an Ace bandage, and today it feels pretty good, but I have limped around a bit.

I have sent home two books recently "liberated" from "our house at Dülken." One is a picture book of German history that Willie might like to tear up. The other is a book about the Nazi Party. One of these books is in every German home. I am sending it because I thought you all, and particularly your father, would be interested in seeing it.

These days without you are difficult. As I have a moment in these busy times, my thoughts inevitably turn to you, and as I think of your loveliness and our life together, my pulse quickens, and I find myself with rapid shallow breath. How sweet and important that day will be when we can once again face the future together. To do otherwise is not to live.

Love, H

1 April 1945
Easter Sunday
3:00 P.M.

Dearest Ginny,

Today has been a windy day, with low, dark, fast-moving clouds and occasional showers and no sign of the sun. Secondly, this is Easter, and our time to weekend at the Eastern Shore. The memories are sweet indeed.

As you know, we are closed, and so have not been too busy. But 50 sick *postoperative patients take about two hours to see adequately in the morning and equally long in the evening.*

They require meticulous postoperative attention, especially the chest cases that must be tapped daily and examined more often for tension pneumothorax or effusion that interferes with respiration. I vary from week to week as to whether it is better to put in tubes routinely. Next week, I think I shall put them in, because this time we have had some men with tension pneumothorax that was neglected.

This afternoon I had to remove a boy's leg that had become gangrenous due to injury of the femoral artery. At the original operation, it was necessary to tie the femoral about 1" below Poupart's ligament, where there was a defect of about 1" in the vessel and no gelatin tubes with which some people have had success in doing anastomoses. I have not yet done a successful vessel anastomosis but will keep looking for a case.

The diaphragm case that turned out so well, and which I mentioned the other day, was an Indian from Idaho [PFC. J. N.]. He had an evisceration of several loops of small bowel just below the 12th rib on the left. I made an upper-left rectus, only to find that the 11th rib was blown away with the attachment of the diaphragm from the midline in front around to a line under the armpit—a distance of a good ten inches.

The evisceration was actually through the chest and was easily reduced and the holes in the small bowel and stomach easily sutured.

But what to do about the diaphragm? Approached through the chest, it would have been easy to sew the remaining edge of the intercostal muscles at the 9th interspace. But, mechanically, I could not get up under the diaphragm through the upper-left rectus incision.

I fiddled about 30 minutes and then was able to pass several sutures from outside through the 9th interspace after having made a skin incision. This suture could then be passed through the edge of the diaphragm, then the needle unthreaded and the other end sent the same way and tied. The skin was closed over these.

The patient is doing well, and I think the diaphragm has held in spite of considerable tension.

The news is good. It now appears as if we will really have to meet the Russians, as there may be no organized surrender. The Nazis are really fanatics, as if we needed any other evidence to prove it.

All my love, H

———————————

H. R. WAS ADMITTED at 4:30 A.M. on 29 March. He registered no pulse or blood pressure. However, the skillful people in the admitting tent gave him one thousand cc of blood. He had a mild chill, but they kept pushing the blood and, in fact, gave him two thousand cc of blood, at which point his blood pressure was 118/50 and his pulse 96.

His problem was that he had had a traumatic amputation of the right leg, two inches above the knee. While he was anesthetized with and under Pentathol, we were able to do a quick amputation of the leg a little above the knee joint. He survived very well and was evacuated on 1 April in very good shape. He was yet another casualty whose life was saved by definitive surgery very near the front line.

PFC M. B. OF B Company, 115th Infantry, provided an example of how a battlefield surgeon sometimes must do things contrary to the way he is supposed to do them in order to save the patient.

M. B. had a penetrating wound of the abdomen. He was in reasonably good shape, but he also had a very large and ugly wound of the thigh extending up onto the abdominal wall. We closed the perforation in the small bowel, but M. B. also had a perforating wound in the cecum that we normally exteriorized.

Because of the extensive wound in his thigh, we elected to close the defect in the cecum in several layers, contrary to the army's instruction. Fortunately, the wounded man did extremely well and was evacuated in good shape. I am confident he recovered.

TECH SERGEANT F. A., from the 8th Armored Division's 58th Armored Infantry Battalion, arrived in terrible shock from disabling injuries of the extremities. He was wounded about 3 PM 28 March. We saw him around 5:40 PM. His pulse was 160.

He immediately received one thousand five hundred cc of blood, at which point his blood pressure was 90/60 and hematocrit 36 with hemoglobin of 12.1 grams. We amputated his right arm at the shoulder and applied a plaster spika [figure eight], which seemed to work very well.

He had hoarse rales throughout his lungs the night following the amputation, but he rebounded strongly and was in good shape when evacuated.

MY LAST OPERATION at Friedrichfeld was Heinrich Hoeck, a prisoner of war. I remember him vividly—a shivering seventeen-year-old child, as were many of the soldiers whom Hitler pressed into service in the closing months of the war in Europe.

Hoeck was wounded around midnight 28 March and admitted to our field hospital at 6 AM. He had a penetrating abdominal wound. He had been given five hundred cc of plasma before admission. On admission, his blood pressure was 120/90, his pulse 100.

As was the custom, prisoners of war were not given priority as far as operations were concerned, so Hoeck was passed over several times before we operated on him at 6 PM. In other words, he had been twelve hours in the admitting tent, receiving plasma. But his general condition was good, and when we began the surgery, his pressure was 120/80, his pulse 90.

He had a Meckel's diverticulum [a congenital outpouch of the small intestine] that had been completely shot off, and multiple perforations of the ileum. I closed many of these perforations and removed about a foot of small intestine, including the Meckel's diverticulum. The continuity of the intestine was reestablished by sewing it end to end. Although his operation had been delayed, he recovered well.

---

2 April 1945
1:30 P.M.

Dearest Ginny,

Another blustery, showery day. I am in the squad tent where eight of us are now living, and the tent is flapping and swaying to beat everything. You just make up your mind that you will not let it bother you or it would drive you crazy.

The enclosed violets I picked up in the city square at Dülken, where we were in bivouac immediately before crossing the Rhine. They came out quickly when we were having the warm springlike spell.

I spent last night rearranging my clothes again. It seems that it is impossible to get a satisfactory distribution between the various pieces of baggage. The truth of the matter is I have too much stuff. Most of it is living conveniences, such as buckets, washbasin, and toaster for over the Army stove, gasoline lantern, and stove.

Every place we go requires a different set of apparatuses, depending on what the place has to offer.

The one night we spent at the evac, for example, we were quartered in a private home of middle-class people who had been kicked out, and the result was that we had everything—bed, bathroom, stove, even a radio and the like, so that some of our portable equipment was not needed.

In tents here, though, I use my cot, bedroll, bucket, basin, radio—and so it goes. The result is that we carry everything and use some at this stop and others at another. The extension cord made from the appliance you supplied gets used almost everywhere.

The clothes I wear daily consist of OD trousers and shirt and combat boots. The only difference from Fort Sam's winter costume is the boots, which have been substituted for leggings. They save time putting on and off. We all got new General Ike suits, which we put on for Easter yesterday.

In the OR, if it is cool, I just roll up my sleeves after putting on cap and mask. If it is warm in the OR, as it has been here at times when we are in a building, I take off my shirt. Almost always I wear a rubber apron, which keeps my trousers fairly free from blood and, particularly, plaster.

When it gets really warm we shall probably wear fatigues or Army pajamas. The laundry continues to be a problem, but I have plenty of everything and can afford to throw away some clothes.

We have had a couple of amusing patients here. One has been our first colored patient. He had a perforation of the stomach and quite a bit of spillage under the diaphragm. He hiccupped incessantly, but slept practically all the time.

Most often we would just go past him while making rounds. But now and again we had to shake him awake and inquire how he was getting along. He said he felt pretty good, but when he was awake, the hiccups bothered him, and so he just slept all the time. Before we asked him how he could turn on the sleep at will, he said he had been working hard for eight months, and this was the first time he had had a chance to sleep.

Love, H

2 April 1945
5:45

Dearest Ginny,

    I spent the time since writing you a few hours ago going over the enclosed review by Nathanson, trying to get an idea for postwar work. Nothing from it, but perhaps if you have not seen it, it might prove interesting. A case of chorio with high pregnanediol excretion is quoted (Ref: 198). Is there anything to it?

    As with other carcinogens, it seems possible to start carcinomas with some known hormones; for example, carcinoma of the cervix in mice with estrogens. But, of course, withdrawal of the stimulus does not stop the growth of the tumor once started. This is the interesting and obviously important thing. Does the body react in any way to combat this growth? And how can we study this part of the problem?

    All my love, H

Wednesday 4 April 1945
2:00 P.M.

Darling Ginny,

    This field is immediately adjacent to a school that was used by the Germans as a hospital. The school was apparently a high school and very modern. The bits of glass lying around (there are still some panes of glass in the windows) are blue, and all rooms have large windows.

    There is but one corridor, and all rooms are on one side of this corridor, the sunny side.

    At any rate, the rooms are kaput, and teaching material is scattered all over the place. Books of all kinds, but no dictionary. I have been trying to find a German one, but so far have not been able to locate one.

    When we first arrived here, the clearing company was using the remains of the school for sleeping quarters, but they have, of course, long since moved on.

    The school had been used by the Germans for a hospital, and a large red cross is painted on the roof. I trust that the damage to the building was done after the hospital left, as I imagine was the case. They had painted signs on the inside of the building, so that it is possible to see that here was the OR, here was the ward, and so on. I imagine it accommodated a field lazaret.

The German graves-registration service must not have been working during the preceding weeks, for over in one corner of the field is a small military cemetery with 31 German-soldier graves, each with a white cross and the man's name and date of birth and death.

The deaths all took place following the crossing of the Roer. I imagine the hospital moved on when we got up to the Rhine. Some of the crosses have been blown to bits by fire of various kinds, and the graves will never be identified. Some of the host of missing men.

The weather continues to remind me of the Jersey Shore in early spring with a Northeaster. It has been squally all day. In spite of the barrage of balloons being hit by lightning, there are just as many up today as ever.

I had to liquidate the car. It ran fairly well for a while, but got something wrong with it. The boys who really looked after it thought that it needed a new carburetor, but, of course, none was available, except from another car. They tried to "liberate" a carburetor from another such car, but there was a nut they could not get off, and about that time we left Krefeld, so the car stayed behind.

My love to our little family, H

Wednesday 4 April 1945
8:20 P.M.

Dearest Ginny,

We are in the midst of a thunderstorm, of all things. The wind blows in big puffs, and the tent feels like it is going to take off almost any time.

We have seen one or two of the barrage balloons get hit by lightning today, as it has been storming on and off all day. The balloons must be filled with hydrogen, as they go up with a big puff, and then the cable burns all the way to the ground. Good show!

Wow! This tent is really swaying. If it ever goes, I will be sitting out in the rain.

The patients are doing well. We have started evacuating and are down to about 30 or perhaps 35 patients. We have one boy with a dislocated spine and have been increasing his lumbar extension gradually.

Tonight we put another blanket under him and gave him a pretty good arch, which was uncomfortable. He complained, and I told him that if he would just put up with it for a few minutes, he would get used to it. He said, "Doc, did you

ever hear the story about the farmer who fed his horse sawdust?" No. "Well, just
as the horse got used to it, he died."

Another patient asked if we had removed his foreign body, and I told him we
had. He said that he was from the engineers, and a friend of his had been
wounded, but he knows the doctor did not remove the foreign body, because when
he got back to the company, he put the mine detector on his leg, and it showed
metal to be present. This must be common practice among engineers on returning
to their command, because I have heard of them doing it before.

This afternoon I spent a little time reading about pneumonectomy. I have
never had a case where I thought pneumonectomy was the proper procedure, but if
the war lasts long enough, a case will come along.

The literature I have is very poor. I was wondering if you could ask Bill
Rienhoff or his secretary to send me any reprints he might have on his technique.

How happy when we will be able to be together again.

Love, H

ACROSS THE RHINE, events moved rapidly. Dorsten, where we
were to go later, was taken by the 8th Armored Division of XVI
Corps, which passed through the 30th Division (one of the assault
divisions). Dorsten also was surrounded by the 6th Guards Armored
Brigade of the British 30th Corps.

Kempen, Germany, 26 March 1945. Team 3 immediately before crossing the Rhine to become the first Ninth Army surgical team in action east of the waterway.

Freidrichfeld, Germany. Lunch using tables "liberated" from school.

Wesel, Germany, 26 March 1945. The Rhine. Riflemen crossing upriver from the pontoon bridge to shoot and explode any floating mines dropped from planes.

Freidrichfeld, Germany, March 1945. School used by Germans as a hospital. The U.S. Army's 48th Field Hospital used tents on school grounds. Ken Tanner is strolling along.

Chapter 12

Letters from Home
24 March 24-4 April 1945

*W*HEN GEORGEANNA WROTE TO ME ON 24 March the largest airborne operation of World War II had taken place east of the Rhine River; 5,051 aircraft and 40,000 men from the British 6th Division and the U.S. 17th Airborne Division participated in the assault. The paratroopers dropped to the north and northeast of Wesel and linked up with British infantry advancing eastward. The several successful crossings of the Rhine in strength by Allied forces raised morale at the front and throughout all countries striving to crush Hitler's Third Reich.

Saturday, March 24, 1945

Dearest Honey Bunny,

I cannot express with what mixed feeling I heard this morning of the 9th Army's crossing of the Rhine. I tell myself constantly that you are, of course, in no danger, but I know it is not true. However, mercifully, all news sources report that casualties are very low. I will live for the day when the mail dated March 25 arrives.

I took Willie to Donnie's for the afternoon and supper. He had a gorgeous time, but he doesn't know how to wrestle, and Harold, who lives in the upstairs apartment, is 7 years old and a very decidedly big-boy influence.

I'll have to give Willie a few lessons, and he likes it while he's on top. But when he's underneath, he's not so sure. Today for the first time, while taking his bath, he mentioned his nipples, and he said, "I have two moles."

Did I tell you B now comes upstairs alone? She is a nice snuggly baby, but has a will of her own.

I have definitely made my plans for a European trip, so don't disappoint me. Perhaps it won't be long now before we can sit together and discuss our future life and work. I live for that day.

All my love, and God bless and protect you, Ginny

Monday, March 26, 1945
5:30 P.M.

Dearest Honey Bunny,

I received four letters today, counting the one V-mail enclosed in March 5, and also March 12 and 13. Mary received her thank-you note, and by the way, I am not at all alarmed about your ETO habits. I will be only too glad to have you drive nails in the wall and break up the china. In fact, life with you is a test and would be my idea of heaven.

We all enjoyed your story of Bill Boukalik's narrow escape and also the Baffin Island narrative. I was glad to hear that you had seen Lehman Guyton. I shall call Benny and tell her. I, too, hope that you do not have to take the evac hospital position, but I feel sure that you would be happier in it than Bill Boukalik. It is maddening to know that already these things (and many others with the new offensive) may have taken place.

Howard at this point is talking a blue streak about "Fort Daniel, which is near Papa in Germany. They have movies and prisoners." He has no idea what all this means; it's just a stream of talk. But it is fascinating how rapidly he piles up new words and phrases.

It is summertime here, and the violets are in bloom. Tonight there is a full moon. A lovely night for our sleeping porch with the sliding roof.

You say that you console yourself by saying it is better thus, and so do I, because I, know that when the children are sick, my place is with them, and really, it seems to me we have been sick all winter, and your letters are so full and wonderful that it is almost as if we were not separated. I couldn't bear to think that a stranger was coming home to me. I don't feel this way at all, and as I have said, in some respects I feel that we are closer, if this is possible.

I am wondering if Elmer drove any of the Ducks [amphibious trucks] across the Rhine? Do look for his outfit if you have a chance.

Your story about the wine bottle and no corkscrew makes me wonder what has happened to all the gadget knives I saw among the officers of the 5th before going overseas. I suppose a lot of such things get lost in the shuffle, and you certainly have had a shuffle recently, and I suppose you are still in it. How anxious I am to get mail after March 24.

We had news that King was still in Bombay March 11, so I presume it will be quite springtime before he reaches home. It's been a long wait, and it makes me realize what is ahead for us. I do hope I will be able to make a trip over there, so that it might shorten things for us a bit. It seems like a dream of wildest delight now, but someday it will be a reality.

In the meantime, all my love, Ginny

Tuesday, March 27, 1945
9:30 P.M.

My darling,

The news continues to be very exciting. I really feel as if the war is over tonight. I do hope the Jap situation is not as bad as lots of people think. Of course, if we move to the Chinese mainland, I suppose that we could use any number of Army troops, but I can't feel that we will do so. Wishful thinking on my part, perhaps.

I can't settle down to anything with you away, and perhaps use this as an excuse. But things do seem to move so slowly without you at home and in the laboratory also. It is hard to keep up enthusiasm for anything—histochemistry of ovarian function or toilet training for B—without your companionship.

All of this just means I miss you dreadfully. You say I sign my letter, "All my love 'til we meet again," and when we meet will actions speak louder than words?

Your letters of March 2 and 14 arrived today, and we are gradually piecing together your interesting chronicle. I was sorry to hear that you had to leave Capt. Hughes, but you are perhaps back with him by now, and things must move rather rapidly.

The books arrived today, and now I am awaiting the charcoal portrait eagerly.

All my love, Ginny

Friday, March 30, 1945
Good Friday

My darling,

Two lovely letters today, and a real surprise, as I was afraid we wouldn't have any today, since I received five yesterday. Last night I was really ill with fever and couldn't sleep properly. I kept dreaming of surgical trucks dashing up long straight two-lane German roads, miles ahead of everything, and getting no mail from you.

I really expect this is true almost, not merely a dream. Today McCardell had an article about a field hospital arriving in a town before any other soldiers, and I thought of your story about Bill Boukalik.

I have been taking my nose drops, and you would be proud of me. But each time I think of the year you gave them to me and I was so sick.

I have also thought of how you treated my chafe so nicely on our honeymoon. How embarrassing that could have been for someone, but not true for us. Do you remember those wonderful rubdowns we used to have in showers after a long day's ride, to say nothing of the lovely nights?

I am going to read Dr. Rich's book on immunity and send it to you, as everyone says it is so good. Perhaps it will give us a lead about lymphosarcoma, Hodgkin's disease, or leukemia.

Today I took Willie to the lab with me to do about one half hour's work. He put stoppers in water bottles, got food checks out of the barrel and put them in the food boxes, and was all in all quite helpful.

He also picked up some pregnant females and very nearly got bitten. He couldn't understand why Eleanor and I could squeeze them and he couldn't.

Gil Vosberg was very much impressed with him, but I still feel that he shows the absence of his father markedly.

He is almost well, and B and I are improving. My temperature is normal tonight.

We have definitely heard that King is coming by boat, so he will probably not be here until the 1st of May.

I just talked to Ess, who sends love. They are well. The news is wonderful, but hours drag for me.

All my love, Ginny

Tuesday, April 3, 1945
4:15 P.M.

My darling,

I have three of your letters at hand, March 21, 22, and 23. I am constantly aware of how fortunate I am with my husband.

Yesterday was a truly hectic day and wasted, as I did not get to write. Both children are sick, and Mother is arriving from South Carolina with opera tickets for the evening. Donnie was coming at 7:00 to look over the children, and then we were going to the opera.

I had just finished all my household tasks and was getting ready to step into the bath (Mary was home and looking after Willie) at quarter of six. Mrs. Ebling called to say Dr. Ebling was very ill, and Karl had asked Father to go over and give him a hypo.

Father was lying down, tired from office hours. Poor Dr. Ebling had obviously had a coronary and was in shock and writhing in pain. They had called Karl twice and had never spoken to him, only to his secretary.

While Father and I took care of the situation, I had time to snatch a bite, wondering how I was going to make it to the opera, as I was to spell Father while he ate. Dr. Ebling solved the problem by dying, but I am disgusted with Karl. He never did get there, or make the effort, or even call us to ask us to look after him.

The opera, when we finally arrived just in time, was lovely. Aida, it was. I believe it to be the best all-around opera performance I have ever seen. The ballet was especially beautiful. You, of course, were with our thoughts, except perhaps in the last entombment scene. I was too busy controlling my wee-wee to really enjoy it properly. In the excitement, I had forgotten to go all afternoon.

I still am unable to answer your Rh question, as I have not been to the hospital, except on odd occasions, since last Wednesday. I hope the children will be well enough tomorrow for me to begin again. I have really got to get myself together for the JHH Medical Society next Monday.

The news is amazingly slow again, and I am terribly impatient. I do think the Jap news is excellent, however.

The weather here must be like yours in training, as it is really like May. This, I think, makes me miss you more. But so did snow, and so does rain, so I guess it's just that I miss you, period.

I find that I miss you physically in great surges on top of the constant steady swell. There is no cure, but thoughts and letters do help until that day. May it not be far-distant.

All my love, Ginny

Wednesday, April 4, 1945
10:30 P.M.

Dearest Honey Bunny,

I finally got back to work after a week of nursing myself and the children and so can answer your Rh factor questions.

Most people believe that sensitivity can be developed within three or four days from transfusions, as this is the method of sensitization. Practically all Rh-negative recipients will develop sensitivity (antibodies) to Rh-positive blood.

The simple method for detection I have enclosed. The catch is you have to have Rh antiserum. Plus, I have written the people in Boston to send the antiserum to you by parcel post. I hope it all arrives after the war is over, but in the meantime it gives me something to do for you (us). Dr. Louis Diamond, 300 Longwood Road, Boston 15, Massachusetts, is the authority on the subject, if you care to contact him.

The Drummond Eatons have another daughter, and both Billie and Drum are doing nicely. Drum lost only one meal this time.

After much delay, we think the Vitamin E method is underway, and so perhaps we will be able to finish that workup.

I am getting very discouraged about the war. I guess the Germans just will fight to the last man, and he will be Hitler. I had so counted on seeing you this spring. How can people stand a three-year separation?

Both Willie and B seem themselves today. I hope we are over these things for the winter. Willie is so sweet when well that it is a shame to have him sick and cross.

I am certainly hoping for news after the Rhine crossing, but I suppose I will have to wait much longer. May the Lord protect you and bring us back together soon.

All my love, Ginny

Method of Typing for Rh Factor

One drop of blood is suspended in about 1 ml of normal saline. In our lab this suspension is spun at not more than 550 r. per min., and the cells resuspended after decanting the first saline. (This step can be eliminated.)

Two drops of the red-cell suspension are placed in a Kahn tube, and one drop of anti-Rh serum (diluted 50%) and one drop of saline are added. Incubate the tube at 37 degrees for one hour (water bath is adequate). Tilt tube gently back and forth (do *not* shake vigorously) a half-dozen times to loosen some of the sediment.

Gross clumping can be seen with naked eye or hand lens. This would be a nice use for those little gadgets of Howie's, in lieu of starting fires or lighting cigarettes.

If no gross clumping is seen, a drop must be examined under the microscope for microscopic agglutination.

Chapter 13

East of the Rhine
4 April-8 May 1945

*T*HE FRONT MOVED SO RAPIDLY THAT WE WERE assigned to the 41st Evacuation Hospital at Dorsten, arriving there to start surgery 5 April. We were there until the sixteenth. During this time, I personally performed 127 operations.

As anticipated, the mix of patients at the evacuation hospital was markedly different from what we were used to at a field hospital. One hundred thirteen of these 127 cases were wounds of the extremities, many of which were comparatively simple (although not to the wounded, of course).

We did have one thoracoabdominal wound, ten abdominal wounds, and three chest wounds, which in the normal course of events would have been treated at a field hospital. But as the war became increasingly fluid, the usual method of handling the wounded became less orderly.

BY 1 APRIL, the Ninth Army met the U.S. First Army at Lippstadt, sealing the Ruhr Valley region and encircling German Army Group B, which shortly surrendered. The two-pronged Allied crossing of the Rhine had deprived the German Army of further supplies from the highly industrialized Ruhr Valley.

On 4 April, Ninth Army reverted to Twelfth Army Group. Germany was swiftly totally occupied. Casualties were few, usually from isolated German units or even artillery, which made traveling dangerous.

On 10 April, Ninth Army's 84th Division took Hanover. Other units continued to reduce the Ruhr pocket.

On 12 April, the 30th Division took Braunschweig, and President Roosevelt died in Warm Springs, Georgia.

On 13 April, the 95th Division of Ninth Army was at Wolfenbüttel, yet another German city we came to know well.

On 15 April, Ninth Army was at the Elbe River, except for a small pocket near Magdeburg. Magdeburg itself was finally taken by the 30th Division and the 2nd Armored Division.

———

5 April 1945
9:00 P.M.

My dearest Ginny,

I am sitting before a potbellied stove in the OR of an evac hospital. As we were eating supper last night, Col. Smith stopped by to look around and said that he thought we would get orders anytime to go to the 41st Evac.

Sure enough, about 6:00 both Henry and I were ordered to proceed "without delay," as the message usually reads. By 7:00 we were loaded and on the way.

The two teams have collected so much stuff that it took one 2½-ton truck for the impedimenta, and we rode in another. Thirteen people, by the way, in addition to the drivers. Henry has had an additional anesthesiologist assigned, as Nicke, his anesthetist, is slow and not so sure on bad cases.

We did not know where we were going, as usual. We knew the number of the hospital, and we found out as best we could the town and location. Often, of course, we get there to find that the hospital is actually ten miles outside the town.

We passed through several bombed-out towns, and it finally got pitch-black, but was possible to see the road, as the trees had white bands on them. We passed through a large town much bombed for the past year or so. At each crossroad I would get out and walk over to the sign and with a shielded flashlight try to figure out how to go.

The MPs get road signs up promptly. As soon as the hospital gets set up, the MPs cover all crossroads with signs for miles around. In this way it is generally easy to pick your way and, by this slow process in the dark, we got here quite uneventfully.

Things do not appear the same at night as they do in daylight. This morning we found that the hospital was set up on a farm and, particularly, in a wheat field. The wheat is about four inches high. We are living in pyramidal tents and not as comfortably as at the field hospital, because there is no wiring in the corridors; therefore, no lights, no radio, etc. The food is better, though, for we do not need mess gear and have a tent especially for mess. This is seldom true of field hospitals.

I started to say that the large town we are near was heavily bombed by the Air Force for some time, and it is thoroughly destroyed. As far as I can see, the Germans, by prolonging this war, are committing a national hari-kari and will end with a completely ruined country—but the present leaders must not care about that. Patients who come in from miles ahead say that every town is the same way.

An evac hospital, compared with a field hospital, is a leisurely place. In a field hospital, you come in, pile your stuff in a corner, help get the OR set up, and buck the first patient through. Here we arrived last night; they made us comfortable for the night in a ward not yet used, and this morning we went around to meet the CO and chief of surgery.

Henry was to be on days and we at nights, so Henry was told that he could come in at 1:00 P.M. and we come in at 8:00 at night, almost 24 hours after arriving. We will be on until Monday, when we change back to days. Of course, we are not busy and have done only one minor case tonight.

The OR here looks a little more like a civilian OR, in that the personnel have made an inner tent from sheets, so that it is entirely white-lined. We also have a white operating suit to wear that covers our ODs but makes it a little chilly when outside.

The weather continues to be rainy and squally, with a thunderstorm and gusts tonight. The news continues to be good, but also bad, in that it appears more and more as if we will really have to continue to fight until we meet the Russians.

Love, H

7 April 1945

Dearest Ginny,

It is now 10 minutes to 4:00 A.M., and I have put everyone else to work and slipped over beside the stove to write this. The airmail arrived today containing the two Bloodgood needles, which I used for the first time tonight on peritoneum and fascia. I never write to anyone else, so do keep everyone informed.

My love as always, H

THE MAJORITY OF our wounded were from the 75th division; fifty of the men treated at Dorsten were from that division. Eight wounded were from the 79th Division, eleven were German POWs, and two were Russian civilians apparently impressed as laborers for the German Army. The remainder of the wounded were from various units attached to 9th Army.

There was one fatality among these 127 patients—a first lieutenant from the 898th Field Artillery Battalion. He had a mortally destructive penetrating wound to the abdomen involving the head of the pancreas, the liver, and the kidney. The damage to the pancreas apparently had caused irreversible shock.

Among special cases of particular interest:

- T. Jerisjanko was the first Russian civilian upon whom I operated. He had a penetrating wound in the shoulder region that was taken care of quite easily with debridement and closure of the capsule of the right shoulder. He seemed to do well.
- The second case was another Russian, Juchim Arkgon. He had a penetrating wound of the right foot, the buttock, and the flank region, as well as the temporal region. These were all debrided, and the patient recovered.
- Private C. D., from the 314th Infantry, was brought in with an

accidental injury. We were seeing more and more accidental injuries. C. D. had a penetrating wound in his left hand, which he received while unloading a pistol taken from a captured German officer.

• Max Alte was a prisoner of war. About fifty years old, he was a member of the Volkssturm—the "People's Militia"—composed of men over the normal age limit for regular military service or possessing partial disabilities and children age sixteen and younger.

Alte had a penetrating wound of the abdomen and was sent, as he should have been, to the 48th Field Hospital's 1st Platoon, but the personnel there were extremely busy, so they sent him on to the 41st Evac, where we operated on him.

He was another one of these cases with eviscerated loops of small bowel on the abdomen. We got at him promptly. He had holes in the small bowel, which were resected with end-to-end anastomosis. He did well in the long run.

• Private V. C., age nineteen, from Company A of the 291st Infantry, was brought in with a thoracoabdominal wound. He was wounded at noon on 13 April, and we saw him three hours and fifteen minutes later.

Why he was not sent to a field hospital, I don't know. At any rate, we took care of him, administering plenty of blood. But we could not operate on him until about twelve hours after admission.

He had five holes in the ileum, a hole in the appendix, and two holes in the bladder. He also had a hemothorax [blood in the chest cavity].

We did a resection of six inches of the ileum with an end-to-end anastomosis and aspirated one thousand five hundred cc of blood from the thorax. We also did an appendectomy, because he had a gunshot wound through the appendix. He also recovered.

---

338   Howard W. Jones Jr. and Georgeanna Seegar Jones

Sunday 8 April 1945
6:05 P.M.

Dearest Ginny,

    I find the evac experience interesting. We do about 15 or 20 cases on a 12-hour shift. This includes one or two big cases, but the great majority are extremities, through-and-through wounds of the legs or arms that require very little treatment.

    Now and again there is more to it than that. We have had one injury to the sciatic nerve and one injury to the popliteal vein, and yesterday we had fun exploring a knee joint.

    A bullet had entered the joint and embedded in the femur. It was possible to extract the bullet and, I think, that gave him a pretty good knee.

    He also had a through-and-through rifle shot in the head of the pancreas. It had caused a fairly extensive retroperitoneal hematoma that I felt I had to explore, because I was worried about the duodenum. It had missed the duodenum by the smallest possible measurement. But the bleeding vessel must have been a large branch of the pancreatic duodenal below the pancreas, and it was with considerable sweat and a little cussing that I was finally able to get the thing clamped.

    Ken and I are living in a pyramidal tent with three of the evac majors, all about 45-to-50 years of age, and I guess you would describe them as a bit set in their ways. It makes living a bit uncomfortable, but interesting, for a change.

    One is a Major Bogel, who was born in Scotland, but who now practices in Littleton, New Hampshire. He is a ski enthusiast and said that Littleton is by all means the place to come. Another is a general surgeon from a small Kentucky town, and another is from Shreveport.

    As usual and always, I miss you painfully and sadly, but I am certainly supported by thoughts of things to come.

Love, H

9 April 1945 (I think)

Dearest Ginny,

    Last night we were busy again, but mostly small stuff, so that we did 22 cases—also many Germans. There is no doubt in my mind that, generally speaking, they are in much worse general condition than are our boys.

It is something more than the dejection of being a prisoner. They are undoubtedly dirtier and their feet are always crusty and smelly; whereas, our GIs, although straight from the front, all seem to be relatively clean about the body, even though they may have a dirty face and need a shave, and not too badly.

Also, the Germans whine and complain more. I cannot remember an American who complained about being handled or troubled, and our soldiers eagerly do what is required of them.

Last night, as Elmer stuck a GI for the Pentathol, the patient mentioned that it was the 9th needle since being admitted, and he was willing and complained only jokingly.

The Germans, on the other hand, complain and whine and always want to do something different. I wish I could talk to them, as they must have been told that they would get poor treatment and perhaps be killed. More than one has asked, "Muss ich stuben?" ("Must I die?").

Also, Germans wounded are troubled with the thought that they probably would do as well untreated. Several wounds through fleshy structures are clean, and probably a prolonged convalescence by incising them would do, but I don't know the end result, and so I continue to slit the fascia for a couple of inches and excise the skin.

All my love, H

9 April 1945
6:30 P.M.

Dearest Ginny,

We are uncommonly busy here at the evac now. There is continuously a backlog of around 50 wounded, which is not tremendously big for an evac, but nevertheless represents continuous work for the oncoming shift. The surprising business about this in all the evacs, I suppose, is that, in spite of being busy, everyone is so leisurely about things.

We work about 12 hours, and then the other shift is there. In the field you feel like someone is chasing you all day, because there is no one to relieve you, and it is a question of getting the patients done yourself. This is, therefore, an altogether delightful experience.

Also, we have been lucky, in that the type of cases has not been as trivial as evac cases have a reputation for being. This is due to the tactical situation, which has been so fluid that the usual field-evac situation has not been maintained or necessary.

Last night, for example, we did a rectal wound with a colostomy, compound-fractured elbow joint, a foreign body in the upper lobe of the left lung, a median nerve and brachial artery [principal artery to the arm], a compound fractured humerus [shoulder upper arm], with radial nerve, a bad leg amputation, a bad compound fracture with rectal and bladder injury. This took us all night.

The first night we had much smaller cases and did 22. It varies and, if things run true to form, the small stuff is much the most common.

However, I am thoroughly enjoying this and experiencing the leisure and would be quite willing to stay a week or two. It gives me a desire to go back to a general hospital on the Continent to see what goes on there. If I do not go to the Pacific, I presume I shall have a chance at a named general hospital in the States.

Most of the cases are transportable immediately after operation, and you do not see the patient before operation and seldom after. Therefore, trying to fill up this hospital is like filling a sieve.

A great number of patients are admitted, but the number who can be here is limited to 450, with expansion possible to 600 in a great emergency. PX rations are for sale and, after buying some candy, canned orange juice, and toothpaste, I shall see my patients, and then into the OR for 12 hours, and so it goes.

Love as always, H

THE LAST CASE we did at Dorsten was W. K. from the 295th Infantry. He had a penetrating wound of the thorax; we resected a rib and had a good look. A foreign body was located in the lobar fissure between the right middle and right lower lobe. This was easily removed.

The patient also had a wound to the head, and while I was doing the thoracotomy, a neurosurgeon at the evac hospital was debriding the wound around the mastoid area. Fortunately, both of these surgeries worked out well; the wounded man was evacuated in good shape.

After the flow of casualties slowed to a pace at Dorsten and the two permanently assigned teams there could carry the burden, we moved on to Schöppenstedt, to the 108th Evacuation Hospital, where we surgically treated five casualties. Three were small cases; two cases were surgically challenging.

We arrived at Schöppenstedt 20 April. Soon afterward the 1st Battalion of the 67th Field Hospital thirty miles away at Gebhardshagen messaged us for help with a case—the auxiliary surgical teams assigned to them had been removed.

So our team went down to Gebhardshagen to operate on W. R., a captain from the 53rd Engineers of the 8th Armored Division. He had been shot accidentally, and he was taken from Wolfenbüttel to the 67th.

He was in shock and bleeding so profusely from the wound that Gene Bennett and Morris Clark, who were the trauma team at the 67th, were afraid to move him. They had given him five pints of blood and put in the call for help.

We got to Gebhardshagen about 5:00 PM. Through an abdominal incision, we ligated the femoral artery just below the profunda (a deep artery); brisk bleeding from the distal part of the vessel indicated that this was the proper surgical response.

An inch-long segment of artery was missing, so an anastomosis was out of the question. The vein was also ligated. At the end of the procedure, W. R. had a warm leg, and later that day he had a warm foot with a palpable dorsal pulse—at least we thought so. He was evacuated on 27 April in very good condition.

THE OTHER CHALLENGING case at Schöppenstedt: A twenty-one-year-old private from the 58th Armored Infantry was accidentally shot in the abdomen with a captured .32-caliber German pistol. I closed numerous perforations in the stomach and small bowel. I felt the bullet under the skin, just below the scapula on the left. I was able to palpate the bullet and simply nicked his skin at the end of the operation to remove it. He did very well.

On the night of 12-13 April, while I was operating on another casualty, the commanding officer burst into the operating room and blurted out that he had just heard on the radio that President Roosevelt had died. We had a brief conversation, the gist of which was that the president's death wouldn't make any difference in the war effort.

The radio soon afterward and *Stars and Stripes* next day reported that the highest military leaders agreed the war would proceed as before. There was also much talk about how the course of the war would have been altered if Hitler, instead of Roosevelt, had died of natural causes. We could not foresee, of course, that nine days later Hitler, who had been momentarily heartened by the news of Roosevelt's death, would die by his own hand.

Saturday 14 April 1945
6:00 P.M.

My darling,

I am sitting in my new home alone on a cot with your Easter box in my right hand and a cookie in my left hand. The mail came yesterday and brought the box and an ad from the yearbook company and nothing else.

The new home to which I refer is a squad tent, i.e., twice the size of a pyramidal, which was put up yesterday for our use. We were so crowded in the pyramidal with five that I asked the hospital to pitch our own squad tent from the PROCO.

The objection to doing it before was that we have no stove, but the weather has been so fine the last few days that a stove is really not necessary. I slept alone here today, but tonight Ken is going to move in, and we will have oceans of room.

We continue to be busy on the night shift. We change tomorrow. The cases have been very good ones, as I said before, and I have been agreeably surprised at the type of work at the evac. It is true that many of the wounds are trifling from a surgeon's point of view, but some of the extremities with fractures and nerve and blood vessel injuries are complicated and entirely different from the abdominal and chest work.

Last night I had a very complicated abdominal and chest case with, incidentally, the first wound of the appendix I have had. We have also had a nice chest case.

By the way, did I tell you of the little German who had a perforating wound of Meckel's diverticulum? In the first 100 laparotomies, we saw five Meckel's divertiula, only one of which was perforated.

It is a strange thing: The 12-hour shift is easy, and we have adequate leisure time, as previously described. But these ten days being on nights have left me indescribably weary, chiefly because I have not been able to get enough sleep. The noise during the day and the light and the heat when the sun is out make the difference. One good night's sleep will fix me up.

We were all stunned by the President's death. As much as I hated him, I was terribly sorry that it had come now, because of his successor, Harry S. Truman, and his successor confirms everything that I previously thought of him for, after all, he picked him. I trust we are all agreeably surprised, but I doubt that Truman can handle the international politicians like FDR. This war, of course, will go on.

My love as always, H

Sunday 15 April 1945
(Really 3:00 A.M. Monday)

Dearest Ginny,

Things here have finally quieted down, and we have caught up with ourselves at the moment. As a matter of fact, we had nothing at all to do last night and spent the night in bed after 1:00 A.M.

Today I felt so good that I made a little trip that turned out to be 100 miles, because bridges are out and it is necessary to go farther than is shown on the map. I had left some equipment at the 48th—some towels, sheets, and gowns—and today was the first chance to go get it.

In the meantime, the 48th had moved forward. We are practically Zone of Interior here, especially since the front has moved 200 miles away in some places, and our local problems seemed to have been almost solved.

This is a pretty part of Germany, somewhat reminiscent of Eastern Pennsylvania, Maryland, and Virginia, with many rivers and canals that make travel difficult if somebody blows up all the bridges.

One of the interesting and pathetic sights is to see a little family cart containing everything that will hold a few possessions being pushed and pulled along by laborers now freed and going home to Holland, France, Belgium, even Italy, and the Balkans. Many of them have the flag of their country on the cart, and one has chalked on it in English, "Going home to Holland. Please do not delay." There are also many liberated POWs of every possible nationality standing along the highways waiting for heaven knows what.

We also saw many factories, as this is a rich industrial area, and outside each one is a camp where slave laborers from Russia and Lithuania are living. This is how Germany solved the manpower problem and used the countries overrun.

At the Krupp works in Essen, there were about 170,000 employees, of whom 50,000 were captured nationals. The Russians were paid five marks— i.e., 50 cents per month—other nationals higher. Major Jim Boyle of this hospital talked to some Russians who told him this.

Tonight a Russian doctor, a captain, visited the "Ewack" hospital. He was captured by the Germans at Smolensk and has been a prisoner four years. He seemed to have been allowed to go loose, as a lot of POWs were, and was taken in by a doctor in one of the divisions who brought him around here for a visit.

One factory we saw was a synthetic-rubber plant that, interestingly enough, had not been bombed, probably purposely, and even now has started to produce rubber products for the Allies. Some factories, as, for example, those at Essen, are flat; nothing left. Everything we heard about the strategic bombing is true, and the effect on German industry must have been colossal.

We had planned to go over to our headquarters, but it had gotten so far ahead that we could not get there.

The boys have time on their hands and are spending it examining their trophies, especially the many German pistols captured. Many of the line outfits have liberated a pistol per man. Each night we have had at least one self-inflicted wound incurred by boys trying to figure out how their trophies worked.

Tonight was the record, and we have had four boys shot through the hand while fooling with unfamiliar weapons. It is a symptom of idleness or lack of fighting.

The war seems to hang on. The Krauts hang on like a prizefighter, down but not out. Perhaps the Russians can kick them in the shins and knock them over— I hope so. Do take care of yourself. Get a good night's sleep now and then for me.

With love and kisses, H

Dearest Ginny,

It is 10:00 P.M. We are bedded down in our own tent at our new location *[Schöppenstedt]* with the same evac (108th) we spent a few hours with at Kempen the night before we crossed the Rhine. The day and the trip have been a beautiful one. We left headquarters at exactly 8:00 A.M. and arrived here at 6:00 P.M., after 175 miles.

We were traveling in three trucks all the way from Dorsten. Two of them were ours—that is, the two PROCO trucks—and the third was supplied for our duffel by the evac belonging to headquarters, and headquarters gave us a third truck to come up here.

Traveling alone in this manner is much more enjoyable than in convoy, and this is the longest trip alone we have made. I drove one truck, and Elmer rode with me yesterday. But he is such a bum map reader that I made him ride in back of the third truck today and took Ken, who is much more sensible about such things than Elmer.

Frenzl and Mac were in the second PROCO, and Elmer and Alice rode in the back of the third truck—the one supplied by headquarters for the move.

We traveled for the most part on the Reich's so-called *Autobahn,* which you can probably see on any map as running through Recklinghausen, Hanover, Braunschweig, and Berlin. The Krauts have done their best to make it an impossible route by blowing bridges over every likely obstruction, principally rivers and canals.

In some cases, we would have to make a short detour of two to three miles to cross over a pontoon bridge, and other times we might go off the road for as many as 15 miles to go around some obstruction. On one occasion, we had a canal to cross and tried four bridges, all down.

It is too early yet to have the roads well-marked. Finally, a six-year-old little German boy ran out as we looked over the bridge that lay in the canal and volunteered the obvious information: *"Die Brücke ist kaputt."* We finally got from him that a bridge was still up some 10 kilometers from there, and his information proved to be correct. This means that some German second lieutenant probably was not on the ball.

This is in contrast to a good bit of the information we would get from GIs, including MPs, who have not been in the place long enough to get accurate information as to roads, etc., and it is most exasperating to have them tell you that they have been that way only to find out that they could not possibly have done so. But with all the misinformation and road difficulties, we and everyone else who had to get through somehow did, and it is amazing that we did.

The countryside was beautiful. All cultivated, except a few pinewoods, and the roads done in good style. The Autobahn is wide enough for three lanes each way, with a parkway in the center. No signboards and very prosperous-appearing farms along the way.

The road misses most of the towns, but we could see them off the road, and they are essentially undamaged in this area, except the large cities like Hanover and Brunswick.

We really had a day touring Central Germany. Many fruit trees in bloom and flowers galore. We often pondered why these people were satisfied to stay and enjoy this land.

We were also amazed at the not-unfriendly reception we received from some of the people. A soldier is a soldier to kids, of course, but the children all along the way would wave and cheer as if we were the Wehrmacht. Many of the older people, too, would salute when they did not have to, and it is barely possible that some of them regarded us as liberators from the Nazis. This has been an interesting day.

With love to all, H

Wednesday 18 April 1945

Dearest Ginny,

This is a beautiful spot. The evac hospital is in tents by the side of the road. It is located in a position that is on top of a hill overlooking the surrounding country.

In the distance is a range of hills, not high, but nevertheless a definite range. The map lists the highest point as 300 meters. This whole area is farm land or pasture, and we are the only visible things to indicate that a war is in progress some 40 miles away. The farmers worked their fields today, and country folk walked up and down the road as if it were peacetime. The weather has been sunny and warm.

Today has been a day of reorganization and straightening-out for me. At the moment, only three of us—Elmer, Ken, and I—are in our own squad tent alone, and we therefore have more than ample room.

This morning we went through the PROCO equipment for the first time and brought back a piece of canvas for flooring and a gasoline lamp, so we are comfortable.

Our trucks were so heavily loaded that the clutch on one began to slip, so I gave away to the hospital a lot of expendable supplies—like plaster, ether, bandages, and the like—that I do not think we will ever use and which will make the truck much more mobile and likely to last longer.

We also had a chance to sweep and clean the trucks. They needed it badly, as we have been on the move so much the last week that they were filthy dirty.

There is little work here. The hospital is located too far back to get battle casualties, except in an emergency, so we shall probably have a few days' rest. Actually, I suppose the casualties are not very heavy. They have got a lot of released POWs, American and British, who had to be admitted for evaluation.

Some of the Americans were captured in the Battle of the Bulge and had to have marched this far. They were in worse condition than the British, many of whom were prisoners for three or four years and had become used to the food and routine.

We are to be on the night shift again and will change to days on Sunday, if we are still here. We have been up most of the day, as we are figuring on sleeping while on duty. I hope we are not disappointed.

Today I also had a day of rearranging personal things. I took a helmet bath, as the hospital showers are not yet running, because there is no nearby water source. Then I washed some accumulated dirty clothes, but got tired in the midst of it after finishing some undershirts and socks.

I thought I had plenty of shirts cleaned, but when I started to dress I found that I had no clean shirts, so I started in again and washed some shirts. Now I am ready for several weeks without laundry.

I said yesterday that I would tell you about our trip. Among the most interesting things are the groups of four-to-a-dozen freed people who, every mile or so, are trudging down the highway toward home—Poles, French, Dutch, Belgians, Italians, Hungarians, British, Australians, and Americans.

The U. S. Army has not been able to take over the prison camps and supply them with food, I suppose, so as the occupying force goes down the road, some *lieutenant unlocks the gate of a prison camp and out the prisoners come. How they get food, I cannot imagine, but I am sure they do not starve.*

We have seen not the slightest sign of disorder on their part, but then, perhaps we would not. Around 12:00 yesterday we stopped for lunch at the 105th Evac Hospital, where Mac now is. He had gone to bed at 9:00, so we did not wake him up. Bill Fuqua was there, so we ate with him. They had been busy, but were doing nothing, as the war had gone off and left them, as it has us here, even before we can start.

It is now about time to go to work, so we will go over and report in, but I hope we will not have anything to do, as a little rest will be welcomed.

All my love and kisses, H

19 April 1945

Dearest Ginny,

Today we did a little sightseeing in a nearby town, and we got into a Hitler Youth School, in which I picked up this armband, which I send home as a little souvenir. Notice that each one is registered by number. Each party man apparently wore one when in uniform, which was practically all the time.

It is now 10:30 P.M., and we have had no work on our shift, which started at 8:00. I had had a wonderful time in going over once again, your recent letters and arranging them in order and filing them away.

I was stimulated to do it, but a distressing fact is that I cannot find two of them that I picked up the other night when we were at headquarters. I am afraid they dropped out of my pocket en route from headquarters. They may still turn up, but I doubt it.

The bad part is, I had read them but once, but I am sure I know the contents. One of them was written on the day the first charcoal portrait arrived, and I thought you had damned it with faint praise.

In the letter I got today, dated April 9, you seemed to like it better, so perhaps you have just gotten used to it. As a matter of fact, I liked it better myself after looking at it for a while, but the first impression is, I believe, not very good. Perhaps you will prefer the one in sanguine that is on the way.

I am hoping very soon to go over to see Lehman Guyton and Tom Ambler, as they are nearby. Their hospital, the 119th Evac, is the one that Bill Boukalik has as chief of surgery. I believe I really was responsible for Lehman Guyton getting to change, but Tom Ambler's transfer was on Col. Smith's desk the day Lehman and I went in to see him.

We all appreciated getting the information you sent about the Rh. As a matter of fact, we have been having a great deal less trouble lately, probably due to the fact that the blood is now coming through faster and is therefore fresher.

We get it for use about nine to ten days from the time it is drawn in Washington, New York, Boston, in contrast to the 14 days previously. If this is really going to make a difference, the Rh assumes a less-important place than it seemed to a month or two ago when we were having many more bad reactions. We should certainly be having an occasional reaction on the basis of Rh.

Your thoughts about the relation of the cervical glands to carcinoma of the portio [a part of the cervix] are good. It strikes me as a neat problem, and we should be able to know the answer.

The trouble with cancer is that knowing the answer about pathogenesis does not further us toward a cure any more than knowing the cause of tuberculosis helps much in treating it. I shall be most interested in seeing Rich's book on immunology. I did not know he had such a book.

It seems a pretty hopeless field, because I can think of so many important ways the body defends itself against cancer. But that may be because we don't know; e.g., it might be worse if there were not some resistance, for why do cancer cells sometimes lie dormant for years and then suddenly go wild?

We have seen breast cancer that developed widespread metastasis 15 years after apparently being cured and still have no local recurrence. Is this an expression of immunity? I have no idea of how to study this problem, but it seems to me an important one.

I have become discouraged again about the war, as it seems certain that the Krauts will not give up until the whole country is occupied, and that will probably take one more good heave—perhaps the Russians can give it. At any rate, it puts off our day of meeting, and that makes it plenty personal.

With all my love, H

20 April 1945

Dearest Ginny,

We were not busy last night, but our three cases were spread out, so that we did not sleep much, with the result that at 2:00 P.M. today we were still asleep when I got a message to come see Col. Weeks, chief of surgery.

While I was getting dressed, Jack Clark, 5th Aux, came in and said that they had a case about 30 miles down the road at the 67th Field Hospital and no surgeon. The hospital was to close at 1:00 P.M., and the Army had pulled out the teams—i.e., Falor and Buehler—in the morning. The result, a patient came in at noon, and no surgeon.

The patient had a bleeding femoral artery, and they were afraid to move him. So Ken, Elmer, Mac, and I got into a 6 × 6 and took off. We did not wake Alice, as we did not think we would need her, and we knew it would be a dusty, dirty trip.

It was a good case—the femoral artery almost completely divided below the profunda and a fracture of the femur. It took us longer to do than I expected, as it always does, and so we are staying overnight and will go back in the morning. Alice will be fit to be tied for our not bringing her, especially as Gene Bennett's team is here and his nurse is her special friend.

The trip was especially dirty and dusty, as we knew it would be, because there was every conceivable kind of vehicle on the road, including tanks, trucks, etc., and the dust was terrible. We put handkerchiefs over our noses and our glasses on and didn't talk at all, because we could not.

The hospital is now closed, and it is farther to the rear by considerable distance than we are in our evac. I hope that by tomorrow we will have less dirt.

We plan to return to our own hospital by ambulance. We are all sitting around in the shock ward talking, and this letter probably makes very little sense. They have fixed up a little coffee to supplement our supper, which consisted of K rations.

We are so far ahead that the dumps have not been able to keep up, but tomorrow we are to have steak, so things are getting straightened out. The news of the Russians as reported by the Germans, is very good indeed. I hope it is true.

With all love and kisses, H

———————

THE RUSSIAN EIGHTH Guard Army entered Berlin's suburbs on the day I wrote the next letter. General Field Marshal Walter Model committed suicide rather than be taken prisoner by the U.S. Army forces that had encircled and forced the surrender of the Fifteenth and Fifth Panzer divisions in the Ruhr pocket; he regarded surrender by a field marshal to be a disgrace. For 325,000 defenders of the collapsing Third Reich, the war was over.

Saturday 21 April 1945
10:00 P.M.

Dearest Ginny,

We came back here this morning by ambulance, so that the ride was not nearly so dusty and dirty. Besides that, it had rained during the night and there was very little dust all day.

Our patient, incidentally, was fine this morning. The right foot, in spite of having the femoral tied, was warm, and both Ken and Elmer felt a dorsal pedis pulse, although I was never sure. The vessel had to be tied, but below the profunda, and there was a pretty good spurt from the distal end of the vessel when we let it go to see.

Alice and Ken were not along when Elmer and I visited the Hitler Youth School the other day, and as they were anxious to see the place and the library, we went back there this afternoon in one of our trucks. It is a fine new building, well-equipped with the latest teaching tricks, and has many movies, slides, etc.

Most of the books there are historical and geopolitical, but there were a few not-too-good books on other subjects, and I liberated a few, which I hope to send off after I have had a chance to look through them. The best is a several-volume work, Musik Wissenschaft. *I selected only books that were well-illustrated, so that if the children paw through the library, they might like to look at the pictures even if they cannot read the text.*

One of them I am sending for its current events interest is, Die Kunst Deutschen Reich. *Unfortunately, the books are in some instances from the 1907-1920 era, and the reproduction of paintings is not as good as it would be if printed at a later date. I hope to get to Paris someday and pick up some reproductions of famous works of paintings, so that the children might have them about the house. There should be some beautiful ones in color.*

While I was looking at the books, two English medical officers came in. One had been taken prisoner four years ago in Africa, and the other in Crete. The latter was a Lt. Col. from Australia and had been in Baltimore for the Diamond Jubilee of the Johns Hopkins Hospital.

Cap Colston took him to dinner. His name is Lesh E. LeSoef, from Perth, Australia. His special friend seems to be Amos Koontz. You might mention him to Cap if you see him. He is also a friend of Hugh Young's and has written him since they were let out of the prison camp nine days ago.

He said that they had had a bearable time of it, but had difficulty in getting things like medicines, vitamins, and the like. Their food allowance was 1,500 calories per day, but they appear to be well-nourished, although they had gained 12 lbs in nine days.

He said that he was more irked at the Germans since being out than while in, because as he looked around it seemed that they had sufficient of everything to have given POWs more. Workers who lived nearby and were employed at a steel plant got about four times as much.

Incidentally, we passed the Hermann Göring Steel Works today, and it was once more obvious that the labor supply was maintained by camps of foreign workers who now are flying their own national flags.

It has continued to rain here most of the day. I hope you kiss B for me on her birthday.

Love, H

Diary Entry: 21 April 1945, Schöppenstedt

We heard on the radio on the 19th of April that the Germans had advanced 15 miles into the northern flank of Ninth Army, trying to reach some of their troops isolated in the Hartz Mountains. We did not know where the advance was, but we hoped it was not in our area.

We had heard that Army and Corps were not worried. However, we were awakened on the 20th by units of the 2nd Armored Division streaming at about 40 miles an hour down the road toward the rear. The conclusion that they were being pulled out of the line to contain this threat from the north seemed obvious.

However, the 2nd Division was being replaced by the 8th Division. Some of the 2nd Armored Division boys had the idea that their fighting days in the ETO were over.

Sunday 22 April 1945
6:30 P.M.

Dearest Ginny,

The news is very good indeed. It will be interesting to see if Hitler et al. sweat it out in Berlin. It may be that we have seen most of our action, and perhaps from a medical point of view our team is about through.

I am happy to have it so. We expect a quiet night here. There were a few Germans in the woods around here, and last night we dropped a few shells there, and this morning several truckloads of German soldiers came out and gave themselves up. Two POWs were brought in here, having been wounded by the shelling.

One of the phenomena of this war is the way no German has been able to stand up to der Führer and call the whole thing off. The two British officers we met yesterday said that their camp had founded a board to examine the political prisoners in the local jail. The poor German people have a miserable choice—be arrested by the Gestapo or play along with the status quo.

This afternoon I boxed up the books I have accumulated and found that I had three 30 x 18 x 12 boxes. Unfortunately, the APO will not accept packages at the moment, but I will get them off when I have a chance. They will probably be two to three months getting there.

One of the favorite topics of conversation just now is what will happen to the 5th Aux come V-E day. The consensus of opinion is that we will go to the Pacific. No one knows, only guesswork, but vitally interesting guessing.

A good bit of my time is spent in daydreaming about our meeting. Where will it be? Under what circumstances? What will I wear? What will you wear? And so on. However, as dim as these things seem now, it is hard to plan as to locale. I am sure that all details will be gone, and that I shall see and experience only you.

All my love, H

Monday 23 April 1945
2:00 P.M.

Dearest Ginny,

   Last night after writing to you, I did a case. It was an accidental shooting, of which there were three last night.

   This was a perforating wound of the anterior and posterior wall of the stomach. The posterior hole was higher in the lesser curvature and about 1½ inch from the esophagus, and it was a bit trying to get it exposed, but not really difficult.

   I learned something, however. The bullet went out above the pancreas, which I could easily feel, but it went below a small structure that, for the life of me, I could not identify. It was about 1½ inch in diameter and directly below the esophagus.

   I thought of a crus [principal attachment] of the diaphragm, but after the operation, I went to Gray's Anatomy *and was amazed to find that the left adrenal is often located just there, much higher and medial than I would have thought. I had never had occasion to identify it before.*

   At this hospital, there are several British and Americans who have been in Stalags (prison camps) and who were admitted here because of malnutrition. I talked this morning to two of them.

   One was a Welshman from South Wales, where I expect my own ancestors came from. He was 34 years old and a reservist. When war broke out, he became a tank man with the Second British Armored Division and was sent to France. He got out through Brest about a week after Dunkirk, [the escaping British] having burned and destroyed all their vehicles before getting on the boat that took them to Plymouth.

   As he said, things then became a little quiet, and unknown to his brid, he volunteered for the Middle East, where he participated in the first British offensive under Wavell, whom he regards as his "general."

   He was captured when the British were forced to send most of their equipment to Greece. We heard the name "Buqbuq" [North African town] while in our cottage on the Magothy River in 1940. He has been a prisoner since, first Italy and then Germany, finally ending up at Stalag IV near Dresden.

   When the Russians were approaching Dresden in their winter offensive, the prisoners were sent west by walking. He was on the road from January to the 1st of April, walking from Dresden and finally ending up in a camp near Braunsweig.

It was on this march that he lost weight and strength by walking 25 kilometers a day, sleeping in barns and wherever they could, eating bread and soup and many days not having that when they did not meet their supplies.

Many men dropped out and were left lying along the road. The guards were old men, the *Volkssturm*, thought to be about 60 years old, and many of these had to be replaced en route. The POWs were finally released when the 2nd Armored Division came down the pike.

The American I talked with had much the same story and was on the same march from Dresden, where he had been taken after being captured near Bastogne, along with his whole battalion.

For the first six days they had nothing to eat and were almost killed several times by American planes before they got out of the Bulge.

He said that the American planes really wrecked the Germans in the Bulge, and that they were terrified of the American planes, particularly the P-47s. The POWs were pushed around from pillar to post, mostly on foot and with poor food, an expression of the bad state of the internal economy of Germany at that time, I think.

They finally heard over the radio that the Americans were coming. Some of the commandos also brought in similar reports. Commandos were POWs who worked. They called them commandos, and sometimes they came back and sometimes they did not.

At any rate, finally they heard firing in the distance, and a French doctor who was in the camp got permission to take off down the road on a bicycle to see if he could contact the American troops. That night he came back with some K-ration biscuits as evidence that he had found the Americans, who came to the camp the next day.

I do not know if Molly has heard from Tom, but I wish that I knew where he was last reported to be. Released prisoners are running around everywhere and continue to come down the road in small groups.

Enough of unpleasantness and personal tragedies, but they form part of the war through which I am now passing.

The work has been so slight that part of the hospital was knocked down this morning. Right now I am going to take a shower, which is in operation, make my bed, and perhaps take a snooze, because I am pleasantly sleepy—wish that you were here.

Love, H

Diary Entry: 22 April 1945, Schöppenstedt

Yesterday afternoon, late, and during the night, there was rifle fire and machine-gun and cannon fire in the nearby woods. We had heard that about 50 enemy armored vehicles had infiltrated this area, and the poor 2nd Armored Division was given the job of clearing them out. They are reported to have put a small detachment in each town and to have surrounded the woods with strongpoints in the form of tanks. We can see one such point along the edge of the woods across a little valley about a mile or so away. I think the firing last night came from there. We have seen no Germans.

ON 23 APRIL, during a conference with the Swedish consul at Lübeck, Heinrich Himmler offered to surrender the German forces to the Western Allies. The offer was rejected, because the Allies had previously decided that they would accept only surrender on all fronts at the same time.

By 24 April the U.S. Ninth Army's XII Corps, with the 29th Division and the 84th Division, was posted along the Elbe River. U.S. Army and Soviet army units met next day at the Elbe, and the Soviet army completed its encirclement of Berlin.

Friday 27 April 1945
9:30 A.M.

Dearest Ginny,

Since I last wrote I have done a little moving around and ended up almost where I started from. First, a little trip to see Bill Boukalik et al., and then a change of hospitals. Bill Boukalik is chief of surgery at the 109th Evac, and fortunately for Lehman Gray and Tom Ambler, they were transferred to his hospital. They all were well.

Lehman is a new man. He has gained 12 lbs. and now appears very much as he did in the hospital days. He is thoroughly happy. Tom Ambler is about the same. He continues with his Presbyterian outlook and takes things as they come.

Tom is an assistant on one of their teams, and Lehman has been given a minor team; i.e., anesthetist, nurse, and enlisted man, but no assistant. Bill is very pleased with the work Tom does and comments especially on his gentleness in handling tissues. Tom hopes to work into bigger things, and he will some of the time, if three years of not operating wears away.

Bill himself is doing a grand job, as he could not help but do. However, he is not happy in his work, in that he has done exactly two cases since he has been there. He has spent his time keeping the wheels turning. I am sure, after having worked in an evac hospital for a spell, that someone must do this, and if the major-domo relaxes even for a brief spell, things go down.

Often after two or three months of organizing, it would be possible, I am sure, to get a system going where the chief could depend on others. But if the war is nearly over, as everyone seems to think it is, our guiding hand has not left us, and we should never cease to be eternally grateful for my lot in this war.

I recently stood on a hill and looked on Magdeburg and the Elbe. Some of the boys have been into town, but the Krauts are just on the other side of the river (perhaps Russians are there now), and they let go with a few shells now and again, and so I would not go. They call me "Cautious Jones," so you can see that I take no unnecessary risks. I love my wife too much, for the thought of her has kept me from doing things now and again that I might otherwise have done.

Bill Boukalik always has a good story. This time he was in a jeep, and he pulled into a village square and was looking around when, at the far side of the square, around the corner came a Kraut tank covered with German infantrymen, then a second tank slowly coming toward him. What to do? Obviously nothing. Finally, a third tank, which was a Sherman covered with Americans who were shepherding the first two tanks full of POWs into view. He said he has not quite recovered yet.

The towns and highways continue to be streaming with soldiers in every describable uniform. You simply could not tell a real enemy from appearance, because some of the ex-POWs are wearing part-German uniforms and part-anything else. Civilians wear parts of any kind of uniform. This is the greatest confusion imaginable, and taking care of prisoners among them is very difficult.

Recently, a nurse saw a man in the dark who had on a respectable German uniform, and she identified him as a German officer. She got a couple of EMs who dragged him into the hospital, from which they turned him in to the MPs who were in town. The next day the hospital got a flip note for turning in a streetcar conductor on his way home from work.

All sorts of queer stories will come out of the war. Another incident, also supplied by Bill: He was going along the road near the Elbe Weser Canal and was stopped by a Frenchman who was wearing and pointing to a watch shouting, "Millions! Millions!"—and pointing to the woods.

They went over and found about 50,000 watches in crates. They took a few samples and went back the next day with a truck, but the watches were mostly gone by that time. A watchmaker in the hospital personally picked up the debris, which contained about $700 worth of watchmaking instruments.

I have not been so lucky, but the camera situation has petered out, and I now have a folding Kodak that takes 620 film, of which I have none. If you are able to buy any of this size, please send it along, and I shall try to get some pictures of my own.

Lehman also thought he could get me a 35mm camera, and I left him $25 to buy one from a friend of a friend, etc., who had one for sale. I was also given a pair of field glasses—a nice pair, too.

I was thrilled last night to get three letters from you, happy about the 19th of April Hurd Hall talk, which went well, as I knew it would.

You asked about coming to Lisbon, and I hope and know you are not fooling. Travel, except by foot or GI truck, is simply impossible. What will happen after the war I do not know, but it seems terribly hopeless to me now. There are rumors of a special mission for the 5th Aux come V-E Day, but I have not seen the Colonel since I heard all that, and I doubt its validity.

Keep your eyes and ears open for opportunities for some sort of official or semi-official trip that will open the door for travel to you. I can't see how I can get to Lisbon now.

I always enjoy hearing about the babies. They do sound alert and sensible. I hope so. Kiss them for me often.

Love, H

ON 30 APRIL, Adolf Hitler committed suicide in the underground bunker at the Reich Chancellery in Berlin. The Soviet army had virtually already conquered the capital city. The day before, Hitler had designated Admiral Karl Dönitz as his successor.

---

30 April 1945
10:45 A.M.

Dearest Ginny,

Today has been one of those days, so far. You know, a lot of people together, everyone wanting something else, and crowded living conditions.

I got the anti-Rh serum. It came official Army emergency airmail from the biological division of the Army Medical Center in Washington, Colonel S. D. Avery. It now appears that we will not have a chance to use it, which is good. But if we do much work, we will certainly follow through.

As a matter of fact, at the last stand there was very little trouble with the blood. I have seen no anemias since Baesweiler, where we were for the Roer Crossing and where we had four patients, who we almost certainly thought had Rh reactions.

The improvement must be due to the fact that we are getting fresher blood, seldom over 10 days old, in contrast to the fourteen to sixteen days before.

As this war draws to a close, everyone is speculating about the Pacific. They all think we will go. It is a good way to look at it.

All my love, H

Tuesday 2 May 1945
11:00 A.M.

Dearest Ginny,

The team is gradually being broken up. Elmer is going to look after some POWs way back near Cologne, and Kenneth is going up to the 109th Evac (Bill Boukalik) on detached service as assistant to Major Cameron, a neurosurgeon. I believe they will all be back at headquarters in a week or two.

I started a rumor last night as a joke, but everyone seemed to take me seriously, and I have carried it on, since it had such a buoyant effect on the party.

Now that I am back in a staff job, everyone thinks that I know what is going on, which I do not, of course. As usual, the conversation got around to what was going to happen to the 5th Aux and whether it would move as a unit, and so on.

I claimed to have seen a very secret letter—and the fact that I said anything about it should have let them know that it was a fake—that directed the theater commander to give the highest priority for return to the Zone of the Interior of those troops who could be useful in the Zone of the Interior, even if it was contemplated using them at some future date in the Pacific.

The "letter" furthermore said that the only troops useful in the Zone of the Interior at the present time were highly skilled surgeons to aid in the reconstructive work and, furthermore, that auxiliary surgical groups were admirably suited to this use.

I told this to about seven people and said it was very secret and not to breathe a word of it. This morning, at least six other people have come to me wanting to know what that letter was about. I told each of them about it and pledged each of them to secrecy, so that by now I am sure everybody has heard it.

Love, H

P.S. We are moving headquarters tomorrow.

> *2 May 1945*
> *1:50 P.M.*

Dearest Ginny,

Kenneth and I are alone in the living room of this small-town German house. He is playing the piano, and quite well, although he makes numerous mistakes from lack of practice.

He has seldom played since he has been with us and long before, but this house belongs to the village organist, and there is an extensive library of Bach, Beethoven, Liszt, Chopin, and others with which he is familiar and which he enjoys.

He is no ordinary pianist though, and while we were in Übach he amused himself by working out the physics of the musical scale and restated a theory of the scale built up on harmonic notes—that is, the 5th is the most pleasing sound with the fundamental and is, in fact, the 3rd overtone, and so on, until the entire scale is derived, and then he showed that the relation could be expressed by relatively simple numbers.

All the while he is doing this, his bed is undoubtedly not made, and I am sure he has no clean laundry and probably has not answered his mail any better than I have.

His home is Rutherfordton, North Carolina, and he went to Harvard Medical School after attending Chapel Hill. As you know, he spent nine months at Johns Hopkins as an intern, and that, I believe, indicates that he was considered a good student, which he is.

As an assistant, he is adequate, but not the best I have had. He, of course, lacks the knowledge of technical procedures acquired by a term as assistant resident, and, therefore, it is often necessary to give him directions throughout a procedure: Hold this, put your hand here, keep the guts out of my way, and so forth.

Knowing what to do, though, he does it admirably and, therefore, will improve as time goes along. Since he has had no experience before, I have not as yet been able to let him do an abdomen or a chest, and I have helped him with extremities and let him do all the small debridements he wants, as they are tedious to both of us, and he can do them quite as well as I can.

He is slow at this and in all things—the Southern approach. In a field hospital it is necessary to keep moving. There is no night shift to take over at 8:00 P.M. The work is often done only when there are no more patients, and it is therefore necessary to constantly hurry the others along.

Is he ready, Elmer? Don't wash his skin off, Mac—Alice has gone after the gowns—Ken throws the sponge stick in the floor—Let's get going, etc., etc.

I have sometimes told Ken to go in and get things going while I continued to scrub away, only to find him still standing beside the table, having been held up by some triviality, like no towel to wipe his hands when he could have used the sponge.

It would be a relief to have someone who could hurry people along. In an evac, it is not necessary to do this, nor is it in a field hospital when not busy. But it is an essential to good work in a busy field hospital.

It is easy to see that Kenneth has a good family background, as he is well-versed in all the courtesies and is, therefore, a delightful person with whom to live. He shares everything he has and has no sense of responsibility in sharing yours, after having previously selected something about which he is sure you will hold no matter. He often offers to do some small task "for the Major"—get the coal, fill up the canteens—things that no one would ever think of or, if he did, not put his thought into action.

After the war he wants to continue with his surgical training. He will make a good doctor and surgeon and a good research man, if he were so inclined, because, as I have indicated above, he has great intellectual curiosity about all *things and the patience to see things through. I do not at all mind his irresponsibility about the mechanics of life, and wish I were more like it, because it would make me more like you and give me time for things much more important.*

The news is good, but so slow. The end has dragged much more than I thought. Germany's professional soldiers have not been able to take over, as I figured they would. Our striker (German) says, "Dönitz ist ein guter Mann und nicht Nazi."

We shall see, but it certainly seems that there would have to be a slow and painful occupation, including perhaps Denmark and Norway. The war in Europe has dragged on so long that even Hitler's death has aroused little enthusiasm, and I think that any attempt at surrender will likewise arouse the same sensation.

We still sit, but things have gone so far ahead that they may set us up to act as a small evac, perhaps soon. The general feeling is that our really busy times are over. I hope so.

It is less than two weeks to Mother's Day. Will you make the necessary arrangements for remembrance?

My love to you and to our family, H

FOLLOWING THE WAR, Kenneth Tanner returned to Hopkins for further training in general surgery, after which he went to his hometown, Rutherfordton. He joined a surgical group founded by his uncle, Dr. Crawford.

The hospital at Rutherfordton was founded in 1900 and grew gradually. By 2000 it had three hundred beds. Kenneth retired at age seventy. In 2001 he was living in a retirement community in Charlotte.

Kenneth met his future wife, Katherine, at a cousin's wedding in 1947. They married in 1950. They had a son who is an accountant and works for a firm in the Charlotte area. There are two granddaughters.

Nancy Garcia, my office assistant, tracked down Ken for me in the latter part of 2000 by using the Internet. I spoke to Ken and Catchy several times before traveling to see them.

When I first spoke to Ken, he said that he was really quite ill and wasn't sure that he could be up to a visit. But after I talked with

Catchy a couple of times, she said that she thought a visit would be possible. She explained that Ken had to use a walker because of spinal stenosis and was on oxygen because of pulmonary fibrosis; his activities were sharply limited. We agreed that Georgeanna and I would limit our visit to one hour.

She and I had the pleasure, along with Nancy and Doris Gentilini, of visiting in June 2001. That was the first time I had seen Ken since he left Hopkins after his postgraduate training after the war. We enjoyed reminiscing together about our wartime experiences.

He told me how he got to join the 5th Auxiliary Surgical Group, a story I had not heard. Following his nine-month internship at Hopkins, he entered the army and was assigned as a medical officer to a replacement depot near Paris.

After he had been at the replacement depot for some weeks without an assignment, he took it upon himself to visit Elliott Cutler in Paris. Cutler was then chief surgical consultant for the European Theater of Operations. Ken knew Cutler, who was his professor of surgery when Ken was a Harvard Medical School student.

Ken explained to Cutler his interest in having a responsible position. Within a very few days he was assigned to the 5th Aux and, in turn, assigned as an assistant in Team 3. He joined the team at Nuth, Netherlands, in the fall of 1944. Ken provided another beautiful example of how it is sometimes possible—indeed, necessary—to go outside regular lines in order to achieve a desirable goal for all concerned.

What a delightful and precious hour! Remarkably, at the end of our stay, Ken was able to get to the automobile, and Catchy drove with him in the car to lead us out of the maze where they lived, so that we could get on our way back to Norfolk.

Following the visit, Ken sent a kind note, which he had typed, saying how much he had enjoyed seeing and talking with us and expressing hope that we could do it again. We planned to return. But in July, a month after our visit, Catchy wrote to say that Ken had died.

8 May 1945
1:00 p.m.

Dearest Ginny,

Yesterday afternoon, late, while on a little trip, we heard the news of the unconditional surrender to the three powers [Britain, the Soviet Union, and the United States] and, therefore, V-E Day. Most people's reaction is the same: And now the Japs.

What will happen to us? Do I go home first, before going to the Pacific?

There is no real enthusiasm in response to the German defeat, and the end has been so gradual that our daily life goes on the same. For the fighting troops is the realization that now they will at last leave here alive, and they too find their enthusiasm dampened by the thought of being sent to the Pacific.

We have had some work. We are the only hospital east of the Elbe River in the 9th Army area and are supporting three divisions and corps troops, so that the accidents and incidentals keep one team moderately busy.

Bill Fuqua and I alternate 24 hours on and off. Today I am on. We have treated two gunshot wounds of the hand and an acromioclavicular [near the shoulder] separation. Perhaps I should say Ken is treating them now while I am writing. I have done one laparotomy with 15 perforations of bowel from an accidental wound.

It is good duty, as over 40 teams are already back at headquarters and I much prefer to stay out until the last. We shall probably stay here as long as there are American troops across the Elbe. I believe this is to be Russian territory.

Yesterday Team 3 in toto started out to see the Russians. They are a few miles up the road. We went to Schwerin. The Russians are five miles from there.

We stopped at division headquarters for lunch, and everyone we talked to advised us against trying to see the Russians. In fact, they doubted that we could get through the lines without a proper escort. The difficulty seems to be that the Russians just have not settled down yet and spend most of their time drinking and shooting. We talked to several people who had the most astonishing yarns about this.

At division headquarters the Russian divisional commander was entertained at luncheon. His aide arrived three sheets to the wind, and spent the time in the back seat of their car. After lunch the band played the American and Russian national anthems. *In the midst of things, the aide comes to, stumbles out of the car, gives a salute with a whoop, and scrambles back in.*

On the first days of contact, three Russian officers were entertained by some officers of the medical battalion of the 82nd Airborne Division. For this occasion, the hosts got out a bottle of bourbon, carried all the way from the States. The Russians grunted and said it tasted like strong wine or weak whiskey.

We have had admitted here two GIs from nearby who were on the opposite side of a picket line from the Russians and apparently cemented relations by handing over some vodka. We had to give the GIs 2,000 cc of glucose and let them sleep for 24 hours.

At any rate, I wanted to go see the Russians, but we did not even go up to the lines yesterday. I am going to try to arrange something of an official trip to see the medical setup. I may not succeed, as I am not well-acquainted with the corps or divisions, but it is worth a try.

I do not know if you have a map of enough scale to follow our little trip, but yesterday we went from here to Schwerin to Ludwigslust to Hagennow to home.

Near Ludwigslust we came upon a concentration camp said to contain political prisoners of all nations. We spent an hour or so there. There were eight or ten buildings of brick with dirt floors. They had been horribly overcrowded and the confinees underfed, because many of them had died of starvation.

We saw at least 50 bodies of individuals who had died in various places about the camp and were just left lying where they had died. Some prisoners were still alive, and we were being escorted while we were there.

The camp was being cleaned up by the German civilians from the nearby town. The victims were to be given a mass burial with military honors in the village square, as a perpetual reminder to the German people of what went on near their village.

It has apparently been the policy of the military government to remind the Germans by such selection of burial places and by employing civilian German labor to clean up the camps that they are held responsible for the deaths of these people. I took some pictures with my new Leica.

I came by the Leica yesterday. I bought it from a British Tommy who needed some money ($90), so now I have more cameras than I know what to do with. I could use some 35mm Kodachrome film.

I have sent home another box of clothing that I do not need and another sleeping bag for future use. In the bag is a box camera with a very fine lens. It can be used for pictures of the babies and can also be used outdoors with a film pack. I believe you will be able to get such a film pack more readily than 127mm film.

We have had no mail since crossing the Elbe. The enclosed photo was taken at Dorsten when we were there with the 41st Evac. It was taken by Alice with her box camera.

Love, H

Ludwigslust, Germany, May 1945. Sergeant Frentzel and one of the concentration camp's many victims.

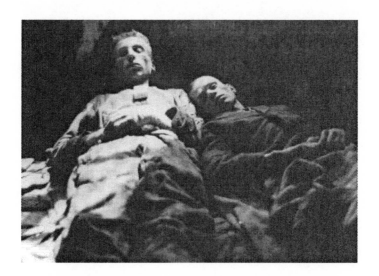

Ludwigslust, Germany, May 1945. These two inmates were alive, although you could tell this only by the movement of their eyes. They were otherwise so weak that they could not move.

Ludwigslust, Germany, May 1945. The military government
required the civilians of Ludwigslust to prepare the graves
for the victims.

Chapter 14

Letters from Home
5 April-21 May 1945

Thursday, April 5, 1945
10:30 P.M.

My darling,

*T*HERE ARE ALL SORTS OF REPORTS OF GERMAN-
civilian sniping at any troops indiscriminately—majors in Medical Corps being killed, etc., so do be careful and don't go tooting around the countryside.

No letters today or yesterday, but Benny Guyton called today to say that she had a letter from Lehman, dated March 26, in which he said his transfer had been effected. He was with Tom Ambler and tickled to death. They both attributed it all to you, and I am sure this is true. Too, I think you are wonderful, and I love to hear other people rave about you.

She also told me something you perhaps already knew: Crampton is out of the Army. He had a severe coronary thrombosis and has had several minor attacks since.

I was especially pleased to hear that Benny's letter was dated the 26th, as perhaps this means there will be no holdup of any mail. This I dread most of all. A day without a letter is a day blank.

We are all much better now, and I trust that in a few more days all will be completely recovered.

I spent the day doing histochemistry. I got also one of my first ideas. Is the cervical secretion carcinogenic or is it only an infection of the cervical glands, that is carcinogenic? Why does cauterization or conization of the cervical glands prevent carcinoma of the portio? Is the content of cervical mucus high in estrogen? Not too good a problem, but something which is fairly easy. I have not expressed it well, but I mean to say, is there a specific carcinogen (estrogen) in the cervical secretions or does an infection produce excessive aging?

Willie has to hear a story about Papa every night, so I tell him about Papa and Willie at Fort Sam. You would be surprised at all the things you do.

Every once in a while he wants one about "Papa in Germany." Then we have to invent a little boy over there for Papa to play with. He is especially interested in what the sick soldier boys do with their guns when they go to the hospital.

I have been getting all sorts of advice about framing my picture of you. I am very anxious to have it done, as I am sure it will be just what I need in the bedroom. It is a trifle sad in expression, but nevertheless I love it. Willie recognized it as Papa at once.

Do be careful and come home well soon to Mama, Willie, and B.

All my love, Ginny

Friday, April 6, 1945
11:00 P.M.

Dearest Honey Bunny,

Now that it's all over but the shouting, it is even harder to wait. I am sure this period must be dreadfully trying for you. Nothing to do and just waiting to hear about what happens next. If you have to wait around, do try to get a leave and visit a general hospital, as you have wanted to. England would be nice, as you could see Tom Auld and perhaps visit Ennal's Hospital.

Of course, I am hoping this won't happen and that they will send the medics home in charge of the wounded. Practically every night I dream that you are here.

Do you suppose I'll ever get used to having you home and not be afraid to wake up for fear you will be gone?

The Signal Corps picture arrived, and I love it. Every detail of your life fascinates me. The head mirror which you had previously described was especially interesting. Most of the other men looked paunchy, but you don't seem to me to have changed a bit.

I was glad to hear that the transfusion reactions are less frequent. If the Rh serum comes, perhaps you could play with it, if they let you go back to a general hospital. But you would do much better back here in this country.

I ran out of ink, so I am finishing this round at JHH. Had an interesting discussion of carcinoma. Wish you were here.

All my love, Ginny

P.S. I am off to surgery to see a breast hypertrophy increased size of organ attributable to cellular enlargement of 24 and 22 lbs.

Sunday, April 8, 1945
9:30 P.M.

My darling,

The war news continues good, but as I have so often said, each hour now is much harder to bear. I am so anxious to receive a letter describing what you are doing and, if possible, where you are.

Last night the TeLindes' party for the Bracks was quite a nice get-together, but the party just made me miss you more. It is nice to see Bozo back and see that he is just exactly the same as he ever was.

I speak at the JHH medical meeting tomorrow. I am really so apathetic about it, I am not even worried. I hope it will go well, but I will get no pleasure out of it without you.

My greatest pleasure, aside from receiving and writing letters, is the memory of our life together. I have recently been recalling our sailboat trip down the bay, cooking and sailing together, swimming, and resting in the beautiful evenings and nights. Do you remember that night at Solomons Island? It was one of my star-

spangled memories. Also, those disgraceful shorts of yours. At the end of the trip, I knew all.

Darling, do be careful and don't take any unnecessary risks or trips. I am as much afraid of a road accident as I am of Germans.

All my love, Ginny

P.S. Ess and Ruth were here yesterday and are well.

Monday, April 9, 1945
12 midnight

My dearest Honey Bunny,

Tonight I gave my paper before the JHH Medical Society at Hurd Hall, and all day I have been sustained by the thought that there were four letters awaiting me at home. The latest was March 31—really record time, and such an interesting letter.

I am so delighted and proud to know that you had the privilege of doing the first operation east of the Rhine. If one must go to war, one might as well have things to talk about afterwards.

Father is all for putting it in the paper, but I dislike such publicity. I might consider Under the Dome *[Johns Hopkins Medical School publication], however. I shall certainly look for the pictures, and do obtain copies from the Signal Corps, if possible.*

I am disgusted about your sprained ankle. Why don't you break it and get sent home? Father says you should have the Purple Heart for it. Seriously, I do hope it isn't too painful and that you will be completely recovered when you receive this. What a pity I can't be there to strap it and love it for you.

Is the tumor of the general's hand a palmar one? Possible a fibroma or neurofibroma?

My speech went off quite nicely, by far the best presentation of the three, I thought. Everyone was quite complimentary and got a great kick when I laughed about getting the right button for the lantern slides.

I really don't enjoy giving a paper without you, however, as it just doesn't seem important. No one is really interested in how I do, and that is the most important thing to me. I just keep thinking, "Howard would want me to be good, and so somehow I manage to be good, but it's no fun." I sat next to Ward Allen, who inquired in detail about you. This, of course, pushed him up 10 points in my estimation.

> *With all my love and oodles of kisses, Ginny*

> *Tuesday, April 10, 1945*
> *12:00 midnight (V-mail)*

My darling,

A V-mail, as I feel that possibly will go better. The news from now on in, I am afraid, will be bad. That is, it will be too slow to suit my racing heart. Everyday my longing for you becomes more difficult to bear.

I saw Mrs. Bucher this afternoon while walking with Willie, and she says Nancy is rather at loose ends. She rather believes that she would like to have a job with UNRA [the United Nations Relief Agency], but I doubt it.

I wish she would come back to JHH. She has had a splendid time in Boston, apparently—skiing, etc. Mrs. Bucher wanted especially to be remembered to you. Don't forget dear, if anything happens to me, Nancy is my next election for you, if she is still available.

Discoveries at the laboratory are still making haste slowly. The thiouracil work should be completed in another month, and I am afraid all will simply prove that rats and guinea pigs aren't humans. I am going to talk to Corner about the possibility of monkeys.

Our histochemistry progresses very slowly because of the lack of supplies. It will probably take quite a spell to collect a good series also. Everything would go faster with Papa at the helm.

> *With a goodnight kiss and a snuggle and*
> *all my love, always, Ginny.*

> *Wednesday, April 11, 1945*

My darling,

Today five letters! A red-letter day. And to think I didn't even know how wonderful you were when I married you.

I am always so interested in hearing about your cases. The through-and-through repair of the diaphragm is indeed ingenious. I am glad that after having worked so hard over so concentrated a period that you do have a resting spell. I don't want your resistance lowered. You've got to be in tip-top shape for our reunion.

I will be interested in reading the reprints you sent and will comment tomorrow. We always enjoy your bits of German literature and are looking forward to the "liberated" books with pleasure. You are truly having a priceless experience, and one which no doubt will be interesting for both of us to look back upon. The living of such an experience is not all pleasant, however.

Willie was very funny this A.M. He hates to dress and takes very decided likes and dislikes to clothes. Today I really had to make him put on some overalls he didn't like. After he got them on, he said, "I'm going to wet them," just as calm and premeditated as you please. He didn't, but I wouldn't have been surprised if he had. He is certainly determined about having his way.

B is now just the age Willie was when he came to San Antonio. She is not as mature as he was in any way. Doesn't look as old, doesn't get around like he did, and doesn't say words, e.g., "clothes" and "shoes," which he did. She is nevertheless a superior baby, and as sweet as they come.

Mrs. [H. S.] (do you remember her case?). Amenorrhea in a marriage eight years ago. Menstruated regularly after H. went overseas (three years). Amenorrhea again now that he has been back three months. She should be put in a case and exhibited.

Had lunch with Donnie, who is well and happy and hears regularly from Joe, who is not in combat. Biddie (Isabel Bittinger) is taking her second baby to her mother-in-law tomorrow. She is even worse than I am, but she also adores her mother-in-law, who adores the babies, who adore her, so all is serene. Biddy claims to have made $14,000 last year, but in New York City that's not much.

My thoughts are always on the time when we will once more be together.

All my love, Ginny

Thursday, April 12, 1945
10:30 P.M.

My darling,

Today the shocking news of the President's death. I am, as usual, speculating on what you think about this. It surely seems at first thought like an irreparable tragedy when we consider the vice president, and I did think that Roosevelt did not delegate authority. The State Department is deplorably weak, and its personnel were chosen on the basis of their ability to be handled, as far as I can see.

However, I have never trusted Roosevelt and have never thought that his policies were in line with those held by the majority of the American people. His death, therefore, may give the people a chance to exert their influence, and I hope that would be good.

I cannot think that the war effort could be interfered with. By now you are undoubtedly in connection with the Russian Army, but Roosevelt's death can, I suppose, unquestionably interfere with the peace. What a blessing that his death was sudden and final, instead of protracted like Woodrow Wilson's.

I frequently close my eyes and try to pretend what it would be like to have you here again. Just the thought makes me goose-pimply—being able to go to sleep at night, cuddled in your arms, and awake in the morning and be conscious of your presence even before I am really awake, or open my eyes and to know all through the day that you are near and, joy above all, to be able to work with you, by you, and for you, and to be able to laugh and tease and plan with you, to enjoy music with you and the children with you. All of this is life's greatest gift.

All my love, Ginny

Friday, April 13, 1945
10:30 P.M.

My darling,

No letter today, and I have contented myself with rereading those five received Wednesday. I am wondering now how near you are to Berlin. Not too near, I trust, as I don't like large enemy cities.

The papers seem to think that this war will be technically over in a matter of days. If this is so, I wonder how our own personal D-Day will be affected. I am becoming discouraged about my ability to come to you. All reports indicate that travel will be just-about prohibited. You can rely on my coming, if possible, however. I keep hoping against hope that our luck will hold and something unusual will happen.

Bill Reinhoff said he would be delighted to send the reprints. Have I also told you that many people have stopped me to say they enjoyed the talk I gave at Hurd Hall? Now I have to work up my lecture for the students in endocrine therapy in gyn for next Monday.

There is not much in the way of news. I have spent the afternoon going over a paper by Pincus that was submitted to the Clinical Journal of Endocrinology for publication. As usual, it is a presentation of chemical methods with no figures to back up the procedures. It looks as if he sat down and wrote it from pure theory.

Your box arrived today, and I'll put the things away for future reference. Elmer writes that he is sending me some perfume, but as yet it has not arrived. I wonder what it will be like. He is still in France.

You have not mentioned Bill Falor recently and have never seen Tom Ambler again, I suppose. Also, do tell me about Martha Smith and Bob Ewing. How are they making out?

All my love, Ginny

Monday, April 16, 1945
11:00 P.M.

My darling,

Our big news is that King is on the West Coast. He called at 2:30 A.M., and Father practically tried to make him hear without the use of instruments, e.g., the telephone. I am sure everyone in the household was awakened, but he burst out of the room calling, "King's in California," practically at the top of his voice. Such excitement was good to see. Jane is coming down Wednesday.

My big news, of course, is that I received your letter of April 9 written in an evac hospital and telling about POWs. They must indeed be a very sorry crew. But I suppose anyone raised under a government like the Nazis would be.

We were all distressed about the Elbe River bridgehead loss of life. At this stage, it seems even more tragic, as it is so unnecessary, really.

The Pounds are really worried about King, who is with Patton, and Leoda Danner about her brother, who is in the infantry and in the 30th Division. He is a 2nd Lt., so look out for him.

Willie and B are fine. Ess and Ruth are well, and I am well, but miss you more and more. It thrills me to even have you mention that there might be a possibility for you to get to a named general hospital.

We are all deeply interested in the news of Truman. He has apparently selected a capable adviser—James F. Byrnes [who had been serving as a director of war mobilization]. We are wondering if he will put in Jesse Jones instead of

Secretary of the Treasury Henry Morganthau Jr. I really believe that he may be better than Roosevelt, but a little time will tell.

I go on dreaming of and planning for the day when you return. Such thoughts are sweet.

All my love, Ginny

Tuesday, *April 17, 1945*
11:30 P.M.

Dearest Honey Bunny,

Two letters today—the 5th and 8th—explaining those of yesterday. I'm so glad for you to have such varied experiences. It is certainly interesting, as well as excellent background. I still thrill when I think of even the remote possibility of a named general hospital.

Everything moved so rapidly last week that I kept wondering if you moved, but I am sure many must have been tied up with the Ruhr, and that probably means you.

Father was so excited and proud that you performed the first operation east of the Rhine that I know he's told everyone. He is also hoping you're right up there ready to enter Berlin first, but that does not appeal to me. He really enjoys your letters almost as much as I do.

Have I ever told you how much I enjoyed your characterization of Elmer? I still reread it and laugh. I will be interested to hear about the majors who are "set" in their ways. Also, I do want a picture of you in the Eisenhower jacket. In fact, I just want a picture, period.

I have spent the last hour cleaning and dusting Jane's room for the expected arrival. Every time I dusted a piece of bric-a-brac, I thought, "Not for me." I really approve of a streamlined household for children and housekeeping in general. Plenty of storage space for sports equipment, but no junk.

Libby is coming up Friday so we will be here for B's birthday. We hope King will make it by Saturday but do not expect him before the first of the week.

I still miss you incredibly. It's unbelievable that such an acute ache won't become chronic, but it just doesn't.

All my love, Ginny

Thursday, April 19, 1945
4:30 P.M.

My darling,

This is the letter of yesterday which I just didn't get written. Auntie Jane arrived, and she does require a lot of attention. Besides not having seen her in three months, we had lots to chat about.

Willie and I drove down to the bus terminal to get her, and Willie went into ecstasy about the porter, his idol. I am worried about keeping him from getting too excited when the whole clan arrives. I hope we have good weather, and I'll just keep him outdoors all the time, away from it all.

I am encouraged about the news, as the newspaper opinion seems to be that the shifting of troops has really already begun. Of course, I am hoping for the best shift, but no matter; the sooner it is accomplished, the sooner it will be over.

I received your V-mail of April 5 yesterday, in which you said the Bloodgood needles arrived and were put to use. I thought perhaps you could make use of some more, so I am enclosing two more.

Do let me know about the Rh plus factor and serum as soon as possible. Dr. Diamond is very interested in hearing about your project and results.

Our case of chorio is a mole, but with some substance which resembles pregnanediol but which we are now in the process of identifying. It is in the amounts encountered in a normal menstruating woman, not a pregnancy, and certainly not in excessive amounts. We have never encountered pregnanediol at all in the other three chorios we have studied.

Our miscarriage work continues to be the most interesting project. I really think we are learning a great deal from it, and not only theoretical, but practical, knowledge. I hope I can persuade Eleanor by the end of the summer that we have enough data to publish. I would like to present it at the JHH and get it put in the bulletin.

B now takes a few steps, so I suppose you could technically say that she walked before the age of one year.

We are at the unfortunate stage of having to change her schedule. She and Willie have begun to conflict in their sleeping habits and will have to be started on a more-similar schedule. After King leaves and the excitement dies down I may take a partial vacation and help reschedule them.

My hopes are always for a break, and perhaps we shall have one. Who knows?

All my love, Ginny

Saturday, April 21, 1945
10:00 P.M.

Dearest Honey Bunny,

King arrived home at about 2:15 P.M. Jane, Lib, and Mother drove down to Meade to get him, and Jane had hysterics all the way down. He looks well, but thin and weather-beaten.

It turns out that Ron Gibbs, who came with him, was ill with dysentery. He was King's roommate, and now I am sure King came by boat to bring him home. He is in the hospital at Meade.

King has the sorriest outlook on the war I've heard yet. I guess the CBI [China-Burma-India Theater of Operations] is a good place to pick it up. He thinks the social setup—China and India—impossible. Has no hope of ever making anything out of people, who, he thinks, are congenitally dishonest. I think distance will mellow him.

He was very pleased with the children. Willie treats him like a puppy and finally got up courage at the table to ask him to sit next to him. Then he said very softly, "How did you get along?"

That broke the ice, and I am afraid he is going to be a nuisance. But he is having so much fun, I hate to interfere, and, so far, King is flattered. He is teaching him all sorts of tricks, which I am afraid will take a long time to unteach.

The house is in a general uproar, and I hope that Father and Mother don't get exhausted. I also hope that the weather is good and I can keep Willie out almost all day to avoid the stairs.

Donnie and Jimmie came over with Spot (the biggest Irish setter you ever saw) and Geneva (the little colored girl), and a wonderful time was had by all. Jimmie and Willie get along famously, and both are very much alike. We are going to try to have them together often, as they both need it.

Having King home is a great comfort, and it makes me think that someday

I'll have you back, and then these months of separation will vanish, and time will begin again.

All my love, Ginny

Wednesday, April 25, 1945
10:30 P.M.

My dearest Honey Bunny,

The second portrait arrived today and, of course, I love it too. They are so different, but I find it impossible to say which I prefer. Of course, any part or sentiments of Papa are exquisitely dear to me.

We are having to make some more shifts in the portfolios, and I am thinking of trying to acquire some more stock. John is sending you copies of all communications.

We are exchanging the government bonds for new issues and making a little something by the deal, apparently. I do hope you get back in time to go over my new acquisitions before the next stock-market crash comes.

We had a very busy day in the dispensary. Did not finish until 1:45 P.M. When you come here, it might be nice to spend some of your leave visiting clinics— tumor and gyn—for ideas. I'd like to see some endocrine and sterility clinics.

Willie needs a father badly. This always comes out after the weather has been bad and he has had to stay in. He had a temper tantrum today because I cut his sausage and couldn't put it together. No other sausage would do, and it had to be that piece.

I left him in solitary splendor until he decided he wanted to eat breakfast, but such a scene is very wearing. Fortunately, they are very rare.

B is getting to the point where she knows her own mind, and we will very soon know more about her personality. My, I do hope that you will get home before too long, as they are both growing so rapidly.

I am so restless for you tonight—sometimes I think reading your letters makes me so—and then when I don't receive them, I think not hearing from you makes me so. I guess the answer is, I just love you always and in all ways.

All my love, Ginny

Monday, April 30, 1945
10:30 P.M.

Dearest Honey Bunny,

Today three lovely long letters, April 17, 18, and 19, all about your trip across Germany and getting established in your new hospital. I do feel that "last heave" which you speak of, has been made and that it is "all over in Europe." I am so anxious to get this first letter in which you say so too. I am so wanting to have an inkling of what and when the next move will be.

You say that you think I did not like the charcoal, but you are wrong—I was deeply moved by it from the start. But at the time I received it we were in such an upset time here, and I am afraid my letters were a bit scattered. I liked both the charcoal and the sanguine, but perhaps the charcoal a bit better, because it represents "you in Belgium" to me.

In other words, it helps me hold a little bit more of the life with you which I have not physically shared. I still have not seen them framed, but I expect that frames will do a great deal for them, artistically speaking. It is hard to hold a drawing up and view it to the best advantage. It really has to be mounted.

King and Jane are back from Hagerstown, and he is deep in the heart of his stamp-and-coin collection, cataloging. They are constantly on the go, and Kay Gibbs says she couldn't understand people going into seclusion. I can, and I don't think I am antisocial, but I'd like to see no one but you for at least the first few days. But I guess being old married people and having babies makes it different.

Willie is his usual comical self. This A.M., while eating bread and jelly for breakfast, he spilled the jelly and said, "Howard, you are a mess." Mother said, "Who says that?"—and he said, "Burgess." Now, he hasn't seen Burgess since before Christmas and still plays with her in his imagination.

I don't think he is a hellion at all. He is noisy, but I don't think you can expect him to be silent at 2½ years. He really minds me very nicely and is quite smart about doing things for himself. He has to be occupied, but if he once gets outdoors he is fine. He does need Papa and, then, so does Mama.

All my love, Ginny

May 9, 1945
12:15

Dearest Honey Bunny,

I am waiting for Eleanor to have lunch and so want to write the letter for last night. Yesterday was V-E Day officially [actually, May 7 was V-E Day], and everything was closed as tight as a drum. No celebration so far as I could see.

Last night we had the Journal Club meeting at Dr. Hundley's, and I certainly wish you could have been here. Joe Hibbitts carried on as usual. He had a paper on the use of testosterone in controlling symptoms of advanced carcinoma of the cervix.

In summary, he said "androgenons" produced beards, acne, and a hoarse voice, but an apparent improvement in "morals." Pop said sub rosa that he supposed it might be anticipated that a beard would be conducive to better morals—no opportunity.

Everyone really talked about the war more than GYN. Dr. Brady told me he had heard that there would be very few medical officers left in the Army of Occupation. I said, "Yes, they are all going to the Pacific," but, of course, I am still hoping for a break.

King and Jane came home about 12:00 midnight and had to talk, so I didn't get to sleep before 1:00 A.M. This life is killing me.

Dr. Wharton's little 18-year-old son has just left for his Army boot camp training, and he feels very low, although he hides it nicely.

My specialty is amenorrhea now. I think I'll have to take up a course in psychiatry or else hypnosis to cope with some of these problems. A number of them are certainly "schizy."

Well, so to lunch and then Vitamin E determinations.

All my love, Ginny

Thursday, May 10, 1945
11:00 P.M.

My darling,

Your sweet little love letter of April 29 arrived today, and I am a new woman. What a difference mail makes in my morale. I do wish the Post Office Department would catch up to you, for both our sakes.

I wonder where you are in relation to headquarters now. The front seems to be so spread out that I can't quite picture relationships. The papers say that things will really start to move Saturday, May 11, so perhaps when you receive this the 5th Auxiliary Surgical Group will be back together again in bivouac. I do hope you won't have to sit around, but can do some interesting sightseeing—not in Germany.

Do give me any news of Dave Monahan, because Louise will be glad to hear any word.

I have just finished my bath and am lying in bed almost content. Do you realize it has been about 10 months since I had my back scrubbed? They'll have to send you home soon to provide the necessities of life.

Our thyroid experiments are just about completed now, and it certainly appears that hypothyroidism has no deleterious effect upon reproduction in the rat or guinea pig. If you get to Switzerland, talk to someone about spermatogenesis in hypothyroidism.

We had a beautiful "Ginny" tumor yesterday. It has every type of granulosa-cell tumor in it, from theca on up to typical Ginny areas. No hyperplasia. I don't mind these tumors not being functional, now that I really believe the granulosa cell is not a secretory cell per se.

Has the Rh serum ever arrived, and if so, do you think you can do something with it? I still hope for a miracle to happen and for you to get here.

All my love, Ginny

Friday, May 11, 1945
7:00 P.M.

Dearest Honey Bunny,

I am waiting for Jane and King to get ready and then we all will be ready to go to Ann Muse's for dinner. They are both slow and try to do too many things at one time. This A.M. King got a telegram to disregard his Asheville orders and proceed to Fort George G. Meade STAT. He had just returned the Asheville tickets when he received a second one. Disregard first telegram and report to Asheville. Just like the Army, eh?

No letter today. Your postal service is going to pot.

Dr. Novak called my beautiful granulosa cell carcinoma (Ginny tumor) a papillary adenocarcinoma. Just what I expected.

I am so hoping for a recent word from you. I wonder how long before we have some inkling of whether you might get home. I hate to think of the approach of our July anniversary.

All my love, Ginny

Saturday, May 12, 1945

My darling,

Today three lovely letters, but discouraging. I am sure from their tenor you do not expect to get home. Actually, I have never really expected it either, but one cannot help but hope. I am now hoping for rapid radical changes in the Pacific War, forestalling any major shift of troops.

I went downtown this afternoon to do several things and looked for an identification bracelet for Elmer. I can't get one for much less than $15, so I think perhaps I will take that out of his savings account. The stores are still decorated for V-E Day and look very pretty. The weather was wonderful, like a day in the mountains. Father had a GI series today, and it is absolutely negative. His blood pressure is good, but he runs a low-grade fever, perhaps gallbladder. It's very distressing to everyone.

Willie graduated to a bed today and is tickled to death. He helped put the bed up, which really pleases him most. He saw the attic storage space for the first time and said, "Bessie, what is it? A garage?"

I am so pleased that you have secured a camera. We will send you film at once. I have also secured some 127mm for me and will try to get some more candid shots of the babies.

I am so pleased to hear about Lehman, and I will call Benny Monday to give her the news. Bill Boukalik has certainly gathered the experiences. I am more than glad that you didn't have to take such a job. And also, may I say that your wife appreciates so much your love of her? I am sure that what pleasures you are deprived of by avoiding danger are doubly made up for by my peace of mind about you. And besides, you know I have felt since the moment you left that you were going to be "Cautious Jones" to comply with my wishes. Again, many thanks, my dear.

We had a very pleasant evening with Ann Muse last night, and I saw King really for the first time since he has been here. He had the time of his life telling tall tales.

*I certainly don't believe the drivel which is written about service personnel
returning from overseas and being reticent about talking about their experiences.
You'll enjoy hearing some of his experiences when you return. His experiences are
apparently widely different from yours.*

*I am constantly hoping against hope that some miracle will happen and I will
see you before long. It is maddening to think that even now you may have some idea
of your future and I don't.*

All my love, Ginny

Friday, May 18, 1945
10:30 P.M.

My darling,

*Today I have had an unusually interesting day and, as usual, miss you
terribly to chit-chat with when the day is over. I saw two ovarian tumors, one a
Meigs Syndrome.*

*Incidentally, I had fun astounding the house staff with both. One they had
diagnosed as a hydatid mole [a cluster of fluid-filled vesicles in the womb] and the
other as carcinoma of the fundus or ovaries. I hope I am right in both of my
diagnoses.*

*Had a little discussion with your friend York about a question of pregnancy
or myomata. He tries to say anything he thinks you are going to say, and I still
think it was a shame to ruin a good anesthetist.*

*Ate lunch with Ruth Murray (you remember her mother's cousin with a
migraine you treated with X-ray). She is Grant Ward's secretary for the Tumor
Clinic now and is fine.*

*Then, who breezes in but Nancy Bucher, down from Boston for the week
and very much as usual, if a trifle thin. She is going to be at the Massachusetts
General Hospital for a time, so we primed her to learn about the current thought
up there along the lines we are pursuing. I still hope that she will come back to us
someday, and I believe she will, if the offer is attractive enough. There is talk of
Astwood going to Tufts.*

*I then advised one of our assistant residents on a current problem. He wants
to know if removal of one ovary interferes with the function of the other. I don't
know how he aims to determine this.*

He thinks if function is not sacrificed, then perhaps the surgeon should remove one ovary at every laparotomy, as a 50% prophylactic measure against carcinoma of the ovary. A little crackpot, I thought, but my contribution was that the right ovary should be removed.

The Vitamin E studies are now progressing nicely, and the histochemistry is at least underway.

Eleanor and I went to the dinner meeting of the OB/GYN Society when Titus spoke on the place of the obstetricians and gynecologists in the Army and Navy. Not so good.

The news about Russia about to declare war on Japan is good. Perhaps the Pacific War will be over before you get there.

All my love, Ginny

Sunday, May 20, 1945

Dearest Honey Bunny,

This time last year we were leaving to rejoin you in Texas. What a short time we had together in actual calendar days, but a wealth in togetherness. My store of memories from those few short weeks is a constant source of strength and pleasure.

The dearth of news is nerve wracking. I vacillate from hope to despair. I hang on to every bit of news about a negotiated peace in the Pacific. Tonight the radio commentators seemed hopeful, and everyone seems to think that more can be expected of Truman than Roosevelt.

I took Willie to St. Agnes this A.M., and it would have pleased you to see how he can climb. It practically turns your hair gray, but he is as agile as a monkey. Almost everyone says what a big child he is, so perhaps he won't be a little squirt. I do hope he isn't too "bratty" by the time you get home.

He loves a change in his routine. Today he went to lunch on the porch so he could "see the birds and flowers." His language is really comical. Today he asked for some, "copryapes," meaning apricots. Did I tell you he pinned a clothespin on the back of B's neck the other day and then ran screaming and crying to Mother, "Come quick, I've hurt B." She too was yelling her head off, of course.

Ess and Ruth came over tonight, and both seemed very well. They took

Willie for a walk, which was a great help, as it allowed me to put B to bed quietly and to make the orange juice without the two of them at my heels.

I am impatient for morning, as I think perhaps it will bring some mail. Is it possible that I love you even more than ever? It seems to be.

All my love, Ginny

Monday, May 21, 1945
11:30 P.M.

Dearest Honey Bunny,

Today four letters, May 2 through 5—Surrender Day—and what interesting letters! They were worth waiting for, but make me all the more anxious for others. Today we learned that the First Army (and perhaps the Third) is on the way to the States, headed for the Pacific.

I somehow feel that many units of the Ninth Army will comprise the Fifteenth Army of Occupation, but I do not see how a surgical group would be necessary. I keep talking myself into getting you home, because I want you home so badly.

Still no news of compromise with or surrender by Japan.

Your description of Ken was charming, and all in all, I presume both Ken and Elmer are not at all obnoxious but perhaps not stimulating to live with.

You should have two packages of hors d'oeuvres en route, and I will start another this weekend. My last, I am afraid, was inadequately packed, due to the excessive weight. I am pleased that you are so nicely fixed for cameras, and I hope that your film arrives shortly.

One of the most serious problems, as I see it, in your mother's getting an apartment (aside from the financial) is the furniture she has. She will have to sell or store it, and storage is really impossible. Don't worry about that problem, because I really doubt if they will do anything about it.

All my love, Ginny

Chapter 15

Europe After V-E Day
19 May-17 July 1945

*T*EAM 3 WAS RECALLED TO HEADQUARTERS ON 19 MAY. When we arrived at 5th Auxiliary Surgical Group Headquarters at Wolfenbüttel, we found that almost all teams were there, although several individuals had been sent hither and yon to look after POWs or displaced persons (DPs).

I was greeted by Lieutenant Colonel Gay with the news that he was glad to have me back as S-4 (supply officer, a headquarters job I had held from the beginning of training at Fort Sam Houston until our deployment into France).

Wolfenbüttel was a relatively undamaged, clean town only about twenty miles from Braunschweig, where Ninth Army Headquarters was. Our personal living quarters were in preempted houses near a modern school, which was used as 5th Aux headquarters.

Bill Falor and I looked through the library attached to the school. It was an imposing library for what we presumed to be equivalent to a high school. Stacks extending over two floors were filled with several-thousand volumes.

We pulled out a book here and there to have a look at it. We found a camera behind one book. Not a very fancy one, but a sort of bellows-type folding camera that might be owned by the average Joe.

This led us to pull out other books. We soon discovered by trial and error that behind the fourth book from the left on each shelf was a camera. Each camera bore a tag with a name, presumably of someone in the school system or in the town.

That day, we collected about a half-dozen cameras—maybe more—and gave them to assorted team members. We returned a couple of days later and collected roughly two dozen more, always behind the fourth book from the left on a shelf. School officials or the townspeople perhaps thought that the advancing occupying American army would confiscate cameras and selected this method of concealing them.

WE STAYED AT Wolfenbüttel only four days before the 5th Aux, except for a small rear section, moved to Weidenbrück. The reason for the move was not clear to 5th Auxiliary personnel, but we hoped it made sense to higher authority.

While in Weidenbrück, Bill Falor, Lou Hall, and I stayed in a confiscated apartment building. Our apartment was comfortable, but also peculiar. It had a sitting room, a living room, bathroom, and so on, but the entrance into the apartment from the hall was through the bathroom.

There was no way to get to the sitting room or the bedroom from the hall, except through the bathroom. If the bathroom were occupied, apparently there was no traffic. It was a very generous bathroom, and we thoroughly enjoyed it, but I have never seen anything like it before or since.

The unhandy aspect of Weidenbrück was its distance from Ninth Army Headquarters at Braunschweig. Wolfenbüttel was twenty miles away, but Weidenbrück. was about 150. At Weidenbrück I was instructed to try to turn in the surgical trucks and the PROCO units. This was England in reverse. I moved back to the 5th Aux rear at Wolfenbüttel for a day or two to deposit the vehicles, which entailed considerable red tape.

The surgical trucks and the PROCO units never fulfilled the purpose for which they were intended. The purpose was straightforward: Because the army figured that an auxiliary surgical team attached to an evac or field hospital would not have an operating room or equipment for the team, the teams were to be supplied with both the room (i.e., a tent) and the necessary surgical equipment.

But we were not in tents all that often, because during the winter we were in buildings, and the operating room had to conform to each building. Even when the teams were pitched in tents, as at Friederichsfeld, for example, adequate surgical facilities were provided by the field hospital.

To be sure, we found the trucks very handy for transportation. When we traveled with a field hospital, we rode in our own vehicles, and this meant the field-hospital commander did not have to beg, borrow, or steal transportation for his attached units.

And the trucks could be used purely for sightseeing. When we were in Wittenburg working twenty-four-hour shifts, we were very rested, because we often slept while we were on duty but weren't busy. Because we had the truck, we went into Hamburg and other places, including traveling to see the Russians.

After Weidenbrück, we moved on to Marburg. The move apparently was dictated by the wish to get most American troops out of the British Sector of Occupied Germany. Somebody discovered an empty field next to a railroad siding and provided us with tents to shelter the whole unit.

In Weidenbrück we learned that we were bound for the Pacific through Marseilles, so a lot of the conversation in the tents at Marburg was associated with how we would go.

By the time we reached Marburg, our team had only two command cars assigned to the 5th Aux and two trucks. But we had other intrinsic 5th Aux equipment, such as the canvas surgical kits distributed to each team and the field kitchens.

While at Marburg, Colonel Gay thought that it would be very desirable to have an advance party in Marseilles to clear the way for arrival of the main group.

This seemed like a good idea, so it was arranged that Joe Redline and I would go in one of the command cars, along with Smokey Stover, a sergeant who would drive us.

The colonel himself followed in the other staff car a couple of days later, and we caught up with each other in Marseilles.

The main unit traveled by train, which pulled into the siding at Marburg and ended up in Marseilles a couple of days later.

The letters below trace the sequence of events, including our trip to Marseilles and some of the happenings in the camp there.

---

21 May 1945
11:00 P.M.

Dearest,

Today Dave Monahan came in. He is about 35 kilometers away and came in for dinner and was persuaded to stay overnight. He is staying with Bill Falor, who is living in the house adjoining.

Dave looks well and has gained perhaps a pound or two. He expressed some sentiments of disillusionment about the war—somewhat different for Dave.

I can say one thing. I think I had no illusions about what the war was for or what it was like. Dave is convinced that the power of politics will have the final say in settling the peace.

He is thoroughly incensed at the attitude of the Army in its disregard for the lives of individuals, as if he had discovered something new, and talks of ways and means of getting out.

He has had perhaps the greatest volume of surgical cases of anyone, doing 188 chests or bellies. I must count mine up.

The pictures enclosed were taken with the Leica. I printed them myself under terrible conditions. They can be greatly improved.

Love, H

Saturday 26 May 1945
8:00 P.M.

Dearest Ginny,

I may be sent to Paris in a few days on an official trip, plus a day or two pass. There are some odds and ends that can be cleaned up by sending someone there, and the Colonel and I have worked out a deal.

It is principally an "inquiry" into the future plans of the 5th Aux trip. I am going to see Colonel Cutler and others to try to find out what is in the wind. I had quite a long, confidential-like talk with the Colonel today, and he is really very unhappy. He feels that two men in particular at headquarters sabotaged efforts he made in behalf of the 5th Aux.

A principal point of argument was against the direct dealings with the other staff sections on the part of the 5th, rather than through the Surgeon's Office; e.g., that office would not like it if it knew I was going to Paris.

As far as the Colonel is concerned, the breakdown finds expression in the fact that he has not been promoted. He would be very happy to be transferred to some other kind of outfit. I really believe, although I hate to say so, that being the CO of an aux group should be a very fine surgeon who would also be the Army surgical consultant.

Incidentally, the Colonel told me that the professional qualifications of the surgeons of the group were recently sent into Cutler's office, and that the 5th had five men with B ratings—B-men are of national reputation or equivalent thereof—and that I was one of them. Not one was in the A group—men of international reputation. I am sorry that I forgot to inquire who the other four were.

The ratings were made by Smith and others. The ratings do not mean anything, except that the higher-ups probably want some statistical record of men, but I thought you might like to know.

We have settled down to a very satisfactory living routine and have a Kraut woman to do our laundry, which is beautifully done for a piece of soap or chocolate. Money is no better to them than it is to us. They are afraid of inflation, such as after War World I.

We have some divided wills among the group about putting these Krauts out of house and home to gain billets for us. All agreed in principle that if anyone has to live uncomfortably, it should be the Krauts. The best is none too good for us.

I subscribe to this view. Those who actually throw the people out—Joe Redline, Bob Ewing—say it is awfully tough to do when they start talking about their four little children or their mother, age 90, and so on—a serious problem important to future American-German relations.

I am going to try to scrape together enough energy to analyze the cases I have handled in Europe in the next day or two. With you, it would be easy. But if you were here, I should not analyze cases.

Love, H

P.S. Have you tried to make inquiries about travel by wives?

Sunday 27 May 1945
8:25 A.M.

Dearest Ginny,

I am back in Wolfenbüttel for the night. Army headquarters is near here, and I am not able to complete my business and so must stay overnight. The 5th Aux maintains a rear detachment here for mail distribution to the teams in this area and a few beds for those who may have business at headquarters.

Today I made arrangements to turn in the surgical trucks and the PROCO units. This will be a tremendous worry off all our minds, as the trucks were never used as intended and there have never been any personnel to maintain the trucks and equipment.

Going around here and there reminds me of England in reverse, for there I was trying to get stuff, and here I am trying to get rid of it. It was easier to get it than get rid of it. This will cut us down to our regular authorized equipment and make us more mobile. It will also cut down on the bookkeeping.

Love, H

June 1945

My darling,

If I knew the day or date it would go at the top of this letter, but the last two days have been so filled with fast-moving events that I have neither the desire nor the ability to keep track of mere time.

At any rate, it is 72 hours since I last wrote, and this, I believe, has been the longest time in 10 years that I have neither written to nor talked with you, and the first time I have avoided doing so.

In the last letter, I think I said that it seemed to me reasonable to believe that we would be going to the Pacific through the States. The very next day we received an order that can leave not the slightest doubt that we go to the Pacific, not by the States, but directly.

Stars and Stripes has said that Marseilles is the port through which units going direct will go, and therefore I suppose we shall go through that southern

French port. It will also be soon—how soon I do not know—possibly before I will have a chance to receive an answer to this letter. Nevertheless, continue to write to this address until further notice.

My reaction of pain and disappointment for both of us at first was so powerful that I could not bring myself to write. I even considered not telling you, but, of course, that would but put off the evil day, and my true feeling could not help but pace whatever words I might write.

Things now seem better, and I feel sure that in years to come we shall look upon this event as but an unimportant incident of the whole war experience.

How can I feel that way? Is it because I must? No, I don't think so. It was inevitable, as we both knew, that the 5th Aux would go to the Pacific, and this being the case, perhaps it is better to have it so.

We have no notion as to where we shall land or even which direction the boat will take. Find out and let me know the exact official title and outfit of some of our Pacific friends, like Ridge Trimble (surgical consultant to General MacArthur) and George Finney (in General MacArthur's office in some capacity). It might be handy to know where they are.

My days have been filled with arrangements, questions, and details. The move in general is old stuff, very much like that to England and across the Channel. I only hope we have comfortable quarters on board the boat.

Kiss the little ones for me. My greatest comfort is to know that you are with them, and my strength stems from the thought that one day we shall again face the world together in work and in love, H

Saturday, June 2, 1945

Dearest Ginny,

The reaction of the various members of the group to the news of the Pacific must have been fascinating to a disinterested party. For fear that my letter of yesterday may not get to you first, I must repeat that we are urgently preparing to go to the Pacific not by way of the States.

I myself have settled down and feel that the situation has become bearable, as it must necessarily be.

In general, the younger and unmarried officers don't care one way or the other. Men like Ken Tanner, Ernie Craig, Clark who have no responsibilities at home are more than willing to go forth to another adventure.

The experiences over here have been neither terrifying nor exhausting, and, for someone who does not have a lover at the other side of the world, I can see that such a trip might have opportunity and allure.

The nurses in general are glad to go. They are young and giddy and, for the most part, do not have good sense, so they are happy to go.

Martha (chief of nurses), who, as you know, does not have average intelligence, had the idea that the girls over 40 should be transferred out of the unit. So with the best motives in the world, she and the Colonel arranged to transfer the five women in that category.

This was apparently without consulting them, because when the order to change came through, there was much dissatisfaction. But the order nevertheless had to go through.

Unintelligent actions by unintelligent people are, of course, one of the troubles with "the Army."

We have acquired several officers who have had up to 32 months of service, and they are terribly disappointed at not going home. I believe they have just cause for complaint, and the Colonel has tried to work out something for them, but nothing very good. They will probably go.

One of the disappointed officers, Rocky Keith, is particularly provoked, because the Colonel did arrange to swap off Phil Johnson and another surgeon to the 3rd Aux. The disappointed officers thought they should have been given preference over those two older men, whom the Colonel judged to be less able to physically stand what may be ahead. Rocky was terribly broken up and cried real tears on several occasions.

At a future time I shall tell more of this, which, as I said, interested me very much. While writing this, I have been talking to Al Eskin, and the letter is probably a jumble. He sends his best to all, and especially to you, my mother, and Miss Smith, whom he remembered by name.

Love, H

4 June 1945

Dearest Ginny,

Our great bulk of work in the supply section has been completed. The instruments have been checked, bad ones thrown out, new ones secured, everything packed, and now we can, I hope, take it a little bit easy.

I have not minded being busy, because it has given me much less time to dwell on my own unfortunate circumstance, which, of course, is no worse, but because of you, many times better than the circumstances of most people.

In general, everyone has quieted down and has prepared himself to go. I did not tell you, I believe, about a few who are simply beside themselves at the thought of going. I did speak about those who, I thought, had a legitimate reason for being upset, but there were a few who had been overseas no longer than any of the rest of us who raised holy hell in one form or another and, I believe, were responsible for making others feel worse.

Dave Monahan was one, Bill Falor, to a lesser extent, and others whom you do not know so well. O'Brien, whom you may remember, was particularly obnoxious. They mostly got good and pickled on the local brew, which is plentiful, but some, like Dave, while stone sober, told the Colonel that he simply was not going.

Dave is over it now. I cannot help but be amazed that people like Dave, and even Bill Boukalik, who were at their wit's end to get overseas, now find that they are just as anxious to get home. Bill Boukalik has been promoted in his new job and is now a lieutenant colonel.

We are having numerous personnel changes, and among the newcomers is a little sharp-faced Jewish boy, by the name of Simon, who graduated from Johns Hopkins in 1936. He remembers you well and claims to know me, but I am not sure that I remember him. He is an eager-beaver type.

My footlocker, which I last saw at Marbury Hall, arrived yesterday, and I have repacked for the umpteenth time.

Love, H

7 June 1945
10:30 A.M.

Dearest Ginny,

In about an hour we are leaving for Marburg. This move has nothing to do with our redeployment, but is an administrative move designed to get us out of the British area.

It has made some extra work for me, because we have to live in a field, and this outfit is authorized no tentage. So we scratched around yesterday and found some pyramidal tents, so that living should not be so bad, provided there are adequate facilities and the like.

The trip is about 100 miles, so that we should be there by 5:00.

Love, H

8 June 1945
12:00 noon

Dearest Ginny,

We are now at Marburg, having had a very pleasant trip yesterday afternoon. The tent-pitching crew had gotten off at 3:00 A.M., and we left at 1:00 P.M., so that when we arrived at 7:00 all pyramidal tents were up, and it took only an hour or so to get straightened out. There was a hot meal at 9:00.

It does not get dark until 11:00. It stands to get light at 4:00 A.M. I spent most of the morning looking up the local supply agencies to see about getting the necessities of living.

We are gradually getting prepared for that long ocean voyage. Colonel Gay had a message last night to come up to Braunschweig today (9th Army headquarters), and we should have some definite news about sailing time when he comes back late tonight or tomorrow. You must prepare yourself for a long interruption. I, too, shall prepare for receiving no mail.

Our trip yesterday was through a much-more-interesting countryside than the flat plains of Northern Germany, rollinglike, almost like little mountains, and this bivouac is in a high plateau with a view reminiscent of some of the views of the Shenandoah Valley and our hiking trip along the Skyline.

We are having more personnel changes. The new rule is that officers with 100 points do not go to the Pacific. We will lose about one-half-dozen nurses. We have one nurse with 69 points, Betty Brocktrup. I have got myself around to a frame of mind compatible with going to the Pacific, and I hope that you will be able to do the same.

With all my love, H

Saturday 9 June 1945

My dearest Ginny,

The Colonel got back about 3:00 A.M., and I am leaving here in the morning as an advance party. Joe Redline is also going.

The Colonel had a very unpleasant day at headquarters. As previously mentioned, the Colonel and headquarters have not gotten along as well as might have been, and the "old man" spoke his piece, as he figured that it was his parting from NUSA (Ninth United States Army).

Colonel Shamboro is at the Riviera, and Frigge is acting chief. It is Frigge and the Colonel who are the most incompatible. At another time I shall try to explain what it is in the Colonel that I think the officer does not like. Frigge told him that he did not like the way the Colonel operated.

We have spent the morning getting this and that from the quartermaster depot. They have a pretty good one near here, and we have been able to pick up some things we needed, such as shelter halves and the like.

With all my love to the little family, H

Sunday 10 June 1945
11:30 P.M.

My dearest Ginny,

We have left Germany for good. I am in Nancy, having arrived just after dark, less than an hour ago. Joe Redline, Sergeant Smoky Stover, and I left Marburg about 9:30 in the command car and have been rolling ever since—Giessen, Frankfurt, Heidelberg, Karlsruhe, Strasbourg, and Nancy.

In Germany we made good time on the Autobahn, which runs down the east bank of the Rhine, but the macadam roads in France are badly beaten up and the last 100 miles was very rough—and I mean very—as it takes some of the pleasure out of what could have been a delightful trip.

We were in Heidelberg for about an hour. Imagine having to "do" Heidelberg with companions who would rather find a brewery in Heidelberg than see the university, even from the outside. We drove through the university, which is, in fact, right in town and on a high hill overlooking the city and the Rhine. There are a million American troops in the Frankfurt-Heidelberg area, and the place simply crawls with them.

It has been the best part of nine months since I was in France, and there is no doubt about it: There is a marked difference from Germany.

When we landed in Normandy, the small towns reminded me of Mexico, only less so, and today the same recollection was evident.

France is more rural and dirty. The small towns have a farmlike odor, more chickens in the street, more cows in the courtyards, and the manure pile by the front door.

One is apt to see a schoolhouse without a blade of grass around it, and we saw several military establishments similar in general appearance to the Mexican ones in that small town 100 miles north of Mexico City.

The countryside is beautiful. The Vosges Mountains are about as high as the Blue Ridge, but more cultivated, and the grain fields look magnificent in the breeze. But one cannot get away from the impression that the German villages appear more orderly, clean, and efficient.

It is also true that French people are naturally friendly. Perhaps the Germans felt themselves as conquered people, but here there are more smiles, more friendly greetings, and, I am sure, much more fraternizing

When we came into Nancy tonight, the streetlights were on, the first I had seen since San Antonio. The light was so unnatural we giggled and laughed about it like children might do around an unexpected piece of candy.

I had got so used to driving in the dark that at first I did not like the streetlights and, therefore, thought I ought to turn off the headlights on the car.

Joe and I have a room in the university dormitory, and I have already had a hot shower. It is just at midnight. You should be here.

All my love, H

Monday 11 June 1945

My dearest Ginny,

We got away from Nancy about 9:00. Joe and I stayed at the Cité Université and had a dormitory room. About 11:00 we came upon a coffee-and-sandwich establishment which had just been set up by the Army in tents to take care of transients on the road. This was some miles north of Dijon. It seems a shame to be so close to Switzerland and not get a look at the place, so we started toward Geneva, knowing full well that we could not go into the place but hoping to see it from a mountain or two.

Popping down the road, we notice that we are in the province of Jura, and, of course, think of Pasteur. Several miles along we came to a crossroad with a sign pointing to Arbois 16 kilometers. It seemed a shame to be so close to Pasteur's birthplace and not go see it, so down the road we go.

Arbois is a beautiful little town and at the foothills of the mountain that became the Alps. No wonder that Pasteur looked with affection on his hometown. His house still stands, and we took a picture or two. We stopped in a store in the village and had a bottle of the very poor beer, which nevertheless tasted good, as the day was very warm and sweaty.

We came upon another fork in the road and found the Swiss frontier, complete with guards and Swiss flags flying. This was at the little French/Swiss town of Rousetta. We stopped and took pictures and found . . . that we could not go in without being interned; so we went to Gex, toward Lyon.

There were more beautiful views toward the west. The road wound around through the hills and we went through a gap to the east, and, to our unexpected amazement, 3,000 feet below stretched Lake Geneva and Geneva itself, with a beautiful range behind crowned by the tallest mountain of all, Mont Blanc.

We could scarcely believe our eyes, it was so unexpected. At first, we missed Mont Blanc. It was a beautiful, cloudy day, and with a naked eye the clouds and mountains all seemed to run together. With the glasses, however, the mountain cap could be seen. I do believe it is the most magnificent panorama I have ever seen.

It was then about 6:00, and it seemed a shame to go on much further, so we stayed in the little town of Gex in the Belvedere Hotel. We shall have a long trip tomorrow, but the time devoted to sightseeing was well worth it.

At the hotel tonight we had an acceptable meal of roast lamb. Food is still difficult to obtain in France.

Joe has talked my ear off tonight, and it is now midnight.

With all my love, H

Tuesday 12 June 1945

Dearest,

We left Gex about 9:00. Mont Blanc was beautiful; almost no clouds about it in the morning sun. I watched it out of the back of the car until we wound around in the mountains around the Rhône Valley, then to Lyon through a hilly, winding road until we reached the Rhône—Lyon appears to be a fine city. Then to Avignon and Marseilles.

Southern France is quite different—cleaner towns with Spanish influence in the architecture, no manure problems, and darker-appearing people. Then there are mountains visible on both sides of the road which hugs the Rhône all the way down. There were many peaches along the way, and we stopped in a small town and bought two pounds at what amounted to 45 cents in American money.

Marseilles is a typical port city, mostly GIs, but also Frenchmen, and particularly "Le Pompon Rouge." The city is a beehive, but 11:30 is the curfew, and I can look out of my balcony and see people streaming out of town. Trucks full of GIs are leaving for the nearby camps.

We have rooms at a small hotel just off the main drag. We had a beautiful double room with long French windows and a little balcony. Being on the third floor, we had a good view. Marseilles, by the way, is a rather pretty harbor, being landlocked by rather sizable mountains.

All in all, we have had a good sightseeing trip within the time limitation. It is too bad you could not be here.

With all my love, H

Wednesday 13 June 1945
11:00 P.M.

Dearest Ginny,

Tonight appears to be our last comfortable sleep. We are at a hotel in town, "De la Poste," as previously mentioned, but the Colonel and the motor element will be here tomorrow, and we will all have to go to our "permanent" area, which is a tent city just out of town. We were there today, and the situation is horrible to contemplate.

I will write more about it after living there awhile. But the difficulty is that the troops are coming in before the place is ready, and the utilities are by no stretch of the imagination able to accommodate their number.

In addition, and making a bad situation worse, is the fact that the camp is located on a dusty plain where the wind seems to never stop blowing. Everything will be ruined.

Tomorrow morning, before the rest of the unit arrives, we want to run over to Toulon to see what's what and perhaps get a look at the harbor where the fleet was scuttled.

Tonight, after a short nap after supper, we walked around town and sat for an hour or so at a sidewalk café. The sights are remarkable.

I figure that you should get this letter about our anniversary time. How different our situation is now than in 1940. Would that we were about to start on our honeymoon that inaugurated our happy life together.

The knowledge of our happiness and the thought of our second honeymoon make prospects like that of our immediate future less difficult and more bearable.

My love, H

Thursday 14 June 1945
10:00 P.M.

Dearest Ginny,

I am writing this just outside my tent in the "dust bowl." We moved out here this morning. The motor element arrived about 4:00 and got settled in good shape.

We had previously located a nearby beach, and so we all went swimming after supper. The beach is about three miles away, and we made use of the trucks that have to be turned in soon. After that, we will be stuck here unless they work out a bus service to the beach.

The water was fine, and salty. It is a little bay off the Mediterranean, and the beach must be characteristic of this region, as it is pebbly.

It has been quite dark as I write, and I have no light.

All my love, H

Tuesday 19 June 1945
6:00 pm.

Dearest Ginny,

Three letters—poor little things. They are almost worn out from being reread so often. It is indeed a pleasantly painful sensation to be so in love. The most wonderful thing about it is that it seems to grow and grow as time passes, and where shall I finally find you?

Yesterday Charley Burbank, Arnold Osterhuis, Haskell, and I went into town for dinner. We had heard that it was possible to get lobster at some of the little restaurants along the waterfront.

They are very expensive, especially for Americans, but, for once, we figured it was worth it. We tried several restaurants. Some are closed. Some claim not to have lobster. But we finally got so hungry after walking around for an hour that we stayed at one which had steak.

We could not quite figure it out, but probably no restaurants are supposed to be open; i.e., the whole restaurant business is black market.

At any rate, the price is 300 francs; i.e., $6.00 each. We had delicious tomatoes, cucumbers, tuna fish, ripe olives, eggs, onions, very good steak and potatoes, and a cookie for dessert. Wine to drink. I was as full as a tick when it was over.

It took us about two hours to get home in the bus, as the capacity is much less than the demand and it is necessary to line up. It was about 12:00 when we got in bed.

This morning at 7:00 Charley came into the tent and said, "Good morning. How are you?" I had to admit that during the night I had a little episode of nausea and vomiting. Then he said that he had the same, so I suppose that puts an end to eating out.

Incidentally, I feel fine tonight, having completely recovered from the restaurant episode, as well as the one of a few days ago.

Did I tell you that I had moved? All field-grade officers were given small wall tents in a nearby area. Mine is a perfect mess, as I have everything scattered over everything, and I cannot find anything. This gives a little more privacy, but it really is not much better than the squad tent.

Love and kisses, H

Friday 22 June 1945

My darling wife,

Five years ago today I did the smartest thing I ever did. It is not right that there should be no special celebration, but all this is postponed, not cancelled.

It is not right that one-fifth of our married life should be spent apart, but we can only hope that that fraction shall become very small indeed as the years go by.

It is not right that you who are so talented should have to struggle with the necessities of living for a family, but perhaps after the war this can be righted.

Nor does it seem right that my dreams of love and work with you, bringing, I hope, happiness to us both, should be long denied. My own personal goal in this war is that our life should be so ordered along the lines we have written, and, if it is perhaps possible, we can look back at these years of separation with some feeling of thankfulness that out of the pain of separation there came a joyful union that otherwise might not have been.

I have two reasons to be especially happy today. The picture taken by Herbert arrived, and the other is your V-mail of June 10. You have probably forgotten what you said exactly, but it is bravely written and makes my journey easier because of knowing that such a partner stays at home.

The changes in personnel are going through. We are losing all with over 85 points; thus, 16 or 17 personnel in all. In addition, Al Eskin is being transferred to a station hospital at his request, so that he has an opportunity for promotion. Grubin has had more trouble with his eye and has entered the hospital and will probably be lost to the unit.

With love and kisses always, H

27 June 1945

Dearest Ginny,

This morning the Colonel asked me to run an errand or two for him while I was seeing a couple of gents about business that I had to see in connection with the travel agency I seem to be running.

Getting transportation is of itself a problem. All our vehicles were turned in the day we got here, and I spent two hours lining up a jeep. This secured, Charley Burbank and I got off about 11:00.

Our personnel replacements for the 85 pointers have been so inadequate in respect to talent that we could put only about 20 teams in the field unless we get better-caliber men.

It is Fort Sam all over again, and I think we will be filled with Tom, Dick, and Harry, letting the new theater of operations make adjustments.

Of course, the new theater people will not know anything about it until we get there, and it will be England all over again. I think Ridge Trimble [Dr. I. Ridgeway Trimble, a Hopkins friend] is theater consultant, in which case it will be largely his baby—but I am ahead of the story.

Yesterday the Colonel talked to Paris (SHEAF Headquarters) about this personnel problem and also the additional equipment requirement under the new T/E, and, during the course of the conversation, the Paris office said that it "understood" we would be reorganizing under the new theater upon arrival there.

Following up that conversation, we today went to see the local people who later found that Paris cabled the difficulties to Washington.

The Colonel also got off a telegram of his own, calling attention to our deficiencies and our inability to function if personnel were not improved and, if necessary, equipment for reorganization were not available in the Pacific.

You see things are in a considerable administrative mess. It is difficult to understand why the Army is unable to prevent these muddles.

So much for my troubles. I anxiously await word about your father. I know it must be a comfort to him and your mother to know that you are there.

With all my love, H

Monday, July 1945
8:00 P.M. (Marseilles)

Dearest Ginny,

I believe this is sometimes referred to as the Blue Mediterranean, and blue it is. Last night Bill Falor, Charley, and a bunch of others went downtown and came home having arranged a fishing trip for today. This morning Bill and I went.

In the very center of the city of Marseilles is the so-called Old Harbor. It is easily recognized on any large-scale map of the area. At the east side and west side of this little bay there are numerous small wharves lined by fishing boats, mostly immobilized by lack of gasoline. Bill had made arrangements for one of them.

The boat was run by two rather young Frenchmen who loved the water and constantly referred to it "comme une belle et très jolie mademoiselle." The boat itself was about 22 feet long and had a generous beam for its length, so that it had a tubby shape, which made it roll at the slightest wave.

I noticed that all the boats like ours had a water baffle extending above the deck, so that there seemed to be about three feet of freeboard, but actually about 18 inches below the scuppers on the deck. It had an engine, but it also carried a mast lying horizontal along the deck and a sail which was improvised into an awning. I believe it was a square sail.

The boats were quite unlike those that we are used to on the Chesapeake Bay, and one cannot help but believe that they differed only slightly from the design of many hundreds of years ago.

Aside from the fishing, the trip itself was fascinating, and I missed you acutely, for I know how much you would have loved it. I even mentioned it to Bill, something I seldom do, because it makes me feel that I am rubbing it in for having such a wonderful, companionable wife, besides other things that I cannot mention anywhere.

The mouth of the old harbor had been completely closed by sinking a French vessel across its mouth. This has now become sufficiently removed to prevent its being a barrier.

In the outer harbor are several large and high islands which are essentially mountain peaks. Bare mountains coming to the shore on all sides and, in that respect, is not unlike Acapulco.

The mountain slopes themselves are bare and brown, and the shore is rocky, like Maine, but with a white rock which appears as if it should be soluble. We fished just outside the last rock, about five miles, I would guess, from the center of town. As we left the dock, we asked if the fishing was good and the waterman said, "Oui, oui." He oui oui'd us to death, saying we would catch a "mille pêche" by 6:00.

But fishing is alike the world over. If you came out at 6:00 in the morning, I am sure it would have been better, but so much explosive was used in blowing up the docks that many fish were killed.

You have probably guessed that we caught no fish. That is, Bill and I were embarrassed not to, while our friends caught about six each, the largest being 5 inches long. The fish themselves were beautiful things, highly colored, tropical-appearing forms. We used clams and some sort of soft snail-like thing for bait.

We fished in about 40 feet of water off the bottom—Chesapeake Bay-style—with hand lines completely of gut. I do not know why, but perhaps because the water is so clear. All in all, it was a worthwhile trip, in spite of no fish, and you should have been there.

Love, H

2 *July* 1945

Dearest Ginny,

Since writing yesterday, I feel like I have been running in one place. On the spur of the moment, Bill and Charley and a few others decided that they wanted to take a boat trip out to another of the islands in the harbor, and so I could not be left out of a trip like that.

Before we left, the wind was blowing noticeably harder, and when the boat got just outside the old harbor it was apparent that there was "beaucoup de mer." The old fellow who runs the boat circled around just at the entrance to the breakwater and then decided that it looked a little rough to go out, so we had to come back.

He has a nice heavy boat that is pointed at both ends, so that it rides the waves beautifully. But there seemed to be water in the gasoline, so that the motor was not thoroughly reliable. His wife was on the boat, and I do not think the old lady cared particularly for the waves.

I know you would have enjoyed it, as it was about as rough and blowy as that night we sailed from Solomons [Maryland] to Weems [Virginia]. However, instead of doing anything like that, he cruised up and down the harbor, and we got a good look at the berths and many ships sunk at the docks and in the harbor.

The Krauts tried to block the harbor, and I am sure they caused a lot of trouble by sinking ships in the channel and at narrow places in the breakwaters. We also saw at least three sunken submarines.

Upon getting back here, we found that the mistral had deposited about ? inch of dust over everything, including bed and clothes, except where it had drifted into piles of an inch or two.

You asked for some recollections of my boyhood, as perhaps being useful regarding Willie. It is surprisingly difficult to think of anything that is of real importance, but perhaps I would like to have had the opportunity to play and meet many different children.

It was always difficult for me to meet new children, and I do not think I quite knew what to do. There was never an adequate number of playmates for me to develop the skills I needed to feel at ease in other people's homes as a child.

I believe this has been overcome in the end, but perhaps it has something to do with the fact that I would much rather have spent the evening alone with Mother than have guests, or is this just because I loved her so much?

At any rate, I would feel it important to have Willy and Ginny not be shy. Try to have them feel at home with other children by being thrown with many other and different children.

This, of course, is not the whole story, and the final outcome certainly depends on the stuff a child is made of. But exposure to birthday parties and other horrible experiences for the mothers might make a happier child.

I also remember getting my head scrubbed and yelling like the devil because my scalp hurt. But Mother must have thought I was goldbricking, because I never remembered anything happening, except getting more shampoos. The moral, I suppose, is that when the kids yell, be sure that they have a good cause for it.

If I think of other things as time goes along I shall write about them.

Love, H

4 July 1945
8:30 P.M.

Dearest Ginny,

This morning seemed like a good chance to go on the rubberneck bus around town, and so failing to interest Charley and Bill being absent at the Riviera, I decided to go alone, and I enjoyed my company immensely.

One of the terrible things about the Army is one's inability to be alone. You live in a glasshouse and cannot do a thing but someone inquires what you are doing.

We saw at least two things that seemed interesting, both churches.

One is up on a high hill and overlooks the harbor in the city. It is Notre Dame de la Garde and is a shrine for shipwrecked sailors. The church has many replicas and paintings of ships that had been on the verge of shipwreck and then saved. I noticed the model of one airplane. The church may be reached by an inclined railway worked by waterpower, like the one at Sainte Anne-de-Beaupre. I think you have seen that.

The second interesting thing is the Church of Lazarus, who landed at Marseilles in AD 42.

The rock hereabout is limestone, and the water of the centuries has dissolved areas that amount to catacombs. These areas Lazarus and the early monks enlarged into a church that can be seen today under the present Abbey of Saint Victor, which itself was built about AD 400 and is the only place I have ever seen where I could actually imagine seeing medieval monks working on manuscripts and the like.

I am now about to go to the movies with Bob Howey. You can see that I live a very busy, though not useful, existence.

With all my love, H

5 July 1945
11:30 A.M.

Dearest Ginny,

The Special Services show I saw last night was the first one I had ever seen in the Army.

There are three outdoor so-called theaters. They consist of a wooden stage, so located that the adjoining hillsides form a naturally inclined plane from which the customers may have an unobstructed, if distant, view.

The seats consisted of the ground, but the GIs have brought all sorts of boxes and have constructed stone and wooden seats, so that there is a great collection of miscellaneous items of junk before the stage.

The show consisted of a master of ceremonies, a magician, and a juggler, who I thought was the best, and two girls, one who sang and one who danced. Type of humor—One strawberry said to another: If we had not been in the same bed we would not be in this jam.

Love, H

THE FOLLOWING LETTER speaks of my assignment to an advance party to Manila. Advance parties were customary in the ETO. For example, Joe Redline and I traveling in the command car from Marburg to Marseilles constituted an advance party for the 5th Aux.

These advance parties were quite useful, particularly for units like the 5th Aux, which had such a cockeye lopsided ratio of officers to enlisted men. The job of the advance party was to ensure that quarters assigned were suitable for the number of personnel to follow, according to rank, and that food and such other essentials were available.

It was therefore with considerable surprise that the colonel learned that the transportation office in Marseilles responsible for transporting the troops to Manila was not issuing advance-party orders.

The difficulty stemmed from the reality that everything in Europe was under General Eisenhower's command and everything in the Pacific was under General MacArthur's. There seemed to be no way for either of these theater commanders to issue orders affecting the other's theater. So, the transportation office in Marseilles could not issue an official order that would have any effect at all on troops scheduled to come under General MacArthur's command.

The colonel was eager to send an advance party, not only to make the housekeeping arrangements that advance parties usually do, but also because he had the idea that there had been no auxiliary surgical group in the Pacific, so it might be of some importance to have someone sound out—and, indeed, find out—whether the 5th Auxiliary Surgical Group would be used in the way it was intended to be used.

This made a little more sense than it might sound superficially, for two reasons.

The first was that the colonel, whose nickname was Steve (and I am not sure where that nickname came from), said he knew quite well General Guy Denit, the chief medical officer under MacArthur. Denit's role in the Pacific Theater of Operations corresponded to the role of General Hawley in the ETO.

Another aspect of the colonel's plan had some importance: I knew Colonel Ridge Trimble quite well. Ridge was the chief surgical consultant to General Denit, and he occupied in the Pacific Theater the same post that Elliott Cutler occupied under General Hawley in the ETO. The colonel's first thought was that he and I would constitute the advance party to ensure "that General MacArthur knew how to use an auxiliary surgical group."

But the attitude of the transportation office at Marseilles seemed to put an end to that thinking. Somehow or other, an alternative idea was suggested. I am not sure I was certain at the time where the idea came from, and even thinking about it now, fifty years later, I am still in the dark.

WE LEARNED THAT units sometimes were transshipped from Marseilles in split delegations; that is, large units maybe couldn't all fit in one ship, so part of a unit might sail in one ship and part in another.

As a rule, only major units, like divisions, were split. But we thought we possibly could split-load the 5th Aux, the first loading consisting of two officers who would be followed at a suitable date by the entire group.

The two officers shipping out before the rest of their unit would still be under the command of the 5th Aux, and, as such, would not violate the theater rule that prevented the issuing of orders to advance parties.

Permission having been granted, we sought out berths for two, which turned out to be for three people in one transport, with the main party of the 5th Aux to follow, presumably in three or four weeks.

Bill Falor, Charley Burbank, and I constituted the advance party. We had a choice of vessels, because many transports had spots for two or three. In order to enable us to spend two or three days at the Riviera before going to Manila, we chose the transport *Admiral Benson*, scheduled to depart 17 July, and procured our loading orders.

We had no official orders. But Colonel Gay did furnish us with a handwritten letter to General Denit. The letter introduced Majors Falor, Burbank, and Jones (commanding) and stated that the three would explain their mission.

We also expected to see Ridge Trimble, the consultant who probably would be the man to talk to about how the 5th Auxiliary Surgical Group teams were used in the ETO.

The advance split-loaded trio saw this as a very good deal, principally because we would not be traveling with the total unit. As noted before, the auxiliary surgical groups' traveling as a whole created a very awkward situation in most ships and other mass-transportation options, because our unit contained more officers than enlisted men; as a consequence, the bed ratio in most boats didn't work out well.

Our *Admiral Benson* accommodations were admirable. Bill, Charley, and I were assigned to a stateroom designed to hold six, but only five officers occupied it—the two other officers being majors from the Engineers.

Saturday 7 July 1945
4:30 P.M.

My darling Ginny,

Yesterday was a day of running around. I went into town no less than three times, 36 miles round trip each time; the first two times making arrangements and the last to a lobster dinner that Charley and I had previously arranged with a local Frenchman.

First, about the dinner. We borrowed the Colonel's car and had dinner about 8:00, hors d'oeuvres, tomatoes, two kinds of pâté, onions, good bread and butter, then lobster, which was like the rock lobster, in that it had no claws, but like Maine lobsters in flavor.

The lobsters were baked with a sauce, but I believe I prefer them broiled with drawn butter.

Then, veal cutlets and cake and peaches for dessert, a bottle of vin rosé each. It took from 8:00 to 9:30 to eat, and I could feel my stomach pressing everything else out of the way.

We were home by 10:30, but it was dark and I could not keep my eyes open, so I fell in bed thinking only of you.

The price: 1,400 francs ($28.00) or 24 packages of cigarettes for the two. We paid in the latter. Total cost: 72 cents each.

The rest of the day yesterday and today was spent in arranging for an advance party that Charley and I are going to be part of. I look upon this as a good deal.

Getting permission to go is a wonderful example of how things happen in the Army. Units are not supposed to send such parties, but because of our Table of Organization changes, etc., the Colonel thought it would be a good thing.

Anyway, I went to a Major Brady, who is G-3, and he said it was not his problem, but Captain Smith could give permission. Captain Smith said Major X was the man.

Major X said, yes, he could put our name on the list, but he would have to have permission from Colonel Weaver.

Colonel Weaver was busy, but his assistant, Major Y, said he could not give permission, but we should submit a letter that would be sent to Paris, etc., etc. After discussing this, he said for us to wait a minute; he would see what he could do by phone. So he called a number, which turned out to be Major Brady.

The result of the conversation was that Brady had no objection, so this Major Y had no objection, so he called Major X and told him it was OK with G-3 to do it and Major X said OK, and so we go.

Puzzle: Figure out who gave permission.

Charley and I are going to the Riviera in the morning. We will spend about three or four days. They say it is wonderful, and that it costs very little.

A big piece of news today is that Bill Falor now has 88 points and will not go with us. He got another Battle Star, just awarded to the 53rd Field Hospital where he was working at the time, and will be happy, I am sure.

Whether he will get home is another question. I hope to get a chance to write again tonight. I love to write letters to you and cherish when I get one from you.

As always, H

Sunday night 8 July 1945

Dearest Ginny,

We arrived in Cannes this morning after a very pleasant train trip. Got up at 5:00 A.M., went to town in a jeep, and got the 7:00 A.M. train, which has a car reserved for American officers. The result was a not-too-crowded ride—and for the Army, that is saying something.

Charley and I do not have the regular leave orders, but have unit orders to go to a local hospital here on detached service, so we are not able to get into the regular leave hotel.

But we are at an "unoccupied" small hotel, Londres et Helvetia. It is about two blocks from the beach and quite nice. It is a family sort of hotel, which would be very satisfactory when we come back with the kids.

The meals we have had are GI food, but mainly prepared by the regular French kitchen staff.

This afternoon we were at Eden Rock, a club really situated across the Gulf from Cannes. It has a swimming pool cut out of the rock along the shore, and you can jump from one spot either into the pool or into the sea. It is very nice, and I miss you greatly.

Love, H

Wednesday 11 July 1945
11:00 A.M.

My dearest Ginny,

We arrived back at 5:00 A.M. today. We left Cannes at 6:30 A.M. and were due in Marseilles four hours later. About 20 miles east of Toulon, the main drive shaft of the engine went kaput, and the engineer apparently took the engine apart.

A second engine had to come from Marseilles to get us. Everyone on the train got out on the track and raided the nearby almond trees until the train showed up 2½ hours later.

The trip was then a slow one, because the new locomotive pushed, and we got home at 5:00 A.M. We were comfortably seated and slept on and off. I feel a nap coming on.

I found two letters awaiting my return. Life so far has been kind to you and me. However, yesterday I could not but help think that it was an unkind fate that denied you the Riviera with me or that kept me from you during a most unhappy period.

I have confidence in our destiny when I remember that we are born to die. And although it is a sacrifice for you to be at home with your family, nevertheless, it is a privilege that you are with your father during what may prove to be his last illness.

One of war's worst aspects is the loss of the individual. You were much smarter than I in wanting to come along, for together with you I am worth much more. I sometimes entertain myself by imagining how you would have reacted to certain situations in which we over here find ourselves.

Bill Falor should have his head examined. He was transferred out to the 43rd General Hospital here in Marseilles. He never was certain that he should go. But after getting there he found that they were not planning on going home until January or February.

He could not stand the place. On his first day, the hospital command had an inspection and spent 55 minutes on whether the patients' robes were clean at the bottom and five minutes on the patient.

He finally volunteered for the Pacific, which is his privilege under regulations, and he is back with us. He figures, and perhaps he is right, that he might get home as quick by way of the Pacific. I would have stayed here and tried by hook or crook to get you over. He wrote and told Ann today.

With all my love, H

Saturday 14 July 1945

Dearest Ginny,

Just one year ago today we spent our time packing up, rolling, and rerolling the bedrolls, packing the Val-A-Pak and musette bag, and today I am doing the same thing, only under much-less-pleasant circumstances, because you are not here.

If I could look ahead one year and know that I should be packing my things for a certain trip to you, which is home, I do not think that I should have any just grounds for complaining. Perhaps circumstances shall be such that that day will come before then, and if so, we are that much ahead.

During this year I have learned a lot, I think. Not of medicine, except how to put together some of those shot on the battlefield, but, rather, about human relations among a lot of people.

It has been constantly brought to mind that those qualities we heard about so much as children are really those exhibited by those who make the most liked and most companionable people here. Honesty, trustworthiness, stability, rather than selfishness, greed, and bigotry are those things admired in a leader and, more important, seem to be possessed by those people who seem to lead happy lives.

This, then, is affirmation that we should bend every effort to teach these things to our children. This is not exactly a childhood recollection, but I had meant it to be an answer to your query about such things.

I guess it is not very practical either, but it comes close to Link's ideas about teaching children the difference between right and wrong before they have sense enough to think about it. I suppose that this cannot be started at too early an age.

This year has done another and quite unexpected thing: I know that our bonds together are stronger than they were before.

This is unexpected, because I had never thought much about it before, and things seemed so perfect that to imagine them any different seemed just plain crazy. Well, I do think I love you more now than last year. Could that be possible?

It is absolutely thrilling to contemplate the year ahead.

Today has been Bastille Day. The holiday has not been celebrated since 1939, and no one can deny that the French have let go with five years' celebration in one.

Last night the sky was full of skyrockets from dark until way after I went to bed. The air-raid sirens blew the all clear every hour, and I, for one, thought that this item could have been left out.

Today we had to go downtown to headquarters, and traffic was in a hopeless mess, due to the parade of military floats and just people milling around in every direction. Many were dressed in clothing of the Revolution.

It is quite possible that this poor little piece of paper will be the last one possible for a while. I know the trip coming up will be an interesting one. You should be here to enjoy it with me.

Do give my best to your family, especially to your father. Kiss the babies and, for you,

All my love, H

16 July 1945

My dearest Ginny,

The advance party now consists of three—Charley, Bill, and me. You can easily see that it took some shenanigans to fix it up this way, but we will have an enjoyable trip, because the three of us are together and because we will be able to get away from the group with all its officers.

I also feel that we have a mission which is of more than ordinary importance and certainly will influence the use to which the group is put.

I expect to stop getting your mail about the time I get this letter off. You and I left San Antonio one year previously. About the 25th of July you could start to write to me through Ridge Trimble.

I am getting off a package today which consists of nothing but maps.

They are now removing all enlisted men from the unit who have 75 or more points. This does not apply to officers as yet, but I hope that it is an indication of a trend. Somehow I feel that in several months they will add up the points again and use 75 as a basis of rotation.

I hate to start talking about this so far in advance, but it is a faint hope that it may materialize before we all realize it. Bill says it may be absolutely right to take his 87 points to the Pacific, as those with under 100 points are staying here.

Love, H

Marburg, 8-9 June 1945. Elmer Carlson does his laundry.

Marburg, 8-9 June 1945. An after-meal cleaning of mess gear. To do it the GI way, the gear is washed consecutively in three garbage cans of boiling water, heat supplied by kerosene-fired immersion heaters.

Marburg, June 1945. Major Henry Swann and Captain
Ernest Craig, who is exercising his talent with a sketch on
the railroad car about to take him to Marseilles en route to
the Pacific.

Chapter 16

Across the Pacific
17 July-22 August 1945

*C*OINCIDENCE CAN BE AN EXTRAORDINARY FORCE in shaping our lives. The coincidence I am about to relate shaped for the better the lives of the three in the advance party to Manila.

The evening before we were to embark on the transport *Admiral Benson*, several of us were having a sort of farewell party in Lieutenant Colonel Gay's tent. In the middle of the festivities, a U.S. Navy captain walked in. He was looking for Steve Gay. The visitor was Captain Gardner, skipper of the *Admiral Benson*, which we were to board the next day.

Gardner was an old friend of the Colonel, and he had found out that Steve was at Camp St. Victoret in command of an auxiliary surgical group and decided to look him up. His ship had been in the harbor for a couple of days.

We were flabbergasted and, of course, explained that three of us were to board his transport next day. We also explained that we were an advance party without any orders except from the 5th Aux, which would linger in Marseilles, and what we were up to. Gardner promised that we would have quarters in the naval portion of the transport and that these would be more comfortable. He said he would speak to the billeting officer, to whom we should report when we got aboard, and let him know that he thought we might be billeted in the naval section of the ship.

We duly reported to the billeting officer, who indeed had been alerted. We were pulled out of the line of boarding passengers and taken to an upper-deck cabin containing six berths—a cabin designed for use by naval officers.

This was a very great privilege. Because it took us away from the large groups of army personnel in the lower decks. We ate with navy personnel in their mess, which doubled as a wardroom.

The wardroom was roomy and had a library. We could lounge there and had access to the deck, which was reserved entirely for those who were operating the ship. We were free to roam around the wheelhouse and other areas of the ship. We had the best possible arrangement for spending a six weeks' trip on a ship. Our only real duty was a routine rotation seeing patients at sick call and in the sick bay.

Diary Entry: 18 July 1945
[At Sea]

Passed Gibralter at about 5:00 P.M. Got a good look at the Rock of Gibralter from the Captain's veranda. Saw dolphins all day. Passed the Balearic Islands to port last night. Amused myself by trying to count the seconds on the lighthouses.

We were very close to the Spanish coast all day, because there is a two-knot current moving into the sea that can be avoided by hugging the shore.

We passed within two miles of the Rock and got a good view of the mountainous country which is Spanish Morocco.

Diary Entry: 20 July 1945
[At Sea]

Captain Gardner amused Charley, Bill, and me on the veranda with stories of Pearl Harbor, where he was a destroyer commander.

Like the time a submarine was coming in from patrol, and someone in the submarine must have pulled the wrong switch and launched a loaded torpedo, which passed just aft of a large carrier, the *Enterprise*, I think—and blew up in the mud nearby, scattering mud over everything.

And the time when a destroyer was warping up to a battleship there and, as the destroyer threw out a line, someone knocked a lever and threw an ashcan depth charge completely across the battleship, landing on the other side between the battleship and another destroyer.

And how when his destroyer and another destroyer both got contact with a sub and he went after it, almost hitting the first destroyer with an ashcan.

And how early in the war a large carrier was torpedoed near Pearl Harbor, and his destroyer went out in pitch-blackness to meet it, along with all destroyers in the harbor (amounting to about 20), and how everyone was jittery and kept getting contacts with subs in the sound apparatus and used practically all the depth charges when there probably were no submarines.

Diary Entry: 21 July 1945
[At Sea]

We see no ships. One of the Lt. Commanders aboard explained the surface-sweep radar to us. It is a wonderful thing. It records the range and course of the ship, enough to pick up a periscope at 4,000 yards and many times at a greater distance. Has many peacetime uses; e.g., in a fog.

On the last trip the ship went into New York in pea soup without slowing down. The surface-sweep radar is very accurate when used for computing ranges for guns, which are effective without ever seeing the enemy. The lieutenant commander told me about the 9 August 1942 Battle of Savo Sound, between Guadacanal and Tulagi islands in the South Pacific, where we lost three cruisers and the Australian cruiser *Canberra*. All of these Allied warships were at anchor—the Japs had been reported by planes, but their ships' speed was not calculated. They were expected at 6:00 A.M. and arrived at 2:00.

Our ships were radar-equipped but were observing radar silence. After this catastrophe, the U.S. secretary of the navy issued orders never to observe radar silence, and Vice Admiral Robert Lee Ghormley was relieved of command.

As I write this we pass a raft about 400 yards to port. The Captain looks at it through his glasses and lets us look. No one apparently is aboard, and we do not even slow up.

Diary Entry: 25 July 1945
[At Sea]

Through Mona Passage. We could see Mona Island and Puerto Rico. Both flat.

Firing practice this morning. The 20mm and 40mm guns knocked down a balloon that the 5mm could not get. We are all given general-quarters stations. Bill's, Charley's, and mine are in the sick bay. They say that once in the Pacific, we have general-quarters drill every day, one hour before sunrise.

――――――――――――――――

At Sea (#1)

My dearest Ginny,

You might like an account of "my day" at sea.

The bugler blows reveille at 0600. This comes over the PA system and, as there is a speaker not far from our door, there is no chance of missing it. This means about 30 minutes more to sleep, as breakfast is at 0700.

There are five to the cabin, and we all have time to shave and wash at our one basin before eating. The wardroom where officers eat does not accommodate all of us at once, so there are time shifts per meal.

I eat at 0700, 1200, and 1700. The meals are cafeteria style, and we eat at long tables. Colored boys keep us supplied with water, coffee, and the like, and take up the trays when we leave.

I have spoken of the meals—they are much better than our regular Army chow. We do not linger long, though, as it is hot and others must eat where we are sitting.

Then, after breakfast, it takes about 10 minutes to straighten up the cabin. We make our own beds. We do have a locker each and adequate storage space, so that it is possible to make the place respectable.

At 9:50 each day, our cabins are inspected, and we take a little ribbing because our cabin has invariably gotten the best rating each day. The ratings are published in a daily bulletin. We have the tidiest cabin because we have only five men where six are supposed to be and, therefore, have an extra locker in which to put the odds and ends which otherwise would clutter up the place.

Most of the morning I spend on deck or in the cabin, either reading or working on the statistics of our group. They drive me crazy.

Dinner at 1200. Then sometimes a little nap, if it is not too hot.

Then on deck to read again, or work a little, very little, on the paper until 5:00

After supper we sometimes play bridge in the cabin, or better, in the ship's officers' wardroom, which is large, airy, and cool.

We have no wardroom, but can use the mess hall as such between meals.

Movies are held around 7:30 each evening, but it is better to get invited by the ship's officers to see their movie, which is topside after dark. The other night, we sat in the moonlight to see Keep Your Powder Dry, *a movie about the Women's Army Corps. Not too good.*

The other two officers in our cabin besides Bill and Charley prefer to play poker and have a game each night. Bill and Charley sometimes play, and I played for about an hour last night and simply could not lose. They probably will not let me play again. I won $22.

We usually go to bed at 11:00. There is a gentlemen's agreement that there will be no cards in the room after 10:30, and so to bed.

About every 5th day we each take our turn in the sick bay, and my turn comes tomorrow. Our daily routine is often broken by drills, tea with the Captain, or a visit to the engine room, such as we are going to have today.

RHIP (rank has its privileges), and since there is little officer rank on this ship, we have fared very well. The ship's officers have been very nice to us and are making the voyage as pleasant as possible. I am hoping to learn a little about navigating, so that when you and I set sail for Bermuda there will be a reasonable chance that we can find the place.

You see, all my plans and thoughts concern what we will do, for I now know that without you life has little meaning and no spark.

Love, H

At Sea (#2)

Dearest Ginny,

They have put out another "Poop Sheet" on censorship, and after saying what you cannot tell it gives suggestions to "help you get started." It is possible to write:

1) That you are on a ship somewhere at sea.
2) Describe the sunrise and sunset, the sea in general.
3) Anything else of a purely personal nonmilitary nature.

You can see that about all I will have left to tell you is love, and I shall certainly run that into the ground.

Today we have had good weather. We have entertained ourselves by watching the playful porpoises. It so happens that because there are very few field-grade officers we have been given half of the Captain's veranda as a deck space.

This is very good, as it is shaded, and best of all, there will always be a seat. I sort of feel like a heel going up there while the others are packed like sardines in the deck below.

This afternoon at 4:00, the Captain has asked us up to tea. He sent a Marine sergeant who saluted and said, "The Captain presents his compliments and requests Major Jones's presence at tea at 4:00 P.M." We are all about to take off for this now. I shall let you know what it is like.

The food continues to be good, and I am planning to see if there is a scale in the sick bay so that I can know just how much I can let myself go.

In the meantime, all goes well, and so far I am enjoying this voyage. It has been hot, but is cooling, and we expect a comfortable night.

Love, H

At Sea (#3)

Dearest Ginny,

At the moment, a GI on deck is entertaining his shipmates by imitating a man at the rail. He seems to be able to swallow a considerable amount of air, and *the reverberations can be heard above the waves, as well as the laughter, which the performance inevitably brings forth. It is positively nauseating.*

We have had much more motion today than ever on the Queen Mary *and I, for one, hope it continues, as it makes the trip seem like a real voyage.*

Yesterday we had a very pleasant tea with the Captain. He had it in his quarters, which are immediately below the bridge.

He has a lovely, large stateroom and adjoining sitting room. We had tea, coffee, and cinnamon toast.

The Captain himself is a relatively young man, about 45. I guess I cannot say more, for fear of the stupid censor.

It so happened that while we were there in the Captain's quarters we came upon a well-known historical and geographical location [Gibralter], and with the aid of his glasses we had a good view. The Captain knows Colonel Gay, having been the skipper of a ship that carried the Colonel somewhere. He saw him again at the staging area, after we had gone to the ship. This gave us something to talk about.

The knowledge that one day we shall enjoy these things together is the force that maintains me. I have squeezed the little picture frame behind a pipe that runs beside my bunk. I can lie in bed and look at you. The substitute for the likeness that is you is a joy that I can carry with me halfway around the world.

Love, H

At Sea (#4)

Dearest Ginny,

Mariners, like ophthalmologists, have a language all their own. It is very entertaining to hear the orders come over the ship's PA system: "Sweepers, man your brooms. Sweep down and clean fore and aft." Or: "Cleaning detail, lay after the stern and dump trash." Or: "Mr. So-and-So, lay down to the mate's office at once."

The most characteristic thing of all is the boatswain's pipe, which is used in lieu of the bugle to give mess and sick call and the like for the ship's crew.

You know how they sound. A shrill pitch, more like the sound of a note, but the gyrations that the boatswains can make with it are something you don't soon forget.

The mess call is the most remarkable, for at the end the boatswain chirps like a bird, and you are sure he has gone hog wild.

It is heartbreaking to b7e getting closer to you and yet not have you, but some day will be different.

Until then, my love, H

THROUGHOUT THE LETTERS written at sea and in some other letters, reference is made to working on the "papers." These papers were intended to be scientific contributions about the experience that we had had treating wounds very near the front, particularly the nontransportable wounds; that is, abdominal, thoracic, and thoracoabdominal wounds.

Charley Burbank, Bill Falor, and I had agreed to keep a record of each case we had operated on. This was not an official requirement, and we did not think that others were necessarily going to do it. But it turned out that some other teams also had kept records.

At the conclusion of hostilities, as the teams were gathered together, Lieutenant Colonel Gay became interested in the results in the treatment of wounded and asked the team chiefs to turn in such material as they had. He knew that Bill, Charley, and I were keenly interested in this subject and he turned all the material over to us.

We agreed that on the voyage to Manila we would attempt to pull the information together. These efforts produced three major and some minor communications summarizing the material.

I took the abdominal wounds and prepared a paper titled, "524 Abdominal Wounds on the Western Front." The paper was published in the October 1946 *Bulletin of the Johns Hopkins Hospital.*

Charley Burbank's paper on thoracic wounds was titled, "374 Acute Wounds of the Thorax." It was published in the May 1947 in *Surgery.*

Bill Falor's paper on thoracoabdominal wounds, "165 Acute Wounds of the Thorax," appeared in the September 1946 *Ohio State Medical Journal.*

We can summarize the principal findings in lay terms. As I have already noted, the auxiliary surgical group was conceived to provide expert surgical care as near as possible to the front; specifically at a field hospital adjacent to the clearing company of a division. Men with abdominal, thoracic, and thoracoabdominal wounds, together with other nontransportable wounded, were to be transferred to the field hospital.

The high mortality rates from such wounds dictated creation of auxiliary surgical groups. In Europe in the early days of World War II—the 1939-1940 period—land activity was limited, but the mortality rate from abdominal wounds exceeded 50 percent. One report of 231 abdominal wounds recorded a 60 percent mortality rate.

In the North African Theater of Operations in 1942-1943, the results may have been a tad better. One report of 381 cases recorded a mortality rate of 33 percent, but several other reports showed mortality rates slightly under 50 percent.

In Russia, where there were few reports, the abdominal wound mortality rate exceeded 50 percent. After the Allies invaded Italy, front-line surgery brought down the mortality rate to 30 percent to 35 percent.

The auxiliary surgical groups were fully operational in Europe during the winter campaign of 1944 in France, Belgium, and The Netherlands, and during the spring campaign of 1945 into Germany. On the ship en route to Manila, I documented a mortality rate of 16 percent for 524 cases on the Western Front. Team 3, which contributed 80 of the 524 cases, had a mortality of 13 out of the 80-16 percent.

Colonel Elliott Cutler, the ETO's surgical consultant, attributed these improved results to several factors. Among these were improved methods of resuscitation (i.e., the treatment of shock), better first aid, use of penicillin and sulfanilamides, improved transport of wounded, the generally good physical condition of our soldiers, standardization of therapy (through the consultant system), and better surgery. As I have noted, we never lacked adequate blood or plasma replacement, and postoperative care was excellent.

The concept of the recovery room came out of World War II into civilian practice.

Prior to the war, surgery patients returned immediately from the operating room to their rooms to be cared for by ward nurses or special nurses.

During the war, field-hospital postoperative patients were transferred to recovery tents, where minute attention to their needs was provided by a relatively small number of staff. After a day or two in the recovery tent, the mended went to the general ward. This practice was subsequently transplanted to civilian hospitals, as were many other innovations inspired by battlefield surgery.

Data of the mortality rates from the chest wounds and the thoracoabdominal wounds before institution of front-line treatment are not as readily available as for the abdominal wounds, but the mortality rate in general for the chest wounds was lower than for abdominal wounds. Of the 374 thoracic wounds that we analyzed, thirty-one proved fatal—about 8 percent. Team 3 had fifty-one of these patients, six of whom died—a mortality rate of 11 percent.

For the thoracoabdominal wounds, the medical literature is not clear about the mortality rate in World War II or in World War I. The toll from such wounds must have been even higher than the very high-toll abdominal wounds.

The mortality rate from thoracoabdominal wounds on the Western Front during World War II was 23.6 percent. Of the 165 casualties with such wounds who reached the operating table, 39 died. Team 3 treated 18 of the 165 thoracoabdominal cases studied. Four of our patients died.

The experience of Team 3 was illuminating in a number of respects having to do with the difference between the field hospital and the evacuation hospital, as the following table shows:

War Experience of Team Three

Casualty Categories	Field Hospital			Evacuation Hospital		
	Cases	Deaths	Percentage	Cases	Deaths	Percentage
Abdominal	68	12		12	1	
Chest	46	6		5	0	
Thoracoabdominal	17	4		1	0	
Amputation	12	2		1	0	
Other	21	1		117	0	
Total	164	25	15.2	136	1	0.73

Total War Experience of Team Three

	Cases	Deaths	Percentage
Abdominal	80	13	16.3
Chest	51	6	11.8
Thoracoabdominal	18	4	22.2
Amputation	13	2	15.4
Other	138	1	0.7
Total	300	26	8.7

The top tables show the difference between the types of patients directed to the evacuation hospital and those directed to the field hospital between September 1944 and May 1945 and how the system was supposed to work. It was generally thought toward the end of World War II that about 25 percent of soldiers wounded in battle would die of their wounds. A wounded soldier who reached a battalion aid station had a 1 percent chance of dying if his wounds were such that he would be transported to an evacuation hospital.

Team 3's experience is illustrative: The mortality rate of the casualties seen by the team at the evacuation hospital was less than 1 percent.

Team 3 treated not only men with abdominal, chest, and thoracoabdominal wounds, but also other nontransportable wounded. Of 164 wounded treated in Team 3 field hospitals, 25 died—for an overall mortality rate of about 15 percent.

There can be no doubt that front-line surgery and effective treatment of shock attributable to adequate supplies of blood and plasma and the ability to combat infection with sulfanilamide and penicillin immensely improved medical care of the wounded toward the end of World War II in Europe. That quality of care was dramatically superior to care available in World War I.

Before 1915, abdominal wounds were treated "expectedly," meaning "no treatment at all"—only a faint hope that some of the wounded would recover. The mortality rate must have been well up in the 90 percent range.

———————

At Sea (#5)

My dearest Ginny,

There is no doubt from the temperature of our cabin that we are getting into the tropics. It is not cool, but pleasant enough on deck, especially on the veranda, where we have the luxury of plenty of room and always a place to sit down.

In the cabin, if the wind is from the opposite side, as it was last night, no clothes at all is wearing too much. I tried our trick of taking a cool shower and getting into bed wet, but it was no go, and so I pulled my mattress off the bunk and put it on the floor. This was very much better, and I slept the rest of the night.

I have, by the way, the upper of three bunks and, therefore, the hottest place. But if I can maintain my right to the floor, I think I shall end up with the best place, as the ventilator sprinkles a good breeze directly onto the floor.

Taking a shower, going to bed wet, and sleeping on the floor reminds of the Magothy and Eutaw Place, as if I needed reminding. These things do seem remote at times, and I previously mentioned I sometimes have to take a second thought to be sure that that life did ever exist.

But you continue to be my star, as a sailor's wife should be, and I shall pursue that star almost around the world, until one day I shall find it again.

Love, H

At Sea (#6)

My dearest Ginny,

It was very delightful and cool on the veranda, where I have just come from. But our cabin gets warmer as we approach the low-numbered latitudes. If it were only possible to sleep on deck, as on the Serene. *Today it is very calm, which no* doubt adds to the warmth. Here we can get full advantage of the breeze created by the speed of the ship.

There is very little I can say about the ship, except that it is new and it is a very nice one. We consider ourselves very fortunate to be able to come on it.

The ship has many things that make a long voyage possible. For example, we have all the fresh water desired for washing and for taking showers. The ship contains a still for making fresh water, and it seems capable of meeting the demands of the entire boat. The hot water is almost too hot. Being distilled water, it is very soft, and any soap makes a beautiful lather. The water spigots in our cabin are reversed. The hot water is marked C and the cold water H.

We have an adequate PX, where cigarettes, candy, and other usual PX items are offered. Coca-Cola is cold and not rationed. Candy is rationed; one box of 24 bars of Hershey every four days. I have steadfastly refused to buy mine, because I weigh 178 on the sick-bay scales. I have eaten some of Bill's, much to his amusement. We also have ice cream, but the smallest amount that you can buy is 2½ gallons, and this afternoon we had a can. It is very good, being made from a mix.

In the ship's library is a volume of Ben Franklin's writings. It is a journal of a voyage taken in 1726. He had an observation interesting to us.

> 'Tis a common opinion among the ladies that if a man is ill-natured he infallibly discovers it when he is in liquor, but I who have known many instances to the contrary will teach them a more effectual method to discover the natural temper and disposition of their humble servants.

> Let the ladies make one long sea voyage with them, and if they have the least spark of ill-nature in them and conceal it to the end of the voyage, I will forfeit all my pretensions to their favor.

Early in our love we put this to the test and found it satisfactory. This would be a wonderful opportunity to make another test, which would not be a test at all, but a fulfillment and renewal of our love, which to me is by far the most important thing in my life.

Love, H

Dearest Ginny,

    This is a little note about Charley Burbank. He is one of the better surgeons of the 5th Aux. Officially, he ranks as a "B." You know that we had only about five of those before reorganization. Actually, Burbank is a fine operator and has good judgment.

    One day Col. Smith walked into the operating room when Shippy, [Burbank's assistant], was putting the dressing on a patient. "What did you just do?" "Just did a pneumonectomy"—and so it was. A whole lung was removed—the first in the ETO, as far as anyone knows.

    The patient was a Kraut who had a bad laceration of the lung. Charley thought he ought to have his lung out, and he went about it and knew how to do it. The patient did well.

    Charley spent eight years at Harvard, graduating in 1938. He finished his residency at Mass General just in time to go into the Army in about 1943. He was originally assigned to the 1st Aux when it was at Fort Sam, but he fell and broke his knee, or something, and spent several weeks in Brooke General.

    The upshot of this was that he was finally assigned to the staff at Brooke General for several months and, on his own initiative, got assigned to the 5th Aux about a month before we came overseas.

    You may remember that he had a house on the post. The last house on the left on Wheaton Road as you went up toward the hospital. We used to see him in the swimming pool with his wife and little girl. You may remember him, as he has a tattoo on his arm. This tattoo he got in London several years ago after a party with a group of friends. He was surprised to find it there the next morning. He threatened to get one as a memento of Marseilles, but never got around to it.

    Physically, he is a big man. He is one of those individuals who has to be very careful of his diet. Since being on the ship he has gone many days with eating but a single meal. But in spite of this he has gained 5 lbs. and now weighs 200.

    He is not really fat. Just big in a general sort of way, but with a very definite waist. He is a nice-looking fellow, and on this voyage he is growing a moustache just for the fun of it. He has turned out to look something like a walrus, and with two tusks the similarity would be more than superficial.

    Charley is definitely a "nice guy" and a good companion. He does not have an important opinion of himself, and you would never guess that he was from Harvard. He enjoys a good time when the circumstances are right, but work comes first. He was the only one of the three who got the least bit lubricated in Panama.

It is hard to know how the illness of his wife has affected him. He seldom talks about it, but recently did show us a letter he received from her written with her left hand. He was overjoyed with the childlike scrawl, and it made my heart ache to see it.

I can notice no difference from the way he was in the fall, but Bill thinks he is less gay. Perhaps so, but I do not think it is evident to his friends.

He comes from a fine family, although I know very little about them. His father is a first cousin of Luther Burbank [(1849-1926) famed American plant breeder and horticulturist], and I guess that makes Charley a first cousin once removed. As a matter of fact, Charley himself seems to know a great deal about fruit and the like, as his family owns large farms in Florida.

All in all, with Bill and Charley I have delightful traveling companions, and we make an agreeable trio.

With love as always, H

At Sea (#8)

Dearest Ginny,

All the medical officers have been given duty with the regular staff. It so happens that there are two of us, and we will do sick call about every third day. The regular officers are very nice indeed, and I believe they run a pretty good service. They bring casualties back on the return trip.

We will do nothing but hold sick call, and they will do any real work. I have never held sick call, except for odds and ends as officer of the day at Fort Sam Houston, and so I shall not mind it very much.

We also get a certain amount of "gravy," as we have free run of the sick bay, which is roomy and airy and therefore cool.

It so happens that there is no laundry facility on the ship, but the ship's surgeon says that since we were not such a large group, it would probably be possible to get our own laundry done through the hospital.

The chief medical officer is apparently a surgeon, as he says they average about 20 operations per trip, from hemorrhoids to strangulated hernias, with appendices a dime a dozen. One of the problems is to keep the men from trying to flock into the hospital, where they find it so comfortable.

With love as always, H

At Sea (#9)

Dearest Ginny,

One of the guys in our cabin is a character. He is major, and we were all unanimous in our opinion that he had been a Regular Army enlisted man who was commissioned after the war broke out. This proved to be the case.

He is everything that one thinks of a Regular Army guy as being. He appears tough, but really isn't. He is a hard drinker, except in the boat, where it is strictly forbidden, and he has by his own admission quite a way with the women. He has told us of many of his escapades in Germany during the nonfraternization era.

Bill asked him today how much education he has, as he is certainly no dummy. He almost finished high school, except for the following episode:

He was selected to give an address to the class at some precommencement exercise and, on the way to the school, stopped at the house of a bootlegger friend who gave him a pint of whiskey, which he put in his back pocket. As he was sitting on the platform waiting his turn to speak, his coat rode up over the bottle, and when he was called upon he delivered the speech OK. But on turning to sit down, the bottle was exposed to the audience and principal, much to the amusement of the former and irritation of the latter, who fired him from school two weeks before graduation. He is a very likable guy with a liberal education. His first name is Stanley.

Last night we made the acquaintance of one of the boat's officers with whom we play bridge. Before the war, he was a music teacher at Hollins College and knew Elizabeth Ender. Incidentally, I bid and made a grand slam.

The news appears to be good, with the fleet apparently able to sail up to Japan at will. Would that the unexpected would happen and the Nips give up, but it is impossible. But someday the day will come, and I shall be flying home to you.

Love, H

At Sea (#10)

Dearest Ginny,

Our trip ashore in Panama came, as I said, as a complete surprise.

The information in Marseilles and on the ship was that no one could go ashore. We (Charley, Bill, and I) had worked hard on the angles all during the voyage. We could never figure out if it laid within the power of the Captain to allow some of the troops, namely, us, ashore.

At any rate, our hints were broad, and I had the feeling, perhaps unfounded, that at the last minute the Captain would ask perhaps a few of us to go. Ship's company was to have liberty anyway. Upon arriving at our first stop, a boarding party came on with the details for sending the entire ship's passenger load ashore, and our problem was at an end.

We did not get to leave until about 8:00 P.M. It was already dark. The time here was Central Western Time. Troops marched. Field officers rode. We went directly to the Officers Club, where our party was put up in a nearby house, which had more than enough beds for the crowd.

The house took me back to Fort Sam Houston. The plan was modified, because of the tropics. The bathroom was very much the same, including the little wall closet over the washbowl. I looked for your leg make-up, but it was not there. We left our belongings, which consisted of a towel.

Then to the club, which being on a peacetime post was an elegant, airy, one-story, rambling building with a lot of tile and rail work. Everyone descended on the bar. The regulations about consuming liquor on the ship were very strict, and so a good many people felt they had stored up a right to a considerable quantity.

On the ship, it had originally been told us that we would be able to go to town if desired, but upon arrival they said that, since the stay was short and that the enlisted men could not go, the general aboard decided that no officer should go.

However, the ship's postal officer, who was being entertained by the local counterpart, made arrangements with the latter for a little excursion, and Bill and Charley and I joined. The postal officer in the Panama Canal Zone had a car, and four months before had married a government worker. But she was home in the States on furlough, and so he was free for the evening.

We went first to the Tivoli Hotel, which is a large, airy, frame building, à la Saratoga Springs. Our intent was to have a sirloin steak, but we were too late and settled for a Tom Collins all around.

Panama is a city of nightlife, and so our host suggested Costa Nova Club as the best. We arrived just in time for the show, which went through three-quarters of an hour and seven or eight acts. It was well-above average, and not as anatomical as you might think, although there was an output by an Ethiopian couple that was pure physiology, as Bill says.

The nightclubs are apparently closely controlled and supervised by the MPs. If the show is considered too bad or prostitution too wild, the place is put off-limits. Some businesses have withered on the vine by this method, and so they are all reasonably respectable places.

After this to a lunch-counter type of place for a bite to eat. The whole place is strictly American—much more so, as Bill says, than when he was there 12 years ago.

I had forgotten that eating places could be clean and that it was possible to order up as desired. I had a steak sandwich and a cup of coffee. It was delicious, and now I am sorry I did not eat more, although at the time I felt pretty full.

We then drove around town a little and, in the moonlight, saw the beautiful homes along the water. These for the most part belonged to local merchants and businessmen. It appeared to be a prosperous city.

The stores are amazing. No more places with dirty windows and dusty cartons of dried ersatz foods, but clean, beautiful windows neatly and abundantly displayed. The place is American.

Other stores had plenty of everything in the windows. Clothes, especially shoes, which are scarce and poor in Europe, hardware, lights, radios, and the like—probably more than the States, as Panama is a free port and a huge crossroad.

And so back to the post about 2:30. Into bed, and the sheet was damp, as is probably always true. Before morning it was necessary to pull up the sheet.

At breakfast we had papaya and fried eggs. We are not used to these, as our eggs are powdered. The cook knew how to fry eggs like Mama, and I had four. Should have eaten more.

On the way to the ship, we picked up some mangos that had fallen off the tree in front of the club. We have enjoyed these. The flavor of a ripe mango is much better than those we had at Fort Sam.

All in all, an enjoyable stop, but lacking in the most important thing—Mama.

Love, H

At Sea (#11)

Dearest Ginny,

Our recent sojourn held at least three surprises.

First, the mail that we received. Being an advance party, it seemed unlikely that we would get any mail unless some snafu stepped in and sent the mail of our entire unit.

We did not bother to go to the mailroom when it was announced that mail was ready for distribution, but about an hour later we thought that we had just better be sure, and it was there: 36 mail bags for the entire 5th Aux.

This means that the mail to the others had been cut off in New York, and we will probably have the entire unit's mail at our destination. This is nice for us, but tough for the rest.

The second surprise was the weather. We figured on a day of scorching sun and breeze cut off by land, but to everyone's delight, it was cloudy and, by comparison, cool during the day and night. The weather has continued to be fine.

The third surprise was going ashore. Local authorities went to a great deal of trouble to arrange accommodations for everyone for so short a stay. Troops and company officers were put up at barracks made available for this purpose, and field-grade officers were put up at an officers club, which compared favorably with Fort Sam Houston.

Whoever is responsible for this policy in regard to directly redeploying troops deserves credit for his good judgment. It was universally approved and had a noticeable effect on troop morale, and more so because it was unexpected.

With love, H

ON 6 AUGUST 1945, the *Enola Gay*, a bomber from the United States 509th Combined Group of the 20th Air Force, dropped an atomic bomb over Hiroshima, Japan. The explosion—its force equivalent to that of twenty thousand tons of TNT—destroyed 60 percent of the city, killing at least eighty thousand of the city's inhabitants and maiming and lethally irradiating tens of thousands more.

President Truman's decision to order the first atomic bombing of a city followed the first successful testing of an atomic bomb at Alamagordo, New Mexico, on 16 July 1945 and the Japanese government's rejection of the 26 July Potsdam Declaration.

The Potsdam Declaration repeated the demand of the United States, the Soviet Union, and the United Kingdom for the unconditional surrender of Japan. The statement asserted that the Allies did not seek to reduce Japan to poverty, but it was silent on whether the emperor would be permitted to retain his throne.

The following letter to Georgeanna addresses the bombing that announced arrival of the Nuclear Age.

At Sea (#15)

Dearest Ginny,

The conversation around the boat has continued on atomic bombs. It has been interesting that during this trip, from time to time, someone would be convinced that the Japs would now have to give up. But it is so similar to the talk of last September regarding Nazi Germany that I cannot bring myself to put much stock in it.

This new weapon does seem to be phenomenal, if we can believe the reports. But even so, it seems to me that the Japs' determination is such that we will have to go ashore before they are willing to quit.

Our possession of the atomic bomb may explain a few things. For example, perhaps we do not care to have the Russians in the war against Japan. We will have better markets for American products in China after the war if the Russians do not come in.

It will be interesting to see how this all works out. Think of how we all might feel had the Japs dropped such a bomb on Honolulu. There have been very few weapons introduced that the enemy did not find out about. I trust we have kept the secret well.

The enlisted men on a troopship are the ones who slug it out. Recently we have been blessed with a quartering breeze that has poured in through our porthole and kept the cabin as comfortable as almost anyplace on the ship. Our mess hall, although hot, has a limited number of people. We have been able to wash our uniforms, so that they are clean, if not pressed.

The GI, on the other hand, is more crowded in the hold where, like many of the officers, he is quartered in compartments without portholes. However, the ventilating system is good, and the air is not stale. We go past the entrance to the EM mess hall en route to ours. The heat is terrific, as the kitchen is nearby. The men are allowed to take off their shirts, and the odor of sweat and body odor that exudes from the doorway is enough to take your appetite.

One of the most difficult things is that facilities for washing fatigues, which are the prescribed uniform, are limited, and this plus the fact that many of them make no effort to wash them anyway, make their uniforms sweaty and dirty enough to stand alone.

In spite of this, they seem to be a happy-go-lucky bunch and spend their time playing cards and the like on deck and throwing cigarette butts and paper around, much to the consternation of the Captain and troop commander, who tear their hair out at this. GIs are impossible, but I can't blame them.

Love, H

ON 8 AUGUST 1945, the United States dropped a second atomic bomb on Nagasaki, Japan. Not as powerful as the bomb that devastated Hiroshima, the second bombing of a Japanese city killed forty thousand inhabitants and maimed and irradiated hordes of others. And the Soviet Union declared war on Japan; Moscow cited Tokyo's spurning of the Potsdam Declaration as its reason for entering the war.

The next letter recounts how the news of the Soviet War declaration was received aboard the *Admiral Benson*.

At Sea (#16)

Dearest Ginny,

And now Russia. We are living in exciting days. I was sitting on the Captain's veranda this morning, waiting for inspection to be over so that I could go below and work on the paper, when a sailor came running out of the radio shack and ran over to a group of his friends shouting something I could not hear, but from their reaction it seemed they were pleased.

And then, B. G., the radio officer with whom we have played bridge these several nights, came out with a big smile with the news. Then in to tell the Captain and put it on the P.A. system. A tremendous roar went up from the GIs and shouts of "Turn her around," and "The Golden Gate by August 8," and the like, and now we await more news.

I can't believe the Japs will give up without an Allied invasion. History tells us that defeated leaders hang on long after everyone knows the jig is up. Most of all, the Japs. I hope I am wrong.

Did I tell you that I bet Charley $10 that the war would not be over by the time the rest of us must get there? I also hope this makes my bets on the war 100% wrong.

We have continued to have pleasant weather. We were all surprised—much better than in Panama. Do kiss the babies for me, and I shall repay them to you that day.

Love, H

Wednesday 15 August 1945
1:00 P.M.

Dearest Ginny,

For several days we have heard on the news broadcasts about false rumors and premature celebrations, so that when the news finally came this morning that the armistice had been announced by Truman, it was an anticlimax.

About two days ago, the Captain told us that, instead of going straight to Manila, he had received orders to proceed to Ulithi, which is only slightly off the route. You may find it just south of Guam.

His instructions were to pick up an escort, and he thought this meant to go to a different destination or at least by a different route. We were going into anchorage at Ulithi when the official word came that the war was over.

Earlier we had a little excitement—the only one on the voyage. Five enemy subs had been reported between Ulithi and Manila, and it was because of this that we figured we were picking up the escort. No enemy aircraft had been sighted.

Soon after daybreak Charley and I were on the veranda, and through the

442   Howard W. Jones Jr. and Georgeanna Seegar Jones

glasses we could just see the tops of coconut trees. They seemed to be growing out of the water. To the right, we could see smoke.

Now and again we saw a giant burst in the water, all at a great distance and visible only through the glasses. I guessed depth charges. And then suddenly, "General quarters!" A mad scramble. Someone saw antiaircraft fire off the starboard bow. Everybody below, gunners topside. Our station at general quarters is in the sick bay. All ports were closed in a few minutes.

Commander Vitt, the ship's surgeon, took two or three of us, and we went on deck, just outside the sick bay. There were several planes on the horizon, and continuing antiaircraft fire. We all remarked how unfortunate to be in this position while waiting for news of peace.

And then, as unexpectedly, release from general quarters sounded before the puffs of antiaircraft fire had blown away. It seemed strange to us that we would be allowed topside, and the gunners sent to their other duties so soon. And then we could see it again. A plane and heavy fire behind it, and then the whole mess was clear. The plane was towing a sleeve, and the fleet was having a little target practice.

Now that the war is really over our (Bill's, Charley's, and my) position is ambiguous.

Will we be diverted to the States, East Coast or West Coast, depending on our position? What do we do?

The best, of course, is that we will have to go back and join our unit. I have dated this letter and mentioned other things forbidden by censorship, but, with the war over, I can't see that it matters.

Ulithi, of which I had never heard until we left Panama, is an atoll which was taken by the U.S. after our march toward Japan began. It was inhabited only by natives, and there was no fight. However, it is our largest naval anchorage in the Pacific.

At the moment, there are over 100 ships here. I counted 130, and there are others. One transport that left Marseilles about five days before us has been here four days. That must mean that something is different from the original plan. We can only wait and see.

With love as always, H

16 August 1945

Dearest Ginny,

We are underway again after spending just about 24 hours in Ulithi, and a hot night it was. There was not a breath of air stirring, and of course we were without the 20-mile breeze stirred up by the ship's way.

They say the war is over, but to us it is a little more real than at any other time in this area. I mentioned yesterday that Jap subs have been reported between here and Manila, and, as a matter of fact, it was over this route that the ill-fated heavy cruiser USS Indianapolis *went a few days ago. We therefore picked up a destroyer escort for this leg of the journey.*

There is only one escort, but it moves back and forth in front of us at about 2,000 yards. The point of it, the Captain says, is to use its sound-detection apparatus. We do not have any.

The destroyer, whose name I have forgotten, is a beautiful thing in the water. It is so fast that its stern seems to be below the waves. It makes some 40 knots, compared to our 20.

As a matter of fact, we are no longer going through the San Bernardino Strait, because it was just there that the Indianapolis *was torpedoed on 29 July 1945 with loss of all but 316 of its 1,100 crew members. We are going to Leyte, discharge some of our troops, as I understand it, and then to Manila. This will increase our journey by a few days.*

There were about 200 ships in Ulithi, including the Admiral Mayo *and the* General Mann. *The* Mayo *left Marseilles five days, the* Mann, *three days before us. We had a choice as to which boat we could take and we selected this so that we could go to the Riviera. And so we left them at Ulithi and will arrive before them—such is fate.*

The other side of it is worse. The scuttlebutt has it that these ships may go back to the States with the present troops aboard.

Whatever our fate I have not yet gotten myself in a postwar frame of mind. We are still at war—the Japs may not know that it is over. Of course, by the time we get to Manila the situation may be different.

Love to all, H

Saturday 18 August 1945

Dearest Ginny,

It is 1:00 P.M. here and we have changed our clock for the last time. We are now on Manila time and exactly 13 hours ahead of you. It is 2:00 A.M. there, and you are sleeping so gently.

We left Ulithi for Leyte, as I previously said. We were due to arrive there this morning, but, instead of going into the harbor, we were given our destination and proceeded directly.

Do you have a map of the Philippines? The one in our map book on page 14 will do. We entered between Malhon Island and Samar, then south through Suriago Strait. It was just as the strait widens that the great surface action of the war was fought and a great part of the Jap fleet sunk. This was soon after the Leyte invasion, when the Japs sent their fleet through Suriago and San Bernardino straits, as well as around the northern tip of Luzon, to try to sink the invasion transports in the Leyte Gulf. The Captain says that the Navy knew from that time on that the Japs had not a single major warship available.

We then go a little south of west between Mindanao and Negros and into the Sulu Sea, then north through Mindanao Strait and into the China Sea. Our port of destination is San Fernando, where we will probably have to go ashore in landing craft, as in Normandy.

We understand that the staging area is at Baguio, which does not seem to be on the map, but may well be shown as Bayombong, which appears to be in the vicinity of Baguio. We are due to debark Monday, having then been on the ship 35 days.

The Philippines are pleasing to the eye after looking at the flatness of Eniwetok and Ulithi. Leyte and Dinagat are mountainous, and the densely wooded hills come to the water. Baguio is, as you know, the summer resort and is in the hills about 2,000 feet high. I would like to get to Manila for the celebration.

We are taking no chances. Our destroyer escort left us at Leyte, but we picked up another as we entered the Sulu Sea. I do hope the 5th Aux is diverted home, as any chance of getting back will be so much greater if this is so.

Love, H

Sunday 19 August 1945
7:30 A.M.

Dearest Ginny,

So we are in the Sulu Sea, but it appears no different from the water we have seen before; that is, except for the rain clouds which hover over every bit of land we saw yesterday and which seem as plentiful today. I suppose we must get ready for wet weather.

Today should be our last one on the boat. We are due at San Fernando early tomorrow and possibly will immediately debark. The 5th Aux is scheduled to be the first unit off the boat. It will probably be a landing-craft job.

I hope that within 48 hours I shall be able to write some definitive word as to our status here and, of course, prospects of getting home. The lack of information aboard ship is discouraging, and I cannot bear to think about the prospect of coming home with things so much in the state of flux. It is as if something that should be attainable is just beyond reach and impossible to take any action. Once ashore we can at least make an effort.

I hope that my not being able to get letters in the mail as soon as the war is over was no cause of anxiety to you. I feel sure, though, that you had our expected arrival time well figured out.

The trip has indeed been uneventful except for news of world history. I had no notion that the end of the war was even around the corner, but the Potsdam Conference attended by the heads of the United States, the Soviet Union, and the United Kingdom, which seemed to accomplish nothing, and then atomic bombs, then Russia, and then the end of the war. Hard to believe it could be.

The boat ride, on the other hand, has been uneventful, so far. We have had no rough weather, one or two days a few land lovers got a little seasick, but nothing for the last 30 days. I was a bit disappointed, for I should have enjoyed a little storm, to see what it was like.

Love to all, H

20 August 1945

Dearest Ginny,

This morning we came into the little harbor of San Fernando. It is a beautiful little place. The hills come down to the water and are covered with several tropical growths. The harbor itself is behind a peninsula, so that it is landlocked on three sides. I don't think there was a large boat dock here before the war. We have built four or five broad piers. The deep water must extend almost to the shoreline, as the bow of the boat almost touches the sand.

Spread along the shore and on to the sides of the nearby hills are supply dumps of all description. Huge piles of boxes, some orderly, some scattered around.

As previously mentioned, this was announced as our destination, but after pow-wows between all concerned only three units got off here, and the remainder, including us, go back to Manila. At the moment we are tied up at the pier. All units have gotten off that are going to, and we are waiting around to get going.

On the other side of the pier, and in full view, is a Liberty ship unloading from all five hatches at once. From one of the ships crated 2½-ton trucks have been coming out for the last four hours, until you are reminded of the clowns getting out of the automobile at the circus. All the other hatches are discharging food.

We talked to one member of the boarding party, who told us direct redeployment has been stopped. I hope the 5th Aux was turned back.

Love, H

Tuesday 21 August 1945

Dearest Ginny,

This morning about daylight we came into Manila Bay. Charley and I got on deck just as we were between Corregidor and Olongapo

Corregidor, like the Rock of Gibraltar, was disappointing. I expected to see a concrete island with gun turrets everywhere, but it appears to be a harmless wooded island. It has a rather flat place on top, where the wreckage of barracks and the like may be seen. A flagpole with the Stars and Stripes and a naval signal station, that flashed at us as we passed were the only signs of life.

As we came up to Manila itself, the weather got thicker and thicker, until the clouds opened, and it rained in torrents for about two hours.

During this time, the shore, which had been visible, disappeared into the mist, and the Captain dropped anchor until he could get in touch with shore.

Finally, a small boat came alongside, and information was passed that troops would be debarked tomorrow.

So here we are, having gotten up at 5:00 A.M. on two mornings to be ready to be off.

Yesterday we stripped our bunks and had nothing but a mattress and pillow. These were quite enough, as I had been sleeping on top of the sheet without the benefit of shorts. Last night, of course, it was cool, and at 4:00 A.M. I got up and slipped on my fatigue shirt. Bill put on his raincoat. For tonight I think I can find a sheet, just in case.

There are many ships at anchor here in the bay. On one side of us is a built-up ship of queer design. It is low and flat, something like a tanker, but has Japanese script on the side. It is sunk and abandoned.

Soon after we came to anchor, the New Jersey, *one of our late large battleships, came in to anchor beside us. It flies the flag of a four-star admiral, perhaps Halsey himself—probably here for the conference with the Nips.*

The news moves slowly. It is maddening not to be able to get any information about the world and us in particular. We can only wait and hope.

Love, H

Chapter 17

Letters from Home
27 July-30 August 1945

*G*EORGEANNA'S 28 JULY LETTER WAS WRITTEN before the atomic bombing of Hiroshima. She alludes to the government secrecy prevailing in an area in Tennessee where her brother, King, had been posted as a U.S. Army medical officer. The reason for the secrecy was revealed following the dropping of the first A-bomb, as she notes in her 6 August letter.

Sunday, July 27, 1945
11:00 P.M.

Dearest Honey Bunny,

I didn't write yesterday, although there was much news, because I just didn't seem to have the heart.

Father continues to be worse, I believe. I gave him intravenous glucose last night and again tonight, as he is a little dehydrated and is really eating practically nothing.

Yesterday Ward Allen told me that Ridge Trimble and George Finney had just arrived for a ten-day conference in Washington, and that hot news was afoot.

I hope to get to see Ridge personally. I guess we were about in this state last year, thinking that the Germans might capitulate at any minute, and I guess I should keep my hopes geared to two years, but it's hard to do.

All my love, Ginny

Friday, July 28, 1945
10:30 P.M.

My darling,

    Today I received your letter of July 12, and so the sun has shone. In it you say start writing c/o Ridge as of July 25. I'll get one off to him tomorrow.
    Even your faint glimmer of hope about rotation has made my day brighter. Yesterday, as I sat waiting for the train to bring Father and Mother in, I could not help think of a far-happier when I shall wait for a train, boat or plane to bring you to me. I have been so emotionally unstable that I'm afraid I won't be able to meet you in public.
    I hate to write a letter like this to you when you are so far away, but after all, it is just these letters that keep us from being far away. And you must and do realize that because I have you everything is possible, and I'm sure I can carry on.
    I don't really see how Father can go through another three months like this. Aside from the emotional strain, which I am sure you appreciate, there are other considerations of practical importance.
    I have never been too familiar with Father's finances, as he is quite self-sufficient, as you know. But it seems that his sister left him property that was mortgaged far above its value. For years he poured money into them, as the mortgage was arranged by poor old-maiden relatives, and he would not let his sisters down. In the Depression his savings were wiped out with the Commonwealth Bank.
    He has been able to carry on with what he has made, pure and simple. But now when he stops, his income stops. The present fixed expenses on the house are $60 a month, food averages $20 a week, and Edward, for cleaning, $4 per week, e.g., $156 per month. The small bit of income Father has been able to accumulate since the Depression will cover insurance policies, but I doubt if it will take care of the two installments of taxes coming up.

I see no way but to assume the $156 running expenses. King and Lib will undoubtedly help with taxes. Father will combat this as long as he is able, but I don't see how, because there is nothing else to carry on with.

This, of course, wipes out some of our backlog, and I'm awfully sorry. Please be frank and say what you think—any suggestions will be gratefully received.

They say that King has done 36 OB cases in less than a month. The government community in Tennessee covers two counties—very secret—and they cater to the patients, as all are, of course, civilians.

The man in charge of Ob/Gyn is Captain Kettel, of the University of Wisconsin, and just a little older than King. King is his senior in grade, but no one receives any promotions.

It is apparently a most amazing place, and they are all very well-satisfied. The folks say that King is very well-domesticated and hangs curtains and pictures like an expert.

Lib wrote about asking Jane to come home for two weeks, and darned if Jane isn't coming.

My dear, you will be awfully lucky to get rid of me for two hours when you get back, and I know I wouldn't consider two weeks.

Kay Gibbs writes that she is thinking of taking her job back and leaving Lou at Fort Benning. I know these girls don't love their husbands like I do mine.

I'm counting the days until September, when I shall possibly hear from you again.

All my love, Ginny

                                                    Saturday, August 4, 1945

Dearest,

As yet I have not seen Ridge, so hope that the mail will go through all right. It gives me a terribly isolated feeling not getting mail and being afraid it will be months before you get mine.

This morning Father had a gallbladder series and they strung it out all day, so that he was dreadfully sick from fatigue, lack of food, and then fatty foods.

He waited and had his usually scattered and copious stool immediately after a fatty meal.

They then gave him 1,500 cc IV. I was so afraid they would give it too fast. I sat and watched it myself, and it took two hours for 1200 cc. Then they discontinued it, as he was weary.

We started home at 7:30 and had a flat tire, but a very nice gentleman helped me fix it.

The children are being perfect angels, and Smitty is really wonderful. I am really emotionally and physically tired, but I want to write my favorite type of letter, a love letter, in the next day or so, because, as always, they help me during these times.

All my love, Ginny

Monday, August 6, 1945
10:30 P.M.

Dearest Honey Bunny,

Today the sun has shone for, lo and behold, I received what I take to be your really last letter, July 15, 1:00 P.M. I had almost forgotten how really wonderful it is to get mail. Just the thought of all my accumulated letters gives me courage and cheer.

Really dear, a furlough at this time would have been very distressing for you, as I am sure you would have had to spend our time trying to do something for Father.

Although I miss your advice and medical knowledge, I really suppose I can struggle along by myself.

When you come home, I do want everything to be as perfect as possible, although with you here, how could it be otherwise?

Donnie says Joe writes illustrated letters to Jimmie (he is no artist; in fact, she didn't know he could make a straight line), and Jimmie adores the letters

Someday, if you have a few spare moments, you might try one of your trips for Willie. I am so anxious for Papa to continue to mean something to him, rather than just a picture.

B goes up and down stairs now without difficulty. She still says only "book," except "bye-bye," "night-night," and "oh, my." She adores fruits and melons of all descriptions.

The secret of Oak Ridge, Tennessee, is out—the atomic-bomb factory, with 75,000 civilians.

All my love, Ginny

Tuesday, August 7, 1945
10:30 P.M.

My darling,

Today a horrible day, but now it is over, and I can concentrate on you and the happier side.

Father was slated for a gastrointestinal series, which they finally concluded at 10:30. No breakfast and no medication up to that point, because the gall bladder series taken Saturday was no good. Question—why didn't they know that two days before?

At any rate, they did a gastric analysis, at my insistence, so the day was not entirely wasted.

I don't know what the result was, as the little intern seems to think it a violation of the Hippocratic Oath to tell me the results of anything, so I have to find out for myself.

Father seems to be more and more uncomfortable and, of course, is terribly depressed and weak now, which is very hard for Mother and me to take. It is so unlike him.

Eddie Edmondson is in the X-ray department, so at least I have a friend at court, and I hope to make his repeat of the gallbladder series easier for him tomorrow. Eddie inquired especially about you.

I also learned that Eddie Richardson is with the 51st General Hospital just outside of Manila. I am enclosing a note to him in case you see him before Ridge gets back.

We are all excited about the atomic bomb, and I hope it will hasten the end of the war. How sick of it everyone is.

I think only of the time when we shall once more be together.

All my love, Ginny

Wednesday, August 8, 1945
10:30 P.M.

My dearest,

Today I feel my usual self again, and I am sure everything is going to be all right.

I am so encouraged about the war news. What with Russia coming in and the success of the atomic bomb, I feel that the Japs surely must capitulate. I have almost promised the kiddies Papa for Christmas, instead of Santa Claus.

Father had a better day, and his X-rays were again negative. His gastric analysis showed no HCL, even with histamine. This is his only demonstrable abnormality, and I am now determined to use this as a diagnosis and treat it for all it is worth.

I somehow feel that I will get somewhere, as he seems in such good shape otherwise. Do wish I had you beside me to advise, encourage and cheer me (also for purposes of recreation).

Beezie—another nickname for B—fed herself two big helpings of squash, Polish sausage, one helping of beans, two saucers of applesauce, and two glasses of milk. Not bad, eh?

I ache to kiss you.

All my love, Ginny

Friday, August 10, 1945
1st surrender-rumor day

My darling, dearest Honey Bunny,

What a day we have spent! I have been certainly wondering where you are and what you are thinking about the possibility of an imminent end to the Pacific War.

I can't help but believe that the end can be counted in days. What will be your status? At least you have had quite a trip, but the only part of it I am interested in is the one to the USA.

This morning at 9:00 A.M., as I was walking up the corridor from seeing Father, who had a good night, Dr. TeLinde signaled me wildly, and when he was within shouting range informed me, "The war is over!" I positively jumped up and down and nearly died laughing. I have been grinning all day.

In addition, my case of hirsutism treated with testosterone (just enough to suppress the adrenal function) came in after six weeks of therapy and she says she is a new woman. She feels fine, and there is definite decrease in her hair. To her this was more important than the end of the war.

I do wish you could have seen B trying to mow the lawn today. She is so cute. I will have to try to get a picture. I think and hope that you will be pleased with both of your offspring, but I do feel that they will both be improved by having a Papa, and Mama will be a new woman.

With just the prospects, I am a new woman, but I do hope I won't be nauseated from excitement from now until you arrive. I have certainly been so today.

All my love, Ginny

Sunday, August 12, 1945
10:30 P.M.

Dearest Honey Bunny Boo,

Everything seems so rosy tonight. I can hardly believe I felt so blue last Sunday, just one week ago. Of course, I realize they may keep you over there as a replacement, but at least there won't be any invasion beach to go in on, thank heaven, and then I can always dream that they will send your boat right on home.

This has been a strange sort of ending to the war, if indeed it is the ending. No one is particularly in the mood for celebrating. I think the gravity of the thing is uppermost in everyone's mind.

Although I said a little prayer of thanksgiving every hour Friday and went about with a Cheshire grin, I am really reserving my celebration for our own particular V-Day when I can celebrate in your arms. May that day be not-too-far distant?

Father continues to improve very slowly, but, I think, definitely. We hope to have him home by Tuesday or Wednesday and begin intensive therapy for pernicious anemia. The ending stages of the war have done a lot to help his morale also.

I am so impatient to hear from you, what sort of trip you had, did you get to see anything, and above all, did you get my letters?

With Ridge in this country and the war almost over, it occurred to me he might not go back, so I thought you would, of course, look up Pat. I hope this train of events occurs.

Also, I suppose you may have some notion of what is to become of you, and that is uppermost in my mind. Will these next few weeks ever pass?

I am waiting for you with ever-growing impatience—when I remember that it took King six weeks after he started, I feel dreadfully frustrated.

All my love, Ginny

Tuesday, August 14, 1945
10:00 P.M.
Surrender Day

My darling,

Our day is surely near at hand, and how really lucky we have been so far. I feel much better about you being on a boat. I would really worry about the celebration at Marseilles or Manila.

Willie shot a temperature last night with no localizing symptoms (throat looked red). Tonight he was much better, so I loaded him in the car with Smitty, B, and Mary and drove down Charles Street to hear the celebration. He was goggle eyed, as indeed we all were, for we had forgotten what traffic is like. I hope they will remember some of it, but I doubt it.

Leoda (a laboratory technician) just called, asking me to come in and celebrate, but I am really not up to it. I am still going to wait for you to stage my celebration. I am just giving thanks that you are well and safe tonight.

Father has been somewhat depressed today, but I hope will be able to do better when we get him home.

I would like to see Fort Sam Houston tonight. If you get into San Francisco with time on your hands, call John Haines at the Marine Hospital.

I am listening to the radio now, and although it is very exciting, there is something missing, and nothing is the same without you to share it.

All my love, Ginny

Wednesday, August 15, 1945

Dearest Honey Bunny,

Today Dr. Pierson finally went all over Father's plates and fluoroscopic examination and decided that there was a lesion on the posterior surface of the stomach at the cardiac end.

He believes it is in the stomach wall, as he says the mucosa is stretched and atrophic over it. But he also says that it could be a lesion in the tail to the pancreas, and this is, of course, what Dr. Hamman had suspected and believes he has.

Everyone thinks that a laparotomy is indicated, as his general condition is good. Dr. Stone has him posted for Saturday or Monday. I hope it's Saturday.

Would that you were here. The mere thought of you, though, gives me infinite courage.

Mother is a dreadful problem, as she is under such a strain and has no relief from it. Of course, she neither eats nor sleeps properly. I have been trying to think of who could come to give her moral support, and I think I will send for Aunt Lil (no relation, but a close family friend living in New Jersey).

Willie is well today, and B, who had a slight temperature today, is also all right tonight.

Your package arrived with the camera, films, and maps, and also the horn for Willie. He adores it and, unfortunately, can blow it. He rides his bike with it slung to the handlebars. He says, "When Papa comes home he will tell me all about it."

The papers suggest that ships "Pacific bound" might be turned homeward in midstream, but I think you are probably way past midstream. Perhaps they will fly you home.

Did I tell you I wanted to make application for a new Ford? I will sell the Oldsmobile if I get the Ford, because the Oldsmobile positively eats gas and oil.

I have so enjoyed looking at the maps, and I am going to pursue them thoroughly while waiting for my telephone call to go through to Lib and Uncle Jim. I have already talked to King.

The thought that I can count the time before I see you in months, my dear, is so thrilling I can hardly stand it.

All my love, Ginny

Wednesday, August 22, 1945
2:30 P.M.

My darling,

It has been quite some time since I have written. Just how long, I am not sure, for one day has merged into the other, and I have had you constantly in my thoughts. I have been spending my nights in the hospital since Friday. I read to Father until 11:30 P.M., when his nurse came in, and then I spent all my time sleeping until 7:00 the next morning so that I can carry on. Lib arrived Friday, and King and Jane Monday. All are a great help and have kept Mother going.

Father's operation this morning was as we all feared—exploratory laparotomy with biopsy of gland. The posterior aspect of the stomach was fixed and immobile— Dr. Stone thinks an infiltrating carcinoma. It is difficult to face, but we are all doing so fairly successfully. We are awaiting the path report to decide about X-ray therapy.

In addition to being so occupied, I have really been hoping against hope that you were not so far out in the Pacific that you could not turn around and start back to California.

Any evening since Monday I have halfway expected a phone call, and the anticipation has kept me going better than any other thing.

In a way, I would like you to wait until this is all over, as it is too bad to have such pure joy mixed with sadness. However, you know that I want you and need you badly always.

Today I received a letter, which also helped. It is, however, one of the most unsatisfactory ones (as far as news is concerned) I have ever received from you. No date, of course, but postmarked August 20.

None of this is your fault, as it is mainly the peculiar circumstances of your voyage. The previous ones had no postmark.

You say you spent the night ashore. You say nothing about atomic bombs or surrender, so I am at a loss to date it at all. I suppose some tomorrow will provide the missing links.

I have sent along one letter to Ridge Trimble and another four or five to Pat Monahan. The rest are addressed to P.O. #339. I shall continue to send to #339 now and nowhere else.

Now as never before, I think I live for your return, and knowledge and remembrance of your love sustains me.

I do wish it could be arranged for me to meet you, and perhaps it can. I am sure that five or six days consumed in cross-country travel will be interminable.

Willie has gone to Myrtle's with your mother. Mother is asleep, I hope, with Seconal, and I am getting ready to go back to the hospital and spell King for a while.

All my love, Ginny

P.S. Beezie has been heckling me and grabbing the paper, thus the crumples and blotches. She does suck her thumb.

Thursday, August 23, 1945
11:00 P.M.

Dearest sweetheart,

All the days drag by, and still no call from California. I have just about given up hoping for the impossible. Tomorrow I shall give up entirely and just start waiting for mail.

The pathology on the lymph node came home today, and it is an adeno-type of carcinoma of, to me, unknown origin. So far Father has not rallied enough to appreciate anything, and I am hoping he will not. Of course, I realize this can go on for a fearfully long time, especially when a person has the constitution Father has.

His circulatory system is remarkable. He was so hoping, even up to Tuesday night, that you would get home. He has always enjoyed hearing your letters and listened with interest and pleasure to the last batch we received, which were written at sea.

Uncle Jim and Aunt Annie arrived today, and we are expecting Cousin Mamie.

Willie and B are both well and doing very nicely under the circumstances. Smitty is a tower of strength. I don't know what we will do without her. Beezie now says "baby" very distinctly, as well as "boy," but "baby" is her first two-syllable word. Poor little Willie really has had his world upset so many times, but he has so many people to love him that I hope it won't mark him for life.

All my love, Ginny

Friday, August 24, 1945
10:30 P.M.

My darling,

Father died this morning at 8:30. I was with him at the time and know that he really did not regain consciousness after the operation, which was a blessing.

We have all gotten through the day remarkably well. Ess took Willie and will keep him until after the funeral on Monday. I spent the evening with him and put him to bed, and Smitty is spending the night with him.

Beezie is really a cheerful little spot in the household and quite easy to manage. Aunt Annie is also help, as she runs on indefinitely, thus keeping everyone's mind occupied.

I now have to look forward only to the pleasant fact of your return. Everyone tells me that it should not be too-far distant.

With all my love and kisses, Ginny

Sunday, August 26, 1945
10:30 P.M.

Dearest Honey Bunny,

Another day gone past—thank gracious. It is really wonderful to have a large family and good in-laws and friends.

I have been most encouraged today, as Elsie Bosley assures me that a friend of hers was transferred from the Pacific, and Georgie Parker tells me it took Girdwood four weeks to go from Hawaii to Okinawa.

Perhaps I shall yet get my phone call from California. At any rate, I feel now that I shall see you perhaps before Willie is three years old. Beezie has been a big help to us all and a real little ray of sunshine. She is so good-natured and sweet that everyone loves to have her around.

Jim Davis, Mason's stepson, arrived today and looks fine. He is much stouter than when he went overseas and is better looking for it.

I love to see these men get back, for it always reminds me that they do return and so shall you.

May that day be near?

All my love, Ginny

August 30, 1945
10:30 P.M.

Dearest Honey Bunny,

Still no phone call and no mail. I am really on pins and needles. Every night I dream of your return. This is a great incentive to go to bed.

Mother sold the car today (as of tomorrow at 11:00 A.M.) for the ceiling price of $975. We thought this very good, and it will help her considerably with the funeral and hospital expenses.

The Fords are supposed to come through in October, so that won't leave us too long without a car. If Mother finds later that she needs a car, perhaps there will be an inexpensive model on the market.

We are putting both pieces of property (1529 Park Avenue and North Avenue) up for sale tomorrow, and I do hope that we are as fortunate with them as we were with the car.

I am also taking Cousin Mamie down to straighten out the bank accounts—put Mother's name on them in place of Father's and also revise her will. I hope that we will have things straightened out in the main by tomorrow.

Mother's insurance is also about straight, and I believe we can get an option whereby she receives about $55 per month. This will use up the principal in 20 years, but I feel that this is not an important consideration, as we would rather have her comfortable than leave us something. As always, we miss you for your advice, counsel, and love.

Lib left for Charleston today, so our household is almost back to normal. Aunt Lil is here and goes tomorrow, but will return Tuesday. Minnie Russell is coming down sometime about next weekend. Mother is doing remarkably well. Ess and Ruth were here for tonight and have offered the use of their car whenever we need it.

Well, my darling, here's hoping you call tonight.

All my love, Ginny

Chapter 18

The Maze of Manila
22 August-30 September 1945

*T*HE PERIOD DURING WHICH THESE LETTERS TO Georgeanna were written encompasses the early days of the Allied Occupation of Japan (which began 28 August) and the official Japanese surrender at a ceremony aboard USS *Missouri* in Tokyo Bay on 2 September.

---

24 August 1945
7:30 A.M.

Dearest Ginny,

We were scheduled to debark yesterday. Our time was to be early afternoon, but about 11:00 A.M. the Captain said he was going ashore in a Higgins boat and we could go along. So Bill and I went down the ladder and fell into the boat in a choppy sea, while a sailor passed down our Val-A-Paks.

Charley remained on board. Manila Bay was rough in the small boat, but pleasant. I snapped several shots en route, including some of the Jap Navy and merchant marine now resting on the bottom of Manila Bay.

The lack of enthusiasm on part of the shore officials is astonishing. They did not seem to care if we came or went. They did not seem to know anything about the 5th Aux, so they said we could go to the transit camp to wait for our baggage.

This suited us fine, for we should have a chance to nose around. So they said a truck was leaving in a few minutes, and we piled on bag and baggage.

Manila smells wonderful, like Mexico. It is reminiscent of the life and diet and lack of sanitation South of the Border. The part we saw was not much destroyed, although it is said that the walled city and the modern Manila have been pulverized.

The camp is about eight miles outside the city and quite satisfactory. We are in a squad tent with wooden floor. It was surprisingly cool last night, and I slept with a blanket for the first time since Marseilles. I also used a mosquito net for the first time.

The other officers in the tent are mostly on their way back to their units after leave or sickness or waiting for transportation to the States. For most of them we were the first Europeans they had seen, and we talked, swapping yarns from the time we arrived until 10 o'clock last night.

There is one doc who has been with an evacuation hospital and who is awaiting transportation to the States. We had a chance to compare the treatment of the wounded here and there and results. All in all, I am sure we had the best theater of operations, although it is somewhat of a privilege to see both, since I could not seem to get home.

In a few minutes we are taking off for downtown, and by night I hope to unearth someone who knows something about the 5th Aux.

Love, H

WHEN THE OPPORTUNITY was presented to go ashore with the captain, the three of us quickly decided that Bill Falor and I would go ashore and Charley Burbank would stay aboard to look after our things.

The plan was for Bill and me to try to locate the main body of the 5th Auxiliary Surgical Group, with the notion that we might somehow or other go back to join up with them, because we suspected that they might have been diverted en route to the U.S. East Coast.

After all, we were officially still under the command of the 5th Aux, and therefore not subject to the command of anyone in the Pacific. We were going to try to stay away from the official aspects of the surgeon's office until we could locate the 5th Aux, because we thought we might be able to hitch a ride from Manila to the States and not get involved in the red tape of the Pacific Command. Charley was to stay on the boat until he heard from us.

But we did not locate the 5th Aux. When we came ashore, we were sent to the casual camp—that is, the replacement depot—without any orders. Each of us was assigned a bed, and we had no problem getting something to eat. But ascertaining the whereabouts of the 5th Aux proved to be very difficult.

We inquired at the transportation office. It had lists of units being diverted to the States. With the permission of the officer in charge, we searched the lists, but the 5th Aux wasn't listed.

About three days after being ashore, we did find a sergeant who was the person who actually received the lists of diverted units. Lo and behold, we discovered that while the 5th Auxiliary Surgical Group was in the mid-Atlantic it had been diverted to Newport News, Virginia.

We attempted to notify Charley Burbank, who was still aboard *Admiral Benson*—at least we thought he was. Wrong. After forty-eight hours Charley had tired of waiting and came ashore.

Not knowing where Bill and I were, he went to the surgeon's office, where the personnel there didn't know what he was talking about. But the office staff referred Charley to the casual camp for a bunk, and we stumbled on to him there. The three of us were again reunited.

We then tried to hitch a ride to the States. We returned to the transportation section in pursuit of a berth, just as we had done in Marseilles. No go. Everything headed homeward was loaded.

We went to Clark Field in hope of flying home, but all transports were loaded with officers traveling under orders; there seemed to be no chance to squeeze in people who lacked orders.

We therefore decided to present the letter that Steve Gay had given us to General Denit. The three of us walked into the general's office, which was in the same three-story white building in Manila that was General MacArthur's headquarters. We found the surgeon's office and encountered a Colonel Robinson, who appeared to be General Denit's chief of staff.

We asked if we could see the general. Robinson asked what we wanted, and we answered that we had a personal message from one of the general's colleagues and wished to present it personally.

This didn't go over well with Robinson, who told us that the general was unavailable at that time. If we came back the next day, he might be able to arrange a visit.

It was about 4 o'clock in the afternoon. We left the office, stepped into the elevator, and a one-star medical general walked in also. I asked him if he was General Denit. He was.

I said, "Well, we have a letter to you from Colonel Elmer Gay." I pulled the letter from my pocket. Still on the elevator, Denit opened the envelope and read the contents, which introduced us and said that we would explain our mission to him.

"Oh," Denit said, "how is Steve Gay?" We were still engaged in small talk when the elevator reached the bottom. Denit said, "This is very interesting, I will be glad to talk to you tomorrow, and please come back."

We did return the next day, but we were not able to see the general. We did not get past Colonel Robinson, who told us that the general had instructed him to handle the matter.

Robinson said our situation was a very peculiar one. He didn't quite know what to do, but he would turn the matter over to the personnel section. We were to return to see him in several days, when he would tell us what to do. My letters to Georgeanna trace how the dilemma was resolved.

The sticking point was that AFWESPAC—U.S. Army Forces, Western Pacific—lacked authority to issue orders involving us, because we were not members of its command.

So AFWESPAC solicited advice from Washington. Washington responded in a telegram, received September 4, authorizing AFWESPAC to "absorb the officers into your command."

If we had not had personal contact with Colonel Ridgeway

Trimble, General Denit's medical consultant, our awkward situation would have become extremely difficult.

———————————

26 August 1945

Dearest Ginny,

I have not written for three days again, and when I do not write to you for that long a time, it must be bad news. But it is really not so bad this time, and a little time will cure it.

My thoughts are with you. How unfortunate not to know how things go at home. I am so afraid that you are having your own great tragedy that it shades my every thought and action.

I shall tell you the story as it is up to the moment.

As soon as we got here, we naturally were interested in the whereabouts of the 5th Aux. We had hoped that its members had gotten home, as I said, because we then thought there was a good chance that, under our present orders, transportation would be provided to get us back to the unit. Our first and still-unsolved difficulty is to find the 5th Aux

We have examined shipping lists galore, and nowhere can we find that the 5th Aux has ever sailed from Marseille. The difficulty is that if a unit has been sent home, it does not have the listing here as yet, although eventually, if a unit had originally been intended for here and cancelled, the information will be available.

In the meantime, we have run across several guys who would be very happy to put us to work, saying that there is a big shortage of doctors here.

So far, I think that we have successfully prevented this, although we may be working against ourselves, because if we stay, and we probably will, it would be better to be in Japan, I think, than here, and soon all hospitals that are going will be full. So that is our dilemma.

In our entire running around, I have come across many more people that I know than I did in the ETO. We knew that Joe Buckman was in the 51st General Hospital, and the second night we were here we went over there. The hospital is about 5 miles from the casual camp where we are staying. Joe is fine, looks perhaps a little thinner, but in reasonably good spirits. The first thing he said was "Here come our replacements; now we can go home."

Ed Richardson is also at the same hospital. He looks well. Also perhaps a little thinner, in good spirits, and wants to go home like everyone else, but takes things as they come and does not really expect to come for some time.

We were also over to see these fellows again yesterday.

In the office of the chief surgeon of AFPAC (the theater name) is Ben Baker, who is a medical consultant for the theater. He was cordial, but little help, and was one of those who were all for putting us to work.

From there we went over to Ridge Trimble's office to see him and see if there was any mail for Papa. Upon walking in, we came upon Hal Thomas.

He was very, very cordial, as usual, and I think is helping to get us straight. He said he would be our snooper, which I think he will be, and find out from others what we may not be able to find direct.

I was amazed at his appearance. He is an old man. What can I do to come home to you as young as I left? He has bad arthritis of his knee and walks with it stiffly. Charley and Bill guessed his age at 55 to 60. He is coming home for good within a few days—perhaps a week.

Ridge was not there, having come home for a meeting, as you know. I went through his mail, which had accumulated, and found nothing for me. I suppose you figured that since he was home, it was no use sending any mail for me to him.

In the same office was Darrell Overpeck who had been at Fort Sam Houston when Georgeanna and I were there. He looks well, but also older. He has gained some weight.

His job at the moment is orthopedic consultant for AFWESPAC, which is the communications zone of the Pacific War. He has the job that George Eaton gave up when he went home.

He has had a good service and is now anxious to get back to a hospital, because since the war has ended there is no call for a consultant, and he spends his time with his feet on the desk.

He also would like to go to Japan, and if it works out that the three of us are going also, to get temporary duty pending the working out of the 5rh Aux, he may be able to arrange it that we get fairly good jobs.

I have not yet looked up Pat Monahan [a native Filipino who was a good friend and resident in obstetrics at Johns Hopkins], but Eddie said that he is here in private practice. Painless delivery for 200 pesos.

Bill also ran across two good friends of his, and Charley found a fellow who was resident at Mass General a few years ahead of him.

About the mail: I see no hope of getting any of the letters addressed to the 5th Aux. I think that the best thing is to send mine to Eddie Richardson, marked for me, 51st General Hospital, APO. 565, San Francisco. I will keep in touch with him if I should leave this vicinity.

All my love, Howard

Monday 27 August 1945

Dearest Ginny,

Still no news as to our status.

Here an interruption of 24 hours. At the moment, a ride to town turned up, and we took off.

We went to AFWESPAC, which has us in tow, and talked to Denit (Brigadier General Guy Denit, chief medical officer to AFWESPAC). Ridge Trimble had just got in from the United States, but had not yet come into the office.

We got a vehicle from Peck and took off to town to tend to odds and ends. We finally found our luggage.

The Benson (our transport from Marseilles to Manila) had been lying in Manila Bay for a week, waiting to get up to the dock. We loaded our baggage onto a truck and brought it out here.

Then I thought I had better look up Pat Monahan, as I had a quiet little hope that you might have written to him. What joy to find a letter from you, dated August 14, as well as the series of letters enclosed in your original letter to him. What a relief to know how things go at home!

Last night Eddie Richardson, Bill, Charley, Joe Buckman, and I went over to Peck's for supper [Darrell Overpeck]. Ridge was there and, I think, looks quite well. He is a little stooped, as is everyone here, from the constant necessity to look away from the sun. He has also lost much of his hair and will be bald as an eagle before many years.

He has a considerable accumulation of points and did not need to return here this time, or last, for that matter. He said he was unfortunate enough to have a conscience, but I think he is unfortunate not to have a woman to go home to.

There was quite a nice party, enlivened by a drawing Peck had just received from Mary. In his absence, she had gone to art school and has, I would say, considerable talent. The drawing is of a beautiful nude in an exotic position with outstretched arms. She said she knew what he was thinking anyway. He has it over his bed.

There was a big crowd around, and we did not have much chance to talk to Ridge about jobs, but we are going into the office in a day or two to find out if he has any ideas. In the meantime, we have ideas of seeing a little of the countryside, Baguio and Corrigedor and the like.

Our coming home does not seem likely in the near future. We will have to think in terms of the winter, and hope. Things will be more definite, I think, come V-J Day, regardless of what is happening to the 5th Aux.

Love, H

P.S. I will repeat what I said in yesterday's letter. Do not write to me by way of the 5th Aux. Write to Eddie Richardson (Capt.), 51st General Hospital, APO 565 San Francisco, Calif.

Wednesday 29 August 1945

Dearest Ginny,

Still no vital news. We will probably see Ridge again today.

Many people have asked us how we thought the two theaters compared.

The fighting was entirely different. The administration is certainly more complicated. They have here a GHQ, which is commanded by MacArthur. This corresponds to SHAEF [Supreme Headquarters, Allied Expeditionary Forces] and controlled the Anzacs [Australians, New Zealanders], Dutch, British, and so forth.

Then there is AFPAC, which is U.S. Army Forces, Pacific and corresponds to the European Theater of Operations. Then there are the armies under this, the same as in Europe.

It is the service section that is different. In Europe it was called COM Z [Communications Zone]. Here it is called AFWESPAC. COM Z. had several base sections. AFWESPAC has several base sections, but has groups of base-section headquarters in between, so that there are additional major headquarters.

Here in Manila this complexity of organization is particularly bad, as there is a representative of each of the five levels, and to start at the bottom and buck anything through is about an impossible job. The local yokels think the trouble derives from too many generals out here with no particular assignment.

The result is particularly disturbing. No one is willing to accept responsibility without referring it to higher headquarters. The explanation of this is that in the Australian days of the Pacific War the whole thing consisted of MacArthur and a few staff officers who had so few supplies that a requisition had to be approved by a general officer before it was honored. The headquarters has not grown with the theater.

MacArthur is a brilliant tactical commander, but has not developed a genuine staff. I suppose it is natural to put less-efficient officers in service jobs. I think the organization in Paris was better. At least, in our dealings, we seemed to be able to get more direct action.

We noticed the difference in the number of POWs. There are some Japs hereabout who are working as stevedores, but nothing compared to the thousands of Krauts who were doing everything, skilled and unskilled.

Incidentally, the Japs appear to be strong and healthy, grown so on good food. They say they were thin and emaciated, just as the pictures show it.

Here the army has employed many Filipinos as drivers, workmen, and the like. This is all to the good, as it will get the GIs home.

I hope you are taking care of yourself. I know what load you are carrying. Wish that I could help some.

Love, H

Saturday 30 August 1945
3:00 P.M.

Dearest Ginny,

No orders yet. We sit and "rest" and wait. I shall not believe that we will get out of here until we leave. For every day we stay, we hear more and more of the inefficiency of the medical setup here. It is too bad.

There has been a long and tiresome struggle between the consultants and Regular Army officers who figure a doc is a doc. The surgeon is an elderly man who is not very forceful, but who seems fond of Ridge, who has some influence with him.

Eddie Richardson and others have said that Ridge is responsible for straightening out the mess to the extent that he has been able. There has never been a consistent policy of medical support for the various operations, and only in the Philippine campaign were auxiliary surgical teams used at all extensively. The consultants had wanted to use this idea before, to effectively use their surgical talent, but only now have they been able to persuade the general.

They complain of never having received adequate replacements. No "B" surgeons had been sent in 2½ years. We were the first to arrive. They have been short on anesthetists; however, part of this is their own fault. They have established no school of anesthesia, such as the ETO had in England.

The three of us, I think, irritated several people in the Regular Army section when we breezed in and told them to whom we would report, and so on and so on, after they started to send us here and there.

I did not like their overbearing attitude, and it got my back up. I really believe it is illegal to keep us here if the 5th Aux has gone home. Anyway, Darrell told us that they were all for giving us dispensary jobs until Ridge stepped in. This would only have proved that they have not properly used the men they had.

A friend of Bill's from Cleveland had us over to dinner. He is writing a medical history of the war out here. He confirmed our impression of inefficiency at the top.

General Martin (former 5th Army surgeon) has just come over. Ridge says that talking to him is like having a fresh breeze spring up after talking to the local yokels. It is too bad he is not theater surgeon. Incidentally, General Martin is the one who said that after V-J Day 85 points gets you home, replacement or not. I hope so.

Love, H

P.S. I will repeat, no mail to the 5th Aux. Send in care of Eddie Richardson, 51st General Hospital.

Friday 31 August 1945

Dearest Ginny,

I finally do have some news, both bad and good, mostly good; all things considered. The bad part is that we have not been able to manipulate it so that we return to the States now to join the 5th, if it is already there. We will sweat it out here until we gain the necessary points.

Ridge arranged jobs for us if it ever becomes legal for the U.S. Army, Western Pacific to write orders on us, and he did exceedingly well by us. I am going to the 54th General Hospital as chief of surgery. This hospital is in bivouac here and scheduled to go to Japan within a month. I certainly hope this is so. The present chief of surgery is about to go home on rotation.

I do believe this is as good a job as is available here now that the casualties have ceased. I know nothing about a general hospital, and today I'm going to move over to the 51st for a little firsthand instruction.

The 54th is a 2,000-bed hospital, and the chief is supposed to be a chicken colonel. Of course, I shall never get this, and I hope I am not here long enough to get to be Lt. Col.

Bill and Charley have really more-important jobs, even if they will get no opportunity to operate. Charley is to be the surgical consultant of the 10th Army and Bill the consultant for the 8th Army. I believe they are well-pleased, and they also get promoted if they stay here long enough.

We have not actually received the orders yet, so continue to send my mail in care of Eddie Richardson, 51st General Hospital, APO 565, San Francisco. Do not write to the 5th Aux.

I am restless again for mail and a picture of you and the children. Perhaps some will catch up to me before long.

Love, H

　　　　　　　　　　　　　　　　　　　　　　　　4 September 1945

Dearest Ginny,

Today we were told that the casual camp where we are staying is to move to another area, and so the three of us moved into the 51st General Hospital, where we now are. There is a nice, open, wooden cottage where Joe Buckman, Eddie Richardson, and others are living, and they are good enough to put up with us. It is actually much more convenient, for we have bus service downtown and the like.

Yesterday we went again into headquarters. Ridge Trimble and Darrell Overpeck were up to Baguio to see the Yamamotos surrender, I suppose, but we talked at length with Charley Mayo and others. They had received an answer to the cablegram to the War Department regarding the 5th Aux and the three officers now in this area.

The War Department said the 5th Aux was not coming (which we knew), but did not say where it was. We still do not know. Furthermore, it said that the theater was to absorb the three officers. This, I suppose, makes it legal for them to issue orders. Until then, I was positive it was not.

They once again confirmed our destinations. Papa, as chief surgeon to the 54th General Hospital; Charley, consultant to the 10th Army; Bill, the same for the 8th.

My love and kisses and everything, H

Wednesday 5 September 1945
8:00 P.M.

Dearest Ginny,

We got to Corregidor today, and for a change, the sun was out most of the day. This means that there were but two short showers while on the island, and one as we were walking home the half mile from the bus stop. The last shower was a tropical one, and this means the heavens open. By the time we got here we were soaked to the skin, except for a little patch of chest kept dry by our raincoats.

It was a very nice trip. Corregidor is about 25 miles from Manila and takes two hours in the boat each way. We went in a Q boat, which is like a cabin cruiser of about 90 feet. Corregidor is about three miles long and a mile wide. On top is a plateau, and here are (were) the barracks, officers quarters, and parade ground. The skeletons of these buildings still stand.

Along the sides of the cliff, a few gun emplacements of the disappearing type, open on top with a gun that is depressed except when firing. They are as out-of-date as yesterday's news—made obsolete by the plane. The ack-ack emplacements are made of earth and sandbags.

The tunnel, which is at one end of the island, is a shambles. This end of the island is honeycombed with shafts from the main tunnel, but the number of gun emplacements is relatively few. Actually, the island was no good, except to shoot at ships at sea, and no good for that since bombers blasted the place. Anyway, it was interesting to see.

There are said to be many Japs still lying around, but they have been removed from the main area where we were. We did see several skeletons and bodies picked clean by the animals. Charley took a radius and ulna. I thought about bringing a vertebra, but didn't.

The best thing about the trip was that it made me physically tired. I am badly in need of exercise. The heat makes it most difficult to take, and I feel so much better for the trip.

Love, H

Thursday 6 September 1945
8:00 A.M.

Dearest Ginny,

I feel so good this morning, I can hardly stand it.

Since coming into the heat before Panama, everyone, especially me, has been lying around in a vegetablelike manner. One's ambition is as nothing, and even plans for the future seem difficult to think about. The postponement of returning home, the enervating climate, and the knowledge of your most difficult situation at home gives me a feeling of frustration never before experienced.

This morning things seemed better. No matter how hard it was, scrambling over the rocks at Corregidor made me sweat as in a Turkish bath and gave us needed exercise whether we wanted it or not.

Last night I was pleasantly tired, and this morning the weather is cool. It sounds like an easy-enough remedy, and one that can be applied as necessary, and I intend to do so, although made exercise is not as interesting as that incidental to other things.

All this has set me thinking, and I looked at a map of the U.S. I cannot help but think that my coming home will be some months yet—next spring, perhaps. By then things at home will probably be straightened out so that you could come to meet me. I assume we will come in on the West Coast, probably Frisco.

What a chance to visit some of those places we did not get to see on our honeymoon. It will probably be off-season for most places, but it might be next summer. I hope not. I should like to go somewhere to participate in some outdoor sports, with modern conveniences.

Now, your part is to keep your eyes open for possibilities and ideas to fit the season. What about Sun Valley, Idaho? What is the season there? We might as well break our necks skiing as anything else.

All this is still months in the future, but thinking about it is exciting, and my heart beats faster.

This morning we are going into headquarters to once again see what is what. We left the paper about our surgical experience in Europe there for them to go over, and probably we can get that off for publication soon.

Love as always, H

Monday 10 September 1945

Dearest Ginny,

Today has been one of those days. This morning we thought it was about time to go into AFWESPAC to get our paper and to see if anything was stirring about our orders. The paper was ready, and we hope to get it off to the U.S. Army Surgeon General for publication.

We called up the personnel officer of GHW who is the one who is actually writing our orders. He said that they had been approved by their office and were being bucked around to the other places that they had to go before the orders were actually cut. He said if we did not hear anything in 10 days to let him know.

Last night we had a sample of the medicine being practiced here, and it made me shudder. Joe called and asked if Charley or I would come over, that they had a depressed fracture of the skull and he wanted someone to scrub with him.

We felt that it was the blind leading the blind, but Charley did scrub. Joe was to fix the skull wound, which did not look bad, and another of the officers was to put on a hip spica for a fractured femur.

They started on the patient before he was ready, with his blood pressure being 90/70, and he had received no treatment for his shock. The anesthetist was a fright. She was a nurse who was supposed to be as good as their regular anesthetist. She could not do a vena puncture, and Joe started the Pentathol for her.

They gave the patient a transfusion through the Pentathol tube, and this got balled up and the needle came out. She asked me to put it in, which I did no less than four times, because she would give him just enough Pentathol to keep him quiet, and then he would wiggle his arm, and out would come the needle. In the meantime, Joe and Charley were taking swipes at the skull as it came by.

Fortunately, the patient did not seem to be harmed by the procedure, in spite of the fact that his pressure was 75 when the nightmare was over. The worst of it was that they seemed to think things went along all right.

Joe, Bill, Charley, and I are about to play bridge. It is a poor substitute for something real to do, but does pass the time.

Love to all, H

11 September 1945

Dearest Ginny,

From talking to several people out here, one gets the impression that this was a five-and-dime war, compared to that in Europe. I believe that the impression we had of the Japs before the war was more nearly correct than we later believed.

They were a stupid enemy. They never developed any area they had conquered. For example, here in the Philippines they maintained an army of some 300,000. No defenses were provided, but more important, no large stockpiles of materials were on hand. The dock facilities and roads were not maintained.

This hospital, which is the station hospital of Fort McKinley, was in a frightful condition. The screens had been allowed to get in disrepair. It was fearfully dirty. The water supply was inadequate. We have moved in and, as everywhere, provided screens, water, and good roads, and developed a place for habitation and expansion.

The Japs were squatters. They had little or no malaria control, although from records here available, malaria was a tremendous problem for them.

The same was true in New Guinea. Those who occupied areas taken by the Japs say that the living conditions were very primitive, in spite of the fact that there was ample time to develop the place. No road system was available to them. The airstrips were adequate, but not suitably developed from our standpoint.

When we went into Lea and Salamauea we made, according to Joe, a road system that was a marvel of engineering, realizing full well that it would be abandoned in due time. The airfields were enlarged and facilities expanded.

Not the least of the things constructed at Hollandia was a home with road for General MacArthur, where he brought his wife and family. The engineers who worked on this project were so infuriated at this construction that, after it was over, they turned in their War Bonds en masse, or so the story goes.

From a military point of view, the Japs did unpredictable things. There was an infantry-battalion commander at the casual camp when we first came, a Col. Kuba. He told of some of his experiences.

He remembered in Luzon one night they had a road covered and were amazed to see coming down the road a company of Japs with vehicle lights on full, talking, shouting, and shooting here and there at what must to them have appeared to be American positions.

From the lights on their vehicles, it was an easy task for Kuba's men to pick off the Japs at leisure who, in spite of losses, kept coming on until they had all been killed.

The next morning Kuba's battalion counted over a hundred dead Japs. They never could figure out what it was all about.

On another occasion, they were dug in and the Japs tried to take one of their machine-gun positions. Over one hundred dead Japs were counted.

Americans or Germans would never pile a hundred men into any machine-gun. We have artillery and mortars to take care of things like that.

You will remember that the 1st Cavalry Division took Los Negros. They went ashore in small numbers for an armed reconnaissance and met with such unexpected success that the operation was immediately enlarged and the island taken then and there.

We talked to one who had been there, an engineer. He said that the Japs had many coastal defense batteries of 5-inch guns and thousands of rounds of ammunition, but for some reason the Japs did not fire a shot with these 5-inch guns. Why? No one seemed to know.

Here in the Philippines we defeated about 30 Jap divisions with half that number. If the Germans had been here in such strength, I am sure it would not have been possible to defeat them.

It will be interesting to read in future years if the historians agree with these impressions.

This afternoon we are going into town to have lunch with a friend of Bill's. He is evacuation officer and should have some interesting things to say.

Love and kisses as always, H

P.S. I weighed this A.M. and am now down to 168, which I think is optimum weight. I am going to come home at this level. While in AFWESPAC yesterday, we found that Ridge had just left for Australia to marry an Australian doctor. This explains why he came back this time. He will probably make arrangements for her to go to the States and then return himself.

Friday 14 September 1945

Dearest Ginny,

Today we called the 5th Casual Camp where we originally stayed and through whom we are to get our orders, as previously arranged with everyone concerned.

They said that they had been thinking it over and they really were not authorized to issue orders on us, as we had never really been assigned to them, and they were going to send the orders back to GHQ when they did come.

What a mess! We are going down again tomorrow and are going straight to General Denit, if I can't get any satisfaction elsewhere. We have to get into some organization to get home.

We have some men here from a station hospital formerly in Italy. They know General Martin, former 5th Army surgeon now AFWESTPAC surgeon. They saw him today on a more-or-less social call, and he told them how confused everything was here.

I have repeatedly mentioned this, but even so, I cannot possibly convey the buck-passing refusal to take responsibility and poor organization that we have found in the medical department here. Furthermore, I am sure the professional care of the patients has suffered.

The enclosed flowers will probably be brown and malodorous upon arrival, but fresh they have a beautiful odor similar to gardenias. I hope they retain some of it.

It is the Philippines national flower. They told me its name, but it is Spanish, and I have forgotten it. I hope the fragrance is still there upon arrival.

These days of idleness when you are so busy gives me a chance once again to think of our reunion and future. These thoughts give me strength and courage to endure this interminable wait.

Love, H

Sunday 16 September 1945

Dearest Ginny,

It now appears that I am finally straightened out. As mentioned in my letter of the 14th, Charley and I went downtown yesterday to get things straight or else.

We traced the order from GHQ to the WESPAC surgeon to the WESPAC G-1. At that office they said they knew nothing about it, but after our persisting they started looking through various files and came across the communication from the AFWESTPAC surgeon, which had sent it on to the replacement command. The latter had sent it back, saying that it had no record of these officers, and G-1 filed it away and forgot about it.

Anyway, it has started on its journey again, and we should have something by Tuesday. We also found out that the 54th will probably not get off until the first, so that I really have plenty of time, although I should like to get down there to get my baggage marked, etc. etc.

I also found out that the 54th is assigned to the 8th Army, which has the Tokyo area and the north. Since it is a 2,000-bed hospital, it seems to me quite possible that it will be sent to Tokyo.

In the meantime, I believe it would be all right to begin sending my mail to the 54th Gen. Hospital, APO 73, San Francisco, Calif.

I was in to Pat's again yesterday, and nothing. I am certainly mystified as to why I have not had any mail for over a week now. Bill got a letter from Ann here at the 51st yesterday, so I suppose mine should not be far behind.

Today Joe has a command car for this afternoon, and we are going to take a ride to Wawa Dam—I suppose that is the way to spell it. There is supposed to be a very nice ridge overlooking Manila and Laguna de Bay. I am frightfully tired of going about without Mama.

Charley, Bill, and I have gotten about more since we have been here than most of the men in this hospital who have been here several months now.

They can't figure it out. It is simply because we are willing to get out and stick up our thumb. They seem to figure that officers should not do this, particularly majors.

We ride in anything and, being officers, I believe, get rides much more easily than normal. The first vehicle that has room usually stops, and we have ridden in everything except the garbage truck. It is by doing things like this that we keep ourselves occupied.

Love and kisses to our family, H

Tuesday 18 September 1945
7:00 P.M.

Dearest Ginny,

Yesterday Bill got a letter from Ann in which she said she had called you, and you had told her of the arrival in the States of the 5th Auxiliary Surgical Group and also the sad news of your father's death. I waited until today to write, because I thought there might be a letter with some details, but there has not yet been time enough to get a letter through the 54th.

It seems as if our guiding star did for this one time desert us. I am particularly sorry that at this time I could not have been there to in some measure comfort and share with you the grief and problems created by this saddest of events so far in your life.

For me, even this darkest event has a silver lining. For being separated, my mind finds peace and reassurance in contemplating that it is you, whom I so love and admire, who will be able to handily cope with every situation.

Even though we know that it is foreordained in the course of human events to outlive our parents, the loss is nonetheless acute. I hope you have been able to some degree to mitigate the loss for your mother, who must feel it more than others. It is perhaps good that the children are around now, for they must be distracting, to say the least. I hope that they behave themselves.

How I await news to tell me how things have worked out and about any plans for the future. I am afraid now that I shall be leaving Manila before any letter gets here. This may mean another month's delay in mail, for the 54th expects to go to Japan around the 1st. In the meantime, I continue to wait here for my orders, which are expected daily.

I am glad that the 5th got home. It was a lucky organization, in that it was the last group over and must have been the first home. It is one of those unfortunate quirks of fate that I got this trip.

It is quite possible to think of advantages to coming here, but they are small compensation for being absent from you for so much as a day. It may turn out to work out better as far as getting out of the Army is concerned and the like. We must wait and see.

I am going to check with Pat and Ridge's office once more before going to the 54th. I hope I will find something. In the meantime, my thoughts are especially with you.

My love and kisses go without saying, H

Wednesday 19 September 1945

Dearest Ginny,

I feel much better today. The biggest reason is that your letters of September 6 and 7 came today.

As you say, in view of the findings at operation, it is indeed a blessing that your father did not survive longer. How my heart has ached not to be able to be there, for I really felt that you must have been going through a most terrible experience and yet, for it all, an experience, which by your presence, I am sure gave comfort to your father.

You say you are wondering if I should be able to settle down and really work when I come home. I don't think socializing will take up any more time than before. I am just not a gadabout, even as much as I think I should be.

I knew Jim Flynn and John Scanlon were in Manila, and it has taken almost a superhuman effort to go over to see them. Yesterday and today Bill and I did go, and I thoroughly enjoyed it.

The sightseeing is another matter. I believe I am an incurable sightseer and traveler, but I think you are too (I don't think it, I know it), so that is no problem. We must try to channel our trips so that they do not interfere too much with our more-serious purpose and pleasure in life. I speak of our work as pleasure, for such I anticipate it to be.

I really cannot imagine any happiness greater than having a medical problem to solve together.

I only hope that we can somehow or other fix the necessities of life so that our time is our own. I, too, have found it difficult to plan for us together while alone, so even planning our future together will be our joy. I do hope that it will work out that you can come to the West Coast so that we can have a few days together— look up Sun Valley and other places.

I hope the mail service continues, for your letters give me pleasure and joy second only to seeing you.

Love, H

20 September 1945

Dearest Ginny,

Well, we have moved again. After much phoning yesterday and this morning, it is apparent that my and Bill's orders are about to be written by the replacement command, and today, therefore, we moved out to the 5th Replacement Depot. It is a tent city, but with all the necessary conveniences. We are eating out of mess gear for the first time since Marseilles.

The tent has no flooring, but it is on a gentle slope, well-ditched, and I believe will be dry. My release, as they call it, has already reached here, and the actual orders are to be cut tomorrow, and I should be on my way the day after.

We are about 25 miles from the 51st Gen, but the hitchhiking is good, and we are going over tomorrow to see about the mail and get some laundry.

I think the news about returning home is still bright. There is a theater order out that all men going home on the 100-point order of about 3 weeks ago must be on their way by 17 October. This means that about 6 weeks will have elapsed between the receipt of the order here and its accomplishment. If the same speed is required on the 80-point-for-doctors orders, I may be on my way before we think. For no reason at all, I think I will start home in December.

As a matter of fact, I have decided to stop feeling sorry for myself for having missed the 5th Aux's good luck. After all, that was a most unique fate enjoyed by relatively few people, so there is no reason at all to feel that we have had bad luck, which we actually have not. We just did not have phenomenally good luck.

I read Hamlet the other day and came across a line that applies to our situation. It was, "Nothing is bad except thinking it so." I am swearing off thinking this is bad and facing forward to enjoy what comes my way in sightseeing and travel.

As mentioned yesterday, we went over to see Jim Flynn, You remember he had lunch with us at Atlantic City when he was there to take his boards.

He had been in Italy for 27 months with the Albany unit, but had only 79 points. He was, therefore, transferred to a field hospital and arrived from Leghorn about three weeks ago.

He is plenty tired of it all and, of course, is anxious to get home. He looks well and asked to be remembered to you. I found out he was here through a fellow who came over on the same boat with him and who was sent to the 51st on D.S. [Detached Service].

We also saw John Scanlon, who was a member of the 5th at Dodd Field and who was transferred about the time of Joe Buckman. He has been on the medical service of the 60th General, which is acting as a holding hospital for patients awaiting transportation to the States. He does not seem to mind the absence of work and sort of vegetates and enjoys the poor liquor available in the Philippines.

I can't tell you how cheering it was to have your letters yesterday. To hear from you is enough. I do not hope like you that your recent letters get lost. I shall love them because they are you. How about the letter to Ridge that came back? Why not send that on. I would like to have it.

With love and kisses, H

Saturday 22 September 1945

Dearest Ginny,

Today we got orders, Bill and I, and are now awaiting transportation. I might go tomorrow, as I have but 40 miles to Batangas (southern Luzon).

Bill goes to Okinawa and might have to wait a few days for transportation.

Charley's orders will be through tomorrow. He is getting a real break. I know the 54th is scheduled to go about the 1st. With no knowledge at all, I am guessing that it will be in the Tokyo area, because it is the only 2,000-bed hospital going through Japan.

Yesterday Bill and I started out to go to town to see a friend of his, and we did not get back until today. We stopped in the 60th for supper, and John Scanlon gave us a jeep to go to the 51st. But a bridge had been washed out, and we would have had to go 25 miles more, so we went back to the 60th all night.

It rained, as you have never seen it, all day. The hospital was an inch or two underwater, and our trousers were soaked to our knees, where the raincoat stops. After a while here you do not mind wet feet. I think it is because it is warm.

There is no doubt that clothes, equipment, and the like go to pieces here much more rapidly than in Europe. Mold appears on all leather within 24 hours, and your clothes are damp and clammy every morning.

You are much more comfortable in a light shower than any other weather, because it is cool and damp. Whenever the sun is out, it is hot and you are just as wet, but with sweat.

I shall be glad to get out of it, and I am glad to have been here to see what it is really like.

I see no harm in planning for our V-J Day (J for Jones). Can you get away from home? It may not be possible to start my leave from California unless I pay our way across the country.

How is travel now? And would you like California for a trip together? Is it practical from a travel-and-reservation angle to plan such a trip, because if you wanted to we will just pay the fare across the country, because heavens knows when we might get a chance to do it again.

How are our finances doing? Did we make any money last year? And will we make any this?

I am sure I must educate you with some plain and fancy spelling in these letters. You no less entertain me and I often chuckle and giggle as I catch a slip in yours, as today—"estatiac."

For these and many other reasons, I love your letters, which bring me some of you. They will have to do for a few months.

Love, H

Sunday 23 September 1945
1:00 P.M.

Dearest Ginny,

You ask in a recent letter if it were really possible that I should want to work. I suppose the actuality of it is the final answer, but I just want to work at something with my head.

Not until the war ended in Europe did I really discover the difficulties of doing nothing. To live, it is certainly necessary to have a task. The writing of the paper on the boat was onerous at times, but in the end, writing it made the journey a pleasure.

When I join the 54th, I must try to set my mind on some project within my possibilities, so that I shall not arrive home with unremovable rust on my thought tracks.

This morning I could not help but feel that I was physically and mentally flabby. The weather is absolutely prohibitive for unnecessary exercise. Today, for a change, it was bright and sunny, with beautiful, thick, drifting, tropical clouds about the mountaintops. But it was, therefore, hot as the hinges of hell, especially in the tent. It is much more comfortable when it rains, as it has been doing for 30 minutes, and I am comfortable lying on my cot with only shorts on, and now and again a spray when the wind blows.

In spite of the hot weather, or because of it, Bill and I got two gloves and a ball and, for about ten minutes, played catch. We sweat like horses, and I was saddened to think about how I was required to puff and blow to accomplish this mild exercise.

When we got back to the tent, our pulses were 110. We were so hot that when I got under the shower I could not be sure that the warm water running down my leg had come from the shower or had been heated by my body or had come from somewhere else.

You cannot believe how hard it is raining now. Charley is just lying back on his cot, sort of exhausted, saying over and over again, "My, this is just delightful, just put your foot out in it." Then he flicked some rain on Bill, who goes wild, of course.

A chaplain moved into our tent, which is a squad tent. He has been overseas for about five months, spending the time in a replacement depot. He was sent here because the records in the office showed that there was an AAA battalion here that had no chaplain.

The office did not know that the AAA boys were running a section of the depot as housekeeping troops. There are no less than 26 chaplains (19 Catholic) assigned to this. Our chaplain says two could do the work. The Chaplain Corps is as snarled as any other corps, I suppose.

It might be best for you to meet me somewhere in the East, but I can't think of a good place. It will almost surely be wintertime. It is fun to plan, and I really do not think it is too far ahead.

Love and kisses, H

P.S. I have sent home another package containing nothing but postwar camping equipment. I hope there is some place to store it.

Monday 24 September
6:00 P.M.

Dearest Ginny,

It has been another sunny day, and that means that we lie on our cots, sans clothes, and gradually reduce to a greaseball. The sun has now just about gone down, and as in Texas, it makes a tremendous difference. Last night I had to get the blanket over me.

We had a letter from Colonel Gay yesterday. He has made a real effort to *get us back, but I am sure it is to no avail, as the War Department has already made a ruling on this point. We won't be here so long, I feel sure.*

He also sent me the news that he had recommended me for a Bronze Star medal. This will take a couple of months to come through, if it does, but will add five points to my score. The medal is for that intangible thing, "meritorious service."

Charley went over to the 51st yesterday and came back with a rumor from Joe that the 54th is embarking today. I brought this to the attention of the proper people today, and they are sending me down there at 8:00 tomorrow. Bill is flying to Okinawa at 6:00 A.M. tomorrow, and so we are finally breaking up. It will be a sad moment for us all, as the friendship has been a comfort to us all, and we will feel alone.

Love, H

> *Tuesday 25 September 1945*
> *10:00 P.M.*

Dearest Ginny,

Today we broke up. Bill caught a plane to Okinawa at 6:00 this morning. We all got up at 3:45 A.M. and went in on the truck to Nielson Field to see him off. There was the usual snafu, and when he got there his name was not on the manifest. After going out on the line and squaring away with the pilot, it was fixed. We left before he took off in a C-46 loaded with cargo for Tokyo.

When we got back to the depot, I checked on the transportation supposed to be arranged for me and found that they had not been able to get through to the 54th, and no one seemed to be doing anything about it, demonstrating once again that in the Army it is necessary to follow up every move.

Searching for some idea, I noticed some ambulances standing in front of the dispensary, and thought I would have a fling at asking the dispensary doc if he would send an ambulance on the 50-mile journey. He said that, as it happened, one of his officers was today going to the 54th, and so it was quickly arranged that I would go with him—Captain Seeley of Burlington, Vermont, who is now transferred to the 54th.

We bumped over the 50 miles to Batangas, stopping en route at the 343rd Infantry Headquarters for lunch.

The 54th is in bivouac in a field near Batangas. They are packed up, waiting to go, but have no good idea of when. Three officers left today. They think they are assigned to the Tokyo-Yokohama area. Most of the officers are still out on temporary duty, so most of the tents are empty.

Captain Seeley and I have been given a separate pyramidal tent near the shower and latrine—very convenient. The tent has an elongated center pole, and the sides are straightened out to let the air circulate. I am afraid it will give similar freedom to the rain.

We have a dirt floor, but can have the Filipinos build us bamboo flooring. There is a shower nearby. I have threatened to throw away my helmet ever since the war has been over, but decided to bring it along once more and am glad I did, as it is the only basin available.

There will be nothing to do here but await our departure. I cannot think of this without realizing how unfair it is for you to have such tasks while I do bunk fatigue.

For the first time since leaving you, I am without friends. It was fortunate I ran into Seeley before arriving here, as we are company for each other. However, I have never been too bored alone and expect to amuse myself by reading, perhaps writing a letter, and planning for our V-Day.

With love and kisses, H

Wednesday 26 September 1945
6:00 P.M.

Dearest Ginny,

We are nicely settled and have, I think, the most comfortable quarters anywhere in the tents, because there are only two of us and because Seeley brought with him a table, two chairs, and a chest of drawers.

I am using my bedroll (air mattress) for the first time since Marseilles and have used my extension to put a light over the bed. Unfortunately, there is no real sign that we are to move in the next few days. I have not found any scintillating personalities among the officers here. Most are still on temporary duty, as previously mentioned. Those still here are interested in the same thing that all of us are—going home.

They seem to expect that when the 80-point order for medical officers comes through, all those eligible will immediately start home. I don't think it will be as *simple as that. I believe we would come home faster by going to Japan first, as there are fewer people there and red tape cannot be any greater than in the Philippines.*

Today the hospital got in 125 new enlisted men just in from the States. Some have three points. Their skin is fair and appears to be fresh and young.

While we were at the 5th Depot there were many casual officers just in from the States. It was possible to spot them a mile off. They did not seem to be relaxed. Like the bride, they have new clothes and appear lost.

Somehow I noticed one day that they seemed to sit on the latrine in a different way, not yet used to the absence of smooth seats and with an expression as if they were afraid of getting a splinter in the rear end.

The mess here leaves something to be desired. We are using mess gear, and the food is just not nicely prepared and presented. It is not at all my idea of what a general-hospital mess should be. I am sure the mess officer is a numbskull MAC who was probably a salesman before the war.

We have movies three times a week: Tuesday, Thursday, and Sunday. Last night we saw A Bell for Adano. *I enjoyed it very much, and it is a pretty good demonstration of how the Army gets snarled up from lack of information.*

Tonight the Manila Symphony is playing in Batangas, and Seeley and I are going. It is an open-air job, and we will almost surely be rained on, as last night it did not rain a drop during the movies.

The sun has been out all day, and we have stayed under cover with our clothes off. I am reading The Education of Henry Adams. *Now a rainsquall and a cooling off.*

Don't forget to let me know where you want to meet me, because that information has to be given here. An order written here takes you to a place in the States. You are in a much-better position to know about travel, resorts, and local conditions.

With love and kisses and everything, H

Friday 28 September 1945
7:00 P.M.

Dearest Ginny,

We have a little goop that is a "tent boy." He makes our bed, cleans, and tidies up, and he is constructing us a washstand of bamboo and is going to make us flooring. He shines shoes and does other work.

We each give him 3 pesos per week. He is a small child—I don't think he is over three feet high. He could pass for about 8 years old, but claims to be 15. The Philps are small people. Pat Monahan is a rather large one.

I find myself being entertained as I go along the roads comparing the numerous Philps children of all sizes to what I think Willie and B are like. This one is too big. This one, too small. This one, too skinny. I half expect our children to have brown skins when I see them.

Somehow I picture Willie as being almost grown up. I suppose I feel as if I have been away for a long time. I picture him larger than he actually is.

In spite of the heat, I joined in a softball game this afternoon and feel very much better for it. I was surprised that I was on my feet at the end.

Papa had a chance to be a hero, two out, three runs behind, and three on base, two strikes. A homer would have won the game. I hit a hard grounder and, fortunately, the guy missed it. Only one run scored, and we finally lost.

Love to all, H

Saturday 29 September 1945
6:00 P.M.

Dearest Ginny,

It is apparent tonight that it is a good thing that I prefer to go home by way of Japan, for we now have a ship in Batangas harbor, and at the moment, the equipment is being loaded. The present schedule calls for personnel to go aboard on Tuesday, and we should be in Tokyo by the 15th of October. The status of the 80-point men is still somewhat in doubt, and unless further instructions are received by the hospital, I am on my way.

Love to all, H

Manila, Philippines, September 1945. Debarking from *Admiral Benson*. The two on the left are Bill Falor and Captain Gardner.

Manila, September 1945. Left to right: Bill Falor, Joe Buckman, and Eddie Richardson.

Chapter 19

Letters from Home
1-30 September 1945

*T*HE BIGGEST INTERNATIONAL EVENT OF 2 September 1945 was the official surrender of Japan to the Allies. General of the Army Douglas MacArthur signed the formal surrender document for the Allied Powers after Foreign Minister Mamoru Shigemisu signed for Japan.

Fleet Admiral Chester W. Nimitz signed for the United States, and other high-ranking officials, in turn, signed for their governments—China, the United Kingdom, the Soviet Union, Australia, Canada, France, Netherlands, and New Zealand.

Later that same day Georgeanna celebrated in a letter to me news of the arrival of the 5th Auxiliary Surgical Group in the United States.

Sunday, September 2, 1945
4:00 P.M.

Dearest,

The big news of the day is that the 5th Aux arrives at Newport News tomorrow. I'm certainly disappointed that you won't be with them. As I frequently said before, that trip across the continent, which you will have to take, is a really hard blow. Five days at least after you are in this country before I see you.

My only consolation is that you are having experiences, and that is a poor consolation. It is getting harder and harder to wait for you, and especially as it seems so unnecessary now.

Everything is so at sixes and sevens now that I feel it will never be straight again. However, I suppose it will all work out. I hope so. If Papa were only here, I'm sure everything would fade into insignificance.

I can't let myself think about the fact that but for a peculiar circumstance you might be in my arms Wednesday. Sometimes those wonderful sensations are part of only a dream, and I can't believe that we shall once again renew them. But I suppose that day will finally come. The nights then will not be long enough for our pleasure or the days for our work together.

All my love, impatiently, Mama

Monday, September 4, 1945
Labor Day

My darling,

To add to my dissatisfaction, Louise Monahan just called to say Dave had talked to her. He is in Newport News awaiting transportation to Dix—thence to his home in Bridgeport for 12 hrs. and back to Washington (I presume to try and get out of the Army).

Louise will wait to see him until he arrives in Washington, and she promises to bring him to see me. After thirty day's leave, they reassemble in Alabama, but not for the Pacific, she assures me. I live in terror now of having you left in the Pacific.

Really—I'll pack up the children and come too. I can't stand this much longer. I'm getting really mad! I have the map before me, and I'm completely at a loss to know where you can possibly be. I want you to fly home, yet I'm terrified for fear you will. What a state!

The babies are fine, and I love you, but I'm just sick and tired of being "a brave woman." I'm not, and I never have been and never will be. I want you home.

All my love, Ginny

Tuesday, September 11, 1945

Dearest,

Your two letters of August 31 and September 1 arrived, and now I suppose I know the worst and can just give up hope.

These last two months between you and Father have done something to me emotionally, which I feel I will never really recover from. Right now I am completely tired out and don't seem to care any way or another.

It just seems impossible that you are ever coming home, and if you are glad about going to Japan, I suppose I should be also, but I am not. I shall be anxious for you the entire time.

I don't see why anyone in his right mind would have the least desire to be stationed in a completely hostile country with 7 million men still in the process of being disarmed and a population famous for their treachery.

The whole thing is a hard fiasco, and I keep thinking it is a nightmare and I'll wake up and find that you really didn't go on the advance party and came home after all.

The children do help, though. Beezie is finally reaching the stage when she tells you "wee-wee." She also tries to say a number of words.

Willie continues to be a character all his own. Mother took him for a walk today and he saw a broken truck. She couldn't budge him for one half-hour while they fixed the truck.

She said he was very talkative to two little boys, saying, "The truck is broken. I don't know what it is—a flat tire or something, but I think they'll get it fixed."

The little boy wanted to know how old he was, and Willie said, "Five."

He was very busy this evening playing "wheely jump." That means he jumped from his hobbyhorse, which has wheels on it, causing the horse to scoot backwards across the floor. Why it doesn't also cause Willie to land on his face I'll never know. Then Beezie has to try the same thing, and between the two they are a circus.

With all my crossness and crabby disposition, I love you still.

All my love, Ginny

P.S. The enclosed letter was addressed to the 5th and just returned.

Wednesday, September 12, 1945
9:45 P.M.

My darling,

Yesterday I wrote a horrid letter, and I'm already sorry. Just disregard it, and check it against a bad-tempered wife. The truth of the matter is, I'm so insane about you and really so jealous of you that I do lose my perspective sometimes.

I really do know that it has been almost as hard for you as I think it has been for me, and that, best of all, you do want to come home, and that you are probably making the best of a bad bargain when you say it will be interesting to go to Japan.

But it's my disposition to resent every minute spent away from me, so I just can't help it.

But I'm sorry I wrote so miserably and promise not to do it again, at least for a little while. But, Honey, remember, don't sit under that apple tree with anyone else but me.

I want you home so badly that it warps my point of view, initiative, disposition, and ability. Life with you is stimulating, worthwhile, and best of all, fun, but without you, it is just something to get along with.

I am trying to institute methods for Vitamin B-complex determinations in the lab to aid in an amenorrhea workup. Vitamin E deficiency, we believe, corresponds to corpus luteum deficiency and thyroid to estrogen areas. Still largely theoretical, but perhaps we'll prove it this winter. Also, I am starting on diabetic rats and reproduction.

All my love, Ginny

Saturday, September 15, 1945
2:30 P.M.

Dearest Honey Bunny,

I am more and more encouraged by the news, but I still realize that it will probably be a very long time before I see you again. I can't help but hope that they will see the folly of putting a 3,000-bed hospital in Japan and send you home instead. Could be. Maybe Dr. Burnam's request that you be released from the service as soon as possible will do some good.

As I ate lunch today, I ached with the thought of you. It was a pickup style meal, much as we used to have Sunday nights, and you would have enjoyed it. Delicious garden lettuce, cold cuts, cheese, and fruit, with iced coffee. It really seemed possible that we will once more live together and derive pleasure from those simple things by just being together.

There was also a piece in the paper warning of the health conditions in Japan—typhus, meningitis, TB, dysentery, etc. Do be overly cautious, and don't eat outside of Army installations. I do want you back as well and healthy as when you went away. I shall try to keep well too, and aside from a few gray hairs, believe I am about in as good shape (with really a better figure) than when you left.

Willie has just wakened, so I will close and take him to your mother's for the afternoon.

Love, Ginny

Saturday, September 15, 1945
10:30 P.M.

My dearest Honey Bunny,

If anyone had told me in my youth that I could ever write to anyone, even my husband, twice in the same day, I would have thought her insane. Jean Stiffler told me last year about this time that I will get over writing once a day, and here I am writing twice a day and loving it.

Really, Honey, I don't think I have changed a bit in the year, except to love you more, if that is possible. Of course, I have attained a sizeable bit of practical knowledge, most of it unpleasant. But this has done little to influence my mode of thought or philosophy. However, after all, my daily routine has been much the same as it has been for years.

I am constantly wondering if your life, which is so vastly different, has changed your mode of thought and philosophy. Do you really think you will be content to settle down to a hard grind again and be happy? From the tone of your letters, I think so, but I like reassurance.

The life that you outline for our postwar one is a rigorous one, and that appeals to me tremendously, and one that I really feel able to cope with. But I sometimes wonder about the Army emphasis on the social, and this I am not sure of.

However, the thoughts do not seriously disturb me, for, of course, I know that life with Papa any way he wants to live it is the most wonderful and exciting thing that could happen to me. There will be time enough to arrange the practical details after we have caught up with some of the philosophical aspects.

All my love, Ginny

P.S. Don't fly any more than you have to.

Monday, September 17, 1945
10:30 P.M.

My darling,

I am constantly amazed at the closeness of our thoughts. Yesterday I asked what would be the possibility of meeting you on the West Coast, and today, in your letter of September 6, you say, "What about meeting me on the West Coast?"

Of course I shall start plans at once, and although they will probably never materialize, yet I will have had the pleasure of thoughts. I still feel that we will be very lucky if you get out of that hole you are in before next August. I hope it's not at the height of the tourist season.

I am glad that you had such a nice trip to Corregidor, and know that you must have needed the exercise. Do try to get more. Again, let me say, if and when you arrive in Japan, don't eat anywhere but in the Army mess. Don't do any private sightseeing, and don't stay out after dark.

Willie suddenly decided today that he wanted his "French books that Papa sent." I kept them put away to avoid spoilage, so out they came, and he has spent the entire evening poring over them. He really has a memory like an elephant.

We are having our usual September hurricane-tail weather. I find it most exciting and invigorating—typical coastal weather. We must someday have a shore place to which we can repair and exhilarate in such things.

At night though, I begin to miss you, Papa, more and more, because it is getting into the cold-feet season.

MacArthur says today only 200,000 troops for occupation after six months. I love that man!

As always, I live for your letters.

All my love, Ginny

Wednesday, September 19, 1945
11:00 P.M.

Dearest Honey Bunny,

You poor darling—your letter of September 10 arrived, and I think you were just about as low as I was at that time. You were not receiving letters because when your Panama letters reached me I thought you meant for me to keep on writing to the 5th Aux. Therefore, for a period of about ten days, I continued to address to the 5th. But now I trust you are once again on schedule.

Some of my letters are so gloomy, I would just as soon you did not receive them, but you know that I am better now, and even more optimistic about "our possibilities."

Dr. Burnam at Johns Hopkins has written a very nice letter, which I am going to take directly to Washington. Here's hoping it helps. I am going to get a letter from Dr. Maxim (head of the Physicians' Selective Service). I have many things to do, and so am much better off than you. I realize this and wish there was something I could do to make things easier for you other than write you letters.

All my love, Ginny

Thursday, September 20, 1945
11:00 P.M.

Dearest Honey Bunny,

Today I had a letter from Colonel Gay, saying he had talked to Washington and also wired to the effect that the three officers should be returned to their home base, Camp Seibert, Alabama. Washington was not very hopeful, as it said General MacArthur's headquarters controlled all men in his theater. However, it was nice of Gay to make the effort.

Sweetheart, I love you to distraction, and I mean just that. I am really distracted when I think how miserable you must have been there, and how miserably unhappy I am back home. I can't feel that this can go on indefinitely, and I believe we may yet get a break.

Colonel Gay tells me you have been recommended for a Bronze Star, whatever that is, and I am sure you deserve a gold one. However, it will give you an additional five points.

I have yet to find anything that's half as good a foot warmer, so do hurry home.

All my love, Ginny

P.S. I hope the moon in Manila is not as lovely as ours is tonight.

Tuesday, September 25, 1945
9:00 P.M.

My darling,

Today two letters, one the 8th, written from Baguio, and the other the 12th, and also your sweet airplane for Willie. Willie was entranced and also kissed Mommie on the spot, not only the 1st reading, but the 4 subsequent ones, so I have five kisses by proxy—a liquid and poor substitute, but sweet. Beezie was beside herself at no mail for her and would not be contented with simply an envelope.

Do let me know if Ridge will be back before he comes home. I'm so afraid if he leaves that you'll really be in for it.

You ask if the "babies" are still babies. Willie, I am afraid, is not. Beezie is still in the cute-baby stage, but is rapidly developing into a wiggle wart.

She has now learned to jump and to bend her knees and straighten them out without getting her feet off the floor and then look surprised. She now says many words when told to, and a few spontaneous—some two-syllable ones, like Howard. We can understand her well, of course, but no one else could, I'm sure. Willie and B now eat at a separate little table, and it is much easier on the family. Everything is quiet by 8:45, as a rule.

Here's hoping for an unexpected break.

All my love, Ginny

Chapter 20

On to Tokyo
30 September-30 October 1945

*G*ENERAL MACARTHUR MOVED SWIFTLY TO DEMOBILIZE the seven million Japanese military in uniform on V-J Day and successfully argued for retention of Hirohito as emperor of Japan against British and Soviet demands that the Japanese leader be tried as a war criminal.

MacArthur contended, "If the emperor were indicted and perhaps hanged, military government would have to be instituted throughout all Japan, and guerrilla war would probably break out."

MacArthur was bent on transforming Japan into a constitutional democracy, and he needed the emperor to attain his objective.

History confirms the wisdom of his decision.

MacArthur's mission was still in its earliest phase as I steamed toward Japan.

Monday 1 October 1945
4:00 P.M.

Dearest Ginny,

Once again I have bulkheads instead of walls, ladders for stairs, and decks for floors. The flying fish are my companions.

I hope the stranger to whom I gave it mailed the brief note I got off yesterday.

At a little before noon we were told that hold baggage must be ready by 3:00 P.M., and we were to be prepared to board by 6:00 P.M.

Later we heard that the ship would leave as soon as we were all aboard, about midnight.

All this seemed in a big hurry after originally planning to go on Tuesday.

What happened was that the ship did not have the hold space necessary to load the entire equipment, and the bulk of that is coming on an LST *[landing ship, tank]*.

Everything was packed before I wrote you yesterday, and I spent the rest of the day reading David Copperfield. We had supper of coffee and two pieces of bread, between which were huddled three small pieces of dried-up, cold pastrami. I was not hungry, thank goodness.

I could not get out of my mind how the embarkation for Japan might have been. Loaded in the same kind of ship, but with equipment stowed to be easily set up and work commenced on the beach. I have the greatest uncertainty and no faith in the ability of the people in the Philippines to have used our group properly.

About 9:30 the trucks came over to the officers' area and, about 10:00, were loaded onto a 6 x 6. I had Val-A-Pak, musette bag, pistol belt, canteen, and a folding chair given to me by Ralph Seeley.

The ship was not tied up to a pier, but anchored some mile or so offshore. An LCVP came on to the shore, and we piled on.

The wind had kicked up a bit of surf, and those without raincoats were prodigiously wet. In a quiet sea, it is a simple matter to step from a landing craft to a boarding ladder, but if the water is choppy when one goes up, a little sport is added.

I was on the verge of throwing the chair overboard, but remembering how handy it might prove for a desk, I tucked it under one arm, holding the Val-A-

Pak so that my left hand and arm would be free. At an opportune moment, I gave a jump and landed safely on the foot of the ladder, easily scrambling to the top.

We got on ship just about midnight. We promptly found out that the time for departure had been set at 10:00 A.M. today. We are now quite out of sight of land.

I see that you are now on standard time. As I figure it, this puts us 14 hours ahead of you. When it is midnight in Baltimore, it is 2:00 P.M. here.

You see, I can keep a constant image of you as you sleep the night through. In the not-too-distant future, I shall keep a close watch, and I shall know by my arms and body when you turn in your sleep, as we can snuggle up close together, if my dreams come true.

Love, H

1 October 1945
6:00 P.M.

Dearest Ginny,

We finally got underway about 10:00 A.M. yesterday, as I said. It did not occur to me that we should turn south after leaving Batangas, for Japan is to the north. A glance at the map, however, shows that it is nearest to go through San Bernardino Strait and up the east coast of Luzon.

We went through the strait during the night, just as the Jap fleet did in October before meeting Admiral Kinkaid's 7th fleet in the second sea battle of the Philippines. About 10 o'clock this morning we found ourselves at Legaspi in a fine bay just up the east coast from San Bernardino Strait.

We dropped anchor and are still here, and apparently will be tomorrow. There are about six other transports in the bay, loading the 158th Combat Team, which assaulted the beach here on Easter Sunday and have been here ever since. Then all six ships are to proceed in convoy.

The idea of a convoy, I understand, is a precaution against mines. The destroyer escorts sweep before us. Some floating mines are supposed to be still at large.

This afternoon, after lunch, the PA system gave forth, "Now hear this—all officers wishing to go ashore be at the gangway in five minutes." I grabbed my camera and took off. We went in an LCP complete with spray.

The little town of Legaspi was badly handled by the bombers before the landing. We heard while in town that the Japs had left just before the bombing. In many ways it is the most interesting of the local villages I have seen, because it is more provincial.

It is 330 miles from Manila by road. The people are Polynesian and Chinese. Here the usual bamboo structures are on stilts, and the town is rapidly becoming rebuilt. I took a picture of a man building his house.

One sees odd things. In the midst of eastern smells and diaperless babies, à la Mexico, we come upon a "beauty shop" and, within, a tremendous rig for administering a permanent wave. We also saw several Singer sewing machines.

We bought a pineapple, the first I have had, and ate it on the dock while waiting for the boat to take us back to the ship.

On the shore of this bay is Mount Mayon, the most symmetrical mountain I have ever seen. It is a volcano, active last in the early 1900s, and the biggest mountain in the Philippines—rising some 8,000 feet.

We were back on board by 6:30 P.M., in time for dinner, and now I am sleepy. It will be hot tonight, as we are not underway. I hope I can hold out until we reach the cooler latitudes of Tokyo.

Love and kisses, H

Wednesday 2 October 1945
6:00 P.M.

Dearest Ginny,

Here we sit. We were supposed to leave Legaspi today at 10:00, but one of the ships in the harbor has not yet completed loading, and we have to wait for her. It is particularly exasperating to have to lay over, because it is very hot when the ship is not underway and every day here postpones by the same length of time our own V-J Day.

Ralph Seeley and I have set up a timetable for coming home. We are both eligible under the 80-point rule. I had planned not to mention it, as it is a little more optimistic than I have previously said, but it has been entertaining to us to compare our programs with the schedule we have confabulated.

We are due in Yokohama the 15th of October. Thirty days from then we are to receive orders to report to a replacement depot for shipment home.

There will be a two-week delay there, and we should be boarding the ship the first of December. Considering the delays in leaving and disembarking, we are not due in San Francisco until the 23rd of December at 8:00 A.M.

The natives here have wonderfully fast sailboats, which they use for their normal transportation from their shoreside homes into the village of Legaspi.

They are very thin, as all boats here, but these more so. To keep them from capsizing, they have permanent outriggers onto which they climb while tacking for better ballast, but the sail has the most local color. It is made of palm leaves woven into a mat of a size to suit the boat. They have but a single sail spread fore and aft; the mast is like our canoe, but instead of a triangular sail, this is trapezoidal. What do you call that shape?

The meals are very good. Much better than at the 54th. We get up at 6:30, breakfast at 7:00, lunch at noon, and dinner at 5:30. Every afternoon the so-called soda fountain is open to officers from 3:40 to 4:00. Why it is called the soda fountain, I can't imagine, because the pièce de résistance and the only item is a Dixie cup of ice cream, price 10 cents, and Philippine pesos are no good.

This leaves me in an unsatisfactory position, as I have no dollars, but have borrowed one until Japan. My finances are in a low state, as I have not been long enough in one place to accomplish the red tape required to receive my $80 per month. I have about 15 pesos left from Marseilles.

It is the cool of the evening now, and a slight breeze has come up into my porthole, so perhaps it won't be so bad tonight after all.

Love, H

Thursday 4 October 1945

My darling Ginny,

Underway at last. This morning, while still horizontal about 5:30, we heard over the PA system the usual chatter preceding departure: "All departments make ready to get underway and report to the officer of the deck on the navigation bridge." And later, "Set special sea and anchor detail." We left at 7:00 A.M., the nine ships in the convoy falling in line and leaving the mouth of the harbor like elephants, trunk to tail.

We have now formed three columns of three ships each, with a destroyer *escort in front of all. The course is northeast, but mostly east. Everyone is in high spirits because we are moving toward home.*

The ship is called an APA [attack transport], the letters standing for "Attack Personnel." I don't know what the final A means. They are similar to other naval transports, except that they have landing craft stored in every possible cranny.

These are the ships that go close to the hostile beach and launch the assault waves. This particular ship has four LCMs [landing craft, medium], which hold about 100 men each. There must be 15 LCVPs [landing craft, vehicle, personnel], which are the ordinary landing craft you see so commonly in pictures like General MacArthur's coming ashore in Leyte. There are also a couple of LCIRs, another type of craft.

They are slung on the deck so that the deck space is cut up and reduced. To walk around, it is necessary to duck rudders and propellers.

Four landing craft are slung over the side and carry something like a lifeboat on davits. Huge cranes move them around and launch them as if they weighed nothing. It is said that it is possible to launch all of them in 12 minutes.

The other night on coming aboard I noticed that the bedspread was an old one of the Baltimore Mail Line. The ship is called the Charles Heywood. *On further investigation it turns out to be the former* City of Baltimore, *which used to run between Baltimore and Europe.*

It is APA No. 6 and was converted early in the war. It has carried troops to Attu, New Guinea, Saipan, Okinawa, Leyte, Luzon, and other places—a real veteran. It was like meeting someone from home.

Once again I feel that at last I have started on the road back. This keeps us ahead of schedule, because we are due on the 10th, five days ahead of time.

Love, H

Friday 5 October 1945
8:00 A.M.

Dearest Ginny,

In spite of being underway, last night was the hottest of all. My pillow and sheet were a sweaty mess this morning. The only breeze is coming from the southwest, and at about the same velocity as the ship moves, so that we are in a sort of doldrums.

It is better this morning, as the sun seems to have come up a little farther to the south, and the breeze is a little fresher and more southerly, so that I believe we have changed course toward the north and cooler latitudes.

There is something about this parboiled sleeping that leaves you like a well-known dishrag in the morning. The result is that, on coming out on deck, where it is much cooler, I immediately got so sleepy that it is miserable trying to get comfortable.

The accommodations here are in many respects better than on the Admiral Benson. *Our cabin is somewhat smaller, but there are only four of us. Once more, it has paid to be a major.*

We have running water in the room, but the cold water is on only from 6:30 to 8:00 A.M., 11:00 to 11:30, 4:30 to 5:30. The hot water is just too damn hot to use alone, but we sometimes beat the racket by drawing a basin full of hot water and allowing about 30 minutes for it to cool. Freshwater showers are the same hours.

The messing facilities are especially good. The troop-officers wardroom will accommodate just about all the officers aboard at one fell swoop. There are about 90. Between meal hours, the wardroom is available for reading, cards, and the like.

There is also a radio, and yesterday we heard a rebroadcast of the World Series, complete with a terrific amount of static and fading in and out à la long-distance short-wave broadcast.

Last night I played bridge, and in between times I read, and thus I have a completely useless day when we—you and I—have so much to do.

All my love, H

P.S. Our new APO is 503.

Saturday 6 October 1945
10:30 A.M.

Dearest Ginny,

It is a beautiful day. The air is fresher, the clouds are not so bulky, and there is a gentle roll to the boat. The wind is moderate from the northeast, which seems to be a fair wind out here.

I am getting to know a few of the officers in the 54th, and especially those in my cabin. Generally speaking, they are not as professionally astute as the group in the 5th, but in some departments they are strong.

In my cabin is a Major William Evans, who graduated from Williams in 1926 and Hopkins in 1930. He has been doing X-ray work with his father in Detroit and should be a very competent man. He has not been back to Baltimore since graduation and was pleased to hear what was happening. Conrad Acton was a member of his class. Evans thought him quite as hare-brained as we did.

Another of the occupants is a Major Morris Lilga, who is a wizened, Mr. Milquetoast type of individual, with an almost bald head and ribs you can count with ease. He is a bit grouchy and says the confinement of a ship gets on his nerves—always does.

He spends a lot of time in the bunk. He was in Baltimore around 1930 as a house officer at Shepherd Pratt (a psychiatric hospital). Since then, he has done medicine, but he could easily pass for a psychiatrist.

The fourth man is a Major Englert, a dentist, who has been in the Army since before Pearl Harbor. He is a pleasant-enough individual with a neutral personality that neither attracts nor repels.

He is tempted to apply to the Regular Army, if they will give him his present grade. Like many of those who have joined the Army from school, I think he has some fear of the uncertainties of individual effort.

With love and kisses and everything, H

Sunday 7 October 1945
10:00 A.M.

Dearest Ginny,

Yesterday the sun rose and set in the same place. Figure that out and you will see that we are getting nowhere fast. While writing yesterday I noticed that we had cut to half speed, and about three hours later the entire convoy turned 180 degrees back toward the Philippines.

Two converging low-pressure areas ahead gave promise of a typhoon, and on orders from Yokohama, we turned around.

This morning, we are still going southwest, but about one hour ago we reduced speed, so that at least we are going nowhere and not quite so fast. This will delay our arrival in Tokyo and home, and may result in our arrival "on time" and before, in regard to the schedule for deployment of HJ.

The weather here is fine. A quiet sea, but an overcast sky. Moderate northwest winds. The absence of the sun keeps it livable.

We now must be back in the area where the northernmost section of the second battle of the Philippines [The Battle of Leyte Gulf, 23-27 October 1944] took place off the northeast tip of Luzon.

That was where Halsey's Third Fleet almost got too far away to get back to help Kinkaid hold the Japs coming through San Bernandino. In contrast to a land battle, a sea battle leaves no debris. There is nothing here but water.

With love and kisses, H

Monday 8 October 1945
8:30 P.M.

My darling Ginny,

The pump handle has nothing on us, for, like it, we go up and down, touching neither sky nor ground.

The sea today is a beautiful thing. I know you would love it, and how I miss you. The wind has blown from a half-dozen directions since this morning, so that the ocean is quite perplexed as to what it should do. The result is substantial rollers from the starboard bow and smaller ones from abaft the starboard beam.

When two such waves meet under the bow or stern, we have an especially nice ride. Overhead, it is overcast, with some showers, but the sun now and then peeps through, and the wind has not assumed a velocity of more than 25 miles or so per hour. We are getting the effect of the storm we ran away from.

Yesterday afternoon, about 3 o'clock, after running backwards some 24 hours, there was great blinking of lights between ships, and the entire convoy once more turned 180 degrees and headed toward Tokyo. Just now we must be about where we were when we turned around two days ago. They say that we will have rougher weather before it gets better. The little destroyer escort out in front is bobbing around like a cork.

I came upon a book of Greek plays and amused myself last night by reading Agamemnon. *You will remember that it begins with the fall of Troy and the end of the Trojan War. The thing that holds your interest now and makes the 25-centuries-old play a modern thing is the similarity of the problems. The 25 centuries have little changed the human side of war:*

> *Dead and wounded:*
>> *The captains and the captors cry*
>> *Tell diverse tales of Fortune's twofold power.*
>> *Those now are fallen about the prostrate forms*
>> *Of husbands, brothers, friends, young children, too,*
>> *Changing to gray-haired fathers—and from throats*
>> *No longer free, lament their dearest slain.*

> *Demobilization:*
>> *Still remains the home-return to round their tumultuous course.*

> *The soldier's story:*
>> *Were I now to tell*
>> *Our toils and hardships neath the open sky*
>> *Lying on various brinks, ill-lined and bare,*
>> *Lamenting each day's lack of every store;*
>> *Then on firm land, still worse, to lodge the field,*
>> *Close under the enemy's wall with rain from heaven*
>> *As dew from the damp meadows drizzling*
>> *Our clothes and bodies and our clotted hair.*

> *And one I like:*
>> *What light is sweeter to a woman's eye than that which floods*
>> *the opening gate when heaven brings home her husband from*
>> *the war?*

But on my return my thoughts will differ from Agamemnon's. Not once does he speak of love for his wife, nor does he have any. I might not say anything. I doubt if I am able. But you will know that that moment holds more joy than I can dare imagine.

Love, H

Tuesday 10 October 1945
10:00 P.M.

Dearest Ginny,

When we left Legaspi, we were due to arrive in Tokyo today. Instead, we are lolling in the ocean some 800 miles from our goal.

This morning, it became evident that we were falling out of the convoy. One of the naval officers said that we had burned out a bearing on a blower of one of the boilers and it would take only about two hours to fix it. The convoy was not over the horizon when we started up again, and we caught up after chasing about three hours.

Then this afternoon the entire convoy slowed to about 6 knots. It seems that the typhoon we have so far avoided is still ahead. We are still lolling at the same speed. I hope we don't have to turn around again.

It is a fine night now. I have just come in. The waves are about 15 feet with a 25-mile wind. Stars clear and bright. We are obviously getting farther north, but I was not yet able to see the northern star.

Orion is up, but somehow he seems to be too sideways. Actually, the stars are not as sparkling in the tropics as in the colder northern latitudes. It may be the warm, humid atmosphere, but I think it is because you are not at my side.

Love, H

Thursday 11 October
8:00 A.M.

Dearest Ginny,

I did not write yesterday. I had planned to wait until I was comfortable in bed, but when I got horizontal I was like the doll whose eyes go closed in that position. It was a dreary day at best, and the letter would have been a sad one.

All yesterday morning we continued to make progress by going slowly. It was rougher than at any other time, with the wind 30 knots and the bow of the ship dipping under now and again. About noontime we noticed the lead ship began to swing, and we did 180-degree turns and, for the second time, turned away from home.

The typhoon has not yet got out of our way. During the night a Liberty ship off Okinawa sent out repeated SOSs, but was afloat yesterday morning. This morning we got word to be on the lookout for wreckage and men, so it must have been pounded to pieces.

Some people on the ship are beginning to wonder what our fate may be. No one has any desire to perish in a typhoon after weathering the other storms of war.

The executive officer of the ship entertained Ralph Seeley and me yesterday with a yarn or two and some facts about the storms. They seem to make up in the region of Yap and Ulithi and travel in a generally northern direction, but describing a gentle circle to China and then eastward across southern Japan.

They are, of course, twisters, with the greatest wind velocity about 50 miles from the center of the disturbance, where the waters are sort of a boiling pot, with waves from every direction, so that it is impossible to put a ship on a quiet course.

They are tremendous things. The one that is bothering us is some 250 miles away, but we had a 30-knot wind here yesterday. This means in an area of 500 miles there is no ship in the ocean.

Our executive, who was master of the President Grant *in peacetime, was in such a typhoon in Hong Kong in 1937, where the wind was recorded at 167 miles per hour. Of 30 large ships in the harbor, all were sunk or grounded.*

When I went to bed last night, the wind had moderated some, and there was but a gentle rock.

My bunk is beside a porthole on the port side of the ship. Great was our disappointment this morning when I could see the sunrise directly out of this peephole. The sea was relatively calm.

While we were at breakfast, the ship began to buck a bit, and we had once again made a 180-degree turn. Best of all, we seemed to have put her to the floor. I hope this time it is full speed ahead, and it will get us to Tokyo. At least we will now arrive on the 16th, one day behind our timetable.

Love, H

Friday 12 October 1945
10:00 A.M.

Dearest Ginny,

Last night Orion was in his place and the Big Dipper visible in the sky. The stars had a sparkle and Vega that brilliant-blue color. The skies appeared familiar, and we are out of the tropics. The typhoon has degenerated into a second-rate storm, and we are going full speed ahead for Tokyo and home.

Colonel John Caldwell, the CO of this outfit, differs from Colonel Gay as night from day. He is aloof from the men and officers and cultivates an unavailability befitting a CO and giving him authority over his command, if not respect. Each night he has a bridge game in the stateroom he has alone, and last night it was my turn to be entertained.

He is a relatively young man—perhaps 40—but appears older, as do many of those who have spent time out here. He spoke in a whiny, nasal voice reminiscent of my Aunt Amy. He wears spectacles, which slide down, on his nose, and is thin with wrinkled skin.

The other officers at the game were long-standing members of the 54th, and I noticed at once that there was no familiarity between them; they referred to him as "Colonel, sir," and generated a forced laughter at nonludicrous situations. I therefore said nothing and waited for the evening to develop, which it never did. It was, therefore, a rather stiff evening, but we played bridge until 11:30.

After it was over, someone mentioned that we were playing for a 1/5 of a cent a point, and I had won 60 cents. Everybody collected except the Colonel. I understand he often supports the party, as his bridge does not show the effects of the long hours of practice common to Regular Army officers.

All in all, I rather liked the guy, who, I think, has developed the attitude toward him with forethought. It represents a possibility for commanding officers and has some of the qualities quite lacking in Colonel Gay. Furthermore, this man seems innately smarter than our late CO but judging from the conversation, there is no team unity among us. He has the reputation at headquarters for running a good hospital, and it is probably warranted.

The latest word is that we will arrive in Tokyo by tomorrow and perhaps be off the boat by the 15th. This will put me exactly on schedule, so perhaps I will make San Francisco by the 23rd of December at 8:00 A.M. I hope to have mail

*in Tokyo, for then, perhaps, we can make more plans for our V-J Day. This is
a remarkably satisfactory time.*

Love and kisses, H

*P.S. Some Japanese invasion money for Willie. I am afraid I shall not be able to
send him anything for his birthday. Kiss him for me.*

*Saturday 13 October 1945
9:00 P.M.*

Dearest Ginny,

*This morning when I awoke there was a rocky shoreline out of the porthole.
From 5:00 A.M. until we pulled into the dock at Yokohama around 2:00
P.M., we all hugged the rail to see Tokyo Bay and the harbor.*

*It has been a rough trip. Even last night the waves were banging around the
side of the ship, and twice during the night a fine spray came in around the edge of
the porthole with a terrific banging of the life raft just outside the hole. The men
in the next stateroom got soaked.*

*There are still many mines loose in this area. The Americans dropped
thousands, and some of the Japanese mines are loose. The night before last, one was
sighted, and the destroyer escort dropped behind and fired at it for about 30
minutes and never did explode it. Apparently, it is necessary to hit one of the
"spikes" that are the contact apparatus.*

*On the way up the harbor we saw innumerable American cargo and transport
ships. We came in with 17 "battleships"—really, 12 destroyers, 2 carriers, and
3 battleships. There must be 25 or more assorted warships in the harbor.*

*On approaching the city, it would be difficult to guess that it was not an American
city. It appears less foreign than many so far seen. The buildings are modern, apparently
clean, from the distance, and scattered here and there are church spires, which I was
surprised to see. Only the peculiar local sampans about the harbor remind me of the
East.*

*We were all amazed to come up directly to the dock. The speed with which
they got the ship unloaded was amazing. The LCVPs, which are stored over the
deck and holds, were launched while we were still underway, and within five*

minutes of tying up, the first truck was taken out of the hold. The units aboard other than the 54th disembarked at once. We will stay aboard until Monday, so that our place will be ready. We have plenty of room aboard now.

The hospital is to be set up in the Doai Memorial Hospital in Tokyo, about five miles from the Imperial Palace. From the verbal description of the advance party, it should be a very satisfactory hospital setup. The living quarters will be in permanent buildings—steam heat, hot and cold water, and the like.

The big uncertainty is to how long I shall have to stay. We are on schedule (exactly) for disembarking, and I have some hope that I shall be on schedule in Frisco. There shall probably be more information on this in the next day or two.

Love, H

Monday 15 October 1945
7:00 A.M.

Dearest Ginny,

This is yesterday's letter. I am still on the ship, but completely packed and ready to leave. We are due to depart at 8:00 A.M. for our permanent location in Tokyo. Incidentally, we are going by DUKW [amphibious truck] overland.

Yesterday we "did" Yokohama. In the morning we walked about the downtown area, which is adjacent to the port facilities. We are docked at Yokohama Pier 1, which is the NYK line that ran to the States in peacetime. In one raid on May 29 the U.S. Army Air Forces put Yokohama out of business. The downtown area apparently consisted of modern, fireproof, American-type office buildings, six-to-eight stories high, and one-or-two-story frame shops with tin roofs.

The latter structures are gone, burned up. The larger buildings undamaged. It is possible to go along the street and find here a bicycle shop with 25 twisted bicycle frames, a hardware store with its myriad of household trinkets, a novelty shop with its assorted junk, which powders when you touch it.

Whole blocks of downtown Yokohama are thoroughly destroyed. In the area immediately adjacent to the docks, the modern office buildings are still standing. The damage was entirely by firebombs.

There is very little debris from this destruction. A bulldozer run once over the area cleaned it up. The reports early in the war about the effectiveness of firebombs on flimsy Japanese cities were the exact truth. With the rusty tin that was the roof, individual Japanese families are building small houses. They will be frightfully cold this winter.

There are a few shops open. They offer trinkets of the ten-cent-store variety at Tiffany prices. I bought a few little cards, which will do for place cards sometime.

In the afternoon we walked along the waterfront to the residential district. The situation there is the same. Whole areas are burned over. Nothing left but the fireplace, as we sometimes see when a farmhouse burns down.

Other sections are intact. In those areas it would be difficult to know you were not in America. It is the exceptional house that shows an Oriental influence in its architecture. They say that Yokohama was completely destroyed in 1923 (by an earthquake).

We saw several Christian churches. The chaplain said that there were 23, of which five are undamaged. We saw a temple, very Oriental, of course. I took some pictures, but it was too dark. Shoes are left outside. We saw an international cemetery, where Russians, Chinese, English, and Americans who died in this area during the last 75 years are buried.

At 5 o'clock, when we got back, I was wet from the hips down. I don't know when I miss you the most, but when looking around, the lack is especially acute. I think you would like it.

Love, H

Monday 15 October 1945
7:30 P.M.

Dearest Ginny,

Today we arrived in Tokyo. If someone had offered to bet me $1,000 to $1 that when we were 50 miles from Berlin that I would get to Tokyo first, I would have thought that he was throwing $1 away, such is fate and the army.

We left the ship at 8:00 A.M., as planned. Five officers and some bedrolls were in the 2½-ton truck I rode in. From the pier in Yokohama to the hospital, it must be 20 miles through downtown Tokyo.

Everywhere is the same—substantial office buildings, except those directly hit, still standing—the two-story frame shops completely consumed by fire. Our hospital here is an oasis in the midst of ruined areas.

Since being here, I have said nothing about the people, who are much more important than the houses they lived in. I hope to encounter someone who speaks

English, as this gibberish they speak is as unintelligible to us as our English is to them.

I have tried to pick out a wealthy or educated Jap—a successful businessman, lawyer, or doctor—and I have either not seen one or did not recognize him. They all appear to be factory workers or laborers.

They all seem to wear a uniform. A dozen kinds, and mixed, but nevertheless a uniform. Perhaps the war regimented the clothing, as they certainly were not all in the Army.

The uniform is an ordinary pair of trousers and coat, with the characteristic Jap Army headgear. About half of them have the tightest-fitting britches you ever saw. Their legs are covered with a roller legging like a khaki Ace bandage, and for shoes they have a rubber-soled, canvas-top, Ked-like affair with a big toe separate. You cannot get out of your mind some web-footed animal—I think of a frog.

There are a few exceptions, as some wear complete Western dress. A few have kimonos. I think I saw two old men with spotless white skirts and wooden shoes sliding along.

A few of the women have Western dress. Most of them have a sort of zoot suit. You would not call it a kimono, but they are cotton or silk and seem to be a one-piece coverall with flowering designs. It gives them a shapeless appearance, like a sack. They seem to have on great layers of clothes. The trousers funnel down like ski pants, and the sleeves are flowing. Those who do not have these suits wear slacks and sweaters. We see very few with skirts; they are quite the exception.

The children, like kids the world over, are cute and healthy appearing, although pudgy. They love running races and have learned to ask for chocolate and gum. The American soldier is the real chocolate soldier. The children wear anything from rags to coveralls to kimonos.

The Oriental custom of carrying a papoose is universally used. It appears to be a very satisfactory means of transportation, and many of the kids are fast asleep, with heads bobbing as if they are about to tumble off.

What do these people think as they trudge along with a load as big as they? You look, expecting to see hate or resentment, as we would feel were the tables reversed. It may be there, but as I looked at the flattened noses, slanting eyes, and wrinkled forearms, I was reminded of Dayton and Evo (two chimpanzees at Hopkins Medical School), and God knows what is on their minds.

I think some former Atlantic City shopkeepers have come to Tokyo. In two or three shops, including one large department store, there are big signs, "Welcome

Americans. "Imagine Hutzler Brothers, "Welcome Japanese," if the Nips were occupying Baltimore.

The Nips are moving out the last of their things as we come in today. The officers' living quarters are in private hospital rooms, two officers to a room. My roommate is Harris Lilga, one of my shipboard roommates. I am happy in that assignment, as he is affable and white, which is something in this half-Indian organization.

We have cots, and I am using my air mattress, side table, cupboard, chest of drawers, and adequate electric light. Nails in the wall and shelves knocked out of the cupboard have given us space to hang our clothes. The water is not yet on, but when it is we shall be very comfortable.

Tomorrow I shall take off to see Tokyo, although I apparently shall have to sit on some sort of examining board, of which more tomorrow.

Love, H

Tuesday 16 October 1945
10:00 P.M.

Dearest Ginny,

There is no sign of mail here as yet. I suppose it is possible that I shall not get any before leaving. If this means that I shall not be long here, I could possibly put up with it, but it doesn't, and I can only hope that it breaks through in the near future.

This morning Bill Eastman and I walked down to the Imperial Palace. This goes through the heart of business Tokyo, which being of large fireproof buildings is for the most part in good shape.

The palace is in a park or palace grounds. The palace area is surrounded by a moat and a wall of Oriental design. Now and again there is a huge gate and bridge. You cannot cross the moat, and all the gates are closed, but we saw the main entrance and the favorite place for hari-kari. It took us 40 minutes to walk it.

I had to be back by 11 o'clock, for at that time Melvin Berlind, who has charge of the detail to do the examinations at the 42nd, was to be back with the dope. It seems that the 54th is furnishing an examining board to meet three days a week to pass on Regular Army officers for promotions. I will have the surgical part. It won't be bad, and we begin tomorrow.

We continue to live here and go there Monday, Wednesday, and Friday. The wiseacres around here say it is another example of someone doing the 42nd's work. The 42nd seems to have a bad reputation in that respect. You might ask some of them about it (the 42nd General Hospital is a University of Maryland unit). There is a considerable chorus of sour grapes among the personnel of both the 51st and 54th about the 42nd's two peacetime setups in the Pacific. I think it is nice work if you can get it.

This afternoon we walked to a park about two miles from here. On the way a sign says, "Imperial Museum." Unfortunately, the museum is closed, but it is housed in a magnificent, graceful, Japanese-type building.

I think of any building as Japanese that has the roof turned up at the edges. It would be interesting to know how this type of architecture developed here. No one I have asked has any sensible suggestion.

One smaller building is labeled in English as the Tokyo Science Museum, and it is closed, but the door was open, and we went in. The exhibits are smashed and scattered. One dinosaur's skeleton is scattered in the yard. What a pity. It will take years to gather it together again.

They got the movie set up today, and tonight we saw Eddie Pyle's picture. It is well done, I think. I suppose his contribution was the description and interpretation of the front-line GI.

Tomorrow I hope to have some dope on coming home. I hope it is good.

Love, H

Thursday 18 October 1945
9:00 A.M.

My dearest Ginny,

This examining board I am on is a joke. It is a board for examining Regular Army officers, and we go to the 42nd General Monday, Wednesday, and Friday afternoons. We went yesterday for the first time, and the 12 of us did four officers. My job was to do the rectals, but I was taking a shower when the four showed up, so I did not earn my last four months' pay yesterday as anticipated.

While we were in the lunch line, a major who appeared vaguely familiar asked me if my name was Jones. He was Everett Diggs, who was resident for Jack Hundley when King was resident in OB at Maryland.

There are but three or four of the original *University of Maryland* group left. *Bowie* is going shortly. *Gundry* is on his way, and so on. He said he heard that *King* was out of the *Army.* I hope so.

He inquired about where I had been, and he said that the same thing had happened to me as to one of their new officers—a *Major Burbank*—and then in walks *Charley,* who is their new chief of surgery!

It seems that *Charley* flew up the day after I left and has been here ever since. The 8th *Army General Rice* decided that they did not need a surgical consultant and sent *Charley* over to the 42nd to take over as chief when *Bowie* leaves.

They have a fine setup in St. Luke's *Hospital,* which was built with a good share of American funds. They have had chiefly accident work, but a few appendices. The only elective work has been hernias. *Charley* says that, except for *Bowie,* the surgical staff does not know from nothing.

He also has to do the orthopedics. He has already been driven crazy by men with pain in the back, running down the legs and arms and out the top of the head. People with painful scars and men unable to lift anything except a bottle of beer or a glass of Scotch. What to do with them? Returned to duty, they bounce back in a day or two, as they will not work, and they have nothing to board them home on.

However, having to stay here for a while, he has as good a job as there is available, in that he does see a patient now and again. We both think *Bill Falor* may be home, as the 10th *Army* has been inactivated, of course, and *Okinawa* evacuated as rapidly as possible, due to the storm. *Bill* may have had to pass up *Tokyo.* In a sense, it is too bad to have been so close and not seen it—slightly sour grapes, I think.

Tonight I am going to have dinner with *Charley* at the *Imperial Hotel.* For 16 yen ($1.07), it is said, it is possible to get a good Japanese dinner. It is run by the *Nips* under *American* supervision. I certainly wish you were here, but that goes without saying.

Love, H

Saturday 20 October 1945
9:00 P.M.

My darling Ginny,

I don't believe that I told you about our dinner at the Imperial Hotel. Thursday, after looking about town, I went over to the 42nd, and Charley and I *went downtown to the Imperial Hotel for dinner. Two of the dining rooms there have been set aside for "transient officers." The food and service are Japanese. They are carrying on just as always, I presume. No civilians allowed.*

I don't think the Army is supplying them with any of the food, and it has considerable local color. Soup, usually sea fish with an elaborate sauce; meat, also with a musty sauce; and cabbage; and eggplant was our dinner. Tea served in a glass. No dessert. Price 16 yen ($1.07).

The waitresses wore kimonos, but they are not in costume, as kimonos on the street are by no means uncommon. It is quite a good idea to have this downtown place for meals, although I am a little surprised that civilian food is allowed to go into Army stomachs, if the food situation proves to be as bad as anticipated.

Today Ralph Seeley and I did a little going-home investigation of our own. He knows the Okinawa port surgeon. It seems that shipping has been very slow recently, due to the diversion following the Okinawa typhoon. However, in the next 30 days shipping to accommodate 53,000 troops will be available at Yokohama.

There is a big backlog, however, at the moment. By guesses and calculations, it seems reasonable to us that we will fulfill our projected schedule calling for arrival in the United States around the 23rd of December. However, there is a good possibility that the port will be Seattle, rather than San Francisco. Some ships make it in about 9 days.

Our living conditions are gradually straightening out here, but oh-so slowly. We had hot showers today for the first time. From 3:00 to 4:00 for officers; no sign of laundry as yet. Almost all of my clothes are dirty. With no hot water, it is almost impossible to do them yourself.

Our food continues to be poor, partly due to the generally inferior 54th mess and partly due to such things as absence of a quartermaster bakery here.

One of the advantages of going to the 42nd for examining three times a week is the good noon meal we get. It was steak yesterday. Except for these three afternoons, I spend my time going about the city, reading in my room, or planning what to do tomorrow.

I have been disappointed at what there is here to buy to bring home. I would like to get some things we could use as gifts, but unless something more turns up, this does not appear promising. The streetcars are running, and that is our usual method of locomotion.

The cars are marked with the local hieroglyphics, which are supposed to represent route numbers, I presume. However, not being able to understand these, we get on, and if it turns out in an undesirable direction, we get off again. No fare.

Thumbing is very poor, as we are constantly commenting on the paucity of GI vehicles and personnel. We sometimes get all the way to town without meeting another American soldier. I try to travel with someone else, although I have heard of no trouble.

With love and kisses to all the family, H

Thursday 25 October 1945
9:30 P.M.

Dearest Ginny,

I have just read 28 letters from you—all received today. In actuality, there were but 14 letters, and I have read them each twice. They were scattered—most of them sent to Eddie Richardson and forwarded, the latest sent directly to the 54th and dated the 3rd of October.

Our mail is still going direct to the Philippines, and then up. This accounts for the 20-day delivery. There were four priceless Kodachromes—3 of B and one with my sweetheart holding B. I take it that my letters are arriving in about 10 days.

You asked for a little word about Pat Monahan to tell Eleanor Delfs. I saw Pat only the once, although I called at his home for mail several times later, when only his mother was home. I believe that you and I could make our home in the Philippines and like it, provided we reoriented our life somewhat.

As I see it, the greatest need in the islands now is for those who are willing to devote the greatest portion of their time to teaching and actually doing the work.

I think you are right in saying that Pat cared not at all for Eleanor. Considering the people she would have been thrown with, I think she would have longed to return to America once the novelty of the thing had worn off. If Eleanor really loved Pat, she might continue to enjoy it, but she is not the type for Pat.

You are absolutely right in not sending a Christmas package. I intended to mention this before. As a matter of fact, Mrs. Jones, I expect to be with you at Christmas, although probably not in Baltimore.

The meeting on the West Coast will be very difficult to coordinate. I will not be able to give you specific instructions until I am about ready to leave the replacement depot at Yokohama, and those instructions may be wrong and will certainly arrive in Baltimore too late for a comfortable trip out. Perhaps you can fly part of the way. I hope it won't be necessary to fly over the Rockies at this time of the year, but more of that later.

In a very sweet letter that I love, you wonder again if I will be changed. You say you don't think you really are. I don't believe that my conception of domestic life has changed any. Having seen the world, so to speak, I have some opinions on international life and the relation of nations that my lack of scope did not allow me to hold before.

For example, what our attitudes should be to participate in foreign affairs. The kind of Army and Navy we should have, and the like. This should entertain us some dull evening.

My ideals may be higher, if anything. The first few months at home will tell if I have any better ability to attain them. I am more than ever convinced of the importance of integrity in the individual. It is of tremendous importance to be honest with oneself and other people, and very difficult. Everyone seems to have a variable truth factor by which you must multiply what they say under various circumstances. I really don't think you will notice any difference.

Am I physically different? While taking a shower the other day, I notice about 10 hairs on my chest. Were they always there? It seems quite an astonishing discovery to me.

You speak about the socialization in the Army. I am convinced that our attitude will remain the same. I am afraid it will still be a tremendous effort to entertain all but a few of our friends. I do think I shall be ready to settle down, but it may take two or three vacations a year to keep me that way.

The only change in my love for you is that it seems more profound and broader than ever before. Although I subconsciously knew it previously, I had never formulated the fact of its complete control of all important aspects of my life. The least to be said is that this is the greatest lesson a man may have. I hope I shall be worthy of it.

Love and kisses, and may I soon deliver them in person, H

26 October 1945
7:30 P.M.

Dearest Ginny,

In my letters, I have not been overly optimistic, for fear of a letdown, but it now appears that it is necessary to let you know of a real possibility, in order that you may make the necessary arrangements for coming out to the West. The plans for meeting I will enumerate as follows:

My schedule could run something like this:

> *2 November—Go to 4th Replacement Depot, Yokohama*
> *6 November—Sail from Yokohama*
> *18 November—Debark*
> *18-20 November—Begin temporary duty.*

Allowing seven days to cross the country and assuming you get this letter on November 5, you may have to leave for the West Coast within 8 days.

1. *I will meet you in Sacramento, California. It is by no means certain where we will disembark. Although some troops are getting off at Seattle, I was told today, by a fellow who should know, that most troops still go to San Francisco and that the ships are not given their final destination until at sea. That destination is dictated by docking facilities and accommodations at the city in question. I selected Sacramento, because it has good rail connection with the East, San Francisco, and Seattle, and because it is somewhat away from the ports, and therefore hotel space should be available. Also, the Frisco POE is at Camp Stoneman, 60 miles from San Francisco.*

2. *About 48 hours before I sail, I will try to send an EFM (telegram). From the date of this (I hope they are dated; if not, figure it was sent 72 hours before receipt), and figure that I will probably debark in about 14 days. Example, EFM received dated at Yokohama the 10th of November; assume that I will arrive about November 24, and, therefore, you should be in Sacramento on this date. If this message gets through all right, you should have five or six days in which to try to get a reservation. You should also be able to tell from the letter about when I will sail; thus the letter confirming the EFM should arrive about the time you are due to leave.*

3. In event the EFM does not get through for any reason, we will have to depend on airmail, in which case there will be no time for reservations. There is a possibility that the EFM will have arrived by the time this letter is received (very unlikely).

4. I do not have a list of the EFMs here, so I do not know what I can send; therefore, consider any EFM as the message referred to in 3 (you can only send certain stock messages).

5. Continue to write, but not after receiving the EFM.

6. Go to the Hotel Senator in Sacramento. Let my mother know for sure where you are by phone. I will call her from the POE. In event you are still en route when I call Mother, I will go to Sacramento after calling home. If you know the time of arrival in Sacramento, leave this information with Mother. Leave note at Hotel Senator in Sacramento saying where you are if you cannot stay there. Should I arrive first, I will do the same. Send a telegram for reservations to the Hotel Senator. The California is also a good hotel, but we will try the Senator as first choice.

7. I presume Jane Auld is still in Stockton. I have the Aulds' address as 1440 North Hunter Street. You might let her know where you are.

8. Letters with late information may arrive in Baltimore after you leave. If any of this requires a change in plan, I will repeat important information in a letter to my mother. Therefore, phone her from Sacramento when you get there. In the event that the EFM does not get through and you leave by mail direction, there is a good possibility I may get there first. Therefore, in this latter circumstance, it might be a good plan to phone home while en route, e.g., Chicago.

I trust this will work out OK. It would be nice if the EFM and this arrived on the same day. You should really be getting the EFM within two weeks of receipt of this letter, unless I am delayed at the replacement depot.

I am told that Sacramento is on the main Union Pacific and Southern Pacific from Chicago, so that it should be necessary to change only in Chicago.

I have gotten this information from a boy who lives in San Francisco. He has suggested that we go to Lake Tahoe for skiing and has given me the name of several hotels. It sounds like a grand trip. He has also mentioned other places to go. We will work this out in Sacramento. Perhaps you could get Miss Einstein *(travel agent) to wire the Senator and to get the train ticket, but I am concerned about the press of time for a comfortable trip on the short notice you will have.*

I got a letter today—September 25—gradually catching up with the backlog. There is another backlog I have to make up, beginning, perhaps, soon after Thanksgiving.

Love, H

Wednesday 27 October 1945
9:30 P.M.

My darling Ginny,

We had a long day of examinations at the 42nd doing 91 men, including three majors and about 14 brigadier generals. Every officer who has anything to do with going home gets a pep talk as he goes through the line.

After the session, Ralph Seeley and Bill Eastman and I went to hear the Nippon Philharmonic Orchestra at Hibyo Hall just outside the Imperial Palace. The concerts begin at 5:00, which is an awkward time, as there is no satisfactory time to get dinner. I was in favor of skipping the dinner, as I can well afford to do, but I was overruled, and we left at 6:45 to make the 7 o'clock deadline for dinner at the Imperial Hotel just across the street.

Hibyo Hall is the lyric of Tokyo and seats about as many as the Baltimore concert hall, but the acoustics are not nearly as good, and it is a very dingy place, badly in need of paint and repair. It has an elaborate modern center of Japanese design representing the busy city. It is a sparkling thing of many colors, but close examination shows it is not a thing of art. Papa could have done as well (joke).

The Nippon Philharmonic Orchestra is the best orchestra, although the Tokyo Philharmonic also plays. The former is completely Japanese, of course, except the conductor, who is a little German about as tall as the Nips.

The orchestra dressed in dark Western business suits, white shirts, and dark hand ties. The conductor wore tails. There were three women playing strings. The program is enclosed. The English has been added to the program since the end of the war, I am sure.

A Siamese student who spoke English sat beside me and said that this was the first playing of the New World Symphony *since Pearl Harbor. They*

*played very well, but actually no better than a just-average American orchestra—
the Baltimore Symphony, for instance.*

*The second selection was Tchaikovsky's B-flat Concerto, played by a woman—
the best in Japan, according to my Siamese friend. Beyond any doubt, she was the
best-looking Japanese woman I have seen. In fact, the only one with any S.A. [sex
appeal]. She must be about 28-30. She was a little stiff, but very good.*

Love, H

————————————

THE COMPLEMENT OF physicians examining officers for promotion
at the 42nd General Hospital was soon enlarged. Although we processed
officers scheduled for permanent promotion in the regular army, someone
directed that we do routine annual examinations of regular army officers,
a practice that lapsed during war. Each examining officer was therefore
presented with a several-page list of regular army officers who would be
coming through for exams.

Heading the list was General of the Army Douglas MacArthur,
followed by Lieutenant General Robert Eichelberger, and then several
other generals, colonels, and others who had had no annual physical
examination when the war was on.

Many officers were processed, but we were told that MacArthur
likely would not appear, although it was thought possible that
Eichelberger might. Neither MacArthur nor Eichelberger appeared,
but many other stars did.

My role was to take a history and deal with the lower bowel, including
a rectal examination. To make small talk after the first day or two of
these examinations, I resolved to ask officers as they came through,
regardless of their rank, whether they had anything to do with issuing
orders for the rotation of officers home.

This small talk usually got a laugh—I asked the question just
before doing the rectal. Word got around. The day after I started
asking the question, several of the officers who came through, including
certain generals, preempted my question by announcing, "I want it
clearly understood before you do this exam that I have nothing to
do with issuing orders to rotate officers home."

This joking helped pass the time, and the examination routine was not all that bad.

Sunday 28 October 1945
9:00 P.M.

Dearest Ginny,

We have just got back from our trip to Fuji-san. We got up at 4:45 A.M. and changed trains three times and were amazed to get where we had planned to go. Some Jap wrote notes for us to flash when we got lost, and they seemed to have the desired effect.

The mountain itself is worth the trip, and remarkable, because it stands alone. It is now snowcapped and appears just like the pictures.

The Jap trains are an experience. We rode part of the way back in a private car—the baggage car. It was the first time I have ever seen people get in and out of a train by way of the windows.

With all love and kisses, H

Tuesday 30 October 1945
5:40 P.M.

Dearest Ginny,

Today has been a day of rest and preliminary packing. I went through my stuff, for that is what most of it is, and threw away enough to get everything into the footlocker that I hope to send straight through to Baltimore.

We had today some advance information that our orders should be through here in three or four days. This will keep us on a good pace, and if we are not held up in the replacement depot here, there is a very good chance of making the 20th of November date in Sacramento.

I got a letter today, written the 20th of October. I hope mine are getting there as well, especially at this time.

Your letter told about taking the children to Mary Jane's third birthday party.

I think I know what to expect in regard to B, for she is just the age Willie was when I left. About Willie, I am not too sure. I fully expect to scare one or both of them to tears when I arrive, and if they do anything but cry, it will be a surprise.

General Maxwell, who is chief surgeon, was over yesterday and apparently hurried the colonel along some, for the hospital is going to open for patients next Monday. I trust that I shall miss this.

I examined a Colonel Douglas Kendrick. He was a member of the 10th Army while Bill was down there. He said that Bill left Okinawa by ship about the 8th of October. By now he is surely home and, I suppose, has called you.

I feel especially sorry for Charley Burbank. While Bill and I were delayed in coming home, we can at least claim that the trip out here was some recompense.

Poor Charley will probably be here until spring. That is too much of a price to pay. He is beautifully adjusted to it, and surprisingly enough, I believe he rather dreads going home, with his wife no better in health than she is. He has never mentioned it, but I know it must be constantly on his mind.

All my love, H

Tokyo, October 1945. The U.S. firebombing air raids left only chimneys and steel safes in neighborhoods of wooden houses.

Tokyo, October 1945. For the survivors, life must go on.

Except for the transient dining room the
Imperial Hotel is supposed to be off
limits to all except those billeted there.
The latter consists of G.H.Q. field
officers mostly generals & colonels.
Tonight Charles & I went into the
cocktail lounge & as one said too to me
no visit to Japan is complete without
trying Sake. It is really a wine I
suppose.

IMPERIAL HOTEL

OFFICER'S COCKTAIL LOUNGE

Hours: 1500-2300

PRICES

Canadian Club	per glass	¥ 6.50
Old Crow Rye	per glass	6.50
Whiskey (Suntory)	per glass	5.50
Beer	per bottle	3.00
Sake	per bottle	2.00
Tansan (Soda)	per bottle	.40
Sweet Soda	per bottle	1.00
Coca Cola	per bottle	1.00

Kindly pay when served.

Set-ups will be provided if you bring your own bottle.

Canadian Club & Old Crow are not available in bottles.

Suntory can be purchased at the Front Desk.

October 1945. Imperial Hotel menu.

Chapter 21

Letters from Home
1 October-3 November 1945

*B*RING THE BOYS HOME! THAT WAS THE CRY OF A war-weary United States of America. That was Georgeanna's cry and also, of course, mine. There were other cries, too, for an end to wartime rationing, price controls, and higher wages. Labor unions were militant in pursuit of better pay for workers and benefits. Georgeanna alludes to labor unrest in the letter below.

——————————

Tuesday, October 2, 1945
9:00 P.M.

My dearest,

I was really getting panicky this morning about not seeing you. I began to wonder what we would do if internal trouble in the States got so bad that there would be a real interruption to communications, etc. I figured in my sleep how we should arrange to meet.

Should I take the children and try to go to Mexico and thence to the Philippines, or what? This evening I have received a letter dated September 17, and Mother has received hers dated September 19, so I feel that perhaps we are almost back in rapport and will once more meet again.

Then, too, your lovely gift from Panama arrived. It is quite the most beautiful bag I have ever seen, and I shall save it to meet you on the dock. You don't know at what a strategic moment it arrived—it has boosted my morale no end.

I do hope you aren't counting on being home close to the first of the year. I am through counting on such things and feel that at the present rate we will be lucky if you are home by early spring.

Sometimes it just doesn't seem possible that I could wait that long, and then the peculiar ache in my tummy and throat would just blow up and burst, but, of course, I know by experience that this will pass.

Please, darling, never stop loving me, because that would be the end of my world. I can work and really derive some pleasure and satisfaction from it without you, but entertainment without you is just so much sawdust.

I have season tickets to the Philadelphia Symphony with Kitten Foote, but I really dread going. Smitty saw (or heard) Rhapsody in Blue and said, as you did, that the movie was wonderful. I just can't bring myself to go and shall wait until you come home.

Do tell me what Army the 54th General Hospital is with, or smaller unit, so I may follow it in the papers, if possible. I am writing to Lieutenant Colonel Gay to give him your address and also to ask him to have your mail forwarded, if possible.

I shall go on working, my dear, but I shall not live again until your arms are once more about me.

All my love, Ginny

Wednesday, October 4, 1945

Dearest Honey Bunny,

This is a letter of finances. I suppose you never received my letter with last year's figures as you ask me did we make money last year.

We were $1,454.88 ahead, but had $300 of taxes to pay. Our check balance is now $1,996.54, and, in addition, we have $1,371.32 more in ground rents.

When Wilkins Ave. went, I took 3 ground rents instead of two. Also have now bought two bonds a month to amortize.

We have the following stocks bought from the checking-account fund: Remington Arms $775; Liquid Carbonate $841.09; S.O. N.J., $963.66.

Our expenses have, of course, risen, for now to pay for all the food, this amounts to about $75/mo.

My total expenses amount to about $180/mo. I do not think this excessive for these times. This does not count clothes, recreation, etc. I think that we are very nicely situated and can afford to spend $1,000 on a trip, if we choose.

I, of course, would love to meet you on the West Coast, if possible. I don't want to have to wait five or ten days for you to arrive home after being in this country. I suppose we really can't make plans until we know something more definite, but I shall at least make believe I am coming to the West Coast.

As I have said before, I do hope you're not counting on getting home too soon, for I'm afraid you can't make it before April or May.

The internal situation continues badly, and I do hope that Truman will do better about the strikes than he has.

With all my very best love and kisses, Ginny

Monday, October 8, 1945
11:30 P.M.

My darling,

Today three letters and your adorable one to Willie: "Papa driving a jeep." You are developing into quite an artist, much to the delight of the entire family.

I am really delighted that it appears you will be off from Tokyo. I did not feel this way about it a month ago, but you are right. You may as well see as much as possible, and after all, it is 2,000 miles closer home.

Right now I plan to meet you in San Francisco. John Haines is at the Marine Hospital, and they live on the Post. I thought I might go out and stay with Jane Auld a few days, until I had some idea of where you would dock, and then move into the Haineses.

You would presumably call home (TUX 2570 and Ess HO 0156 for me), and any change in plans would then be communicated (that is, if I don't meet you on the dock).

I would like to know the name of your boat, if possible. I suppose that if you do not hear from me, we will have to let you come through to Fort Meade. How *long will it take you to come from Japan? Long enough for me to hear from you and get to the Coast?*

Willie and I had a wonderful time this morning. He awoke fresh as a daisy and decided to go see the train, so we meandered out at 7:00 o'clock. It was fun.

All my love, Ginny

> October 25, 1945
> 9:15 A.M.

Dearest Honey Bunny,

Yesterday I received 17 letters. I thought I would, so passed up my ride to wait for the mail, and it was worth it. Your story of the tornado is fascinating, and I am sure it was a remarkable experience which you do not regret having.

Your statement about December 23 at 8:00 A.M. intrigues me, but I cannot take it seriously. I shall, however, be in California, if I receive the go-ahead signal from you.

We are almost ready for Willie's birthday, and I expect to have fun.

If you should come about Christmastime, I think there is some nice place up in the California mountains where we would go and spend a "White Christmas." Also, perhaps, stay over until the holiday rush is over. I will not even let myself think about being with you once more, because it is more than I can bear, and I'm so afraid of being disappointed because you will be delayed again.

All my love, Ginny

> Thursday, November 1, 1945
> 10:00 A.M.

Dearest Honey Bunny,

I think I had better plan to go to San Francisco, even though you do come in at Seattle, for I have friends in Frisco and could motor up to Seattle, as you could come down.

I trust that by now you have received all the information and are planning accordingly. Clara Ward Haines's address is #1 Grijalza Drive, Park Merced, San Francisco.

I do not know what to do for a place to live, as everything is way out of sight. People think that the market will hold for perhaps two years.

We will apparently have to stay at Hawthorne Road until you get here and can help make such decisions. These decisions with you will be vitally interesting. Without you, they seem impossible. If Jane's baby and you arrive at the same time, what excitement!

I can hardly believe and really do not allow myself to hope that perhaps in less than two months I will see the flash of your smile and hear the warmth of your voice.

I only hope I don't disgrace myself and burst into a flood of relief-filled tears. If I shall be so rash, I trust and know that you will understand. Perhaps I will be so anxious to look my prettiest for you that I can avoid such emotions. I hope so.

I, too, am glad that you will be coming home when it is cold and cuddly.

All my love, Ginny

> *Monday, November 5, 1945*
> *11:15 P.M.*

Dearest Honey Bunny,

Just think, I may not be doing this much longer. Instead, I will be warming my feet on your legs. I still can't believe it.

Seriously, darling, do you know how excited and divinely happy and eternally grateful I am to have you coming home soon? I guess you do, for you must be all these things too, except you never seem to get as excited as I do.

I wonder if this time I'll be on the platform watching you pull in, or will my first glimpse of you be like my last—you standing on the platform watching the train pull out.

I saw R. W. Travel Agency today, and they are making my reservations for November 13. If they have to be changed, OK. Also the agency is wiring the Senator.

The two hotels open in the California Mountains are at Tahoe and at Arrowhead, so they are investigating possibilities. Also suggest we stop at Grand Canyon (and) or the Santa Fe Trail. Sounds good, eh?

Asbury was back today, and you can't imagine what a difference that makes to me. It's all the difference from existing to really enjoying life. I'll be willing to

534	Howard W. Jones Jr. and Georgeanna Seegar Jones

skimp on the other things to keep him or Elmer. I'm paying him $20/week now, but that isn't what most of them are getting, and I will probably have to up this. But he said that will do until the first of the year.

Have cleared space for your things, so all you have to do is move in. My impatience rises with every 24 hours.

All my love, Ginny

Chapter 22

Home at Last
30 October-22 November 1945

31 October 1945
11:00 A.M.

Dearest Ginny,

I HOPE I SEE YOU BEFORE YOU GET THIS LETTER. THIS *is to say that we go to the replacement depot at 1:00 P.M. tomorrow. There is a possibility that I can be in Sacramento by the 16th of November, so if you have not had any previous word, you should leave Baltimore to arrive by that date.*

Stay either at the Aulds' or Hotel Senator, Sacramento. In any case, I am giving my destination as Sacramento, but if when I call from Seattle or San Francisco, I find you are at Stockton, it will be easy to get there.

Things are happening sooner than I thought.

Love, H

1 November 1945
11:00 A.M.

Dearest Ginny,

I am now at the 4th Replacement Depot at Atsugi.

535

Yesterday I found an officer who was returning by air, and I asked him to send you a telegram from California to meet me there about the 16th of November.

It now appears that this will be too early, as the stay here seems to be at least a week. I had calculated on two days. At any rate, if you are still in Baltimore to get this, you should now plan to go there as soon after the 16th as possible.

Love, H

P.S. Either Aulds' or Hotel Senator, Sacramento.

AS CAN BE seen from the letters, we necessarily jury-rigged an elaborate system for trying to meet on the West Coast at the end of the war. I had no way of letting Georgeanna know exactly where we were coming in, and she, therefore, the soldier that she was, brought skiing equipment, except for skis, and headed for the West Coast.

This was not easy to do, as one had to have a priority to travel on the train. But somehow she managed to do it and ended up staying in Stockton with friends of ours—with, actually, the wife of Tom Auld, a classmate of mine at Amherst College.

I, of course, did not know exactly where she was going to be, but the plan called for her to stay either at a hotel in Sacramento or with the Aulds.

As it turned out, I arrived in Tacoma, Washington, and Fort Lewis on 18 November 1945. At Fort Lewis, I got on the phone and soon connected with Georgeanna at the Aulds. We agreed that Georgeanna would take a train to Tacoma. She was scheduled to arrive at the Tacoma station the day before Thanksgiving.

Train travel was difficult enough at that time. With Thanksgiving vacation thrown in, space on trains was scarce. Georgeanna rode a train from Sacramento to Portland; then she rode a second train from Portland to Tacoma. She had to stand part of the way.

Changing trains in Portland, Georgeanna almost lost her luggage. She had brought her ski equipment, as well as personal things, and the equipment was too much to carry, she required the services of a porter.

Porters also were scarce, and they looked after more than one passenger at a time. Fearing she would miss her train, Georgeanna left her baggage with the porter, with the understanding that he would bring it to her.

She ran ahead to board the train, coming upon a car where she could stand in the vestibule. She waited for the porter to come along as the time for the departure approached.

She had resolved that if the train left before the luggage arrived, she would remain on the train and abandon the luggage. Just when she was despairing of seeing her luggage again, the porter and his cart came into view. She waved to him. He placed the luggage in the vestibule as the train began to move.

An officer who was also in the vestibule helped her with the bags and ski equipment and asked where she was going. She told him she was meeting her husband in Tacoma. He led her into a compartment he was sharing with several other officers who made room for her.

I met the train at the station. I passed through the main station and placed myself where it appeared that all passengers had to exit. Everyone seemed to have left the train, but no Georgeanna. I dejectedly turned around to walk back to the station. About halfway down the long corridor, I saw her from a distance. She was heading from the station back to the train. We had unknowingly passed in the crowd. Within moments, we were joyfully together again.

Processing my release from the army took several days. I thought by the time Georgeanna and I were reunited that I might already be out. But the actual release was not affected until the next day, Thanksgiving. Our Thanksgiving dinner was at Fort Lewis, at the officers' mess.

We traveled from Tacoma to Mount Ranier and the Paradise Inn, which was halfway up the mountain. For a few precious, unforgettable days, we skied, we feasted, we talked, and we refreshed our love for one another.

And then to Baltimore. But not easily. Reserving a train berth exacted considerable effort. Our reservation from Tacoma to Milwaukee was for an upper berth.

I asked the railroad ticket agent if he could sell an upper berth for two. "Yes," he said. "I can sell you an upper berth for two, but whether you can sleep in it is another matter." We managed to do that. We reached Baltimore in mid-December to begin our new life together in postwar America.

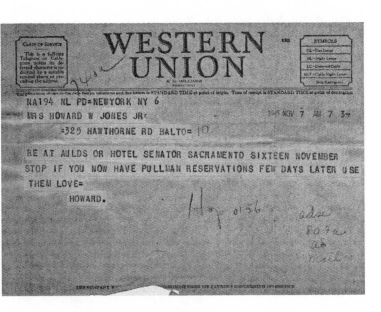

NA194 NL PD=NEWYORK NY 6

MRS HOWARD W JONES JR=   1945 NOV 7   AM 7 3=

=325 HAWTHORNE RD BALTO=

BE AT AULDS OR HOTEL SENATOR SACRAMENTO SIXTEEN NOVEMBER
STOP IF YOU NOW HAVE PULLMAN RESERVATIONS FEW DAYS LATER USE
THEM LOVE=

    HOWARD.

A final plan.

Tacoma, Washington, 21 November 1945, where we met in the Tacoma train station the day before Thanksgiving.

Paradise Inn, Mount Ranier, November 1945.

Thoughts About War

WORLD WAR I WAS LABELED "THE WAR TO END All Wars." Battle deaths totaled 8.5 million; wounded numbered more than 21 million. From the ashes of this global tragedy arose the League of Nations, which was intended to defuse international disputes without going to war. World War I ended in 1918. The League of Nations, provided for in the Treaty of Versailles, came into existence in 1920. World War II started in 1939 after but nineteen years of world peace marred by regional wars.

Worldwide, World War II claimed the lives of fifteen million soldiers, sailors, marines, and pilots and air crewman, nearly twice the combat deaths in World War I. And 38.6 million civilians also were killed. U.S. combat deaths totaled 292,131; wounded 671,268. I operated on three hundred wounded, of whom twenty-six perished, numbers that pale in comparison to the immense toll exacted by the global war.

During great battle activity, as in the 1944 winter offensive inside Germany to the Roer River, I was so engrossed in treating the wounded that I gave no thought to the phenomenon of war. During times of inactivity, discussions among fellow officers centered on topics of the day, such as the Allied tactical and strategic effort, and usually with someone characterizing one or another of these activities as stupid action on the part of higher command.

We generally agreed that the Allies' cause was just, because our side fought to champion liberty by eliminating the dictatorships of Hitler in Germany, Mussolini in Italy, and Tojo in Japan. We were participating in a war to defend and advance life, liberty, and the pursuit of happiness. Everyone seemed to be content and, indeed, proud to be a part of it.

While World War II flowed in part from failings of the League of Nations, the United Nations emerged from the ashes of the second global conflagration. The dream of a world body dedicated to ameliorating and/or peacefully resolving conflicts lives on.

THE GHASTLY TRAGEDY of World War II ignited the desire to recapture the purpose of the League of Nations. The covenant of the United Nations was signed in San Francisco on 26 June 1945, almost within one month of the surrender of Germany and three months before the surrender of Japan.

Item 1 of the Preamble states, "We the peoples of the United Nations are determined to save succeeding generations from the scourge of war, which twice in our lifetime has brought untold sorrow to mankind."

Humankind has thus far been spared a World War III. The Western nations did engage in the (sometimes hot) fifty-year Cold War to contain the expansionist drive of the Soviet Union and Communist China, and ethnic, religious, territorial, and liberation wars abound. Since World War II, the United States has fought in five major conflicts in Korea, Vietnam, and the Middle East. The United States has taken military action in Panama, Granada, Kosovo, and elsewhere. Alas, humankind is not yet prepared to banish war.

CAN WE EXPLAIN the continued lack of consideration for the lives of others?

Perhaps.

After all, *homo sapiens* is but one of the millions of species in the animal kingdom in general, and but one species among thousands of mammals.

Books and other publications and still and moving photography chronicle mammalian behavior. Virtually all mammals engage in four primary, inherent, instinctive activities: eating, sleeping, reproducing, and fighting.

Most mammals, including humans, eat other species of the animal kingdom; some eat only vegetation, which, after all, is also life. It seems that all life above bacteria and other plants ingests life.

Present knowledge indicates that all mammalians sleep, each in a specific territory offering relative protection from predators.

Reproduction is essential for the preservation of the species, and perhaps the urge to reproduce is the most powerful force in the animal universe.

Animals fight, either singly or in groups, over one or another of the previous three activities.

Homo sapiens follows this simplistic pattern. But the human species' brain power has complicated the pattern. While humankind is prepared to fight for many reasons, its brainpower has led it to produce weapons of mass destruction capable of wiping out billions of people and rendering the planet Earth uninhabitable.

This former battlefield surgeon believes that we humans have not yet reached a level of civilization that would allow us to master, rather than be mastered by the destructive behavior common to all mammals.

I do not mean to say that efforts of the likes of the League of Nations, the United Nations, and myriads of advocacy groups and the religious vision of "Peace on Earth, Good Will to Man" are doomed to failure forever. Such organizations and the vision of a peaceful world are essential to the civilizing process—a process whose progress is measured in millennia, rather than human lifetimes.

How lamentable that this is the human condition. But how blessed are the peacemakers among us, for they light the path to a happier future.

Epilogue

GEORGEANNA CONTINUED TO DIRECT AT JOHNS Hopkins the Division of Reproductive Medicine while I was away at war. She had founded the division in 1939. In addition to responsibility for running the newly established hormone laboratory, she developed a substantial private practice in the treatment of problems related to reproduction.

Our highest priority after the war was given to devising an arrangement that would allow Georgeanna and me to work side by side. But we had to overcome a major obstacle to realize our dream.

Before going off to war, I had had a residency in general surgery. Although that residency involved gynecological surgery, I was necessarily on the staff of general surgery while Georgeanna was on the gynecological staff. At that time, obstetrics was a separate department.

All members of the gynecological staff had been residents in gynecology at Hopkins. My best chance to be appointed in gynecology and accepted by all was to have a residency in gynecology.

Richard TeLinde, the gynecology department's chairman, received Georgeanna and me at his home one evening. We expressed our hope. He was receptive. I was appointed chief resident in gynecology for a six-month period. Upon completion of this attenuated residency, I was duly appointed to the department and resigned from the Department of General Surgery.

During this era at Hopkins, all members of the gynecological faculty, including the chairman, were part-timers. This meant that faculty received no remuneration from the university. There was a bit of an exception to this, in that Georgeanna was full time, at a salary of $1,200 a year, and had an office in the hospital. I opened an office in the medical section of downtown Baltimore. Georgeanna and I maintained separate and distinctively different medical practices. Georgeanna dealt with problems of reproduction, i.e., infertility and like, while I saw patients with general gynecological problems requiring surgical attention, but with emphasis on gynecological malignancy.

Prior to the war, I had spent three years at Baltimore's Kelley Clinic, which had a large supply of radium and treated many patients with malignancies, including all such patients from the Johns Hopkins Gynecological Service.

After a while, Georgeanna referred to me her patients requiring surgical therapy—patients suffering tubal obstruction, ovarian cystic problems, endometriosis, congenital anomalies, and more.

Referrals from Georgeanna and others became so numerous that by the mid-1960s I was doing essentially nothing but reparative gynecological surgery. Thus did Georgeanna's clinical and scientific interests and mine fuse.

EACH OF US was busy. But although we derived considerable satisfaction in correcting this or that problem for individual patients, we yearned intensely to involve ourselves in the cutting-edge study of infertility and the quest for cures.

While still a medical student, Georgeanna exhibited this investigative eagerness.

During her time as a medical student, the origin of the pregnancy hormone was generally thought to be the pituitary gland. The principal investigator in this area was Bernhard Zondek of Berlin who, with Selmar Aschheim, had developed a biological test for the pregnancy hormone.

Zondek conjectured that the pregnancy hormone came from the pituitary gland. But an assay of the pituitaries of pregnant patients failed to disclose the presence of the hormone. Zondek explained this phenomenon by asserting that during pregnancy the hormone was excreted immediately, because of the body's strong demand for it, and he cited the great rise of the pregnancy hormone in urine.

Georgeanna suspected that the pregnancy hormone did not originate in the pituitary gland. She cultured placental cells in vitro (in a glass dish) to determine whether the cells produced the hormone. She showed that the Aschheim-Zondek test was negative in the culture medium, but that after the tissue grew, the pregnancy test became increasingly positive. Her experiment clearly indicated that the pregnancy hormone was produced by the chorion, i.e., a part of the placenta.

Her report on her work was published in 1943, after a preliminary note in *Science* a few years before. In her report, she referred to the hormone as "chorionic gonadotropin," and this name has stuck to this day.

Early in her laboratory experience she developed, along with Theodore Astwood, a test for the production of progesterone. This was done by assaying twenty-four-hour urine specimens for pregnanediol, an excretion product of progesterone. Employing this new test, she showed that some patients who had repeated miscarriages or occasional incidental miscarriages had greatly deficient pregnanediol excretion, suggesting a deficiency of progesterone in some pregnancies, thus causing spontaneous abortions. Administering progesterone prevented such abortions.

She first presented this work in 1949, in a paper at a meeting of the American Medical Association.

GEORGEANNA IDENTIFIED YOUNG patients with amenorrhea (inability to menstruate) who also had menopausal levels of gonadotropin in their urine. She discovered that these patients' ovaries were insensitive to the gonadotropin hormones that normally regulate the menstrual cycle. This is known as the "ovarian insensitivity syndrome," but a good many of our colleagues thought that it ought to be called Jones Disease. In 1967 Georgeanna published her discoveries with a fellow, Maria de Moraes Rheusen, as coauthor.

Alex Brunsweig, general surgeon, was chief of the gynecological service at Memorial Hospital in New York. He introduced a very radical operation for cancer of the cervix; in suitable cases, bladder, rectum and the female generative tract were removed. Being a general surgeon, I thought I should train to perform the operation. After a month in New York at the Memorial Hospital with Alex Brunsweig, I persuaded Richard TeLinde to allow me to do the exenteration at Hopkins, and I did the first one at that institution.

Being in New York led to an unexpected opportunity for Georgeanna and me to move to the city and join the team of George Pack, chief of the Mixed Tumor Service at Memorial Hospital. We carefully considered the offer, but decided against making a change.

MORE AND MORE patients presented themselves to me for surgery designed to overcome infertility. Patients came not only from Georgeanna, but also from other members of the department interested in other surgical challenges.

Operating on wounded soldiers had demanded surgical innovation to overcome unusual difficulties. Having been compelled to innovate while in the fields of Europe, I continued to innovate in the postwar years. Among the innovative procedures I developed, I cite the Jones Metroplasty for removal of the uterine septum.

IN 1950 LAWSON Wilkins, then professor of pediatrics at Johns Hopkins, made the brilliant discovery that the consequences of congenital adrenal hyperplasia could be overcome by administering cortisone. Previously, female patients with hyperplasia were masculinized, experienced serious metabolic problems, were amennorheic, and had uncorrected ambiguous external genitalia. They were called "female hermaphrodites."

Cortisone reversed the metabolic aspects of the disease— menstruation and breast development occurred and serious hirsutism gradually disappeared. Repair of ambiguous external genitalia required surgery.

Wilkins asked if I would take on these cases. I would, and over the years I performed many operations and published a series of papers on the subject. In 1958 I coauthored with William Scott, professor of urology at Hopkins, a book titled *Hermaphroditism, Genital Anomalies and Related Endocrine Disorders.*

My passion for reparative surgery resulted in many operations for tubal defects, polycystic ovaries, and the like, all of which prompted a series of publications over two decades.

JOHN MONEY, A psychologist at Hopkins, became an authority on the physiosocial aspects of sexual identification. He interviewed essentially all patients with ambiguous external genitalia, regardless of their gender. And he encountered many patients with transsexualism; i.e., people possessing no identifiable defect, either male or female, but who considered themselves individuals of the opposite gender.

John regarded this anomaly as incurable psychologically. He argued that the best possible solution was to reconstruct the genitalia to correspond to the gender to which transsexual patients believed they belonged. Along with members of the plastic surgery department, a series of what the press called "sex-transforming operations" were performed on willing patients. These operations triggered medical-research papers and widespread and often sensational publicity in the 1970s.

TO BETTER STUDY these problems of sexual development, we established a cytogenetics laboratory (a laboratory to study chromosomes).

With several fellows, I coauthored a series of papers on the chromosomal status of sexual abnormalities. Dr. Theodore Baramki was coauthor of several of these and author of a textbook, *Medical Cytogenetics.*

While Georgeanna and I were busy with heavy clinical schedules, we were invited to prepare textbooks and edit *Obstetrical and Gynecological Survey.*

Obstetrical and Gynecological Survey is a monthly publication established after World War II by Nicholson Eastman and Emil Novak. Novak died in 1958. Professor Eastman asked Georgeanna and me to consider taking over the gynecological aspect of the journal. We were editors in chief for gynecology of the periodical for three decades.

Emil Novak had written a very successful textbook of gynecology. After his death, his son, Edmund Novak, produced a revised edition. He invited Georgeanna and me to be coauthors with him for subsequent editions. We worked with him to produce the seventh, eighth, ninth, and tenth editions of the work.

In addition to the book about hermaphroditism, Georgeanna and I wrote other books. Georgeanna published a volume on menstrual disorders in 1954. Richard Heller, a pediatrician, and I authored a textbook of pediatric gynecology. John Rock and I published two editions of a book on pediatric gynecological surgery. Georgeanna and I wrote a biography of Richard TeLinde that was published in 1986.

DURING THESE ACTIVE years at Hopkins, we reared three children. Howard III—"Willie" in *War and Love*—was born in 1942. Georgeanna—"Beezie" in Georgeanna's letters (nickname derived from Howard III's efforts to say "baby")—was born in 1944. Our third child, Lawrence, was born in 1947.

After graduating from Amherst College, Howard III gained his M.D. from Duke University, took his residency at the University of Colorado, and was a fellow in oncology at the M. D. Andersen Hospital in Houston. At this writing he is professor of obstetrics and gynecology at Vanderbilt University and director of the Division of Gynecological Oncology. With John Rock he edits the well-known *Operative Gynecology* textbook founded by Richard TeLinde.

Daughter Georgeanna also studied medicine at Duke after graduating from Mount Holyoke College. She is professor of pediatrics at the University of Colorado, where she is a pediatric endocrinologist, with a special interest in diabetes.

Lawrence, our third child, graduated from Amherst College. Not disposed to practice medicine, he pursued a business career in Denver. He is principal of his own firm of financial advisers.

We have seven grandchildren—Kathleen Jones O'Connor, Howard Jones, William Klingensmith IV, Theodore Klingensmith, Tyler Jones, Nathan Jones, and Adrienne Jones. At this writing, there is one great-grandchild—Thomas O'Conner.

While rearing our offspring, we were very busy with patients, investigative opportunities, editorial duties tied to a journal and a textbook, and traveling to national and international conferences to speak and teach. Along the way we were awarded honorary memberships in more than a score of foreign medical societies and collected between us nine honorary degrees.

HOPKINS MANDATED RETIREMENT at age sixty-five. For me this occurred at the end of the academic year—30 June 1976. The dean sent me the customary retirement letter expressing appreciation for past services, noting that I no longer needed to take on committee assignments, and wishing me well.

Full-time members who had offices in the hospital were required to vacate them. But the director of the hospital telephoned to say that since Georgeanna and I occupied the same office, the hospital would not object if I continued to share the office until her retirement two years hence. No paperwork spelled out this arrangement, but I was accepted and carried on as before the retirement until Georgeanna retired 30 June 1978. Both of us then had to depart Johns Hopkins Hospital.

What to do next? Friends urged us to continue in private practice in Baltimore in the downtown medical district. But another longtime friend, Mason Andrews, of Norfolk, Virginia, presented us with a compelling option.

Mason was the principal initiator and driving force of the civic movement to establish a medical school at Norfolk, the city at the center of a metropolitan region with more than a million people. The fledgling Eastern Virginia Medical School specified no retirement age. Would we join the faculty there? Yes! We were delighted to seize the opportunity to pursue our academic work by joining the then-three-man Department of Obstetrics and Gynecology. We were appointed to develop a Division of Reproductive Medicine within the Obstetrics and Gynecology Department.

While we were en route to Norfolk, the first in vitro fertilization baby was born in Oldham, England. Patrick Steptoe and Robert Edwards had effected this historic advance that defeats infertility.

As a fellow at Hopkins in 1965, Robert Edwards attempted to fertilize human eggs in vitro. He had come because Hopkins could provide him human eggs, which he had had difficulty getting in Great Britain. His effort in the United States yielded two scientific papers describing the IVF process, one by Edwards in *Lancet* in 1965 and another by the group at Hopkins in the *American Journal of Obstetrics and Gynecology* in 1966.

Interviewed by the local newspapers on our arrival in Norfolk, we were asked whether in vitro fertilization could be carried out at Eastern Virginia Medical School. We replied that it could, with adequate financial support.

The published interview prompted a telephone call from a woman with a reproductive problem who had been referred to Georgeanna in Baltimore. As Georgeanna's patient she had been rewarded by the birth of a daughter. She offered us funds to start an in vitro fertilization program.

Our program was successful. The first in vitro fertilization baby in the New World was born in Norfolk in December 1981. A textbook and a lengthy list of papers describing our experience and lessons learned followed that achievement.

Georgeanna and I and other members of our team, both at Johns Hopkins and Eastern Virginia Medical School, have trained hundreds of fellows from the United States and foreign lands in reproductive medicine. To our immense joy, the results of this new specialty have been replicated repeatedly at clinics around the globe. The ultimate reward to mentors is to see their colleagues and students succeed.